Psychology

A Behavioral Overview

APPLIED CLINICAL PSYCHOLOGY

Series Editors:
Alan S. Bellack, *Medical College of Pennsylvania at EPPI, Philadelphia, Pennsylvania,*
and Michel Hersen, *University of Pittsburgh, Pittsburgh, Pennsylvania*

Current Volumes in this Series

THE AIDS HEALTH CRISIS
Psychological and Social Interventions
  Jeffrey A. Kelly and Janet S. St. Lawrence

BEHAVIORAL CONSULTATION AND THERAPY
  John R. Bergan and Thomas R. Kratochwill

BEHAVIORAL CONSULTATION IN APPLIED SETTINGS
An Individual Guide
  Thomas R. Kratochwill and John R. Bergan

THE CHALLENGE OF COGNITIVE THERAPY
Applications to Nontraditional Populations
  Edited by T. Michael Vallis, Janice L. Howes, and Philip C. Miller

HANDBOOK OF BEHAVIOR MODIFICATION WITH THE MENTALLY RETARDED
Second Edition
  Edited by Johnny L. Matson

HANDBOOK OF THE BRIEF PSYCHOTHERAPIES
  Edited by Richard A. Wells and Vincent J. Giannetti

HANDBOOK OF CLINICAL BEHAVIORAL PEDIATRICS
  Edited by Alan M. Gross and Ronald S. Drabman

HANDBOOK OF SEXUAL ASSAULT
Issues, Theories, and Treatment of the Offender
  Edited by W. L. Marshall, D. R. Laws, and H. E. Barbaree

HANDBOOK OF TREATMENT APPROACHES IN CHILDHOOD
PSYCHOPATHOLOGY
  Edited by Johnny L. Matson

PSYCHOLOGY
A Behavioral Overview
  Alan Poling, Henry Schlinger, Stephen Starin, and Elbert Blakely

---

A Continuation Order Plan is available for this series. A continuation order will bring delivery of each new volume immediately upon publication. Volumes are billed only upon actual shipment. For further information please contact the publisher.

Psychology

A Behavioral Overview

Alan Poling

Western Michigan University
Kalamazoo, Michigan

Henry Schlinger

Western New England College
Springfield, Massachusetts

Stephen Starin

Health and Rehabilitative Services
Developmental Services Program Office
Miami, Florida

and
Elbert Blakely

Western Michigan University
Kalamazoo, Michigan

Plenum Press • New York and London

Library of Congress Cataloging-in-Publication Data

Psychology : a behavioral overview / Alan Poling ... [et al.].
        p.   cm. -- (Applied clinical psychology)
    Includes bibliographical references.
    ISBN 0-306-43432-6
    1. Psychology.   I. Poling, Alan D.   II. Series.
BF121.P798   1990
    150.19'43--dc20   90-35603
                                                                         CIP

First Printing—June 1990
Second Printing—January 1991

© 1990 Plenum Press, New York
A Division of Plenum Publishing Corporation
233 Spring Street, New York, N.Y. 10013

Printed in the United States of America

Foreword

Psychology: A Behavioral Overview is an introductory text with an orienting perspective that is frankly behavioral rather than eclectic. This focus is made quite clear in the first chapter of the book, but in the remainder it also becomes clear that such a focus permits coverage of most of the topics found in the more common introductory text. Actually, the next five chapters (dealing with psychology as a science, methodology, evolution, physiology, and learning) are in many ways comparable to the treatments provided in more eclectic introductory texts. The behavioral focus and the departure from traditional approaches become most significant in the last six chapters which deal with traditional psychological topics (e.g., language, child development, and personality)—but deal with them systematically in terms of the concepts and principles introduced in the chapters on evolution and physiology, and especially in the chapter on learning. Using the concepts provided early in the text to interpret complex aspects of human behavior provides valuable justification for those concepts, as well as an opportunity for improved understanding of them.

Although students will not make extensive contact with the variety of theoretical approaches found in the typical text, they will become especially competent in the use of behavioral concepts and principles to interpret and understand many of the topics of traditional importance in psychology. As a result, they will be better prepared to attempt a scientific interpretation of behavioral phenomena encountered after they complete their introductory course.

Students who use *Psychology: A Behavioral Overview* will be ideally prepared for further work in a behaviorally oriented undergraduate major, and because of the coverage of traditional topics, they will not feel out of place in later courses taught from a nonbehavioral perspective. The integrated and systematic nature of their understanding of psychology may well constitute a better base from which to explore other theoretical approaches than the knowledge that results from an eclectic introduction to the field. In any case, if they master the material of this text, they will have learned much about the science of behavior.

Jack Michael
Department of Psychology
Western Michigan University
Kalamazoo, Michigan

v

Preface

There are many things that the world obviously needs, but another introductory psychology book is not among them. Dozens of such books are available, and some, like Neil Carlson's *Psychology: The Science of Behavior* (1987), are quite good. Carlson's text is impressive in breadth, depth, and clarity of coverage, and the same can be said for a handful of its competitors. They admirably serve the needs of students and instructors who desire a panoramic perspective on psychology.

Psychology: A Behavioral Overview is more limited in scope than those texts. Most introductory psychology books are lengthy and detailed; they contain too much material to be covered in one semester. Thus, the instructor must ignore substantial sections of the text and forgo consideration of significant topics. This should not be a problem with *Psychology: A Behavioral Overview,* for the book is relatively short.

Moreover, it is a focused volume. In contrast to most introductory psychology texts, the book was not written from an eclectic perspective. Instead, it opts for a generally scientific, and specifically behavioral, orientation. In the absence of such an orientation, the student is given no means of evaluating alternative conceptions, no strategies for imposing order on the tangled web of data and theory encompassed by psychology. This text does not ignore conceptual systems other than behavioral analysis—some have considerable merit—but greatest weight is assigned to those that have a legitimate scientific status. Despite their intuitive appeal, many questions concerning human behavior cannot be answered scientifically, and some explanations of human behavior are meaningless.

Although the orientation is *Psychology: A Behavioral Overview* does not simply describe basic es of behavioral psychology or clinical applications of those principles. one with admirable clarity in other texts (e.g., Fantino & Logan, 1979; Lutz & Martin, 1981). These books do not, however, address many topics that constitute an important part of psychology as laypersons and many professionals envision it. *Psychology: A Behavioral Overview* deals with nearly all of the content areas that are deemed important by laypeople and covered in traditional introductions to psychology.

Organization of the Book

Psychology: A Behavioral Overview contains 12 chapters. The first three introduce psychology and scientific analysis. Chapter 1 describes the discipline of psychology as a whole and introduces behaviorism. Chapter 2 considers what a scientific approach to the study of behavior entails. Such an approach has much to recommend it, but much of contemporary psychology is not scientific. Chapter 3 deals with psychological research. Research plays a crucial role in the development of a science of behavior.

Chapters 4, 5, and 6 consider at very different levels what causes humans and other organisms to behave as they do. Chapter 4 provides an introduction to evolution and considers its significance in the study of behavior. Like most scientists, we accept the evolution of humans and other species as fact, arguments about precise mechanisms notwithstanding. Evolution is important to psychologists because it determines the range of behaviors that members of a species can acquire and their ease of acquisition. In a real sense, all of the behavior we exhibit depends on evolutionary history. We would not, for example, be able to learn about psychology had not central nervous systems adequate to the task evolved in our ancestors. Chapter 5 deals with the role that the central nervous system and other physiological structures play in controlling behavior. Changes in behavior cannot occur without changes in physiology; hence, there is good reason to explore brain–behavior interactions. There is, however, also reason to examine how behavior is affected by events outside the organism, that is, by environmental variables. This is the level of analysis characteristic of behavior analysis, which is summarized in Chapter 6. Learning is its topic.

The remainder of the book builds on principles introduced in the first six chapters to deal with topics traditionally of importance to psychologists. Language, consciousness, and memory have long fascinated psychologists and are the topic of Chapter 7. Chapter 8 addresses child development, the changes in behavior that characteristically occur during the first few years of life. Personality is explored in Chapter 9. It begins by considering the meaning of personality, then proceeds to an examination of significant theories of personality. The behavior of people in groups—that is, social psychology—is the subject of Chapter 10. Chapter 11 deals with abnormal behavior, broadly construed to include mental illness, mental retardation, and drug abuse. Diagnosis, etiology, and treatment are addressed. Applications of behavioral psychology is the topic of Chapter 12. This chapter considers how behavioral interventions are used to solve problems in many areas.

Three themes run through the book. First is that many traditional explanations of behavior are fundamentally inadequate. The second is that behavior is controlled by evolutionary variables, physiological variables, and environmental variables. The third is that an effective behavior-change technology based on manipulation of environmental variables has been developed. If the reader is convinced that these themes are legitimate, our primary objective has been attained.

Limitations of the Book

The reader should be forewarned that some of the material in *Psychology: A Behavioral Overview* may prove difficult. Human behavior is remarkably diverse and complex; thus, it should come as no surprise that it is not easy to explain. Although we have endeavored to emphasize fundamentals, not details, and to write without undue embellishment, the concepts of a science of behavior are no less challenging than, for example, those of chemistry.

Unlike the concepts of chemistry, which generally do not conflict with lay notions, the concepts of behavioral psychology frequently clash with everyday conceptions in which behavior is assumed to be the result of mental activity: thoughts, feelings, desires, cognitions, and so on. This clash may trouble some students. We beg their forbearance. Gleaning anything of value from *Psychology: A Behavioral Overview* requires two things from the reader. The first is a willingness to accept an analysis of human behavior that shares little with folklore or commonsense notions. The second is a willingness to accept the fact that human behavior is complex and is controlled by evolutionary, physiological, and environmental variables.

Our coverage of how behavior is controlled occurs is rudimentary, in part because no one understands behavior completely and in part because of spatial limitations. As noted earlier, *Psychology: A Behavioral Overview* is not encyclopedic in its coverage. Some phenomena of interest to more than a few psychologists are ignored completedly; others are no more than briefly described. No single topic is covered completely—books could be and have been written about each chapter topic, and about most chapter subtopics. Surely experts in behavior analysis, or in any other area we address, will not be enlightened by our coverage. But except to avert their ire by avoiding egregious errors, we did not write the book for experts. We wrote it instead for the vast number of people interested in, and largely ignorant of, why we humans behave as we do.

Many people made substantial contributions to this book and we are grateful to each of them. Special thanks are due Shery Chamberlain, Sue Keller, Herman Makler, Vicky Pellettiere, and Roger Ulrich. We appreciate your help.

Contents

CHAPTER 1

The Study of Behavior

This book obviously deals with psychology, but what is that? This chapter addresses the question and also summarizes the historical development of psychology as a discipline. Primary emphasis is placed on the development and defining characteristics of behaviorism, a unique approach to the study of behavior.

What Is Psychology?

The term **psychology** comes from the ancient Greek *psyche*, which refers to the "breath of life" present in living people. Although the psyche was not directly observable, Aristotle and his associates assumed that it was never present in inanimate objects, and that it departed the living at the moment of death. Contemporary psychologists concern themselves not with the psyche, but with something else that distinguishes living and nonliving beings: behavior. Psychology is often defined as the **scientific study of behavior,** although much that passes for psychology is neither scientific nor directly concerned with behavior.

People who call themselves psychologists are specially trained and hold advanced (e.g., M.A., Ph.D., or Ed.D.) degrees.[1] They do many things. Some perform clinical services. Others teach or conduct research. A few do all three. The results of a 1983 survey indicated that the primary placements of doctoral-level psychologists, in descending order, were in (1) academia (i.e., colleges and universities); (2) independent practice; (3) hospitals and clinics; and (4) business, government, and other settings (Stapp, Tucker, & VandenBos, 1985). For masters-level psychologists, the ranking of placements was (1) secondary and elementary schools; (2) hospitals and clinics; (3) academia; and (4) business, government, and other settings.

Psychologists work in many places, and they do many different things. The diversity of psychology is evident in Table 1-1, which lists the 45 divisions of the American Psychological Association (APA). The APA is the largest and most powerful organization of psychologists in the United States.

[1]Psychiatrists, who are sometimes confused with psychologists, hold the M.D. degree. Unlike psychologists, psychiatrists can legally prescribe drugs.

Table 1-1
Divisions of the American Psychological Association[a]

Division number	Division name
1	Division of General Psychology
2	Division on the Teaching of Psychology
3	Division of Experimental Psychology
5	Division on Evaluation and Measurement
6	Division of Physiological and Comparative Psychology
7	Division on Developmental Psychology
8	The Society of Personality and Social Psychology—A Division of the APA
9	The Society of the Psychological Study of Social Issues—A Division of the APA
10	Division of Psychology and the Arts
12	Division of Clinical Psychology
13	Division of Consulting Psychology
14	The Society for Industrial and Organizational Psychology, Inc.—A Division of the APA
15	Division of Educational Psychology
16	Division of School Psychology
17	Division of Counseling Psychology
18	Division of Psychologists in Public Service
19	Division of Military Psychology
20	Division of Adult Development and Aging
21	The Society of Engineering Psychologists—A Division of the APA
22	Division of Rehabilitation Psychology
23	Division of Consumer Psychology
24	Division of Theoretical and Philosophical Psychology
25	Division for the Experimental Analysis of Behavior
26	Division of the History of Psychology
27	Division of Community Psychology
28	Division of Psychopharmacology
29	Division of Psychotherapy
30	Division of Psychological Hypnosis
31	Division of State Psychological Association Affairs
32	Division of Humanistic Psychology
33	Division of Mental Retardation
34	Division of Population and Environmental Psychology
35	Division of the Psychology of Women
36	Psychologists Interested in Religious Issues—A Division of the APA
37	Division of Child, Youth, and Family Services
38	Division of Health Psychology
39	Division of Psychoanalysis
40	Division of Clinical Neuropsychology
41	The Psychology-Law Society—A Division of the APA
42	Division of Psychologists in Independent Practice
43	Division of Family Psychology
44	The Society for the Psychological Study of Lesbian and Gay Issues—A Division of the APA
45	The Society for the Psychological Study of Ethnic Minority Issues—A Division of the APA
46	Division of Media Psychology
47	Division of Exercise and Sport Psychology

[a]There are no Divisions 4 or 11.

Even psychologists within the same specialty area may differ widely. Consider two Ph.D.-level clinical psychologists. Each is licensed in New Mexico, is a member of APA Division 12 (Clinical Psychology), and is engaged in private practice. One is trained in rational-emotive psychology in the tradition of Albert Ellis; the other is trained in behavioral psychology in the tradition of B. F. Skinner. Both are attempting to help a depressed client; their goal is the same. How they pursue that goal, however, will differ widely. Although both are well-trained and competent clinicians, they will in all likelihood disagree about the causes of depression, how it should be treated, and the appropriate techniques for evaluating a patient's reaction to treatment. Each of them will succeed with some clients and fail with others, but in all cases, they will go about their business in unlike fashion.

Scientists who use the same conceptual framework and share a body of assumptions, methods, and values adhere to the same **paradigm.** Thomas Kuhn (e.g., 1970) popularized the use of the term *paradigm* in this sense, and he posited that science proceeds not in a smooth progression but rather in a series of rather dramatic **paradigm shifts.** In a paradigm shift, one way of examining and explaining a part of the world is usurped by another. The usurper is usually a paradigm that, in some sense, better accounts for observations than the one it replaces.

Astronomy provides a clear example of a paradigm shift. Before the sixteenth century, it was widely believed that the earth was stationary and that the sun and planets revolved around it. This geocentric (earth-centered) conception of the solar system is usually termed the *Ptolemaic system* in honor of Claudius Ptolemy, an astronomer who lived in Egypt during the second century A.D. For many years the Ptolemaic system appeared to be perfectly adequate. It accounted rather well for the observed positions of heavenly bodies, and moreover, it made good sense. Humans, divinely and uniquely created, lived on earth, and it seemed eminently reasonable that their home should be centrally located and immobile.

In the mid-1500s, however, the Polish astronomer Nicolaus Copernicus and others came to believe that the earth and the other planets revolve around the sun and that the turning of the earth on its axis, not the rotation of heavenly bodies around the earth, accounts for the apparent movement of the stars across the sky. This heliocentric (sun-centered) conception of the solar system is termed the *Copernican system.*

More than 200 years passed before the Copernican system was widely accepted. At the time it was conceived, there was no overwhelming reason to accept it over the Ptolemaic system, for both accounted reasonably well for the apparent movement of heavenly bodies. The clergy and most scholars and laypersons staunchly supported the Ptolemaic system and considered advocates of the Copernican system heretics. Among the alleged heretics was Galileo Galilei. Galileo helped to invent the telescope, which he used in astronomical observations. Those observations led him to believe in a heliocentric solar system, a belief that led the church to excommunicate him. Excommunication in those times was no laughing matter.

Copernicus had been dead for a century and half when, in 1669, the English physicist Robert Hooke provided confirmation that the earth revolves around the sun. Hooke measured the position of the star Gamma Draconis and found clear evidence of stellar parallax (a perceived difference in the position of a star due to the motion of the earth around the sun). But subsequent attempts to demonstrate parallax with other stars produced conflicting results, and the controversy continued. Only with the coming of better telescopes and more refined measurement systems did doubt cease: There is stellar parallax, and the earth does revolve around the sun.

This example of a paradigm shift demonstrates four important points:

1. *Scientists often disagree*. In many cases, legitimate scientists hold different opinions.
2. *Scientists are influenced by their culture.* The opinions of scientists are determined in part by the society in which they live.
3. *Science is fallible*. The opinions of scientists may be in error.
4. *Science is self-correcting*. Erroneous conceptions, if significant, are eventually demonstrated to be in error and are replaced. In many cases, a modification of existing paradigms may be sufficient to correct erroneous conceptions. Occasionally, scientific progress demands a complete paradigm shift. When this occurs, disagreements are likely to be frequent and rancorous.

At the present time, psychologists accept many different views of behavior; no one paradigm is dominant. Some authors see the field as being encompassed by two general and competing paradigms, the **behavioral** (or behavioristic) and the **cognitive**. As Barber (1976) pointed out:

> the behavioristic paradigm emphasizes objective descriptions of environmental events, operational definitions, and controlled experiments while the cognitive paradigm emphasizes internal information processing and programming. The investigator who adheres to the behavioristic paradigm seeks antecedent environmental and situational events that can be related to denotable behaviors. On the other hand, the investigator who adheres to the cognitive paradigm seeks to construct a model of internal processes and structures that can lead to the observed output. These contrasting paradigms lead to different questions and to different ways of designing and conducting investigations. Furthermore, even if psychologists who adhere to these divergent paradigms obtain similar data—which is highly unlikely since they will conduct quite different studies—their paradigms will lead to divergent interpretations of the data. (p. 8)

As indicated by its title, *Psychology: A Behavioral Overview* was written by authors who accept the behavioral paradigm. The remainder of this chapter summarizes the historical development of that paradigm and outlines its essential features.

A Brief History of Behaviorism

Behaviorism is a unique and recent approach to the study of behavior. Psychology is rooted in philosophy and it is possible to detect antecedents to behaviorism in the writings of René Descartes (1596–1650), who attempted to provide a mechanistic explanation of behavior, and Auguste Comte (1787–1857), who founded the movement called **positivism**. According to Comte, the only valid knowledge stems from objective observations. Observations are **objective** if the events of interest can be observed by more than one person, **subjective** if they cannot. In part, early behaviorism arose as an objection to the subjective methods that characterized psychology in the early 1900s.

Psychology was very young at that time; most scholars agree that it emerged as a separate discipline in Germany around 1875. Wilhelm Wundt (1832–1920) may fairly be considered the founder of psychology as a formal academic discipline. He founded the first psychological laboratory, edited the first psychology journal, and initiated psychology as a science (Schultz, 1975). Wundt investigated sensation and perception, attention, feeling, and association, areas that continue to be important to psychologists today. He approached these topics from a perspective that later came to be known as **structuralism.** Structuralism was one of two major schools of thought in the early days of psychology. Like most other early psychologists, Wundt was concerned with the nature of the mind, which he believed was responsible for behavior. For him, the appropriate goal of psychology was to discern mental structures and processes. Using a method of self-observation called **introspection** (see Sidebar 1-1), Wundt and other struc-

---

Sidebar 1-1
What Is Introspection?

The term *introspection* comes from the Latin *introspicere,* meaning "to look into." In the vernacular of today, introspection refers to self-examination, the contemplation of one's own feelings and thoughts. Introspection is commonly considered a means of accessing mental activity, which is revealed to others in verbal statements. A friend asks, for example, "What are you thinking about?" You introspect briefly, then reply, "I was thinking about how to study for my biology final next Friday." Your friend has no way of knowing whether this is true—you may have been thinking about how you'd like to be left alone—or of determining what is responsible for the thoughts you reported. Nonetheless, the report may be of some practical value: It may, for instance, suggest that you are more likely to study Thursday evening than to go dancing.

The introspective techniques used by Wundt, Titchener, and other early psychologists were far more tightly structured than the example above. These techniques used well-trained subjects who were taught to use a limited range of words to describe their conscious response to specific items, perhaps a word or a color, presented under tightly controlled conditions. These refinements were intended to make the techniques less subjective and more scientific. To some extent, they did so, but these intro-

spective techniques were still widely criticized for several reasons (Schultz, 1975):

1. The reports of well-trained subjects frequently were not in agreement.
2. The use of well-trained subjects raised questions about whether they were actually reporting conscious happenings or were only saying what they had been trained to say.
3. The act called *introspection* was actually retrospection; subjects were looking backward in time.
4. The appropriate interpretation of verbal reports was unclear: How do verbal statements relate to mental events?
5. The use of introspective techniques was limited to highly verbal adult subjects. No complete psychology could be built on the study of such a limited group.
6. Introspective techniques yielded information only about conscious mental processes. Much of behavior, however, occurs without conscious correlates.

Contemporary psychologists do not deny that people "talk to themselves," or that they can report their internal states. They recognize, however, that introspection does not provide a useful window to the mind.

turalists, among them Edward Titchener (1867–1927), investigated private activities such as sensations, images, and feelings. The objectives of structuralism as expressed by Wundt were three (Schultz, 1975): "(1) to analyze the conscious processes into their basic elements; (2) to discover how these elements are connected; and (3) to determine their laws of connection" (p. 61). These objectives were not attained, and structuralism died with Titchener in 1927. It is important, however, as an early attempt to apply the methods of science to the study of behavior.

The primary alternative to structuralism, termed **functionalism** (or functional psychology), was concerned with the mind as it is used in the adaptation of the organism to its environment (Schultz, 1975). Primary questions for the functionalists were: What does the mind do? And how are these things accomplished? Charles Darwin, Francis Galton, and William James were intellectual ancestors of functional psychology; G. Stanley Hall, James McKeen Cattell, Harvey Carr, and John Dewey were its foremost practitioners. Psychology in the United States today is definitely functional in orientation, even though functionalism is not recognized as a unique paradigm.

Functionalism clearly influenced John B. Watson (1878–1958), who is generally credited with making the first clear statement of the behavioristic position. Most functionalists (e.g., Carr, 1925) contended that there was good reason to consider practical applications of psychology. Moreover, certain functionalists argued for an objective psychology, one that emphasized overt behavior rather than consciousness, and they suggested that the study of nonhumans[2] could play a valuable role in such a psychology. The psychology that Watson developed was to be objective, practical, and based in large part on the study of nonhumans.

Before the publication in 1859 of Charles Darwin's *On the Origin of Species by Means of Natural Selection*, there was general agreement that little could be learned about the mind (or behavior) of humans through the study of other animals. As Schultz (1975) put it, "[Prior to Darwin] there was no reason for scientific interest in the animal mind because animals were considered to be soulless automata with no point of similarity to or commonality with man" (p. 125). A major implication of Darwin's work is the absence of a sharp mental or physical discontinuity between humans and other animals. To test this notion, a search for evidence of similar mental processes in humans and nonhumans was begun. Because actions of the mind cannot be directly observed but must be inferred on the basis of overt behavior, the actual search was for similar behaviors in different species. Darwin (1872), for example, provided many examples of behavioral continuity between humans and other primates.

Early studies of nonhumans influenced Watson, who once stated that "Behaviorism is a direct outgrowth of studies in animal behavior during the first decade of the twentieth century" (1929, p. 327). Ivan Pavlov (1849–1936) and

---

[2]When humans are compared to other species, many authors, including some whose writings we quote, have designated the latter collectively as *animals* or *infrahumans*. There is nothing beyond precedent to recommend this practice. Humans are in fact animals, and other species are not clearly inferior to us. Therefore, when comparing humans and other species, we will designate the latter as *nonhumans* or as *other animals*, not as *animals* or *infrahumans*.

Edward Thorndike (1874–1949) bear special mention as researchers whose work affected Watson.

Pavlov was a Soviet physiologist who in 1904 won a Nobel Prize for his work on digestion. He is best known, however, for an offshoot of that work, the study of conditioned reflexes. Interestingly, much of his important work began with a fortunate, but accidental, discovery. Pavlov knew that placing food in a hungry dog's mouth elicits salivation as a reflex. Moreover, his observations showed that the sight of food, or the sight or sound of the man who brought it, also elicited salivation. Somehow, these **stimuli** (forms of energy) had come to bring about salivation, just as did the food: The unlearned **response** (measurable unit of behavior) of salivation had been conditioned to stimuli that reliably preceded food presentation, or to put it another way, the reflex had been conditioned, or learned. After considerable deliberation, Pavlov set out to investigate this phenomenon. His investigations, conducted over a span of more than 20 years, were remarkably objective and precise. Pavlov found no value in subjective or mentalistic explanations of behavior. He wrote:

> [In our first experiments] we conscientiously endeavored to explain our results by imagining the subjective state of the animal. But nothing came of this except sterile controversy and individual views that could not be reconciled. And so we could do nothing but conduct the research on a purely objective basis. (Quoted in Cuny, 1965, p. 65)

Pavlov recognized that speculations about the internal state of subjects were of little value in explaining the changes in behavior observed in conditioning. Of far greater explanatory value were the relations between stimuli that were responsible for the conditioning. Pavlov and his many collaborators explored these relations with great care and discovered the basic principles of classical (or respondent) conditioning. These principles, outlined in Chapter 6, basically describe how learning can occur through the correlation, or pairing, of neutral stimuli (e.g., the sight of food) with stimuli (e.g., food in the mouth) that reflexively control responding (e.g., salivation). Note that, in respondent conditioning, events outside the organism—that is, stimulus–stimulus pairings—are responsible for changes in behavior. The work of Pavlov is significant in the development of behaviorism because it shifted the search for causes of behavior from inside the organism to events in the environment. It is also significant in its objectivity, its use of nonhuman subjects, and its demonstration of respondent conditioning. The same is true of the research conducted by two other Soviet physiologists, Ivan Sechenov (1829–1905) and Vladimir Bekhterev (1857–1927). Although less well known than Pavlov, both of these men championed the objective study of reflexive behavior. Bekhterev (1907), in fact, went so far as to attempt to explain psychiatric disturbances and complex mental events in terms of conditioned reflexes. His writings appear to have exercised considerable influence on Watson's early work (Moore, 1987).

Edward Thorndike was a contemporary of Pavlov and Bekhterev. Like them, Thorndike was interested in learning, used objective methods to study overt behavior, and attempted to explain learning in terms of environmental events. Although he came to favor human subjects in his later years, much of Thorndike's early research involved the study of cats in an apparatus known as a **puzzle box.** This was a relatively small slatted enclosure equipped with a door that was latched in place. In a typical experiment, a cat would be deprived of food for a period, then placed in the puzzle box with food located outside. A specified response, such as pulling a chain or pushing a lever, unlatched the door and allowed the cat to reach the food. Thorndike observed the cat and recorded the amount of time it required to unlatch and open the door. When this had occurred and the cat had eaten, it was returned to the puzzle box for another test trial.

Thorndike found that, in early trials, the cats escaped through trial and error; many behaviors occurred until one unlatched the door. With repeated exposure to the puzzle box, however, the subjects learned to respond correctly. The time required for them to escape from the box diminished greatly, as did the number of wrong responses (i.e., behaviors that did not unlatch the door) they emitted.

Thorndike speculated that learning occurred because of the consequences of particular responses, as described in the **law of effect** for which he is famous:

> Any act which in a given situation produces satisfaction becomes associated with that situation, so that when the situation recurs the act is more likely than before to recur also. Conversely, any act which in a given situation produces discomfort becomes disassociated from that situation, so that when the situation recurs the act is less likely than before to recur. (Thorndike, 1905, p. 203)

According to Thorndike, the consequences of behavior stamp in (strengthen) or stamp out (weaken) connections between stimuli (the situation in which the behavior occurs) and behavior. Because of this orientation, Thorndike is sometimes called a **connectionist.**

Watson favored the objective methods used by Thorndike. In part as a rejection of the introspective methods of his time, Watson (e.g., 1930) proposed that psychology should confine itself to the study of observables. He excluded mental events from analysis because such events are not directly observable; therefore, it is impossible to measure them precisely, or even to determine with assurance whether or not they have occurred. A person introspecting surely can describe her or his mental activity, but how is one to know that the description is accurate? Watson solved this problem through what has come to be known as **methodological behaviorism,** an approach to psychology in which all assertions are based only on directly observable events.

Watson appreciated Thorndike's objectivity, but he did not accept Thorndike's law of effect. In a discussion of how habits (learned responses) are acquired, Watson (1930) complained:

> Most of the psychologists, it is to be regretted, have even failed to see that there is a problem. They believe habit formation is implanted by kind fairies. For example, Thorndike speaks of pleasure stamping in the successful movement and displeasure stamping out the unsuccessful movement. (p. 206)

One can understand Watson's displeasure with the "stamping in and out" metaphor. Nonetheless, the fundamental message of the law of effect—that the consequences of behavior can powerfully influence learning and performance—is a cornerstone of contemporary behavioral psychology.

It did not play such a role in Watsonian behaviorism. Watson was strongly influenced by Soviet studies of respondent conditioning, and he largely discounted the role of consequences in learning. Perhaps as a result, Watson failed to develop a satisfactory explanation of how environmental events influence behavior. He was, however, convinced that environmental variables,[3] not genetic inheritance, were responsible for nearly all of human behavior, and he voiced strong arguments in favor of this position. In perhaps the most famous passage he ever wrote, Watson (1930) asserted:

> Give me a dozen healthy infants, well-formed, and my own specified world to bring them up in and I'll guarantee to take any one at random and train him to become any type of specialist I might select—doctor, lawyer, artist, merchant-chief and, yes, even beggarman and thief, regardless of his talents, penchants, tendencies, abilities, vocations, and race of his ancestors. I am going beyond my facts and I admit it, but so have advocates of the contrary and they have been doing it for many thousands of years.[4] (p. 104)

According to Watson, the only way to make sense of human behavior is to analyze it scientifically. He wrote, for instance, "It is the business of behavioristic psychology to be able to predict and control human activity. To do this it must gather scientific data by experimental methods" (1930, p. 11). These methods demand directly observable data, and Watson argued for a psychology concerned only with how overt behavior (responding) changes as a function of other observable changes in the environment (stimuli):

> The rule, or measuring rod, which the behaviorist puts in front of him always is: Can I describe this bit of behavior I see in terms of "stimulus and response"? By stimulus we mean any object in the general environment or any change in the tissues themselves due to the physiological condition of the animal, such as the change we get when we keep an animal from sex activity, when we keep it from feeding, when we keep it from building a nest. By response we mean anything the animal does—such as turning toward or away from a light, jumping at a sound, and more highly organized activities such as building a skyscraper, drawing plans, having babies, and the like. (1930, p. 6)

For Watson, dualistic explanations of behavior, in which an unobserved mind (or soul or other hypothetical entity) is used to explain behavior, were simply and absolutely unacceptable. This does not mean, however, that Watson ignored what are traditionally regarded as cognitive events, such as thinking. In fact, he wrote at some length concerning thinking (e.g., 1930), but unlike his contemporaries, he regarded thinking as behavior, not as an explanation of behavior. This position is still held by most behaviorists.

Watson used experimentation as well as reason in his analysis of complex human behaviors. He claimed, for example, that emotion simply involved a special class of conditioned responses, and he purported to demonstrate this claim in a well-known investigation of an 11-month-old child, Little Albert (Watson & Rayner, 1920). In the first phase of the study, Albert was presented with a white rat, which produced no adverse response in the boy. In the second phase of the study, crying was conditioned by making a loud noise (produced by striking a metal bar with a hammer) immediately after presenting the rat to

[3]A variable is any object or event that can be measured in physical units that are not immutably fixed, and that are, in principle, capable of changing.
[4]The last sentence of this passage, which is rarely cited, indicates a recognition that human behavior is not endlessly subject to modification. In fact, Watson goes on to discuss variables that could, in his opinion, limit the effectiveness of training.

Albert. After seven rat–noise pairings, the rat was presented alone: Little Albert gave a start, fell over, and started to cry. This reaction, according to Watson was conditioned fear. Interestingly, the behavior generalized to items similar in appearance to the rat, such as a rabbit, a dog, cotton, and a Santa Claus mask, although these items had not controlled such responses before conditioning.

Watson was a skilled polemicist who clearly articulated the virtues of an objective science of behavior; in fact, he went so far as to propose at the end of *Behaviorism* (1930, pp. 303–304) that such a science could foster a utopian society. His arguments affected laypeople as well as psychologists, although not all agreed with him, and it is fair in view of his lasting influence to consider Watson the founder and early leader of behaviorism. His role as leader lasted for less than two decades; scandalous divorce proceedings brought against him in 1920 led to his resignation from Johns Hopkins University and effectively ended his academic career. After the divorce, Watson married his laboratory assistant and went on to a successful career in advertising.

Perhaps Watson's greatest contribution to psychology was his advocacy of a completely objective science of behavior, one in which observations of overt behavior—what an organism actually does—form the basis of all conclusions. Most contemporary psychologists are methodological behaviorists in the sense that they base their conclusions on overt responses (Schultz, 1975).

Several people built on the foundations laid by Watson to develop psychological systems. Among them were Edward Tolman (1886–1959), Edwin Guthrie (1886–1959), and Clark Hull (1884–1952). Tolman is known as the developer of purposive behaviorism. In this system, behavior is assumed to be the result of (1) environmental stimuli; (2) physiological drive; (3) heredity; (4) previous training; and (5) age. Tolman proposed that these things did not affect behavior directly but influenced internal processes in the subject (called *intervening variables*), which in turn affected behavior. Although Tolman's approach is termed *purposive behaviorism*, it is actually cognitive in that mental events are posited as intervening variables. For example, Tolman proposed that rats learned a maze by constructing a "cognitive map." Unlike Tolman, Guthrie was not interested in intervening variables. He was a theorist who proposed that learning occurred because connections were formed when a stimulus and response occurred together in time. There was relatively little empirical support for the theoretical position that he advocated, and it did not long endure.

In the tradition of Watson, Guthrie did not emphasize the role of consequences in controlling behavior. Hull, in contrast, recognized the importance of consequences. To account for their effects, and for those of other events, Hull constructed a complex and formal theoretical system based on need reduction. The system was constructed as a set of detailed postulates and corollaries, all presented in verbal and mathematical form. Most of Hull's work involved testing theoretical predictions and modifying his system to incorporate experimental results. These modifications made the system elaborate and cumbersome—there were 18 postulates and 12 corollaries in his last version (Hull, 1952); yet it failed to provide a good general description of the phenomena of interest. Nonetheless, Hull was committed to the objective and scientific study of behavior, his model was responsible for a great deal of experimentation, and his attempt to develop a quantitative model is noteworthy. His work influenced many contem-

B. F. Skinner in 1961. (Photo
courtesy of Roger Ulrich.)

porary psychologists, but most of them are not associated with the branch of
contemporary psychology we term behaviorism.

*As the term is used in this book, behaviorism is the approach to the study of behavior
popularized by B. F. Skinner* (1904–). The terms **behavior analysis, behaviorism,
the experimental analysis of behavior, radical behaviorism,**[5] **Skinnerian psychology,** and **behaviorology** are also used to refer to this general approach.
Applied behavior analysis and **behavior modification** are more specific terms;
they refer to the use of behavioral principles in the treatment of practical
problems.

Table 1-2 describes several important events in the development of behavioral psychology from the time Skinner laid out the rudiments of his approach in
The Behavior of Organisms, published in 1938. Among the most important events
before 1960 were (1) the founding in 1946 of the Society for the Experimental
Analysis of Behavior, an organization committed to behavior analysis; (2) the

---

[5]The *radical* in *radical behaviorism* designates not a desire for social revolt or political upheaval, but a
behaviorism that is taken to the limit in the sense of attempting to account for most, if not all, of
what organisms do.

publication in 1950 of Keller and Schoenfeld's *Principles of Psychology,* a clear introduction to behavioral psychology; (3) the publication in 1953 of Skinner's *Science and Human Behavior,* discussed below; and (4) the founding in 1958 of the *Journal of the Experimental Analysis of Behavior (JEAB),* the first journal devoted to behavior analysis.

Science and Human Behavior was especially important, for in it Skinner described how a scientific approach could be of value in understanding human behavior, and in changing it for the better. According to Michael (1980):

Table 1-2
Some Important Events in the Development of Behavior Analysis

Year	Event
1938	Skinner publishes *The Behavior of Organisms,* which sets forth the basic principles of behavioral psychology.
1946	The Society for the Experimental Analysis of Behavior, which publishes the *JEAB* and the *Journal of Applied Behavior Analysis (JABA),* was founded.
1948	Skinner publishes the controversial *Walden Two,* a novel describing a utopian society built on the principles of behavioral psychology.
1950	Keller and Schoenfeld publish *Principles of Psychology,* an influential introduction to behavior analysis.
1953	*Science and Human Behavior* appears. In this book, Skinner extends to human behavior the analysis outlined in *The Behavior of Organisms.*
1957	*Schedules of Reinforcement,* by Ferster and Skinner, and Skinner's *Verbal Behavior* are published. The former is a detailed examination of how consequences affect behavior; the latter is a behavioral analysis of verbal behavior.
1958	*JEAB,* the first journal devoted entirely to behavioral psychology, is founded.
1960	The research philosophy and methodology characteristic of behavior analysis are described in Sidman's *Tactics of Scientific Research*
1961	Bijou and Baer publish Volume 1 of *Child Development,* which offers a behavioral approach to a field traditionally dominated by cognitive theories. A self-instructional text describing basic principles of behavior analysis also appears (Holland & Skinner, 1961)
1964	Division 25 of the American Psychological Association, the Division for the Experimental Analysis of Behavior, is formed.
1965	*Case Studies in Behavior Modification* by Ullmann and Krasner is published. This text describes the application of behavioral principles to the solution of socially significant problems.
1966	Two important texts appear, one providing reviews of basic research in many areas of behavioral psychology (Honig, 1966), the other (Ulrich, Stachnik, & Mabry, 1966) describing clinical applications of behavioral principles.
1968	*JABA,* the first journal dedicated to publishing reports of the clinical application of behavior principles, is inaugurated.
1969	Skinner publishes *Contingencies of Reinforcement,* a book in which several important conceptual issues are addressed.
1972	The journal *Behaviorism* is founded. It is devoted primarily to theoretical and philosophical issues.
1974	The Midwestern Association of Behavior Analysis is founded. Its name was changed in 1978 to the Association for Behavior Analysis (ABA). Skinner's *About Behaviorism,* a good summary of his position, also appears.
1978	The inaugural issue of *The Behavior Analyst,* official journal of the ABA, appears.

In *Science and Human Behavior,* using only the basic concepts of behavior analysis that appeared in *The Behavior of Organisms,* some results of his subsequent work with pigeons, and the material that subsequently went into *Verbal Behavior,* he managed to deal with a wide variety of human situations from a completely behavioral point of view, and very convincingly at that. It was this extension to all aspects of human activity that, I think, provided behaviorists with the encouragement necessary for them to begin contributing to the areas of mental illness, mental retardation, and other applied fields. (p. 4)

Science and Human Behavior encouraged behaviorists to apply themselves to the solution of human behavior problems, but they did so only sporadically in the decade following its publication. Before the mid-1960s, most research in behavioral psychology used nonhuman subjects and was intended primarily to increase understanding of the variables that control behavior. By 1965, however, behaviorists were steadfastly attempting to explain and treat problem behaviors in a variety of human populations. These early clinical endeavors were reported in a number of sources, including texts edited by Ullmann and Krasner (1965) and by Ulrich, Stachnik, and Mabry (1966). In 1968, a new journal appeared, devoted entirely to the publication of articles describing behaviorists' attempts to deal with practical problems, and entitled the *Journal of Applied Behavior Analysis (JABA).*

Contemporary behavior analysts are engaged in a very wide range of activities. The scope of the field is evident in Table 1-3, which lists the 16 general-interest areas represented at the 1988 Association for Behavior Analysis (ABA) Convention. This organization, founded in 1974 as the Midwestern Association of Behavior Analysis, is an interdisciplinary group interested in behavior analysis. A perusal of Table 1-3 will indicate that their interests cover most of psychology as traditionally defined. Although behavior analysts are not equally active in all areas, it appears that any problem involving the behavior of organisms can be appropriately dealt with from the behavioral perspective.

Table 1-3
General-Interest Areas Represented
at the 1988 ABA Convention

Behavioral Clinical Interventions
Behavioral Community Interventions
Behavioral Family Interventions
Behavioral Gerontology
Behavioral Medicine
Behavioral Pharmacology and Toxicology
Behavior Analysis in Business and Industry
Computer Applications
Developmental Disabilities
Educational Technologies
Ethical, Legal, and Social Issues
Experimental Analysis
Sport Behavior Analysis
Staff Interventions in Human Service Settings
Theoretical and Philosophical Analysis
Verbal Behavior

The Behavioral Perspective

Behaviorism rests on three assumptions that, when considered together, differentiate it from other approaches to psychology. Behavior analysts assume that:

1. *Psychology should be scientific.* Accepting a scientific approach to the study of psychology requires the acceptance of several additional assumptions and imposes limits on how information is collected and interpreted. Chapter 2 is devoted entirely to science and its relation to psychology.

2. *Environmental variables play a key role in controlling behavior.* **Environmental variables** are events that occur in the world outside an organism, or within its own body. Behaviorists emphasize the importance of environmental events in controlling behavior, and in this, they differ dramatically from cognitive psychologists, who stress the role of cognitive events in controlling behavior. The difference in the two approaches is readily apparent in the following passage by Skinner (1974):

The human environment is remarkably complex. What kinds of variables may be affecting the behavior of the students in this picture? Remember that the environment comprises living beings and their actions, as well as inanimate objects. (Photo courtesy of Neil Rankin.)

A behavioristic analysis rests on the following assumptions: A person is first of all an organism, a member of a species and a subspecies, possessing a genetic endowment of anatomical and physiological characteristics, which are the product of the contingencies of survival to which the species has been exposed in the process of evolution. The organism becomes a person as it acquires a repertoire of behavior under the contingencies of reinforcement to which it is exposed during its lifetime. The behavior it exhibits at any moment is under the control of a current setting. It is able to acquire such a repertoire under such control because of processes of conditioning which are also part of its genetic endowment. In the traditional mentalistic view, on the other hand, a person is a member of the human species who behaves as he does because of many internal characteristics or possessions, among them sensations, habits, intelligence, opinions, dreams, personalities, moods, decisions, fantasies, skills, percepts, thoughts, virtues, intentions, abilities, instincts, daydreams, incentives, acts of will, joy, compassion, perceptual defenses, beliefs, complexes, expectancies, urges, choice, drives, ideas, responsibilities, elation, memories, needs, wisdom, wants, a death instinct, a sense of duty, sublimation, impulses, capacities, purposes, wishes, an id, repressed fears, a sense of shame, extraversion, images, knowledge, interests, information, a superego, propositions, experiences, attitudes, conflicts, meanings, reaction formation, a will to live, consciousness, anxiety, depression, fear, reason, libido, psychic energy, reminiscences, inhibitions, and mental illnesses. (pp. 207–208)

The foregoing passage does not imply that behavior analysts reject the existence of what is commonly termed *mental activity*. Skinner has long contended that a complete account of human behavior must include thinking, self-awareness, and related events. These activities are, however, viewed as behaviors to be explained, not as explanations of other behavior.

3. *Behavior is of interest in its own right, not as a sign or symbol of anything else.* That behavior is important in and of itself may seem obvious, but many psychologists are primarily concerned with behavior as a reflection of some underlying process or condition, such as mental illness. The behaviorist, in contrast, assumes that behavior is a rich and fascinating subject matter in its own right. Consider, for example, someone who is considered mentally ill. The interesting thing about such a person is how she or he behaves. It is on this basis and no other that the person is considered mentally ill, assigned a diagnostic label, and exposed to treatment. Take the case of Jim[6]:

Jim was born in a small town and had an apparently normal childhood. An above-average student and a good athlete, he was popular through high school. Though Jim encountered most of the problems characteristic of youth, his parents, teachers, and friends considered him generally warm and well adjusted. In the fall of 1986, at 19 years of age, Jim enrolled in the business administration program at State University. Shortly thereafter, he began to change. At first, the change was subtle: Jim started spending more time alone in his dorm room, reading occult books and listening to music. Over time, his attendance at classes became increasingly sporadic, and on those rare occasions when he did talk to friends, he appeared preoccupied with a spirit, Megog, but was reluctant to answer questions about it. By the end of the fall semester, Jim was spending almost all of his time in his room and rarely interacted with other people.

---

[6]This case is hypothetical in its details, but it is based on events similar to those that actually occur in schizophrenic disorders, although such disorders do not necessarily or characteristically involve violence.

At home for the Christmas holiday, Jim largely avoided his family and old friends. When interactions did occur, they were often painful, as on Christmas Eve, the traditional time for his family to decorate the tree. Instead of helping his parents and older sister with the task, as he had done with evident relish for many years, Jim chastised his family for constructing a graven image, then delivered a rambling and meaningless monologue on Megog, enlightenment, and what he called monothereal karma. Attempts to calm him failed; Jim eventually burst into tears, ran upstairs, and locked himself in a bedroom. An hour later, he came down, apologized, and helped put on the last of the ornaments. Jim was his old self for the rest of Christmas Eve and the next day, and the family had a good Christmas. It was the last good day they were to have for quite some time. Jim's grades—three E's, a D, and an I—arrived the next day, and their arrival precipitated a long and bitter argument. When Jim's parents asked for an explanation of his poor performance, Jim cursed them—something he had never done before—and proclaimed them eternally damned. He did so in phrases odd and disjointed: "Megog knows, tells me, damned bitch-bastards. There isn't much, but we know with the waves. Why is it you make me king? Does the crown fit? Squeeze my skull in, like always. Stretch my soul, too, if its plastic pleases. Isn't one prodigal son enough? Your god isn't mine, isn't yours, isn't anyone's. It's coming back to you; the karma is long-suffering, eternal. The last A you made was mine."

Around noon on December 28, Jim struck his father in the face with a brass candelabra, knocking him unconscious. Two hours later, Jim's mother returned and made two calls: one brought paramedics; the other, the police. Both came and left with appropriate burdens. The next few days were hell for Jim's mother and sister. What they were for father and son is unknowable, for one screamed incoherently in a locked ward and the other lay unmoving in a hospital bed. Each suffered from a condition that could be diagnosed and labeled: Psychiatrists determined Jim to be in the active phase of a schizophrenic disorder, paranoid type. Cerebral concussion was the name assigned his father's primary injury.

In time, both improved. The elder man regained consciousness on the fourth day and suffered no lasting impairment. His son has done less well. Two years after the Christmas of 1986, Jim is living at home. Each day, he takes 400 milligrams of thioridazine (Mellaril), an antipsychotic drug. Jim makes no mention of Megog and has no trouble with his parents. But he seldom interacts with other people and spends most of his time alone. Though Jim occasionally talks about getting a job or returning to school, he has made no progress toward either.

Why is Jim noteworthy? It's tempting to answer, "Because of his schizophrenia." And that is true. But it is important to recognize that schizophrenia is nothing more than a general label for a set of troublesome behaviors that meet certain diagnostic criteria. Jim was labeled schizophrenic because of what he did: Over time, his speech became progressively more bizarre, he failed to meet responsibilities, and his interactions with other people diminished. Finally, he violently assaulted a close relative. In essence, Jim caused a problem for himself and for those around him because he stopped behaving in desirable ways and began behaving in undesirable ways. It was on the basis of his behavior and nothing more that he was diagnosed and treated as a mentally ill person.

As discussed in Chapter 11, behavior defines mental retardation as well as mental illness. Behavior is also the basis of fame and infamy. You undoubtedly are familiar with Henry Aaron and Adolph Hitler. Aaron is famous, Hitler infamous. Why? Because of what they did. Aaron batted well enough to hit over 700 major-league home runs; Hitler acted in ways that led millions to their death. Both outcomes are unique and significant enough to be widely known.

The behavior of most people never attracts widespread attention, but it is important nonetheless. What we do defines us as saints or sinners, friends or fiends—in a word, as individuals. For that reason if for no other, behavior is a fascinating subject.

Defining Behavior

But what, exactly, is behavior? *In a general sense, behavior refers to anything that an organism does.* Many behaviors are **overt** in that they are detectable by other organisms and can be measured objectively. *We can define overt behavior as measurable displacement in space through time of some part of an organism* (see Johnston & Pennypacker, 1980, p. 48). Walking, talking, writing, and eating are examples of overt behaviors. We can easily discern whether one of these responses is occurring, for each involves physical events accessible to people other than the behaver.

As the case of Jim emphasizes, overt responses are both interesting and important. A psychology concerned with such responses and nothing else might well be of practical value, for many of the problems that beset humanity involve overt actions. But, you're probably asking, what about nonpublic events, things that each of us is aware of in ourselves but can't see in others—thinking, feeling, imagining, and the like? Two general positions are possible concerning such events.

One position is simply to exclude from analysis all private phenomena (i.e., those accessible to only one person) on the grounds that science deals only with public events. This position, sometimes caricatured as *black-box* or *empty-organism psychology,* is not widely held today. Many critics nonetheless, and wrongly, consider it characteristic of all behaviorists.

The second position is that private events must be dealt with in any adequate analysis of behavior. Radical behaviorists and other psychologists hold this position. They differ, however, with respect to their interpretation of the nature of the private events. For psychologists who are not radical behaviorists, the private events do not necessarily parallel the public events through which they are indexed, and the former can be physiological, psychic, or metaphorical in nature. Psychologists who take this tack frequently make assertions about cognitive processes (e.g., information retrieval) on the basis of observed relations between overt behavior and environmental events. This position is consistent with traditional approaches in which behavior is assumed to be of interest not in its own right, but only as a reflection of some other process or condition. It differs, however, from the behavioristic approach. As Moore (1987) noted:

> Genuine [or radical] behaviorism advocates the study of the interaction between behavior and the environment as a subject matter in its own right, at the level at which it

occurs. Organisms are held to live in the world and behave with respect to its features. Behavior is not considered as a manifestation or expression of inner acts, states, mechanisms, or processes, and behavior is not explained when observed instances of behavior are cited as the index for postulated organocentric phenomena. Behavior is a function of physical variables, although some of these variables may not be publicly observable. Language, thinking, and such other traditionally mental phenomena are construed as fundamentally behavioral in nature, although not necessarily public. Private phenomena may therefore be dealt with as real, actual *behavioral* phenomena, accessible only to the person involved, rather than as logical inferences. Some private phenomena are bodily states that have a variety of functions, from discriminative to motivational. Others may be understood as covert responses that, by virtue of specific events in an organisms's lifetime, have come to exert discriminative control over subsequent responses. There is an explanatory homogeneity throughout, for public and private behavioral processes as well as for the observer and the observed. (p. 463)

As Moore indicated, radical behaviorists do not deny the existence of what are conventionally termed *feelings, sensations, ideas,* and *thoughts.* They do, however, treat them as behaviors, not as causes of behavior. This position may not be easy to grasp, but a passage by Skinner (1974) should help to make it clear:

> [Radical behaviorism] does not insist upon truth by agreement and can therefore consider events taking place in the private world within the skin. It does not call these events unobservable and does not dismiss them as subjective. It simply questions the nature of the object observed and the reliability of the observations. The position can be stated as follows: what is felt or introspectively observed is not some nonphysical world of unconsciousness, mind, or mental life but the observer's own body. This does not mean . . . that introspection is a kind of physiological research, nor does it mean (and this is the heart of the argument) that what are felt or introspectively observed are the causes of behavior. An organism behaves as it does because of its current [physiological] structure, but most of this is out of reach of introspection. At the moment we must content ourselves, as the methodological behaviorist insists, with a person's genetic and environmental histories. What are introspectively observed are certain collateral products of those histories. (pp. 16–17)

Many of the internal events that we experience and report involve physiological changes in our body of which we are subjectively aware. For instance, a person may say, "I'm hungry," when her stomach "rumbles." It is reasonable to assume that physiological changes also accompany covert behaviors. For example, neurochemical activity undoubtedly occurs when you say to yourself, "I hate calculus," and it is logical to assume that the activity differs from that associated with thinking, "My lab partner is cute." It is also logical to speculate that the physiological activity that is correlated with a covert response (e.g., thinking, "I hate calculus") is similar to that associated with a comparable overt response (e.g., saying out loud, "I hate calculus"). Perhaps the only difference between the two is that the latter involves obvious activation of effectors (muscles or glands). At present, however, we know far too little about neurophysiology to relate discrete actions in the central nervous system to specific behaviors, whether overt or covert.

Three Myths Concerning Behaviorism

Perhaps because they confuse contemporary radical behaviorism with methodological behaviorism, critics of behaviorism frequently misunderstand the role that behaviorists assign to private events, genetic variables, and physiological processes. These misunderstandings have lead to the perpetuation of three myths:

Myth 1: Behaviorists ignore private events. As discussed in the preceding section, this is not true. What is true is that behaviorists do not assign any special status to such activities: they are not seen as explanations of overt behavior or as indicators of mental activity to which unobserved characteristics are ascribed.

Myth 2: Behaviorists consider genetic variables unimportant. This is not the case. Behaviorists know that genetic variables are powerful determinants of what an organism does. Evolution, which acts at the level of genetic material, has determined the behavioral characteristics, as well as the physical structure, of every species. Chapter 4 is devoted entirely to evolution and genetic variables as they relate to behavior.

Myth 3: Behaviorists consider physiological variables unimportant. Again, not so. Behaviorists recognize that everything an organism does is determined by physiological processes. For example, when a child learns to recite the alphabet, there undoubtedly are changes in the central nervous system that parallel the changes in behavior. At present, changes in behavior cannot be related precisely to changes in neuronal activity. Nonetheless, much is known about the structure and function of the brain and other parts of the body, and it is possible to analyze some aspects of behavior in terms of physiological processes. Chapter 5 is devoted to the biology of behavior, that is, to the role of physiological processes in determining what organisms do.

Behaviorists recognize that genetic and physiological variables play a role in controlling how an organism responds in a given situation. They emphasize, however, that environmental variables also influence behavior, and it is the relation between environmental variables and behavior on which they have focused most attention. They have done so because:

1. *Environmental variables clearly influence behavior.*

2. *Environmental variables are directly observable and can be studied with the technology now available.*

3. *Many environmental events that affect behavior are subject to direct manipulation; if they are arranged appropriately, desired behaviors can be fostered.*

Three characteristics of behaviorism result from an emphasis on environmental variables as causes of behavior: Behaviorism is **pragmatic** in that it directs attention to variables that can be directly observed and manipulated. It is **optimistic** in that these variables can be manipulated to help humans behave in desirable ways. It is **parsimonious** in that it explains relations between behavior and the environment in a simple and straightforward fashion. And, as discussed in the next chapter, it is also scientific in its approach to collecting and interpreting information.

Study Questions

1. Be able to (a) describe paradigm and paradigm shift; (b) illustrate the latter with the example of Copernicus; (c) list the four points about science demonstrated by the example; and (d) briefly describe the two general and competing paradigms in psychology.

2. Discuss functionalism (in contrast to structuralism) and how it influenced John B. Watson.

3. Describe the implication of Darwin's work concerning continuity between humans and nonhumans and how it influenced the early development of behaviorism.

4. What was Pavlov's role in the development of behaviorism?

5. Describe Thorndike's role in the development of behaviorism, especially his law of effect and the experimental results explained by this law.

6. Be able to describe how Watson was influenced by Pavlov and Thorndike.

7. What was Watson's greatest contribution to psychology and the development of behaviorism? Was it primarily scientific or philosophical?

8. How is the term *behaviorism* used in this book, and what are some of the other terms that are often used as approximate synonyms? What is the distinction between experimental behavior analysis and applied behavior analysis?

9. What is the point of listing the wide range of activities of contemporary behavior analysts (see Table 1-3)?

10. It is essential that you know the three assumptions that differentiate behavior analysis from other approaches to psychology, and why the example of Jim is noteworthy.

11. How is behavior generally defined, what are the two possible positions on private events, and what is the behavioristic position? (The answer is contained in the quote by Moore.)

12. Be able to (a) state the three myths concerning behaviorism as if you were a critic; (b) provide counterarguments against each of them; (c) provide the three reasons that behaviorists emphasize the role of the environment; and (d) list three characteristics of behaviorism that result from an emphasis on the environment.

Recommended Readings

Leahey, T. H. (1987). *A History of Psychology.* Englewood Cliffs, NJ: Prentice Hall.

There are many scholarly books on the historical development of psychology. This one is relatively easy to read and more interesting than most.

Skinner, B. F. (1974). *About Behaviorism.* New York: Knopf.

Who better to describe behavioral psychology that its premier spokesperson, B. F. Skinner? Several books by Skinner are worth reading, but *About Behaviorism* provides an especially good introduction to his position on a number of important issues. Although it is not easy reading, the richness of its content will reward the dedicated student.

CHAPTER 2

Science and Psychology

Science is not sacred, but it is an especially powerful way to obtain and organize information about objects and events in the natural world. This chapter considers what science is and is not, and it differentiates scientific and nonscientific approaches to explaining phenomena, including behavior.

Characteristics of Science

Like laypeople, psychologists want to understand behavior. But what is understanding? Consider attempting to explain how babies are made. Would you explain the process in the same way to a small child, your roommate, and your biology teacher? Not likely. But how would you know if your explanation satisfied any of these people, that is, if they understood procreation? Probably by noting whether they continued to query you. The small child asks, "Where do babies come from?" and you say, "Storks bring them." No more questions. The child goes blithely forth, secure in understanding. In time, she'll be back: "Come on, level with me. Mom just had twins and the only birds around the hospital were pigeons." And that stork story would never have washed with your roommate. Obviously, what passes for adequate understanding of a phenomenon varies from person to person and, in some instances, over time for the same person.

In many cases, we feel that an event is understood if we know what causes it. A cause in this sense is that which produces an effect or result. Causes occur along a temporal continuum from proximal to distal. A proximal (or immediate) cause is one that is near its effect in time; a distal (or historical) cause is one that is far removed. Consider what causes a person to say, "That's a springer spaniel," when a medium-sized brown-and-white dog appears. One obvious answer is the appearance of the dog; this is a proximal cause. But the situation is surely more complex: The dog's appearance will evoke this response only in a person who has had particular experience with respect to the English language and the naming of springer spaniels. The special events that constitute this experience are causes, just as surely as the appearance of the dog, for the stimulus–response relation (dog–naming) would not have occurred in their absence. The appearance of the dog and the person's experience with respect to the English language and the naming of spaniels are **ontogenetic variables,** for they occurred within the life span of the individual whose behavior is being explained. Most people recognize that proximal and distal ontogenetic variables are important determinants of behavior.

So, too, are phylogenetic variables, which are always distal with respect to a bit of behavior. **Phylogenetic variables** reflect historical (i.e., evolutionary) happenings that determine the characteristics of a species. These characteristics, in turn, determine an organism's response to proximal and distal ontogenetic variables. For a human to respond verbally to the appearance of a dog, she or he obviously must be able to detect the dog visually and to verbalize. Moreover, she or he must be capable of learning. The capacity to see, to speak, and to learn are not present in all species, but they are present in most humans. This is so because of the unique evolutionary history of *Homo sapiens*. The variables that constitute this history are certainly important causes of behavior, although the manner in which they determine a person's verbal response to a particular animal becomes apparent only with reflection.

Psychologists recognize that behavior has many causes. Their attempts to discern and make sense of these causes often closely resemble those of non-specialists; the appeal of many schools of psychological thought is a close parallel to commonsense explanations of behavior. Even so, many psychologists claim that their efforts to explain behavior are scientific and are therefore somehow different from, and perhaps better than, lay explanations. Determining whether this is so requires us to examine what science is and is not.

The word *science* comes from the Latin *scientia*, meaning "knowledge." But as Medawar (1984) so aptly puts it:

> no one construes "science" merely as knowledge. It is thought of rather as knowledge hard won, in which we have much more confidence than we have in opinion, hearsay and belief. The word "science" itself is used as a general name for, on the one hand, the procedures of science—adventures of thought and strategems of inquiry that go into the advancement of learning—and on the other hand, the substantive body of knowledge that is the outcome of this complex endeavor, though this latter is no mere pile of information: Science is organized knowledge, everyone agrees, and this organization goes much deeper than the pedagogic subdivision into the conventional "-ologies," each pigeonholed into lesser topics. (p. 3)

Science, then, is a general strategy for collecting and ordering observations; these ordered observations constitute scientific knowledge. Although science takes many specific forms (the methods of chemistry obviously differ from those of astronomy and paleontology), all scientific disciplines share certain characteristics. Five of the most important characteristics of scientific inquiry are discussed below:

1. *Science deals primarily with empirical phenomena*. The natural world is the source of all scientific information (**data**), and that world consists of **empirical phenomena.** These are objects and events that can be detected through observation or experimentation. Most scientists agree that good data are objective, reliable, and quantitative. As noted in Chapter 1, data are **objective** if the events of interest can be observed by more than one person, **subjective** if they cannot. They are **reliable** if independent observers can agree on whether the events

have occurred. And they are **quantitative** if they can be scaled in physical units along one or more dimensions (termed **parameters**).

Historically, psychology has been plagued by subjective and unreliable data, in part because many phenomena of interest to psychologists can be observed directly only by the person who experiences them. For example, only you are directly aware of your thoughts and feelings, although you can report them to other people and they may be able to observe indirect correlates of them (e.g., the public act of throwing a book may accompany the subjective emotion of anger). The fact that some events are not directly available for public observation does not mean that they do not exist or make these events trivial or uninteresting. It does, however, pose serious problems for scientific analysis.

A long-standing religious and philosophical tradition in which humans are considered **dualistic** beings, made up of body and mind (or soul), also poses problems for a science of behavior. As traditionally conceived of, the mind, which is nonmaterial and subject to control by nonmaterial forces (e.g., deities), determines what the body does (i.e., behavior). The nonmaterial is beyond the realm of science, and insofar as behavior is controlled by nonmaterial phenomena, a science of behavior is impossible. No one can conclusively evaluate the role of the nonmaterial in controlling human behavior; some assign it great weight, others little or none. If, however, one acknowledges that some aspects of behavior are lawfully related to environmental events, those aspects can be analyzed scientifically. A person may place considerable weight on the importance of the nonmaterial yet recognize that much of what we do can be analyzed scientifically. Therefore, it is possible for a behavioral scientist to be religious, and some are. Science is secular, but not necessarily incompatible with religion. Only when religious beliefs are paraded as scientific, as in the recent debate over scientific creationism, is conflict inevitable. Unfortunately, such conflict is not easily resolved, for the evidence that supports scientific belief has little relation to that which supports religious conviction.

2. *Scientific understanding rests primarily on the disclosure of orderly relations between classes of events*. Collecting data is not a unique characteristic of science; all people, scientific or not, gather information about their world. What characterizes scientific analysis is the way in which information is collected and ordered. As noted earlier, understanding an event often involves specifying the variables that caused it to occur. Although there is room for debate about what constitutes a cause-and-effect relation, it appears that we usually conclude that A causes B if the relation between them is as follows: If A, then B, predictably. What laypeople term cause-and-effect relations are called *functional relations* by scientists. When a **functional relation** is evident, the value of one event, termed a *variable* (because its value can vary) determines the value of a second variable. For example, the position of a light switch (up or down) determines whether a light is on or off. Thus there is a functional relation between the position of the light switch and the condition of the light with respect to illumination.

As discussed in Chapter 3, in psychology functional relations are usually demonstrated through experimentation in which the researcher manipulates the value of one variable (termed the **independent variable**) and determines whether doing so changes the value of another variable (termed the **dependent variable**). If the value of the dependent variable varies systematically with the value of the independent variable, the two are functionally related. As Eacker (1972) pointed out, a causal relation "is the relationship between an independent and a dependent variable when the independent one may be prior to or contemporaneous with the dependent variable. In short . . . a causal relation is a functional one" (p. 562). In the example of the light, the switch position causes the light to be on or off.

Figure 2-1 provides graphic representations of sets of data in which functional relations are evident. Four kinds of functional relations are shown. In one, termed a **direct relation,** the value of the dependent variable increases with increases in the value of the independent variable. In another, termed an **inverse relation,** the value of the dependent variable decreases with increases in the value of the independent variable. For instance, body weight increases as caloric intake increases; these variables are directly related. And body weight (the dependent variable) decreases as the number of calories burned increases (the independent variable); this is an inverse relation. Both relations are linear because all of the data points fall along a straight line. Functional relations may also be nonlinear, and two such relations are depicted in Figure 2-1. One of these nonlinear relations is S-shaped, the other takes the form of an inverted U. Many other nonlinear functions are possible, and some are quite complex in form. Nonetheless, in all functional relations, the value of the dependent variable varies lawfully with the value of the independent variable.

Functional relations can be described in verbal statements as well as in graphic representations, as in the statement "Reaction time varies directly with amount of alcohol consumed." Such statements summarize how an independent variable influences a dependent variable, and they are useful to the extent that they do so accurately.

Functional relations between variables are the raw material of science, but to be of value in understanding the world, these relations must be organized and

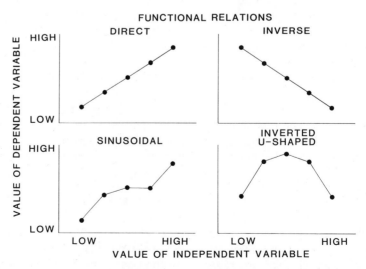

Figure 2-1. Hypothetical data showing four types of functional relations.

classified according to the general principles that they portray. For example, behavioral psychologists have repeatedly demonstrated that the consequences of behavior powerfully influence whether such behavior will recur. Some kinds of consequences weaken behavior, others strengthen it. This general relation has been observed in many species with a wide range of behaviors and consequences and was summarized years ago in Thorndike's law of effect, which appears on page 8.

The law of effect, like all scientific laws, expresses a general relation between classes of variables—responses and their consequences in this case. Scientific laws are based on observation and vary from quite specific to very general. As McCain and Segal (1988) noted, however, four criteria must be applied to any statement before it can be accepted as a scientific law:

> (1) The statement must be about kinds of events and not directly about any singular event. (2) The statement must show a functional relation between two or more kinds of events ("kind of event" refers either to things or to properties of things). (3) There must be a large amount of data confirming the law and little or none disconfirming it. (4) The relation should be applicable to very different events (although there may be limiting conditions). (p. 52)

3. Prediction and control are the goals of scientific analysis. Once it is clear that an independent variable is functionally related to a dependent variable, prediction and control of that dependent variable become possible. Prediction is possible because the value of the independent variable determines the value of the dependent variable. Thus, all other things being equal, the probable value of the dependent variable can be predicted given knowledge of the value of the independent variable. Moreover, the value of the dependent variable can be controlled by selecting the value of independent variable. The practical value of science rests in large part on the isolation of independent variables that are subject to manipulation and that change important parts of the world (i.e., dependent variables) in a manner that benefits humanity.

Some people object to the notion that human behavior can be predicted and controlled. They fear, perhaps, an inhumane world in which a few powerful people manipulate the actions of others to evil ends. Such fear is natural; historical and current events provide too many examples in which control equals oppression. Nevertheless, we can only hope to improve the lot of humanity if it is somehow possible to change what people do. And though we may not like the term, whenever we act to change the behavior of someone else, we are acting as controllers. Consider an alcoholic who comes to a clinical psychologist seeking treatment. In order for the clinician to help the alcoholic, he or she must be able to predict how the client will respond to particular interventions. Moreover, for the intervention to work, the clinician must be effective in controlling the client's behavior with respect to alcohol. Most of us are not opposed to this kind of control; what we object to is control that involves unpleasant means (e.g., privation or corporeal punishment) or leads to undesired ends.

4. Science presupposes an orderly and deterministic reality. As noted above, scientific prediction is possible because some variables are lawfully related to other variables: If A has occurred, then B is likely to follow. Knowing this allows one to predict when B will occur (after A). Such knowledge is dependent on an orderly world, one in which relations revealed in the past (e.g., B follows A) will recur.

Moreover, it requires a deterministic world, one in which the value of some events depends on (e.g., is determined by) the value of other events. This relation holds true regardless of the subject matter of the science. As Skinner (1953) noted:

> If we are to use the methods of science in the field of human affairs, we must assume that behavior is lawful and determined . . . that what a man does is the result of specifiable conditions and that once these conditions have been discovered, we can anticipate and to some extent determine his actions. (p. 6)

The notion that human behavior is determined by specifiable events is contrary to many lay, philosophical, and religious conceptions. In these conceptions, humans are given volition: They behave in a particular fashion because they choose to do so. Often, an unobservable entity—the soul, spirit, mind, intellect, unconscious, or persona—is considered somehow responsible for the choice; it directs the behaving body as a captain pilots a ship. The controlling entity is free and unfettered and can act to change behavior in dramatic and unpredictable fashion.

Causal observation seems to support such conceptions. At present, no one is able to predict accurately all of human behavior. In fact, behavior sometimes appears chaotic rather than orderly. Nearly every day we hear of upstanding citizens who, without warning, destroy themselves and their loved ones. We also hear of reprobates saved, their behavior shifted dramatically from reprehensible to saintly. Moreover, each of us is aware of being confronted with behavioral alternatives from which we seem to freely select an option. Should I study for the exam or go skiing? Is J.B. or B.J. a better date for the party? Are condoms really something my partner and I need to use? We mull our options, talk to ourselves and others about them, sweat, agonize, and eventually choose. The choice, when made, appears to be ours alone: we typically are aware of what we did and felt before making the choice, but not of historical events that affected the process.

The fact that we are not aware of these events does not mean that they did not influence our behavior. Although it is not possible to demonstrate that *all* of human behavior is controlled by antecedent events, it is abundantly clear that *some* of what we do is determined by our past experiences. A science of human behavior is possible only with respect to those actions that are determined in the sense of being lawfully related to other empirical variables, for these actions can be described in terms of functional relations, and hence predicted and, in principle, controlled. Other actions fall outside the scientific domain.

The notion that important aspects of human behavior are determined may be vexing on first glance, for most of us are taught from childhood to emphasize nonempirical causes of behavior and to believe in free will and conscious, unfettered choice. That view is hopeful, for it admits the possibility of miraculous change and mystical intervention. It is troublesome, however, for it provides no clear directions for how a person can bring them about.

In contrast, knowing that behavior is lawfully related to specifiable events often suggests strategies for changing a person's actions in desired directions. Scientific knowledge characteristically is practical knowledge: it lets us change our world, to develop useful technologies. The truth of this assertion is evident in the dramatic medical advances made within the past 100 years. Consider infectious diseases. For millennia, their causes were not known and they were not treated effectively. As a science of medicine arose, it became clear that microorganisms caused infectious diseases and that these tiny invaders could be thwarted with antibiotic drugs, serums, and vaccines. These interventions produced dramatic results. In 1900, for example, pneumonia, tuberculosis, infections of the gastrointestinal tract, and diphtheria were among the 10 leading causes of death in the United States of America, collectively accounting for more than one third of all fatalities. Whooping cough, measles, scarlet fever, meningitis, and typhoid fever also killed an impressive number of people (Dowling, 1977). Though these scourges have not been completely mastered, relatively few people succumb to them today. No comparable gains can be cited for the success of psychologists in dealing with behavioral problems, perhaps because the scientific study of microbes is well established and has yielded a good data base, whereas the scientific analysis of human behavior is a recent and controversial development.

5. *Scientific assertions are tentative and testable.* Observations of real events are the raw material of science. Relations among these observations form the basis of scientific laws. These laws, in their turn, are related to one another through higher order principles and concepts. Scientists recognize that observations are necessarily inexact and that important relations among variables are not easy to detect or to summarize meaningfully. Therefore, scientific assertions at all levels do not reflect absolute truth; they are instead tentative and subject to revision.

This does not mean that scientists know nothing or that scientific assertions are so imprecise as to be useless. Consider the law that describes how far a falling body will travel in a given period of time:

$$S = \tfrac{1}{2}gt^2$$

where S is meters travelled, g is a constant that varies with location and altitude (this accounts for variations in the force of gravity), and t is time in seconds. This equation enables one to predict with very good accuracy how far any object will fall in a given time at any place on earth. Other kinds of scientific knowledge allow for equally good prediction of other phenomena. In fact, when it comes to predicting natural phenomena, scientific information is usually far superior to any other kind.

In large part, this is so because scientific knowledge is not fixed but changes over time to reflect observations more accurately. We noted in Chapter 1 that science is both fallible and self-correcting. It is fallible in that scientific assertions made at a given time may subsequently be modified or rejected; it is self-correcting because these changes lead to a progressively refined worldview, one that provides better integration of observations and allows better prediction of important phenomena. A mature science is **internally consistent:** its assumptions, laws, and general principles hold together and make sense in light of the observations that it attempts to explain. Moreover, they do not violate the findings of other scientific disciplines. For example, any science of behavior that posits neurological mechanisms that do not correspond to those recognized by contemporary neuroscientists is automatically suspect. Finally, an established science is **deductively ordered,** in that principles, laws, and other general statements are established so that accurate descriptions of particular happenings are possible. These statements take the form of predictions, and as Medawar (1984) noted:

> [A] Property that sets the genuine sciences apart from those that arrogate to themselves the title without really earning it is their predictive capability: Newton and cosmology generally are tested by every entry in a nautical almanac and corroborated every time the tide rises or recedes according to the book, as [they are] also corroborated by the periodic reappearance on schedule of, for example, Halley's comet (due, 1986). I expect that its embarrassing infirmity of prediction has been the most important single factor that denies the coveted designation "science" to, for example, economics. (p. 4)

If the criterion of accurate prediction is robustly applied, psychology is not scientific. No psychologist, regardless of his or her theoretical persuasion, can consistently and accurately predict all of human behavior, although some can make accurate predictions in certain circumstances. Science is not all or none, however; disciplines exist along a continuum from highly scientific to completely unscientific. Psychology as a whole is certainly more scientific than, say, astrology or palmistry, but less scientific that chemistry or physics. Some psychologists, including those who call themselves behavior analysts, study behavior in a manner that reflects to a goodly degree each of the five characteristics of scientific analysis. Whether they will succeed in building a science of human behavior that emulates the mature physical sciences in compass, integration, predictive utility, and emergent technology has yet to be determined. As the remainder of this text will demonstrate, they have at least taken some steps in that direction.

But what, you may ask, is the value of a science of behavior? Is a scientific psychology really any better than a nonscientific approach? The answers are straightforward: The scientific approach has been uniquely successful in allowing people to predict and control natural phenomena and may provide a means by which we humans can understand and better our lot on this earth. In holding that promise, a scientific psychology is superior to its competitors.

Inadequate Explanations of Behavior

We have previously discussed how scientists attempt to explain events of interest, namely, by determining functional relations among those events and other variables. There are, of course, many other kinds of explanations, and some of them are often applied to behavior. The purpose of this section is to explore types of explanations that are fundamentally inadequate. Though the problems with these types of explanations become apparent on close scrutiny, they are so common that few recognize them as flawed.

One inadequate explanation is termed the **nominal fallacy.** A person guilty of the nominal fallacy assumes that simply assigning a name to a phenomenon explains it. Consider, for example, a severely mentally impaired, institutionalized resident who is observed by an aide to chew and swallow cigarette butts. The aide, understandably troubled, seeks an explanation from the ward psychologist, who asserts that "consuming nonfood items is an example of pica, and pica is fairly common in this population." The aide has learned a technical term, *pica,* but is no better able to predict or control the resident's behavior. Hence, the explanation is a useless and inadequate one.

The aide realizes this and returns to the psychologist for more information: "Hey, I've been thinking about the patient who eats cigarette butts. Why does that pica occur, anyway?" The psychologist isn't sure but suggests that the resident "is probably eating the butts in order to gain attention from other residents." Beyond the fact that it is speculative, do you see anything wrong with this explanation? Most people won't. There is a problem nonetheless, and the problem is that the explanation is teleological. In a **teleological explanation,** a future event (attention from other residents in our example) is assumed to cause a current event (eating butts). This is obviously illogical; causes must precede effects. It is reasonable to speculate that the resident eats butts because doing so in the past has resulted in attention from other residents. But it is teleological to speculate that the resident eats butts *in order to* gain attention.

A third kind of inadequate explanation is termed a **circular explanation.** In a circular explanation, the cause is inferred from the same information that con-stitutes the effect.[1] Envision a schoolchild who often fights with other students, spits at the teacher, and throws books and papers. These behaviors share certain characteristics; many of us would group them together as "aggressive re-sponses" and assert that the student behaves aggressively. There is no problem with this label as long as we recognize that *aggressive responses* is simply a short-hand designation for the behaviors observed. Problems arise, however, if we posit that something termed *aggression* causes the fighting, spitting, and throw-ing. There is no evidence of aggression apart from these behaviors; therefore, the cause and the effect are one and the same and the explanation is a circular one: fighting, spitting, and throwing are assumed to be caused by aggression, but there is no evidence of aggression apart from the fact that the child fights, spits, and throws.

This example clearly shows the fallacy of circular reasoning. It also demon-strates reification, which has long been a problem for psychology (Eacker, 1972). In **reification,** an abstraction is treated as if it has material existence. Although aggression in the foregoing example is offered as a causal variable, it is a non-material abstraction, not a real object or event. Therefore, if we accept that only empirical phenomena can enter into functional relations, aggression in this sense cannot cause anything.

Both circularity and reification are evident in the example of the aggressive child. Reification can, however, occur without circularity. You have probably heard of the id, ego, and superego; they are the primary structural elements of the psychoanalytical theory of personality developed by Sigmund Freud (e.g., 1933) and discussed in Chapter 9. In essence, Freud claimed that the id, the ego, and the superego each accounted for a different aspect of a person's behavior. The id, ego, and superego have no physical existence; Freud created them as mechanisms to account for the behaviors he observed in therapeutic interactions with well-heeled clients. Nonetheless, they are often construed as real and

---

[1]Some behavioral psychologists use the term **explanatory fiction** to refer specifically to explanations of behavior in which the cause cannot be observed independently of the effect for which it is the explanation. When used in this sense, *explanatory fiction* is not synonymous with *inadequate explanation.*

causal entities. For example, Lefton (1979) wrote in an introductory psychology book that:

> the id is demanding, irrational, selfish, and pleasure loving . . . the ego is patient, reasonable. . . . The superego acts to tell the id and ego whether an approach toward gratification is moral and ethical. If a child seeks her ice cream cone and asks her mother for it, her superego will indicate that this is morally correct. This approach toward obtaining ice cream will not invoke guilt, fear, or anxiety in a child. In contrast, a child may see candy on the table and may know her mother is out of the room. Her ego knows that taking the candy would be very simple, and this would satisfy her id. However, the superego holds the child back from taking the candy; it has taken over the role of conscience and parental authority. (pp. 384–385)

The foregoing passage illustrates reification in a form that is readily apparent. The id, ego, and superego are treated as things and are also imbued with human qualities: The ego "knows," the superego "holds back." A man or woman can do these things, but a nonmaterial abstraction cannot. Nonetheless, perhaps because such an approach is consistent with traditional dualistic conceptions in which a mind or soul controls the body, it is tempting to explain behavior in terms of alleged structures (usually assumed to be located in the brain or mind) that control our behavior as we control that of a pet or a small child. The behavior of this **homunculus** (little person) is usually not explained,

Higher education should alert students to fundamentally inadequate explanations of phenomena. (Photo courtesy of Neil Rankin.)

and ascribing our behavior to its actions allows us neither to predict nor to alter what people do.

Explanations of behavior that involve reification, circularity, teleology, or the nominal fallacy are automatically suspect because they are usually of little predictive value. Moreover, their acceptance tends to stop inquiry into the actual causes of behavior. In view of these limitations, it is important to recognize fundamentally inadequate explanations for what they are. Perhaps the best way to do this is by asking a series of questions, as shown in Figure 2-2. This figure, prepared as a flowchart, is intended to help you evaluate various explanations of behavior. Note, however, that an explanation of behavior can be free of reification, circularity, teleology, and the nominal fallacy and still be inadequate. This would be the case if the explanation posited a relation between real historical events and behavior that was simply wrong. Logical analysis cannot detect inadequate explanations of this sort; only an empirical test of the proposed relations will suffice. Explanations of behavior based on posited relations between behavior and current or historical events are, in principle, adequate, but particular explanations may be incorrect and of no value in predicting and controlling behavior.

In reification, abstractions are treated as physical entities, a practice that is generally unproductive. That this is so does not diminish the importance of

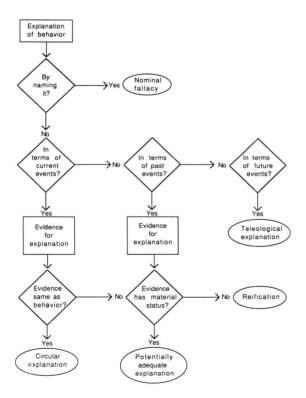

Figure 2-2. Flowchart showing a series of questions designed to help determine whether an explanation of behavior is fundamentally flawed or potentially adequate.

abstractions, which are terms used to summarize functional relations. *Gravity* is an example of a profitable abstraction. The term refers to the attraction (a functional relation) between any two physical bodies, one of which is often the earth. This attraction can be scaled in physical units and is well understood by physicists. For example, they have ascertained that the force of attraction (gravity) between two bodies of sufficient mass is directly proportional to the product of their masses and inversely proportional to the square of the distance between them. (This is why a person is heavier on the earth than on the moon.) Moreover, the force of attraction between the earth and bodies near it is such that the distance that the body will fall in a given period of time can be precisely specified (by the equation discussed on page 27, $S = \frac{1}{2}gt^2$).

Gravity is not a material entity, but the term has purely physical referents. When a physicist speaks of gravity, she or he does so for convenience: The term has no meaning apart from the empirical functions that it summarizes. Although the term *gravity* does not in and of itself explain anything, knowledge of the functional relations encompassed by the term allows physicists to predict (and in some cases control) the attraction between physical bodies. Abstractions are often used in accounting for human behavior, and they play a valuable role in psychology.

Psychological Theories

The term **theory** is used in many and conflicting ways, but it refers in general to a system of rules and assumptions used to explain and predict observations. Some psychological theories are formal, detailed, and specific; others are loose and informal. All of them are designed to make sense of—that is, to order—observations. As discussed earlier and portrayed in Figure 2-3, scientific analysis involves ordering observations at several levels of specificity. At its most specific, the analysis is at the level of a functional relation between a particular behavior and some other event. At its least specific, it is at the level of the paradigm, which orders observed relations within the context of a general conceptual framework and a body of assumptions, methods, and values. Between these end points in decreasing order of specificity are general functional relations between classes of variables, scientific laws, and theories.

As McCain and Segal (1988) observed, "The purpose of a theory is to describe and explain observable and observed events and to predict what will be observed under certain specified conditions" (p. 96). Freud's theory of person-

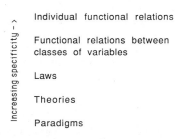

Figure 2-3. Levels of specificity in the ordering of scientific observations.

ality, for example, was intended to explain certain behaviors, in particular those that were of clinical significance in his patients. The id, ego, and superego are cornerstones of the theory. If one is willing to accept these constructs, and to ascribe to them the characteristics specified by Freud, certain predictions about behavior follow. Moreover, observed behaviors can be attributed to the actions of the id, ego, and superego, which may in some sense explain them. Despite these features, Freud's theory is constructed in such a way as to be essentially untestable, and it is accepted by few psychologists today. Other psychological theories that assign similar weight to hypothetical constructs are, however, currently in vogue.

Many theories borrow their hypothetical constructs from other disciplines. For example, some theorists, among them the Nobel laureate ethologist Konrad Lorenz, have developed hydraulic models of motivation. Lorenz's model was designed to account for certain kinds of species-typical behaviors termed fixed action patterns. **Fixed action patterns** are stereotyped response sequences that are characteristically controlled by environmental stimuli termed *releasers*. If, for instance, an egg rolls out of the nest of a goose, she will use a stereotyped bill-rolling behavior to return it; the egg is a releaser, and rolling the egg with the bill is a fixed action pattern.

In Lorenz's model, pictorially represented in Figure 2-4, motivation is represented as a fluid that is stored in a reservoir. When released, the fluid causes certain behaviors (fixed action patterns) to occur, much as hydraulic pressure causes mechanical devices to operate (e.g., brakes to close). Certain stimuli (releasers) act to open a valve and release the motivational fluid, or it can simply build up and eventually leak out. In that case, a fixed action pattern would occur in the absence of a releasing stimulus.

Because most of us are familiar with simple hydraulic systems, the model shown in Figure 2-4, which resembles a flush toilet, is easy to understand and to talk about. Moreover, it appears to allow for predictions about behavior (for instance, releasers will engender fixed action patterns only if sufficient motivational fluid is available) and may serve to generate reasonable research projects. How, for example, could production of the motivational fluid be increased? What features of a releasing stimulus allow it to open the valve?

Despite these appealing features, Lorenz's theory of motivation is only of historical interest to modern ethologists, for it is actually of questionable merit. The same is true of other theories based on **analogy,**[2] such as those that liken the function of the central nervous system to that of a telephone switchboard or a computer. As Eacker (1972) pointed out:

> the diagram of a hydraulic system for motivation, or comparison of the human nervous system with a telephone switchboard, or the human brain with an electronic computer do not explain motivation, the nervous system, [or] the brain; they may only make them more familiar. They do not explain because they, in turn, must be explained either by another science or by another model. If the former, there is the problem of a finite regression back to one science left unexplained. If the latter, there is the problem of an infinite regression of models or analogies. (p. 559)

[2]Analogy involves describing something by comparing it with something else. An analogy is involved when we say, for example, that K.C. "eats like a pig" or "goslings are to geese as kittens are to cats."

Nevertheless, computer models of brain function (or of mental activity) are quite popular today. These models use a diagram of electronic circuitry to represent "cognitive architecture." Although a model based on the modern computer has more panache than one based on a flush toilet, the brain contains no more electronic circuitry than plumbing fixtures.

Models based on analogy are not without value: they may help us to talk about and predict how an organism will function in a given situation. But

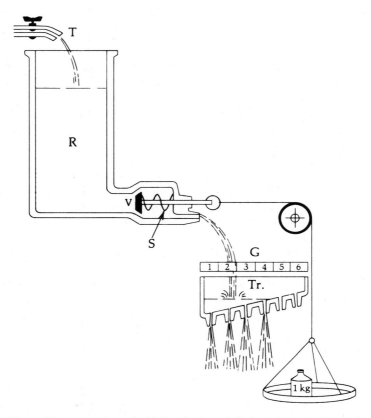

Figure 2-4. Konrad Lorenz's "psychohydraulic" model of motivation. Hypothetical motivational waters flow from a tap (T) into a reservoir (R), where they are stored. The water represents what Korenz called "action-specific energy." A releaser (stimulus) placed on the scale at the lower right pulls open the spring-equipped valve (V) so that the waters can "turn on" the behavior. The gradual nature of the behavior, which makes the response stronger as the interval between performances increases, is analogous to the graded water pressure that produces a stronger flow when the valve is opened. Lorenz illustrated this process with the graded trough (Tr). The lower threshold (smaller weight) necessary for releasing a behavior after prolonged abstinence is a consequence of increasing water pressure over the spring (S). "Vacuum" activities (which occur in the absence of a releasing stimulus) are a consequence of the water pressure's finally exceeding the spring tension, so that the system triggers itself internally. (From *Ethology: The Mechanisms and Evolution of Behavior* by James L. Gould, 1982, p. 186. Copyright 1982 by W. W. Norton. Reproduced by permission.)

behaviorists rarely use them for the reasons described by Eacker. In contrast to building theories based on elaborate models, behaviorists prefer to account for behavior by summarizing observed relations between real events and changes in behavior. They do so without recourse to analogy and without positing constructs that do not and cannot have an empirical basis. These and other theories can be evaluated according to several criteria (see, e.g., Bachrach, 1972). The following five are of particular importance:

1. *Empirical support.* In judging a theory, one must consider the observations that relate to it. Are there any? If not, the theory is automatically suspect. If there are, the theory is suspect if the observations do not support it. A theory is also suspect if it is framed so generally or so imprecisely as to be able to account for any possible set of observations. Such theories are deemed **untestable.**

2. *Logical support.* The mechanisms proposed by a theory must be plausible. If, for instance, a theory accounts for language in terms of posited activity in the central nervous system, this activity must be consistent with what is known about the nervous system. Moreover, the explanations of behavior associated with a theory must not be fundamentally inadequate; that is, they must not involve reification, circularity, teleology, or the nominal fallacy.

3. *Generality.* The generality of a psychological theory refers to the range of behaviors it purports to explain, and to the range of conditions under which it does so. A theory of learning that attempts to account for the acquisition of many kinds of behavior is, for instance, more general than one that attempts to account for verbal behavior alone. Similarly, a theory of depression that explains the phenomena in all depressed humans is more general than one that explains it only in, say, adult children of alcoholics. All other things being equal, general theories are preferable to specific ones.

4. *Parsimony.* Good theories do not invoke complex mechanisms when more simple ones will suffice to explain a phenomenon. **Occam's razor,** named after the English philosopher William of Occam (c. 1285–1350), is the name assigned to the principle dictating that, all else being equal, the simplest explanation of a phenomenon is the best one, or in terms more akin to those of Occam's day, "what can be done with fewer [assumptions] is done in vain with more" (Thomas, 1981, p. 979).

5. *Utility.* The goal of scientific analysis is prediction and, if possible, control of the subject matter. If psychology is to be scientific, a good theory must allow for accurate prediction of the behaviors it covers. Depending on the nature of the events assumed to control behavior, it may also suggest strategies for changing behavior in desired ways. In evaluating a psychological theory, it is useful to ask, "Does knowledge of this theory allow me to better predict behavior?" And if so, "Does it suggest any procedures for changing behavior in desired ways?" If the answer to the first question is yes, then the theory has explanatory value. If the answer to the second question is also yes, the theory has practical merit as well.

Objections to a Science of Behavior

All approaches to psychology, including behaviorism, are theoretical in the sense that we have been using the term. Skinner has acknowledged this, as in his reply to a question concerning the appropriate role of theory building in psychology:

> It depends on what you mean by theory. I have been called an antitheorist, probably because of a paper I wrote entitled, "Are Learning Theories Necessary," even though I carefully defined what I meant by theory. I defined theory as an effort to explain behavior in terms of something going on in another universe, such as the mind or the nervous system. Theories of this sort I do not believe are essential or helpful. Besides, they are dangerous; they cause all kinds of trouble. But I look forward to an overall theory of human behavior which will bring together a lot of facts and express them in a more general way. That kind of theory I would be very much interested in promoting, and *I consider myself to be a theoretician.* (Quoted in Evans, 1968, p. 88; italics ours)

Given this stance, it is of interest that Skinner has repeatedly been chastised for being opposed to theory (Schultz, 1975). What he actually opposes are certain kinds of theories, as well as research strategies designed to test these theories. He does not oppose gaining general information about behavior and its controlling variables.

Opponents of a science of behavior have not limited their criticisms to issues of theory. As Skinner has often pointed out (e.g., 1974), many objections (including those based on the three myths discussed in Chapter 1) involve serious misunderstandings of behaviorism. Others, however, cannot be dismissed entirely on that basis. One real objection is that a science of behavior as proposed by Skinner is impossible. A second is that such a science is possible but is unde-

No one can accurately predict this little girl's future. But a science of behavior identifies some of the variables that will affect her development. (Photo courtesy of Roger Ulrich.)

sirable. A third is that a science of behavior is fatalistic and could not possibly be used to benefit humanity because the deterministic world it requires renders humans incapable of acting to improve themselves or their world. Each of these objections are considered here:

Objection 1: A science of behavior is impossible. Many who raise this objection assert that humans have free will; hence, their actions cannot be predicted or controlled. The absence of free will cannot be demonstrated empirically: no one can show that all of human behavior is controlled by environmental (or other) variables. What can be demonstrated is that some responses are in some circumstances so controlled. This demonstration indicates that a science of behavior may be possible, although its proper scope remains subject to debate.

Even if it is granted that behavior is lawfully related to other events, it does not automatically follow that a science of behavior is feasible. Human behavior is in many instances the product of multiple and interactive variables, and it may appear that the very complexity of human behavior and its controlling variables renders a scientific analysis unfeasible. Surely it makes such an analysis difficult. Nonetheless, it is possible to discern classes of variables that generally influence behavior in predictable ways. We know, for example, that the outcome of a particular response is likely to determine whether or not that response will recur. This knowledge can be put to good use to change behavior in desired ways—to teach, for instance, a child to read or a politician to avoid racial slurs. Although behaviorism may never provide us with knowledge sufficient to create the utopian society envisioned by Watson (1930) or Skinner (1948), it has enabled us to deal rationally with a wide range of problem behaviors. To that extent, a science of human behavior is more than possible; it already exists.

Objection 2: A science of behavior is undesirable. Critics of a science of behavior have deemed it undesirable on two counts. One is that such a science is unethical and could be used to oppress people. The other is that such a science is dehumanizing. Each of these contentions merits attention.

With respect to ethics, it is important to recognize that all sciences are ethically neutral. Science is not a direct source of ethical principles; the practice of science provides no guidelines for determining what is right or good. As Karl Popper (1978) noted:

> It is important to realize that science does not make assertions about ultimate questions—about the riddles of existence, or about man's task in this world. This often has been well understood. But some great scientists, and many lesser ones, have misunderstood the situation. The fact that science cannot make any pronouncement abut ethical principles has been misinterpreted as indicating that there are no such principles while in fact the search for truth presupposes ethics. (Quoted in Medawar, 1984, p. 58)

The wise application of scientific knowledge also presupposes ethics. General guidelines for professional conduct by psychologists are set forth in the American Psychological Association "Ethical Principles of Psychologists" (1981), and behaviorists characteristically adhere to these standards. In so doing, they make oppression neither their goal nor their accomplishment. History indicates that there is no need to fear behaviorism; it is neither unethical nor oppressive.

But is there any reason to embrace behaviorism? Can't the case be made that the scientific conception of humanity is intrinsically dehumanizing? In one of two common usages (*American Heritage Dictionary,* 1984), to dehumanize is to deprive of human qualities or attributes. In the other, it is to render mechanical and routine. Scientific knowledge is dehumanizing only if we accept traditional conceptions in which humans are given central and privileged status relative to all other natural beings. As Carl Sagan (1987) contended:

> In the history of science there is an instructive procession of major intellectual battles that turn out, all of them, to be about how central human beings are. We could call them battles about the anti-Copernican conceit. Here are some of the issues: *We are at the center of the Universe. All the planets and the stars and the Sun and the Moon go around us.* (Boy, must we be something *really* special.) That was the prevailing belief—Aristarchus aside—until the time of Copernicus. A lot of people liked it because it gave them a personally unwarranted central position in the Universe. The mere fact that you were on earth made you privileged. That felt good. Then along came the evidence that Earth was just a planet and that those other bright moving points of light were planets too. Disappointing. Even depressing. Better when we were central and unique. *But at least our Sun is at the center of the Universe.* No, those other stars, they're suns too, and what's more we're out in the galactic boondocks. We are nowhere near the center of the Galaxy. Very depressing. *Well, at least the Milky Way galaxy is at the center of the Universe.* Then a little more progress in science. We find there isn't any such thing as the center of the Universe. What's more there are a hundred billion other galaxies. Nothing special about this one. Deep gloom. *Well, at least we humans, we are the pinnacle of creation. We're separate. All those other creatures, plants and animals, they're lower. We're higher. We have no connection with them. Every living thing has been created separately.* Then along comes Darwin. We find an evolutionary continuum. We're closely connected to the other beasts and vegetables. What's more, the closest biological relatives to us are chimpanzees. It's an embarrassment. Did you ever go to the zoo and watch them? Do you know what they do? Imagine in Victorian England, when Darwin produced this insight, what an awkward truth it was. There are other important examples—privileged reference frames in physics and the unconscious mind in psychology—that I'll pass over. (pp. 42–43), italics in the original)

Behaviorists don't pass over the unconscious mind or, for that matter, the conscious mind. They do, however, refuse to give them special status as tangible entities or as explanations of overt behavior. Thus, another intellectual battle is joined. In contrast to most other psychologists and laypeople, behaviorists contend that what organisms do is determined by environmental variables, genetic variables, and physiological variables. This holds true for all animals, including humans. Our behavior is determined by the same classes of events that control the behavior of other animals; therefore, we cannot argue for human uniqueness on the basis of a discontinuity of behavioral processes.

Science does not allow us the favored position that we once arrogated to ourselves, and it may be disheartening to accept the conception of our place in the universe that science provides—indeed, most people are unwilling even to consider it. Nevertheless, that conception does not strip us of the human characteristics that are truly valued—of the ability to love, to pity, to create, to laugh, and to cry. Science strips away illusion, but it does not render life mechanical and routine. Life is the delight of the living, and Skinner has long argued that we humans can—indeed, must—create a humane and just world, a rational society without excess or oppression, in which life can be lived to the fullest. This position, which is shared by many behaviorists, is that of a thoroughgoing secular humanist, one who values life and hopes to make it better.

Objection 3: A science of behavior is fatalistic. But opponents of a science of behavior object: Isn't the deterministic world that behaviorism requires inconsistent with the notion that people can improve themselves and their world? Is not the lot of each individual as immutably fixed by historical and current variables as the course of a train by the rails beneath its wheels? No, and no again. Determinism is not the same as **fatalism**, which is the name assigned to the philosophical doctrine that all events are predetermined by fate and therefore unalterable. From the perspective of fatalism, all events that have occurred and all events that ever will occur are fixed and capable of being predicted. A being with sufficient knowledge could therefore predict whether you will have great-great-grandchildren and, if so, exactly what they will be doing at 11:05 A.M. on April 12 in the year 2117. One can conceive of such an omniscient being, or even of an omnipotent being that is capable of controlling as well as predicting all that ever will occur; many religions are based on their posited existence. Such beings are, however, neither human scientists nor accessible to humans acting as scientists.

From the modest perspective that science affords, there is no world clock, no preordained sequence of events that automatically unfolds. There are, of course, lawful relations between classes of events, and it is a scientist's work to discover and interpret them. When they are discovered, these relations are often not exact, but probabilistic. Thus, predictions cannot be made with certitude. Consider, for example, the half-life of a radioactive isotope, such as plutonium-238. The half-life is the time required for one half of the atoms in a sample of an isotope to decay (i.e., become nonradioactive); this value is about 50 years for plutonium-238. Knowing this, one can predict with confidence that about 50% of the atoms in a given sample of the isotope will decay over a period of 50 years. The time at which a given atom will decay cannot, however, be predicted accurately; some will do so in less than 50 years, others in more than 50 years. Although accurate prediction of the half-life of plutonium-238 is possible at a global level (that is, when one is dealing with changes in a sizable quantity of the isotope), accuracy decreases when an isolated atom is considered. The best prediction is that it will decay in about 50 years, but that prediction often misses the mark, and sometimes by a wide margin.

There is demonstrated uncertainty of prediction regarding nonbehavioral events; many deterministic relations are "soft" and probabilistic, not "hard" and exact. Logic and data indicate that the same holds true with respect to behavior. There is simply too much slop in the causal chain for the world clock to keep ticking. Moreover, as bumper stickers accurately if inelegantly proclaim, shit happens. Significant events occur that no human can foresee, predict, or control, and they influence behavior. We usually call them accidents. The occurrence of these events, coupled with a world in which determinism is, in many cases, soft and probabilistic, removes men and women from the fixed destiny that fatalism demands.

Phylogenetic and ontogenetic variables surely limit behavioral options, but as we have repeatedly emphasized, it is impossible to resolve the free-will–determinism issue on the basis of data. It is also impossible to resolve the issue on the basis of philosophical debate. It is, however, possible to ask, "Under what circumstances do we humans call ourselves free?" That question can be answered: We call ourselves free when we have response options and are not exposed to aversive circumstances at the hands of other people. A science of behavior can be used to increase human freedom in this sense, and to improve the quality of human life. As Duane Schultz (1975) rather whimsically put it:

> The free will-determinist controversy cannot be resolved at this time and may never be. A point worth noting is that many determinists, notably Watson and B. F. Skinner, have made "determined" efforts (no pun intended—I think) to bring about improvements in the individual and society. (p. 221)

If they have not succeeded, there is no world clock to blame.

Science and Pseudoscience

The virtues of scientific analysis become crystal clear when we contrast them with other approaches to understanding behavior. When science is absent, nonsense abounds. This is abundantly clear in the field of parapsychology and related pseudosciences. We consider these fields not because they explain human behavior, for they do not, but because they provide such good examples of illogical and nonscientific analysis.

Parapsychology refers to the study of behavioral phenomena that are not explainable by known natural laws. Parapsychologists have claimed that many such phenomena exist; four that have preoccupied them in the past 5 years are telepathy, clairvoyance, precognition, and psychokinesis, which Hansel (1980) defined as follows:

> **Telepathy,** a person's awareness of another's thoughts in the absence of any communication through sensory channels.
> **Clairvoyance,** knowledge acquired of an object or event without the use of the senses.
> **Precognition,** knowledge a person may have of another person's future thoughts (**precognitive telepathy**) or of future events (**precognitive clairvoyance**).
> **Psychokinesis** [PK], a person's ability to influence a physical object or an event, such as the fall of a die, by thinking about it. (pp. 3–4, boldface added)

With the exception of psychokinesis, each of these phenomena involves perception and is independent of sensory activity. Hence telepathy, clairvoyance, and precognition are grouped together as subtypes of **extrasensory perception (ESP).** This term was coined by J. B. Rhine, whose experiments at Duke University in the 1930s kicked off the modern ESP craze (Gordon, 1987). The term **psychic** (or **psi**) **phenomena** is widely used to cover ESP and all other parapsychological happenings.

Parapsychology is only one aspect of the **paranormal,** which refers in general to supernatural or extrasensory abilities or events (Randi, 1982). As Hines (1988) noted, "paranormal phenomena include extrasensory perception (ESP), telekinesis, ghosts, poltergeists, life after death, reincarnation, faith healing, human auras, and so forth" (p. 7). Astrology and UFOlogy (belief that unidentified flying objects are piloted by extraterrestrial visitors) also qualify as paranormal. Many people accept the existence of some paranormal phenomena as fact. For example, a 1984 Gallup telephone poll of 506 United States teenagers 13–18 years old revealed that 59% believed in ESP and 55% believed in astrology; 28% believed in clairvoyance, 24% in Bigfoot (Sasquatch), 20% in ghosts, and

18% in the Loch Ness monster (Frazier, 1984–1985). The paranormal phenomena that are generally accepted in a culture change over time. The Bermuda Triangle, pyramid power, and Eric Von Daniken's extraterrestrial astronauts are passé whereas channeling (receiving information from spirits through mediums) and UFOlogy are currently hot. And though the Age of Aquarius is past, astrology continues to have its proponents: there is hardly a daily paper anywhere in the United States that does not include a daily horoscope.

Even though belief in the paranormal is widespread and extends backward in time to prehistory, skeptics abound. Sidebar 2-1, which contains an article by Paul Kurtz, makes it clear that there is good reason to be skeptical. Kurtz is a philosopher and the chairman of the Committee for the Scientific Investigation of Claims of the Paranormal (CSICOP), an organization with a stated purpose "to encourage the critical investigation of paranormal and fringe-science claims from a responsible, scientific point of view and to disseminate factual information about the results of such inquiries to the scientific community and the public" (*The Skeptical Inquirer*, 1988, back cover).

In general, skeptics bring two kinds of criticism to bear on parapsychological claims (Kurtz, 1985b):

> The first are analytic and logical objections to the conceptional framework of parapsychology, which seems to conflict with or contradict well-established principles of common experience and the natural sciences. Hume's argument against miracles has proven to be a powerful one. If a claim violates the regularities discovered by experience, then we ought to weigh the possibilities and accept the explanation that has the highest probability. At the very least, skeptics insist that extraordinary claims made by paranormalists should be supported by extraordinary evidence. If psi phenomena exist, then it is important that there be conceptually coherent hypotheses or theories to explain them. Perhaps this is not possible at the beginning stages of a science, but it is the ultimate goal. Parapsychology has not progressed in this area. Although it has postulated several constructs—e.g., ESP and PK—there is no developed theory, and what has been presented is in contradiction to the physical sciences.
> The second and even more fundamental criticism concerns the data themselves. The crucial question is whether or not there is a sufficient degree of evidence to support the claim that ESP, psychokinesis, or any other psychic phenomenon exists. Parapsychologists maintain that there is; skeptics deny it. The key issue, therefore, is whether there is adequate data, objectively obtained and capable of replication in the laboratory by neutral and independent scientists. Before we can ascertain whether psychic phenomena exist, we need to carefully examine the fund of experiential and experimental data. And here is where the dispute rests, because skeptics deny that the evidence is strong enough and suggest that, where anomalies are uncovered, normal explanations can be given to account for them. (pp. xix–xx).

Kurtz goes on to discuss how fraud has been a serious problem in parapsychology. Many people with alleged paranormal powers have in fact been magicians, skilled tricksters capable of fooling scientists and laypeople alike. Uri Geller is of this ilk (see Randi, 1982). Fraud is not, however, limited to mere pranksters; a number of researchers in the area have been found guilty of fakery and fabrication. The case of Walter J. Levy, Jr., is an interesting case in point (see Rogo, 1985). In the early 1970s, Levy reported a remarkable string of successes in parapsychological research. He published 20 studies in the area from 1969 through 1974, and in 1973, J. B. Rhine made him director of the Institute for Parapsychology at Duke University. Among other noteworthy findings, Levy demonstrated

Sidebar 2-1
Is There Intelligent Life on Earth?

Paul Kurtz

In recent months, we have witnessed a sharp rise in uncorroborated paranormal claims—much to the dismay of skeptics who thought they were making some headway in the case for rationality. The level of credulity seems to have reached new heights.

Shirley MacLaine's gushings have lured millions to join her out on a fantasy limb. Her deja vu experiences, regressions to earlier lives, precognitive visions, channeling, UFO visitations, and astral projections have been touted far and wide in best-selling books and in a TV miniseries. Large segments of the public are impressed by the "profound spirituality" of her accounts.

Uri Geller is back again after virtually a decade of hibernation, back to moving compass needles by means of hidden magnets and claiming "psychokinesis," and secretly peeking at pictures he has asked various subjects to draw and then claiming his ability to duplicate these drawings is due to "clairvoyance."

Incredibly, Geller secretly met in Washington with Senator Claiborne Pell, chairman of the Senate Foreign Relations Committee, and Congressman Danta Fascell, chairman of the House Foreign Affairs Committee, in an attempt to convince them—with some apparent success—that the Soviet Union is ahead of the United States in the "psychic arms race," even alleging that skeptics are doing the work of the KGB by discouraging such research by the U.S. government. CSICOP's [Committee for the Scientific Organization of Claims of the Paranormal] facetious response was to suggest that the United States launch a "skeptics' rapid deployment force"—for, if it is the case, as psychics maintain, that skeptics inhibit real "psychic energy" by their negative vibes, then this could defend the Western democracies against enemy intrusion!

Launched by his publisher to sell his new book, *The Geller Effect*, Geller's recent highly publicized tour included not only the United States, but France—where he appeared virtually unchallenged for two hours on national television—Great Britain, Canada, and other countries.

In addition to these antics, the discredited spiritualism of the nineteenth century has returned as "trance-channeling." Channelers claim to go into trances and communicate with spirits on the "other side" who reveal information "they could not possible have known in any other way."

The 35,000-year-old "Ramtha" speaks through a woman known as J. Z. Knight, while other channelers call upon "Dr. Peebles" (William Rainan) or other discarnate spirits, inspiring the adulation of thousands, perhaps millions, of uncritical New Agers. *Channeling* is just a new word for "spiritualism," but today there is not even a pretense of providing hard evidence—no darkened seance rooms, no levitating tables, no ectoplasmic emergences—but simply the claim of instantaneous communication with the spirit world, without any kind of objective verification.

Last, but not least, is the sudden revival of UFOlogy after a period of quiescence. Three major new UFO books have been launched: *Communion: A True Story*, by Whitley Strieber; *Intruders*, by Budd Hopkins; and *Light Years*, by Gary Kinder.

Communion (published by Morrow/Hearst Corporation) has been on the best-seller list for several months. Whitley Strieber, who has written many fictional horror stories, claims to have been in touch with semi-divine extraterrestrial beings. Budd Hopkins's *Intruders* (Random House/Newhouse Publications) is based on the author's "careful analysis" of 125 frightened "abductees" who have been hypnotically regressed under the eye of the artist-sculptor-author (he now claims to have talked to 140 of them). Some of his hysterical women subjects claim that the extraterrestrials are engaged in genetic engineering and have impregnated ova taken from their bodies; and Strieber has intimated that even he has been raped. Random House publisher and CEO Howard Kaminsky was so taken by *Intruders* that he placed a full page ad in the *New York Times* personally recommending the book to "all open-minded people."

The new UFOlogy is based on largely uncorroborated events, often revealed in hypnotic sessions. The paucity of evidence is unnerving: a scar, a lost hour, some bright lights in the sky, and—oops!—someone claims to have been abducted by aliens from outer space. Usually the subject has no memory of the abduction until it is revealed in all its stark terror under hypnosis. In April, I challenged Whitley Strieber (on the Tom Bauerle Show on WGR-Radio in Buffalo) to submit his evidence to us for scientific investigation. He adamantly refused, claiming that CSICOP was "biased."

On "Good Morning America" (ABC-TV, May 19), I asked Budd Hopkins to provide a list of the names of his "abductees," but he said that most of them were "fearful of ridicule" and hence preferred to remain anonymous. However, he promised on the air to promptly send me a list of the "scientists who support" his work. As we go to press, I still have not heard from him.

Hypnosis is an unreliable method for eliciting the truth. As Martin Orne, a leading authority on hypnosis, points out, it may evoke a vast store of unconscious dreams and imaginative fantasies mixed with reality. In many instances, the subject's "memory recall" is influenced by suggestive questions from the hypnotist.

In regard to Hopkins's "abductees," many of those he hypnotized had read his earlier book *Missing Time* and had been influenced by its extraterrestrial interpretation. CSICOP is of course open to the possibility of intelligent life elsewhere in the universe. We devoted an entire session to this subject at our 1987 conference in Pasadena in April. But *possibility* does not translate into *verified actuality*, nor does it mean that we are being visited by extraterrestrials who engage in kidnapping and rape.

It is clear that the communications industry must shoulder a good deal of the responsibility for the current spate of New Age nonsense. Today's media conglomerates have apparently abandoned all reasonable standards of credibility in an effort to package and sell paranormal claims; they leave little doubt that they are more interested in achieving high profits than in pursuing the quest for truth. At the annual American Booksellers Association convention held in Washington, D.C. over the Memorial Day weekend (May 22–26, 1987), some 52 publishers announced the formation of the New Age Publishers Alliance to promote the sale and distribution of occult, paranormal, and spiritual books.

Today, uncorroborated subjective claims are being heralded as unvarnished truth. In regard to trance-channeling and hypnotic regression, alternative states of consciousness are being offered as special paths to another reality. The quasi-religious character of channeling is strikingly similar to classical mystical trances by means of which seers and prophets allegedly received revelations from gods and angels. In the case of UFO abductions, the entities are science-fiction extraterrestrials, and the analogy to the ancient gods of classical religions who impregnated mortals is unmistakable. Any demand for confirming evidence from true believers falls on deaf ears, often eliciting angry retorts.

UFO pundit Jerome Clark, associate editor of *Fate* magazine and editor of the *International UFO Reporter*, has derided skeptics. He berated me in the *IUR* (January/February 1987) for asking the question "What is the difference between claiming that you have been raped by an extraterrestrial and claiming that you have seen a pink elephant?" Clark attacks skeptics for being closed-minded and dogmatic, yet he is easily impressed by questionable evidence. Since extraordinary claims require substantial evidence, skeptics have a right to be cautious. Reports of individual subjective experiences are hardly sufficient in themselves. One cannot and should not reject these reports out of hand—prime facie, they are the data given. What is at issue is how to *interpret* such subjective reports. The interpretation that the subjects have been abducted by aliens from outer space is highly suspect. There are viable alternative explanations. One would think that a dash of common sense would dictate some careful checking. But this is apparently foreign to the many UFO buffs who have climbed aboard the media bandwagon.

Skeptics have embarked on an uphill journey. Every time we think we are making progress, a new wave of nonsense overtakes us. Perhaps the "transcendental temptation" (i.e., the tendency for magical thinking) is too strong to be overcome, but can it not be tempered by rationality? To borrow from William Blake's chastisement of the skeptics of his day: We "throw the sand against the wind, and the wind blocks it back again."

I must confess that I have asked myself several times in recent months whether the task that CSICOP and the SKEPTICAL INQUIRER have set for themselves—to raise the level of rationality—is insuperable. Yet I write this just after CSICOP convened its most successful conference, in Pasadena, California, where more than 1,500 people attended one or more sessions and which received considerable worldwide coverage. Moreover, local and national skeptics groups that share CSICOP's aims are now experiencing an unparalleled period of growth. We seem to have crystallized a point of view, and we have strong support from a growing number of scientists, scholars, and other skeptics.

Perhaps the recent surge of untested paranormal claims can be attributed to the effort by the media to sensationalize and exploit them as marketable products. Still, although the scientific search for extraterrestrial life goes on, as it should, given the mass of uncorroborated beliefs, we wonder sometimes to what extent intelligent life exists on Earth!

From "Is There Intelligent Life on Earth?" by P. Kurtz, 1987, *The Skeptical Inquirer*, vol. 12, pp. 2–4. Copyright 1987 by the Committee for the Scientific Investigation of Claims of the Paranormal. Reproduced by permission.

precognitive clairvoyance in mice. That is, they appeared to recognize through nonsensory means a forthcoming electric shock and behaved so as to avoid it. Psychokinesis in chicken embryos was another of Levy's impressive demonstrations. These powers were revealed by placing fertilized eggs in an incubator where heat was turned on and off by a randomizing device designed so that the incubator would be heated about half of the time. Levy's data indicated that the incubator was on significantly more than it was off, which led him to conclude that the chicken embryos had influenced the randomizing device through psychokinesis, presumably exercised because of the reinforcing effects of heat. A control group of hard-boiled eggs provided no evidence of psychokinesis. (You laugh, but this was big news.)

By 1973, there were suspicions that Levy was cheating. A year later, co-workers caught him red-handed fabricating data indicating that rats use psychokinesis to obtain reinforcing brain stimulation. A scandal ensued. Researchers at the institute could not replicate any of Levy's findings, and it became apparent that his cheating was widespread. This discovery was revealed to the public, although in a less than straightforward fashion, with the result that interest in psi phenomena in nonhumans plummeted. Ironically, the scandal did not end Levy's career as a researcher. As Rogo (1985) related:

> Dr. Walter J. Levy did not go into medical practice, as everyone had expected. He completed an internship in Georgia and then embarked on a career in medical research, specializing in neurology. He eventually took a research post in the Midwest, where he continues to publish in the field of neurosurgery. (p. 324)

Levy is, of course, only one researcher, and it is unfair to dismiss an entire field on the basis of a single cheater, or even a bevy of them. It is, however, fair to point out that fraud has been very common in the history of parapsychology. So common, in fact, that Henry Gordon (1987) pessimistically concluded that "Extrasensory perception, the so-called ability to perceive or communicate without using normal senses, would be better named extrasensory *deception*. The history of parapsychology, of psychic phenomena, has been studded with fraud and experimental error" (p. 13).

To put it baldly and boldly, in view of current evidence (reviewed in Hansel, 1980; Hines, 1988; Kurtz, 1985c), there is no reason to accept telepathy, clairvoyance, precognition, or psychokinesis as real phenomena. That may surprise you. Are there not dozens of experiments demonstrating them? Indeed there are. Psi phenomena have been investigated for over a century, and hundreds of experiments, case reports, and anecdotes have been published. Nonetheless, these phenomena simply cannot be reliably reproduced under controlled conditions.

Similar status can be accorded most if not all parapsychological phenomena. Astrology, for instance, does not provide a means of predicting human behavior or the events that will befall an individual. There is no plausible mechanism whereby the position of heavenly bodies at the time of one's birth can influence one's fate, and there are no data indicating that astrological forecasts provide accurate and specific predictions of human affairs. As Kurtz (1985a) noted, astrology has absolutely no scientific merit. It, like most of parapsychology, is a **pseudoscience,** a term applied to fields of inquiry that "(a) do not utilize rigorous experimental methods in their inquiries, (b) lack a cohesive testable conceptual framework; and/or (c) assert that they have achieved positive results, though their tests are highly questionable and their generalizations have not been corroborated by impartial observers" (Kurtz, 1985a, p. 506).

Pseudosciences are not effective in determining the variables that actually control human behavior, and they provide no rational basis for changing behavior in desired ways. It is, of course, true that unorthodox notions not widely accepted by scientists may eventually prove valid and may be incorporated into a scientific paradigm. Alfred Wegener's theory of continental drift, which was proposed early in this century but accepted only in the 1960s, is a case in point. But it is also true that unorthodox notions will be accepted only if there is compelling empirical support for them. As Stokes (1985) noted, it was the overwhelming preponderance of geological evidence that finally forced the acceptance of Wegener's theory. If in the future a preponderance of good evidence supports some notion currently advanced by parapsychologists, legitimate scientists will take that notion seriously. In the interim, they will be rightly skeptical.

At present, it appears more interesting and profitable for psychologists to examine *why* people believe in paranormal phenomena than to investigate the phenomena themselves. A major advantage of this strategy is that belief in the paranormal is certainly real, which is more than can be said for the phenomena.

Study Questions

1. In general, when is an event understood?

2. With respect to the temporal continuum, what are two kinds of causes? Give an example of each.

3. Be able to name and describe the five characteristics of scientific inquiry.

4. How are functional relations demonstrated?

5. Traditionally, the causes of behavior have been attributed to nonempirical entities such as the "free will," "soul," or "mind." In contrast, the science of behavior seeks empirical causes. What is the advantage of discovering empirical causes (compare with advances in medicine)?

6. Be able to list, describe, and give an example of each of the four inadequate explanations of behavior.

7. What is the purpose of a theory?

8. What is a hydraulic model of motivation? Give an example.

9. The hydraulic model is one of many based on analogies. Such analogy-based explanations of behavior, according to Eacker, have a disadvantage. What is it?

10. List and describe the five criteria for judging the adequacy of a theory.

11. In what way is Skinner a theoretician? In what sense is he not?

12. List and describe each of the objections to a science of behavior. What is the rejoinder to each?

13. What are Kurtz's two criticisms of claims of paranormal phenomena?

**2. SCIENCE AND
PSYCHOLOGY**

McCain, G., & Segal, E. M. (1988). *The Game of Science*. Pacific Grove, CA: Brooks/Cole.

This little volume, now in its fifth printing, provides an entertaining and enlightening discussion of the general characteristics of science. Using examples from many disciplines, the authors demystify science and show it for what it is: a unique human enterprise, with pitfalls as well as promise.

Randi, J. (1980). *Flim-Flam.!* New York: Lippincott & Crowell.

There are many good books debunking the paranormal, but this is one of the best with which to begin. The author, a professional magician and skilled skeptic, does a good job of demystifying much that appears to be beyond natural explanation. Quality work by Randi and other skeptics also appears regularly in *The Skeptical Enquirer*, a periodical that offers rational alternatives to New Age psychobabble.

CHAPTER 3

Research Methods

There are many ways to gain knowledge about natural phenomena, including human behavior. One method that is invaluable to scientists is research. The present chapter describes general research strategies, with special emphasis placed on experimentation. Errors that commonly occur in experimentation are highlighted, and two general experimental strategies (within-subject and between-subjects comparisons) are contrasted.

What Is Research?

Research is a systematic way of asking questions and gaining information. The information gained through research, called **data** (a plural noun), forms the foundation of all of the experimental sciences, including psychology. Psychological research can be classified either as **applied research,** in which the questions asked are of direct and immediate practical significance, or as **basic research,** in which this is not the case. If, for example, a psychologist attempts to answer the question, "Can high blood pressure be lowered by teaching patients self-relaxation?" the research is applied because it directly addresses a clinical problem (hypertension). In contrast, a study designed to evaluate whether an experimental drug improves memory in monkeys is basic research, for no conceivable outcome is of direct clinical significance. Basic research may, however, yield findings that are by implication and extension clinically important. If, for instance, the experimental drug improved monkeys' memory without producing adverse reactions, one might reasonably posit a future role for it in treating Alzheimer's disease and other conditions involving deterioration of memory. Testing that speculation would require further, and applied, research.

It is sometimes difficult to determine whether a given study is applied or basic. One way to make the distinction is to ask, "Is this study intended to benefit the subjects directly?" If the answer is yes, then the study is applied. In some cases, there can be legitimate disagreement about whether a particular study is basic or applied, for the terms really represent the end points of a continuum, not a true dichotomy. Table 3-1 provides examples of basic and applied research.

Basic research can be conducted with humans and with nonhumans alike. This student is pressing buttons under complex experimental procedures. (Photo courtesy of Sue Keller.)

Table 3-1
Examples of Basic and Applied Research

Basic research

1. A study evaluating the effects of ambient temperature on the air speed of honeybees.
2. A study using respondent conditioning procedures to bring eye blinks in humans under the control of a tone.
3. A study demonstrating that the "runner's high" can be blocked by administration of the narcotic antagonist naloxone
4. A study showing that monkeys deprived of maternal attention early in life fail to develop normal patterns of sexual behavior as adults.
5. A study evaluating whether electroconvulsive brain stimulation interferes with short-term memory in dogs.

Applied research

1. A study using nicotine-fading procedures to eliminate cigarette smoking.
2. A study showing that a self-monitoring procedure can be used by students to increase time spent studying.
3. A study using contingency contracting to increase the productivity of factory employees.
4. A study demonstrating that the narcotic antagonist naloxone dramatically reduces self-injury in autistic children.
5. A study showing that electroconvulsive brain stimulation is effective in reducing depression in adult humans unaffected by other treatments.

There are many ways to conduct studies; the methods of science are re-markably diverse. The research strategies used by a psychologist are influenced by many things, perhaps the most important being that person's training and experience. The research methods favored by a cognitive psychologist are likely to differ substantially from those used by a behavioral psychologist; so, too, are the research questions they ask. The research question is a second variable that influences how a study is conducted. Although it rarely dictates specific pro-cedures, it surely limits the range of the general strategies that are tenable. A third factor that influences how research is conducted is the availability of re-sources: personnel, time, money, equipment, and subjects. Practicality neces-sarily guides the researcher. Ethical and legal considerations also affect how research is conducted. Obviously, a researcher interested in the effects of child abuse on subsequent sexual activity could not conduct a controlled investigation in which some children were intentionally abused and others were not. Rather, existing groups would have to be examined, and the nature of the study would be determined, in part, by legal and ethical concerns.

General Research Strategies

Several general research strategies are available. We will briefly comment on three: naturalistic observation, correlational research, and case studies. A fourth, experimentation, is covered in greater detail. The important characteristics of these research strategies are summarized in Table 3-2.

Naturalistic Observation

In **naturalistic observation,** the behaviors of interest are simply examined as they occur in the subject's usual environment. That environment is not inten-tionally perturbed by the researcher, who may or may not use structured tech-niques to quantify observations. Most of us are familiar with the use of natu-ralistic observation by Jane van Lawick-Goodall (e.g., 1971) in her studies of chimpanzees, and by Margaret Mead (e.g., 1928) in her studies of Samoan youth. Psychologists as well as ethologists and anthropologists use the tech-nique to good advantage. Consider, for example, a researcher who is interested in the behavior of people who call themselves witches. Strange as it may seem, some do, and many of us know little about them. A lot of people, including

Table 3-2
Characteristics of General Research Strategies

Strategy	Independent variable manipulated?	Outcome measures precisely quantified?	Functional relations
Naturalistic observation	No	Sometimes	Suggested only
Correlational research	No	Usually	Suggested only
Case studies	Usually	Sometimes	Suggested only
Experimentation	Yes	Usually	May be demonstrated

psychologists, might wonder, "How do self-proclaimed witches behave?" That is a broad question, probably too broad to allow a meaningful answer. "How do witches behave in their covens?" is of more manageable scope and might merit investigation.

How would one interested in the behavior of witches in their covens proceed? Obviously, the first task would be to find some witches, no easy task in itself. That done, the researcher might ask to watch them in the coven, a request that, if granted, would provide a means of discerning how those witches behaved. This information could be provided in a simple narrative and might serve to satisfy most people's curiosity about witches. Others might want more information: Is it possible that the witches behaved differently because they were being watched? If not, is it safe to assume that the behavior of this group of witches is similar to that of others? If the behavior of various witch groups shares certain features, why does this occur?

As the foregoing example indicates, naturalistic observation can provide valuable **descriptive information** and can also serve to generate interesting research questions. By systematically noting events that occur before and after particular classes of behavior, one can often form reasonable speculations about what is controlling certain actions. Consider, for instance, a boy diagnosed as autistic who frequently bites his left hand and wrist. A psychologist has been consulted to deal with the problem and, as an essential first step, is simply watching the child.

The boy is initially observed throughout an entire day at school. Self-injury occurs several times and the psychologist discerns a pattern: It appears that a particular aide is present when self-biting occurs and that, when it does, the aide rocks the child and offers verbal reassurance. The psychologist is not sure that this sequence of events always occurs and therefore decides to keep a formal record of self-injurious behavior and the events that occur immediately before and after it. In doing so, the psychologist is using an **antecedent–behavior–consequence (A-B-C) analysis** (Worell & Nelson, 1974). Such an analysis is often used by behavior analysts who are attempting to quantify behavior and to determine the variables that control it.

An A-B-C analysis, conducted over the course of two days, reveals that biting the hand or wrist has occurred 19 times. The aide was present during 18 of these incidents. After each of them, the aide rocked the child and talked softly to him. Seeing this, the psychologist hypothesizes that self-biting is, in this case, a learned response, maintained by its consequences (the rocking and/or verbal reassurance provided by the aide). How the response has been acquired is unclear, but its appropriate treatment seems straightforward: Train the aide to ignore self-biting. Given the manner in which self-injury is apparently controlled, this intervention should be effective.

Correlational Research

As in naturalistic observation, the researcher engaged in **correlational research** does not intentionally alter the environment of the subjects that he or she is studying. The researcher does, however, attempt to determine the relationship between two variables. The general purpose of correlational research is to determine if and to what extent the value of one variable is related to the value of the second. Does the value of *A* increase with the value of *B*? Does it decrease? Or are their values independent?

Two variables are **positively correlated** if the value of one increases with the value of another. They are **negatively correlated** if the value of one decreases as the other increases. They are **uncorrelated** if there is no systematic relation between them. Figure 3-1, which depicts scatter plots with the value of one variable along the vertical (*Y*) axis and the value of the other along the horizontal (*X*) axis, shows examples of positively correlated, negatively correlated, and uncorrelated variables. Note that in Figure 3-1, there are two scores for each subject: one score on each of two variables.

Relatively simple mathematical procedures allow the degree as well the as direction of correlation to be determined. These procedures yield a **correlation coefficient** that can vary from −1.0 through 0 to +1.0. The value of the correlation coefficient specifies the strength of the relation between two variables. When the correlation coefficient is close to −1.0 or +1.0, the relation is strong, and one can rather accurately predict a subject's score on one variable given the score on the other. As the correlation lowers (i.e., approaches 0), the accuracy of prediction lessens. Figure 3-1 provides examples of sets of data that would yield correlation coefficients of +1.0, −1.0, +0.68, and 0.0. Sidebar 3-1 provides an example of the steps involved in calculating the degree of correlation between two variables.

Correlational research is useful for quantifying the relation between variables. Interpreting these relations is sometimes a problem. Consider a situation in which a moderately high positive correlation (.56) is obtained between the number of bars and the number of churches in United States cities. How can this finding be interpreted?

Cautiously. The data obtained tell us only that there is a general but imperfect relation between the variables of interest. Why this relation occurs is uncertain. Perhaps the number of bars somehow determines the number of churches. Perhaps the reverse is true. Perhaps both are determined by the action of some other, unknown variable or set of variables. This is probably the case in this example: the size of the city is likely to determine both the number of bars and the number of churches. Large cities have many bars and many churches, whereas small cities have few of each.

As a general rule, *causality cannot be inferred from simple correlation.* Nonetheless, there are surely instances where a correlational relation can *suggest* a causal one. This occurs when the relation is a strong one and there is a plausible mechanism whereby the value of one variable could determine the value of another. The adverse effects of environmental contaminants, for example, are often initially discovered by epidemiological studies in which the prevalence of certain disorders are compared across groups that differ in level of exposure to the agent. If a significant positive correlation between prevalence and exposure is evident, then there is good reason to examine further the effects of the substance and, in the interim, to institute steps limiting exposure to it.

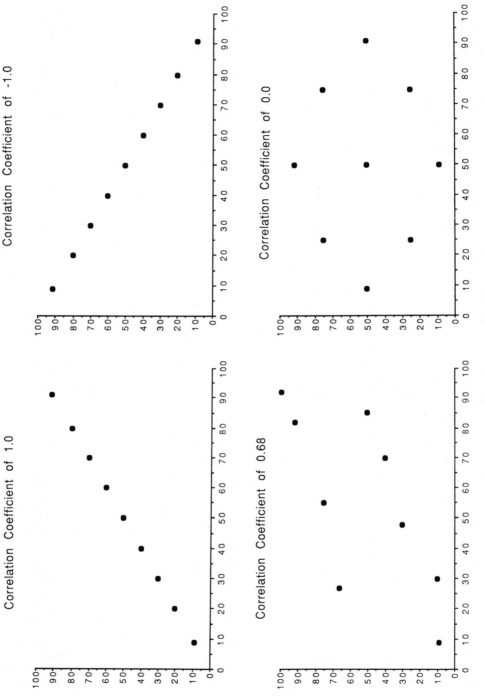

Figure 3-1. Plots of data that yield correlation coefficients (Pearson product-moment) of +1.0, −1.0, 0.0, and 0.68.

A **case study** involves a rather detailed description of the behavior of a single person, most often a patient who is exposed to some clinical intervention. Case studies were once quite popular among clinicians. Many early claims about the success of psychoanalysis (e.g., Brill, 1909), for instance, rested largely on the results of case studies. But it is now widely recognized that the case study technique does not support strong conclusions concerning the relation of treatment to observed changes in behavior. Consider again our example of the self-injurious child and the treatment recommended for him. Assume that the aide is taught to ignore the self-biting and does so consistently over a one-week period.

Sidebar 3-1

Calculation of the Pearson Product–Moment Correlation (r) for Height and Weight Based on a Sample of 10 Freshman Students

The whole-score method is used in this example; other methods are available and yield comparable results. The formula for calculating r by the whole-score method is:

$$r = \frac{(N)(\Sigma XY) - (\Sigma X)(\Sigma Y)}{\sqrt{(N)(\Sigma X^2) - (\Sigma X)^2} \ \sqrt{(N)(\Sigma Y^2) - (\Sigma Y)^2}}$$

where Σ = sum, $\sqrt{}$ = the square root of, N = the number of subjects. We will consider height (in inches) as the X variable and weight (in pounds) as the Y variable. The first three steps in determining r are to (1) list each student's height and weight; (2) square the height and weight of each student (calculate X^2 and Y^2); and (3) multiply height by weight for each student (calculate XY). After this, the sum of X, the sum of Y, the mean of X, the mean of Y, the sum of X^2, the sum of Y^2, and the sum of XY are determined. These simple manipulations yield the following table:

Student	X	Y	X²	Y²	XY
1	60	115	3,600	13,225	6,900
2	66	149	4,356	22,201	9,834
3	69	165	4,761	27,225	11,385
4	76	230	5,776	52,900	17,480
5	72	189	5,184	35,721	13,608
6	68	167	4,624	27,889	11,356
7	62	102	3,844	10,404	6,324
8	70	183	4,900	33,489	12,810
9	66	167	4,356	27,889	11,022
10	67	159	4,489	25,281	10,653
Sums:	676	1,626	45,890	276,224	111,372
Means:	67.6	162.6			
N = 10					

These values are then inserted into the formula:

$$r = \frac{(10(111,372) - (676)(1,626)}{\sqrt{(10)(45,890) - (676)^2} \ \sqrt{(10)(276,224) - (1,626)^2}}$$

$r = 0.96$

This correlation is high and positive; height and weight were strongly and directly related in these 10 students. As this example shows, the correlation between two variables can be determined through straightforward operations involving only basic arithmetic. The difficulty with correlations involves interpretation, not calculation.

During that time, self-injury gradually decreases to zero frequency. Does this mean that the treatment was effective?

Possibly, but not necessarily. Any of a number of other variables may have led to the result. For example, it is conceivable that the self-biting is cyclic in nature and that the intervention was fortuitously instituted at the beginning of a downward trend. If this were so, the pattern of results described above would have occurred quite apart from any effects of treatment. The primary weakness of the case study design is readily apparent. A single case study may suggest that one variable (e.g., treatment) is affecting another (e.g., a problem behavior), but it does not provide convincing evidence that this is the case. A series of case studies reporting similar findings provides more compelling evidence that one variable affects another, but there are better strategies for examining the effects of interventions than conducting multiple case studies. Therefore, the primary role of case studies in a science of behavior appears to be to generate hypotheses worthy of rigorous test.

Experimentation

Psychologists search for variables that lawfully influence behavior. Experimentation aids in this search by providing an especially powerful method for discerning relations between behaviors of interest and other events. The behavior of interest in an experiment is termed the **dependent variable,** and the event that is manipulated in an attempt to alter behavior is termed the **independent variable.** The dependent variable in a psychological study is also termed the **criterion measure** or the **target behavior. Intervention** and **treatment** (sometimes **experimental treatment**) are other terms used as synonyms for *independent variable.* If you confuse independent and dependent variables, just remember

Table 3-3
Research Questions with the Independent Variable Underlined
and the Dependent Variable Italicized

---

1. How is *speed of maze running* in food-deprived rats influenced by amount of food delivered?
2. How does methylphenidate influence *attention span* in normal adults?
3. Does participating in an exercise program alter *self-ratings of mood* in mildly depressed college students?
4. Does *reported condom use* by male homosexuals change as a result of reading a pamphlet about AIDS?
5. What is the relation between the number of violent episodes in a cartoon viewed by preschool children and their subsequent *verbal aggression* toward peers?
6. Does *water intake* by weasels change as a function of electrical stimulation of the ventromedial hypothalamus?
7. Does the *amount of merchandise stolen* from a convenience store change as a function of posting warning signs?
8. What is the relation between amount of sleep deprivation and *reaction time* in adult humans?

---

that the former is the intervention (the clinical treatment or experimental manipulation of interest) whereas the latter is the behavior of the subject that the researcher measures and assumes will be influenced by the intervention. Table 3-3 lists several experimental questions in which the independent variable is underlined and the dependent variable is italicized. It is important to recognize that the terms *independent* and *dependent* are appropriately applied only when a variable is actually manipulated and its effects are measured. If this is not the case, as occurs in correlational research and in naturalistic observation, there is no independent variable or dependent variable.

Many principles of behavior have been understood through experimentation with non-humans in controlled environments. This picture shows an operant chamber, which is just such an environment. The pigeon pecks one of the three circular disks on the front wall and occasionally receives access to food through the rectangular aperture below the disks. Note the speaker on the back wall, which masks extraneous sounds, and the houselight on the ceiling, which supplies ambient illumination. (Photo courtesy of Sue Keller.)

Relations among Variables

Although specific experiments differ widely and some are quite complex, the logic of the experimental method is straightforward: One determines whether an independent variable affects a behavior of interest by comparing levels of that behavior (the dependent variable) when the independent variable is and is not operative or is operative at different levels.[1] The researcher controls the value of the independent variable and also ensures that **extraneous variables,** which are factors other than the independent variable that might alter the dependent variable, are eliminated or held constant across conditions. Therefore, if levels of the dependent variable differ when the independent variable is and is not operative (or is operative at different levels), it is logical to assume that the independent variable has influenced the dependent variable.

As discussed in Chapter 2, if the value of a dependent variable varies systematically with the value of an independent variable, the two are **functionally related.** Once it is clear that an independent variable is functionally related to a dependent variable, prediction and control of that variable—the goals of science—become possible. Prediction is possible because the value of the independent variable determines (at least in probabilistic fashion) the value of the dependent variable. Thus, all other things being equal, the probable value of the dependent variable can be predicted, given knowledge of the value of the independent variable. Moreover, the value of the dependent variable can be controlled by manipulating the value of the independent variable. The practical value of scientific research rests in part on the isolation of independent variables that are subject to manipulation in the natural environment and that change behavior in a clinically significant fashion. Chapters 11 and 12 provide many examples of how human behavior can be improved by manipulating variables that behavioral scientists have determined to be important.

Internal and External Validity

When a study is designed so that changes in the dependent variable can be attributed, with little or no ambiguity, to the effects of the independent variable, the study is said to be **internally valid.** Many factors may compromise the internal validity of a study; several are listed in Table 3-4. No single experimental configuration controls for all of the potential threats to internal validity. Thus, researchers are forced to make decisions concerning the threats that appear most important. Even very good researchers sometimes err in making these decisions and unknowingly conduct studies that are not internally valid. Such investigations may support erroneous conclusions concerning the relation between an independent and a dependent variable. Erroneous conclusions are, in most cases, revealed as such through attempts to replicate the reported studies.

---

[1]Researchers often measure two or more dependent variables in a single study. This procedure complicates data analysis but does not change the logic of experimentation. To facilitate our exposition, we will emphasize studies in which the effects of one independent variable on one dependent variable are evaluated.

There are two kinds of replication: direct and systematic. Sidman (1960) used the term **direct replication** to refer to the "replication of a given experiment by the same investigator" (p. 73) and noted that replicating an experiment with the same subject increases confidence in the reliability of the findings but does not preclude the possibility that this individual is more or less sensitive to treatment than other subjects. Direct replication of an experiment with additional subjects also increases confidence in the reliability of findings and, in addition, begins to address the issue of generality of results.

Systematic replication (Sidman, 1960) is the term used to describe attempts to assess the range of conditions under which a dependent variable is influenced by an independent variable:

> We can define systematic replication in applied research as an attempt to replicate findings from a direct replication series, varying settings, behavior change agents, behavior disorders, or any combination thereof. It would appear that any successful systematic replication series in which one or more of the above-mentioned factors is varied also provides further information on generality of findings across clients since new clients are usually included in such efforts. (Hersen & Barlow, 1976, p. 339)

The term **external validity** refers to the generality of results from a given study. That is, under what conditions can the results obtained be reproduced? Generality of results is usually evaluated across the dimensions of subjects, settings, behaviors, and treatment parameters. Consider, for instance, an applied study that demonstrated a clear relation between exercise and weight loss in obese adolescents. The subjects were at least 40 pounds overweight at the start of the experiment and were highly motivated to reduce; their treatment involved exercising vigorously in a group class for 45 minutes per day. The class was held during the lunch hour at the school they attended. The most important questions concerning the generality of results is whether similar findings can be produced by other researchers under conditions comparable to those in the original investigation. If so, will the procedure work with younger or older individuals? More or less obese people? Outside the school setting? Is it neces-

Table 3-4
Eight Threats to the Internal Validity of a Study[a]

---

1. *History,* the specific events occurring between the first and second measurement in addition to the experimental variable.
2. *Maturation,* processes within the respondents operating as a function of the passage of time *per se* (not specific to the particular events), such as growing older, growing hungrier, or growing more tired.
3. *Testing,* the effects of taking a test on the scores in a second testing.
4. *Instrumentation,* in which changes in the calibration of a measuring instrument or changes in the observers or scorers used may produce changes in the obtained measurements.
5. *Statistical regression,* operating where groups have been selected on the basis of their extreme scores.
6. Biases resulting in differential *selection* of respondents for the comparison groups.
7. *Experimental mortality,* or differential loss of respondents from the comparison groups.
8. *Selection–maturation interaction* and so on, interactions of two or more of the extraneous variables listed above.

---

[a]As described by Campbell and Stanley (1966).

sary to exercise 45 minutes each day, or are other values equally or more effective?

Before attempting replications, it is nearly impossible to determine how widely the results of an investigation will generalize, for there are many threats to the external validity of a study; several of them are listed in Table 3-5. Researchers often say that a good study raises more questions than it answers, and many of the questions raised concern external validity.

Because internal and external validity can rarely be evaluated accurately on the basis of the published description of a study, *the results of any one experiment should be regarded as tentative.* Scientists sometimes report findings that cannot be replicated and, on the basis of these findings, posit phenomena or relations between events that actually do not exist. For instance, French scientists in the early 1900s believed in the existence of N-rays, emanations first reported to be produced by X-ray sources, and later by gases, magnetic fields, certain chemicals, and the human body. In 1904 alone, over 100 papers reporting the characteristics of N-rays appeared in a single French journal (de Solla Price, 1961). N-rays have no physical status. As Barber (1976) explained, "all of the effects attributed to N-rays were due to wishful thinking and to the immense difficulties involved in estimating by the eye the brightness of faint objects" (p. 7). Nye (1980) suggested that some French scientists continued to argue for the existence of N-rays even in the face of seemingly unassailable evidence to the contrary, in part because of fierce national pride. Apparently, the reputation of French scientists in the early 1900s had suffered much at the hands of the Germans. N-rays became almost a national *cause célèbre,* and French researchers whose work affirmed their status were rewarded accordingly. Nonetheless, by 1910 N-rays had lost legitimate scientific status. The fact that N-rays were once widely accepted as real but were eventually recognized to have no physical existence provides concrete evidence of an important point about science introduced in Chapter 1: *Its methods are not infallible, but they are eventually self-correcting.* And that is their greatest strength.

Experimental Designs

In general, behavioral experiments involve either within-subject or between-subjects designs. In a **within-subject design,** the level of the independent vari-

Table 3-5
Four Threats to the External Validity of a Study[a]

1. The reactive or *interactive effect of testing,* in which a pretest may increase or decrease the respondent's sensitivity or responsiveness to the experimental variable and thus make the results obtained for a pretested population unrepresentative.
2. The *interactive effects of selection biases and the experimental variable.*
3. *Reactive effects of experimental arrangements,* which would preclude generalization about the effect of the experimental variable on persons being exposed to it in nonexperimental settings.
4. *Multiple-treatment interference,* likely to occur whenever multiple treatments are applied to the same respondents, because the effects of prior treatments are not usually erasable.

[a]As described by Campbell and Stanley (1966).

able is varied and comparisons are made within individual subjects. Typically, each subject is exposed to all values of the independent variable. In a **between-subjects design,** the level of the independent variable is varied and comparisons are made across different subjects. Typically, each subject is exposed to only one value of the independent variable. Between-subjects designs are often presented as entailing a single observation of each subject and statistical data analysis, whereas repeated observations of each subject and visual (graphic) data analysis are associated with within-subject designs. There is some justification in the psychological literature for this conception. For example, most studies published in the *Journal of the Experimental Analysis and Behavior (JEAB)* and the *Journal of Applied Behavior Analysis (JABA)* involve a within-subject experimental design, repeated observations of behavior across conditions, and visual data analysis. It should be recognized, however, that nothing prevents a researcher from statistically analyzing data from within-subject designs or using repeated measures in between-subjects comparisons. The manner in which subjects are exposed to the various conditions of interest and the procedures used to analyze data should be determined by the kind of information the researcher desires. A good experiment fits the research question and provides data that are acceptable to the intended research consumer.

Experimental Questions

There are many sources of experimental questions. Some arise from the experimental literature, others from day-to-day experience and observations. As Johnston and Pennypacker (1986) noted, "A good experimental question is a limited and carefully worded expression of all of the investigator's best judgements about the direction and focus of that investigator's interests in a particular aspect of behavior" (p. 70). The experimental question determines the nature of independent and dependent variables and limits the range of subjects, experimental designs, and data analysis strategies. It also influences the manner in which obtained data are interpreted. Some experimental questions are relatively open-ended; they posit no specific outcome. Others, even if they deal with the same general topic, propose specific relations between independent and dependent variables.

Consider a situation in which a psychologist, Dr. Jay, is generally interested in the variables that affect athletic performance. Dr. Jay has read two journal articles suggesting that caffeine may improve times in middle-distance running events and has talked with several competitors in 10-kilometer road races who drink a cup or two of coffee (a cup of brewed coffee contains about 150 milligrams of caffeine) an hour before racing in the belief that their performance is improved. On the basis of this information, Dr. Jay formulates an experimental question, which might take either of the following forms:

1. What are the relations between caffeine intake and performance in 10-kilometer races?
2. Will ingesting a small amount of caffeine improve performance in 10-kilometer races?

The first question is open-ended, whereas the second intimates a specific outcome (improved performance). Experimental questions that posit specific outcomes are easily converted into hypotheses. A **hypothesis** is a declarative statement of prediction. Although every researcher who begins a study has some notion about the probable effects of the independent variable on the dependent variable and, in that sense, has formed a hypothesis, some researchers place a great premium on the formal testing of specific hypotheses, whereas others do not.

Six Steps in Experimentation

The preceding example has outlined the first two steps in conducting an experiment: (1) making general observations before formulating an experimental question and (2) formulating a question. The third step is designing a study. The fourth is conducting it, and the fifth is evaluating the data. The final step is

Most scientists agree that computers can play a valuable role in experimentation, but whether they also provide a useful analogue of human behavior is vigorously debated. (Photo courtesy of Sue Keller.)

determining the theoretical and practical implications of the study: What, if anything, of significance has been learned? Table 3-6 lists and briefly describes these steps.

Table 3-6 captures the essential logic of experimentation, but remember that each step in the sequence represents nothing more than a labeled set of researcher behaviors; science is what scientists do. The specific behaviors that occur at each step may vary widely, even if similar experimental questions are asked. As an illustration, let us consider two possible strategies for pursuing Dr. Jay's interest in the effects of caffeine on running. One, which we will consider first, involves an open-ended question, a within-subject design, repeated observation of each subject, and graphic data analysis. The second hypothesizes a specific outcome and entails a between-subjects design, a single observation of each subject, and statistical data analysis.

Let us assume that Dr. Jay has completed his initial observations and hopes to explore how a low dose of caffeine affects running. To do this, he must make provisions to ensure that:

1. The dependent variable is adequately defined and measured.
2. The independent variable is adequately defined and consistently implemented.
3. The sequencing of conditions (experimental design) and the method of data analysis allow the observed changes in the dependent variable to be attributed with confidence to the independent variable.

Table 3-6
Six General Steps in Experimentation

1. *Making initial observations.* The researcher initially gains information about the general phenomena of interest through day-to-day activities, contact with other scientists (in person or through the literature), specialized training, or naturalistic observation. This information suggests that some measurable variable may affect behavior in an interesting fashion.
2. *Formulating the experimental question.* The researcher decides to explore whether the posited relation between the behavior and the independent variable holds. The researcher then formulates an experimental question. The experimental question orients the study; it dictates the kind of data to be collected.
3. *Designing the study.* The researcher carefully defines the independent and dependent variables and chooses an experimental configuration that will provide the desired information concerning their relation. In designing a study, one deals with issues of subject selection, the configuration of the conditions, data collection, and data analysis. One also considers possible threats to the internal and external validity of the study and makes provisions to control those that seem the most important.
4. *Conducting the study.* The researcher carries out the investigation. Often, the design will have to be changed across the course of the study as interesting data or unexpected problems are encountered.
5. *Evaluating the data.* The reseacher examines the data in light of the experimental question and determines how and if the independent variable affected the dependent variable.
6. *Determining theoretical and practical implications.* The researcher examines the study in its totality—the question asked, the design used, the data obtained, and the problems encountered—and makes a judgment concerning its importance and, consequently, how (and if) the study should be presented to other scientists. A particular study is not often of earth-shaking importance, but a series of studies can indeed have important implications and benefits for society at large.

To avoid ambiguities concerning what is meant when they refer to a particular behavior, psychologists typically use operational definitions. Simply put, the **operational definition** of a variable is an exact specification of the way in which it is measured. In our example, the operational definition of running speed is simple: The criterion measure will be the time (in minutes) required to run 10 kilometers on an 800-meter track as recorded by a trained observer with a stopwatch.

Good procedures for quantifying behavior are **empirical** and **quantitative**; that is, they assess real (observable) events that are measured in physical units. They are also valid, reliable, and sensitive. A procedure is **valid** if it measures what it purports to measure. It is **reliable** if it yields a consistent value when the behavior of interest does not change. It is **sensitive** if that value varies as a function of the independent variable. Many procedures for quantifying behavior are available. Among them are self-reports, direct observation, questionnaires, checklists, and standardized tests.

Experimentation requires decisions concerning the definition of the independent as well as the dependent variables. Moreover, the value(s) of the independent variable to be examined must be determined. Let us assume that Dr. Jay has decided to study only one value of the independent variable: 300 milligrams of caffeine. This amount of caffeine, which approximates that typically consumed by runners, will be dissolved in a cup of decaffeinated coffee, to be drunk within a 5-minute period beginning 30 minutes before running.

Within-Subject Designs: An Example

A relatively simple within-subject strategy could be used to investigate the effects of caffeine on running speed. Dr. Jay has four friends, two men and two women, of similar age (35–45 years) and running ability (38 to 44-minute times for 10-kilometer races) who have agreed to participate in the study. The effects of caffeine on the performance of these runners could be determined by having them run 10 kilometers twice, with the runs separated·by a week to control for fatigue. Each runner would ingest caffeine before the second run, but not before the first. (This would be an A-B design, with *A* designating the absence of treatment, or **baseline,** condition and *B* designating the treatment condition.) To control for any possible effects of drinking in and of itself (i.e., apart from caffeine intake), each runner would drink a cup of decaffeinated coffee 30 minutes before the first run. To prevent their expectations from affecting the outcome of the study, the participants would not be told whether the coffee contained caffeine.

Pretend that this study has actually been conducted and that each runner ran faster after drinking coffee. Would you, on this basis, conclude that caffeine improved performance?

Probably not. Consider this possibility: the weather was cool and pleasant during the second run (when caffeine was ingested), but it was hot and humid for the first run (no caffeine). This difference in weather, an extraneous variable, could easily have accounted for the observed difference in running times. The runners ran faster the second time not because they drank coffee, but because the weather was cooler and less humid. The A-B design has one important weakness: Because of its logical structure, the design can provide only weak and equivocal confirmation of the behavioral effects of an independent variable. When a A-B design is used, one can never be confident that a change in behavior that occurs coincidentally with the onset of the intervention is not the result of other, unknown factors (extraneous variables) that became operative at the time the intervention was instituted.

Adding a final baseline (A) phase to the A-B design strengthens it immensely. The A-B-A design is a withdrawal (or reversal) design, and its logic, like that of all such designs, is straightforward and compelling: If the dependent measure changes appreciably from the baseline level when the treatment is implemented and returns to at or near the initial baseline level when the treatment is terminated, there is good reason to believe that the observed changes in the target behavior reflect the actions of the treatment of interest. It is, of course, possible that some extraneous variable will begin to impose on the subject when the treatment is conducted and will cease when the treatment is terminated. Unless the extraneous variable is actually associated with the treatment, however, the odds that this will happen are small and grow smaller with each additional implementation of the treatment.

Dr. Jay could have made his experiment much stronger by using a withdrawal design, perhaps an A-B-A-B configuration. With this design, the four runners would run the same 10-kilometer course for time once a week for 12 weeks. Each runner would ingest caffeine 30 minutes before running in Weeks 4, 5, 6, 10, 11, and 12, but not before running in Weeks 1, 2, 3, 7, 8, and 9. Other than exposure to caffeine, the conditions would be the same throughout the study. If performance during the weeks when caffeine was ingested was consistently superior, as shown in Figure 3-2, it is reasonable to attribute this outcome to the actions of caffeine. If this pattern was not observed, the intervention would be considered ineffective.

Between-Subjects Designs: An Example

Between-subjects designs can be generally divided into single-factor and factorial designs. In a **single-factor design,** the effects of a single independent variable are evaluated. In a **factorial design,** the effects of two or more independent variables are evaluated simultaneously. Factorial designs allow treatment interactions to be evaluated and are effective in the sense of providing much information from a single study. Two independent variables **interact** if the effects of one independent variable differ depending on the level of the other independent variable. Interactions can be evaluated by within-subject as well as between-subjects designs, although the latter appear to be more often used for this purpose.

The simplest between-subjects design is the single-factor design (also termed *completely randomized* or *parallel groups*). With this design, the independent variable is arrayed along a single dimension, each subject is exposed to one value along that dimension, and data are compared across different individuals. The single-factor design could be used by Dr. Jay to evaluate the effects of caffeine (300 mg) on running times. In this case, the caffeine dose would be the dimension of the independent variable of interest; some subjects would receive 300 mg and others would receive 0 mg (decaffeinated coffee), and the performance (running times) of the two groups would be compared. Ideally, a sample of runners would be selected at random, and each would be assigned to one of the two groups. In **random selection,** each person to whom results of the study are to be generalized (i.e., each member of the **population** of interest) has an equal and independent likelihood of being selected for participation. **Random assignment** occurs when each person selected as a subject has an equal and independent probability of assignment to each experimental group.

In reality, random selection almost never occurs. Dr. Jay is interested in the effects of caffeine on middle-distance runners in general, but he is unlikely to study the effects of the drug on a sample randomly selected from that population. Instead, the effects of the drug will be studied in subjects to whom access is

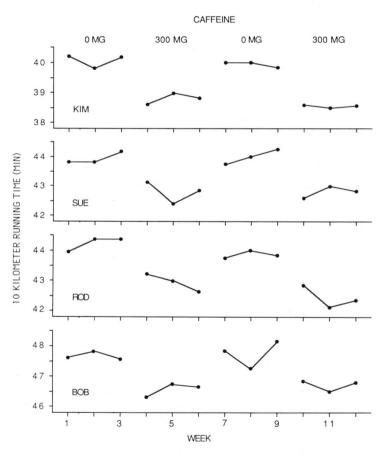

Figure 3-2. Hypothetical data collected in a within-subject (A-B-A-B) experimental design demonstrating that ingesting 300 milligrams of caffeine improved running time in each of four subjects. Note that the change from baseline (0 mg) to treatment (300 mg) is small but consistent for each subject.

available, perhaps in members of Dr. Jay's running club. Because these individuals may differ from other runners in their response to caffeine, it is important that Dr. Jay describe the sample carefully along multiple dimensions and that attempts be made to replicate the investigation in other settings and with other samples.

This caution notwithstanding, let us assume that Dr. Jay has decided to study 20 runners selected at random from the club; 10 of them will be given caffeine, and 10 will not. Before conducting the study, Dr. Jay specifically hypothesizes that, on the average, those who ingest caffeine will perform better (i.e., will have lower 10-kilometer times) than those who do not, and he decides to use a statistical test to evaluate this hypothesis. This hypothesis will be accepted as true if the statistical analysis (a t test) reveals that the difference in the mean (average) running times of the two groups is statistically significant at the .05 level. This means, in essence, that the likelihood of a difference in sample means of the size obtained would occur because of sampling error (chance) alone no more often than 1 time in 20.

In order to test the hypothesis fairly, it is important that the subjects in the sample be randomly assigned to the two groups. If the assignment is truly random and the groups are sufficiently large, there should be, at the onset of the study (i.e., before the introduction of 0 or 300 mg of caffeine), no significant differences between the groups with respect to relevant variables. Therefore, one can assume that a significant difference between the groups after exposure to different levels of the independent variable (i.e., 0 or 300 mg of caffeine) reflects a real treatment effect.

After having appropriately selected and assigned subjects to groups, Dr. Jay conducts the study and obtains the results shown in Sidebar 3-2. On average, runners who ingested caffeine ran 10,000 meters in 44.1 minutes, whereas runners who drank decaffeinated coffee ran the same distance in 45.6 minutes. Calculation of the t statistic is relatively straightforward, as shown in the sidebar. In the case of Dr. Jay's study, $t = 0.42$, with 18 degrees of freedom. To interpret this outcome, we must consult a statistical table, which tells us that the t value must exceed 2.1 to be significant at the .05 level. The value we obtained, 0.42, is less than 2.1; therefore; the results of the study are not significant at the .05 level. This means that Dr. Jay cannot confidently assert that the mean scores of the two groups differed. Therefore, on the basis of the study, caffeine does not appear to affect running times.

There are, of course, many other specific designs that could be used to investigate the relationship between caffeine and running—our examples could be greatly elaborated. Nonetheless, these simple experiments demonstrate the general logic of within-subject and between-subjects designs, both of which play a valuable role in a science of behavior.

Data Analysis: Type I and Type 2 Errors

When the effects of an intervention are relatively large and consistent across subjects and conditions, it is easy, on the basis of a visual inspection of the graphed data, to decide if and how the independent variable affected the dependent variable. Although there are no formal rules for analyzing data by visual inspection, researchers generally respond to changes in trends and levels of behavior across conditions (Parsonson & Baer, 1986).

Regardless of whether the data are analyzed by visual inspection or by statistical analysis, a researcher can err in two ways, termed *Type 1* and *Type 2* errors. A **Type 1 error** occurs when a scientist concludes that an independent variable affected a dependent variable, when in actuality it did not. A **Type 2 error** occurs when a scientist concludes than an independent variable did not affect a dependent variable, when in actuality it did.

The probability of committing a Type 1 error is inversely related to the probability of committing a Type 2 error: as one increases, the other decreases. Kazdin (1982) contended that researchers who use visual data analysis make

---

Sidebar 3-2

Calculating of *t*-test

Ten randomly selected runners ran 10 kilometers 30 minutes after ingesting 300 mg of caffeine. Ten others ran the same course without ingesting caffeine. A researcher has decided to use a *t* test to compare the performance of the two groups. To do this, a simple table would be prepared:

| | Caffeine ingested | | No caffeine | |
	X (time in min)	X^2	Y (time in min)	Y^2
	36.5	1,332	49.9	3,588
	60.0	3,600	32.0	1,024
	48.1	2,314	47.6	2,266
	53.2	2,830	38.1	1,152
	46.4	2,153	39.9	1,592
	42.7	1,823	40.2	1,616
	41.8	1,747	51.1	2,611
	39.1	1,529	57.8	3,341
	38.2	1,459	44.2	1,954
	35.4	1,253	45.1	2,034
Sums:	441.4	20,040	455.9	21,174
Means:	44.1		45.6	
N = 10				

From these values, the standard error of the difference in means (SD_m) can be determined:

$$SD_m = \sqrt{\frac{S^2}{N_x} + \frac{S^2}{N_y}} \quad S^2 = \frac{\Sigma X_x^2 + \Sigma X_y^2}{(N_x - 1) + (N_y - 1)}$$

$$\Sigma X^2 = NS^2 \quad S^2 = \frac{\Sigma X^2}{N} - m^2$$

$$S_x^2 = \frac{20,040}{10} - (44.1)^2 \quad S_x^2 = 59$$

$$S_y^2 = \frac{21,178}{10} - (45.6)^2 \quad S_y^2 = 39$$

$$\Sigma X_x^2 = (59)(10) \quad \Sigma X_x^2 = 590$$

$$\Sigma X_y^2 = (39)(10) \quad \Sigma X_y^2 = 390$$

$$S^2 = \frac{590 + 390}{(10 - 1)(10 - 1)} \quad S^2 = 54$$

$$SD_m = \sqrt{\frac{54}{10} + \frac{54}{10}} \quad SD_m = 3.3$$

The formula used to calculate *t* is:

$$t = \frac{M_x - M_y}{SD_m}$$

Thus, *t* is equal to:

$$\frac{44.1 - 45.6}{3.3}, \text{ or } 0.42 \text{ (the } - \text{ direction is irrelevant)}$$

In this example, the degrees of freedom are ($N_x - 1$) + ($N_y - 1$), or 18. Consulting a statistical table for the distribution of *t* reveals that this value is not significant at the .05 level. The appropriate interpretation of this outcome is described in the text.

> Researchers typically give higher priority to avoiding a Type 1 error, concluding that a variable has an effect when the findings may have occurred by chance. In statistical analyses, the probability of committing a Type 1 error can be specified (by the level of confidence of the statistical test). With visual inspection, the probability of a Type 1 error is not known. Hence, to avoid chance effects, the investigator looks for highly consistent effects that can be readily seen. By minimizing the probability of a Type 1 error, the probability of a Type 2 error is increased. Investigators relying on visual inspection are more likely to commit more Type 2 errors than those relying on statistical analyses. Thus, reliance on visual inspection will overlook or discount many reliable, but weak effects. (p. 242).

Kazdin is not alone in describing visual analysis as largely insensitive to small effects. But Huitema (1986) made the case that visual analysis may, in some situations, be more sensitive than statistical analysis. Be that as it may, studies that use only visual data analysis have appeared primarily in journals oriented toward behavior analysis (e.g., *JABA* and *JEAB*).

Rules pertaining to statistical data analysis are widely available. When data are analyzed statistically, it is imperative that an appropriate test be used, that the mathematical calculations be accurate, and that the assumptions underlying the test not be violated.

Regardless of how data are analyzed, experimental and clinical significance must be distinguished in all applied studies. A treatment is **experimentally significant** to the extent that a researcher is confident that it altered behavior. It is **clinically significant** to the extent that the alteration in behavior actually benefited the treated individual in a therapeutic way.

Clinical significance can be determined in three ways:

1. Comparing levels of behavior during treatment with predetermined **criterion levels** (treatment objectives that constitute a solution to the behavioral problem).
2. Comparing the behavior of the individual(s) undergoing treatment to that of a similar individual who does not manifest the behavioral problem for which the treatment was applied.
3. Having those who defined the problem rate the success of its treatment.

In applied investigations, the response of individual subjects to treatment is always important and can be determined only by monitoring behavior before and during the course of the treatment. Consequently, for most clinical applications, designs that involve repeated measures of the dependent variable are superior to those that involve a single observation of each subject.

Study Questions

1. What is research, what are data, and what is the difference between basic and applied research? (Be able to say why the examples in Table 3-1 are basic or applied.)

2. List the four factors that influence the research strategies of psychologists.

3. Using Table 3-2 as an outline, describe (and contrast) the four general research strategies.

4. What is the point about causality and correlation?

5. Discuss the essential characteristics of experimentation.

6. Define and give examples of dependent and independent variables, and of functional relations.

7. What is the difference between internal and external validity, and what is the role of replication in experimentation?

8. Why should the results of any one experiment be regarded as tentative? Do experiments prove theories?

9. Compare within-subject and between-subject designs.

10. List the six steps in experimentation and explain the following statement: Each "step in the sequence represents nothing more than a labeled set of researcher behaviors; science is what scientists do."

Recommended Readings

Barber, T. X. (1976). *Ten Pitfalls in Human Research*. New York: Pergamon Press.

Although far from new, this book provides a still-current discussion of the general problems that can befall anyone who attempts to conduct research with human subjects.

Kazdin, A. E. (1982). *Single-Case Research Designs*. New York: Oxford University Press.

This is a clear and straightforward overview of the procedures characteristically used by behavioral psychologists in clinical settings. In it, Kazdin shows how relations between variables can be revealed through a number of different experimental strategies, and he makes it clear that there is no one best way to do applied research.

Sidman, M. (1960). *Tactics of Scientific Research*. New York: Basic Books.

One of the first defenses of the research strategies characteristically favored by behavioral psychologists, it remains one of the best. Perhaps a minor classic, but not easy reading for the beginner. Recommended only for students with a good basic understanding of the logic and methods of behavioral research.

CHAPTER 4

Evolution and Behavior

On June 19, 1987, the United States Supreme Court, by a 7–2 vote, struck down as unconstitutional a Louisiana act requiring its teachers to devote equal time to "creation science" if they discussed evolution in their classes. This case, which was well publicized, is but one in a long series of legal battles over the teaching of evolution in public schools. Those battles are instructive in demonstrating the great reluctance with which scientific fact is accepted when it conflicts with traditional belief. And make no mistake about it, that evolution occurred is a fact. Consistent observations and inferences by the thousands indicate that, as Stephen Jay Gould (1987–1988) affirmed:

> The earth is billions of years old and its living creatures are linked by ties of evolutionary descent. Scientists stand accused of promoting dogma by so stating, but do we brand people illiberal when they proclaim that the earth is neither flat nor at the center of the universe. Science *has* taught us some things with confidence! Evolution on an ancient earth is as well established as our planet's shape and position. Our continuing struggle to understand how evolution happens (the "theory of evolution") does not cast our documentation of its occurrence—the "fact of evolution"—into doubt. (p. 186)

But what is evolution, and why is it relevant to the study of behavior? By way of a simple definition, **biological evolution** refers to "change in the diversity and adaptation of populations of organisms" (Mayr, 1978, p. 47). The essence of evolution is descent from common ancestors. This implies that all life forms traced backward eventually converge. For example,

> if we go back about 20 million years, we ourselves are connected to all other apes. Likewise, about 150 million years ago our lineage converges with those of all other mammals. And finally, if we go back a half billion years, all vertebrates are seen to have sprung from a single common ancestor. (Trivers, 1985, p. 10)

The historical connectedness of various animals is often represented pictorially by the kind of diagram shown in Figure 4-1, which depicts the evolution of our own species, *Homo sapiens*. In this figure, time is represented along the vertical axis and offshoots from a lineage along the horizontal axis. Because species become differentiated and branch off from one another over time, the diagram resembles a tree. (A **species** is a group of actually or potentially interbreeding organisms, which do not interbreed with other organisms). Sometimes, the earlier species still exist alongside the more recent species, but more often than not they become extinct. For example, chimpanzees and gorillas are the closest living relatives of modern humans; all three species evolved (i.e., branched off) from a common ancestor that is now extinct. In becoming extinct, it shared a fate common to most of the species that have occupied earth. In fact, even though scientists estimate that 2 million species exist today, this number represents only

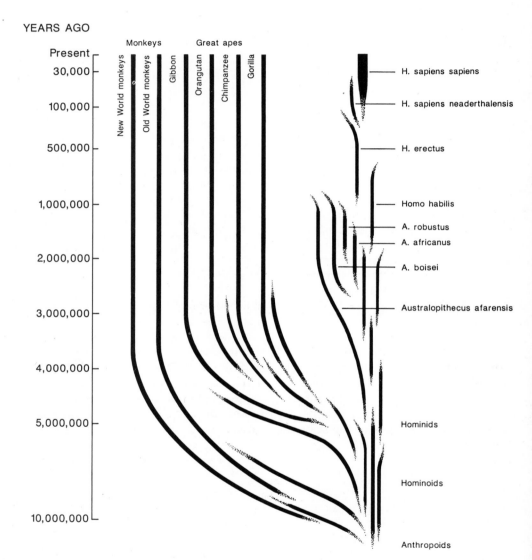

Figure 4-1. The anthropoid evolutionary tree beginning about 10 million years ago and leading up to present-day anthropoids, including *Homo sapiens*. Shown is the evolutionary branching of monkeys from hominoids (10 million years ago) and of apes from homonids (5 million years ago). There is debate about the specific ancestors of modern humans. (Adapted from *Tools and Human Evolution* by S. L. Washburn. Copyright 1960 by Scientific American, Inc. All rights reserved.)

about 1% of those that have ever lived. This means that approximately 2 billion species have existed since life on earth began.

When we speak of biological evolution, it is easy to think only of physical structures such as the brain, muscles, or skeletal system evolving. But behavior is also a part of the biology of all animals and consequently a product of evolution. Therefore, any book on psychology that fails to provide at least an overview of evolution is incomplete. Evolution by natural selection forms the basis of all the biological sciences and is the great unifying concept of biology. Unfortunately, it is widely misunderstood, misquoted, and misapplied despite its simplicity (Gould, 1977). This chapter gives an overview of the **neo-Darwinian** theory of evolution: *Darwinian* because it rests on Darwin's theory of natural selection, and *neo* ("new") because it uses post-Darwinian theories of heredity.

Historical Overview

The historical antecedents of neo-Darwinism can be summarized by five major events:

1. Development of the theory of natural selection by Darwin.
2. Discovery of the fundamental principles of genetic inheritance by Mendel.
3. Discovery of chromosomes and cell division.
4. Discovery of the molecular structure of the DNA (deoxyribonucleic acid) molecule by Watson and Crick.
5. Synthesis of the principles of genetic inheritance and those of natural selection.

Many people believe that Charles Darwin invented the concept of evolution. In actuality, evolution in one form or another had been written about since the time of Aristotle. By the time Darwin left on his famous scientific voyage aboard the *HMS Beagle* in 1831, the idea of the evolution of species was being cautiously advanced by a few naturalists and philosophers in Europe, even though most members of the scientific establishment still vigorously embraced the antievolutionary notion that all species had been created in fixed and changeless form. What popularity there was for the concept of evolution was an outgrowth of the Enlightenment philosophy that nature was constantly changing and progressing up the ladder of life, the *scala naturae*, toward "nature's crowning perfection, humankind" (Leahey, 1987, p. 148). The dominant theory of evolution before Darwin, that of the naturalist Jean-Baptiste Lamarck (1744–1829), reflected this philosophy.

Lamarck proposed that species are generated spontaneously, as in the biblical view of creation, but that they are not perfectly suited to their environments. According to Lamarck, organisms innately strive toward perfection, which they achieve by adapting to their environments. (You should recognize this as a teleological explanation of evolution.) As they strive to adapt, organisms use some body parts (e.g., muscles) more or less than others, thereby changing the structure of those parts. When these changed organisms mate, their offspring inherit the changes that the parent(s) has acquired. Thus, Lamarck's theory stressed the **inheritance of acquired characteristics.** For example, the long necks of giraffes can be explained from a Lamarckian perspective as follows: By attempting to reach leaves high on trees, an ancient generation of short-necked giraffes stretched their necks, making them slightly longer. When those giraffes mated, their offspring were born with slightly elongated necks. This process was repeated across generations until longed-necked giraffes, perfectly suited to eating leaves from tall trees, were the norm. At that point, evolutionary change ceased. Through similar processes, each and every species on earth allegedly evolved into its present and presumably perfect form.

Lamarck's theory did not withstand the test of time and scientific discovery. One of its weaknesses was an inability to account for the acquisition of many important characteristics (e.g., color vision) by self-adaptation. A second, and fatal, weakness was the falsity of its central premise, namely, that characteristics acquired in an individual's lifetime can be passed on to offspring. They cannot: a woman and her mate can do bench presses until their pectorals bulge like melons, but doing so will have absolutely no effect on the muscularity of their children.

Inheritance of acquired characteristics failed as an evolutionary mechanism and was eventually replaced by a theory of evolution based on natural selection. This theory was derived independently by Charles Darwin and Alfred Wallace in the 1850s. But it was Darwin's 1859 book, *The Origin of Species by Means of Natural Selection,* that focused attention on evolution by natural selection and initiated what is now referred to as the *Darwinian revolution*. In general, natural selection theory states that some individuals are more successful in surviving and producing healthy offspring because of the specific traits they inherited from their parents. Individuals with other traits are less successful and produce fewer healthy offspring. Darwin's theory placed great emphasis on inheritance and therefore required a cogent theory of it. Darwin did not, however, develop one.

In 1866, an Austrian monk, Johann Gregor Mendel, did. Mendel proposed a theory of inheritance based on the results of years of breeding experiments with pea plants. Contrary to the prevailing belief that inheritance involved the blending of hereditary material (a notion accepted by Darwin), Mendel proposed that hereditary factors are discrete units (particles) transmitted from each parent to the offspring. Each individual thus inherits two hereditary units, one from each parent, for each physical trait. Mendel discovered that these heredity units, which we now call *genes,* could assume slightly different forms. If an offspring inherited different forms of a gene, one form, which Mendel called **dominant,** would always override the other, which he called **recessive,** and determine the resulting physical trait. In order for the recessive gene to determine the physical trait, an individual would have to inherit two copies for it. For example, with Mendel's pea plants, yellow color was dominant over green. Thus, a plant with one green gene and one yellow gene would produce yellow peas even though it possessed a green gene; only plants with two green genes would produce green peas. Mendel's discovery suggested for the first time that an organism's full genetic composition, called **genotype,** is not always evident in its physical appearance, called **phenotype.** In other words, you can't always tell what genes an organism carries by simply looking at the organism; that is, you can't judge a genotype solely by its phenotype. Mendel's findings were consistent with Darwin's observations that offspring differ from their parents and his suggestion that these differences are inherited. Unfortunately, Mendel's discoveries were unknown to Darwin and were lost to other scientists until 1900, when they were rediscovered.

Just as some important features of Darwin's theory were explained by Mendel's laws of inheritance, Mendel's laws were, in turn, supported at a different level by the direct observation of cells under the microscope, which occurred around the turn of the 20th century. This observation revealed not only the process of cell division, but the presence and role of **chromosomes** ("colored bodies," so named because they respond so easily to the colored dyes used by scientists to make cell contents visible under the microscope), which are the physical carriers of genetic information.

Mendel's findings had important implications for the concept of natural selection, and they were incorporated into a reasonably comprehensive theory of evolution in the 1930s and 1940s (Mayr, 1978). But two questions concerning the basic nature of the hereditary material remained unanswered: (1) How is genetic material copied so that traits can be transmitted from parents to offspring? And (2) how do genes control the development of individual organisms? These questions were finally answered by a chemist, Francis Crick, and a biolo-

These siblings share a similar genetic makeup that produces similar physical characteristics. They also share an environment that interacts with genetic makeup to determine behavior. (Photo courtesy of Sue Keller.)

gist, James D. Watson, with the Nobel-prize-winning discovery in 1953 of the molecular structure of DNA.

Natural Selection

According to Darwin, natural selection is a two-step process. The first step is the production of **variation.** In his observations, Darwin noticed that offspring resemble but are not identical to their parents. In other words, the characteristics of offspring vary from those of their parents. Darwin posited that offspring somehow inherited all characteristics from their parents, including those that the parents did not exhibit.

The second step of Darwin's process is **selection through survival.** Darwin noticed that most species produce many more offspring than actually survive. He must have asked himself, "What makes the survivors special?" His answer was that those individuals that possessed the best combination of characteristics for a given environment would have a greater chance of surviving and producing offspring, which, in turn, would have a greater chance of surviving. As a result, over time those favorable characteristics would gradually become more numerous in the population.

The notion of environment in Darwin's theory is crucial, because it is the physical environment that shapes species (i.e., genotypes) and directs evolution. The importance of the environment and the process of selection was suggested to Darwin during his travels to the Galápagos Islands off the shores of Ecuador. The initial clues came from a type of bird called a finch. Darwin discovered 14 species of finch on the Galápagos Islands. The various finch species varied along several dimensions, but one obvious difference was in the size, shape, and, therefore, the function of their beaks. Each beak was "exactly appropriate" for particular eating habits of the species of the finch in which it appeared. The variation in beaks in this small, intimately related group of birds intrigued Darwin, and he eventually concluded that the variations in beaks had been selected because of the special advantage they conferred on the individuals possessing them.

This description of evolution by natural selection can be summarized in terms of two undeniable facts and an inescapable conclusion (Gould, 1977):

1. Organisms vary, and these variations are inherited (at least in part) by their offspring.
2. Organisms produce more offspring than can possibly survive.
3. On average, offspring that vary most strongly in directions favored by the environment will survive and propagate. Favorable variation will therefore accumulate in populations by natural selection. (p. 11)

The variations to which Gould referred can involve any aspect of the organism's structure or behavior, so long as the variation is favorable. As variations accumulate, populations develop that are increasingly unlike each other, and new species emerge. Of course, evolution proceeds slowly relative to the human life span, but there is reason to believe that a species often emerges from an ancestral stock over a relatively short period of geological time and then does not change greatly through the course of its existence (Eldredge & Gould, 1972).

Although evolution shapes species, *it is erroneous to assume that all of the characteristics of a species, whether physiological or behavioral, are the result of natural selection and somehow enhance the ability to survive and produce offspring.* A given characteristic, or trait, may occur not because it has adaptive value but because (Futuyma, 1986):

1. The trait is a consequence of the action of the environment or of learning.
2. The trait is a simple consequence of the laws of physics or chemistry.
3. The trait is genetically correlated with another trait that does have adaptive value.
4. The trait may be an anachronism. Such traits had adaptive value in the world in which a species evolved, but not in the current environment.

There are several other, more complex, mechanisms that may account for the occurrence of a trait without adaptive value. But the important point is one made clearly by Futuyma (1986), "Adaptation is an onerous concept, and the adaptive value of a trait should be demonstrated rather than assumed, for numerous factors other than adaptation can influence the evolution of a trait" (p. 283).

Genetics

Organisms are composed of one or more cells; the human body contains over a trillion. Each cell consists of an outer part, or **cytoplasm,** where proteins are manufactured, and an inner part, or **nucleus,** where most of the genetic material of each cell is located. Much of the activity of cells consists of cell division. Cell division is an ongoing process that is involved in the growth, repair, and replacement of tissue. As we will see, cell division results from genes' making copies of themselves.

Most cells, called **somatic (body) cells,** divide via a process called **mitosis** (duplication and division). During mitosis, the chromosomes first duplicate and then the cell divides; the result is two daughter cells, each with the same genetic information as the parent cell. For example, human cells contain 46 chromosomes (23 pairs). During mitosis, all 46 chromosomes in the parent cell duplicate and divide, and the result is two daughter cells, each also with 46 chromosomes. Figure 4-2 shows the process of mitosis, beginning with the fertilization of an egg by a sperm, each with one chromosome (for simplicity). In the first stage (duplication), the chromosomes duplicate, and in the second stage (division), they divide; the result is two cells.

Some cells located in the gonads (testes in men and ovaries in women) divide through a process called **meiosis** (lessening, or reduction and division) which results in daughter cells called **sex (germ) cells** or **gametes** (the sperm in men and the ovum in women). Gametes have half as many chromosomes as the parent cell. If through sexual intercourse a sperm (with 23 chromosomes) is joined with an ovum (also with 23 chromosomes), the result will be a fertilized egg with the normal human complement of 46 chromosomes, one half from the mother and one half from the father. Figure 4-3 shows a cell with 2 chromosomes

(for simplicity) undergoing meiosis. In the first stage, the chromosomes duplicate. The resulting cell then undergoes two divisions, each of which reduces the
number of chromosomes by half. The result is four gametes, each with only 1
chromosome.

DNA and the Genetic Code

Chromosomes are long strands (molecules) of **deoxyribonucleic acid (DNA).**
The DNA molecule contains the genetic information that is the recipe for the
production of the proteins that make up all organisms. And its storage capacity is
immense: if the *Encyclopaedia Britannica* could be genetically encoded, the DNA in
a single human cell could hold all 30 volumes of it three or four times over
(Dawkins, 1986). How is it possible for something so small to store so much
information? To find the answer, we must examine the structure of this nucleic
acid. The structure of the DNA molecule is like a **double helix** (Watson & Crick,
1953); that is, two threads, or "backbones," are twisted around one another like a
spiral staircase (see Figure 4-4). Each DNA strand consists of a long sequence of
molecules called *nucleotides:* adenine (A), thymine (T), guanine (G), and cytosine
(C). This is DNA's four-letter alphabet. The strands are connected at regular
intervals (the rungs of the DNA ladder) where two nucleotides meet.

DNA molecules have two important functions: they make copies of themselves, and they carry the instructions (or blueprints) for making organisms.
During DNA **replication** the two strands of nucleotides "unzip" and separate,

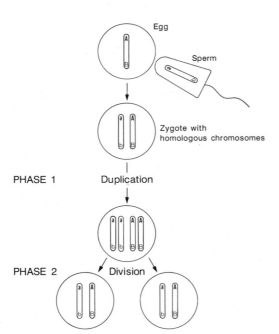

Figure 4-2. Mitosis, the process of cell
division for somatic (body) cells. In the
first stage, the chromosomes duplicate. In the second stage, they divide;
the result is two daughter cells, each
with the same number of chromosomes as the parent cell.

each strand acting as a template for the construction of a new strand identical to the original (see Figure 4-5). A new strand of DNA is formed when each nucleotide on the template bonds to a complementary nucleotide from the surrounding area (bonds are formed only between A and T, and between G and C). The result is a strand of DNA identical to the original. This process occurs from birth to death in every cell of all life forms. The precision of DNA self-copying explains why every cell in the body carries the same genetic information and how genes can be transmitted without change over countless generations. For this reason, DNA self-copying has been called the essence of heredity (Futuyma, 1979). Mistakes, however, do occasionally occur during DNA replication when one kind of nucleotide becomes accidentally substituted for another, an event that constitutes a mutation (see discussion below). But the probability that such an accident will happen is extremely low.

The second function of DNA is to direct the construction of organisms via the **genetic code.** It does so by making protein molecules, which are the building

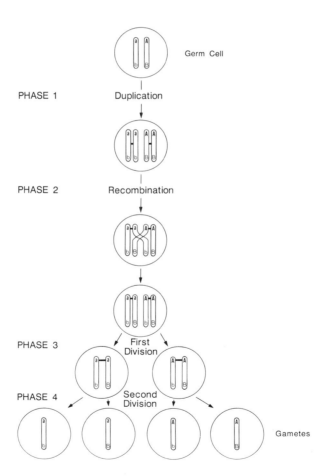

Figure 4-3. Meiosis, the process of cell division for gametes. In the first stage, the chromosomes duplicate. In the second stage, recombination occurs in which homologous chromosomes exchange corresponding segments. The resulting cell then undergoes two divisions, each of which reduces the number of chromosomes by half. The result is four gametes (eggs or sperm), each with half the number of chromosomes as the parent cell.

blocks of living beings. The nucleotide alphabet of DNA (A, C, T, and G) is copied in the cell nucleus and then transported out of the nucleus into the cell's cytoplasm, where it is translated into another alphabet, that of amino acids, which spells out words of protein molecules. Proteins are nothing more than long chains of (100 or more) amino acids. The protein molecules, in turn, determine the structure and function of cells, for example, whether cells become liver, bone, or brain cells.

In all of this talk about DNA replication and protein synthesis, you might be asking, "Where's the gene?" The term *gene* is used very liberally nowadays, almost to the extent of becoming meaningless. What do geneticists mean by *gene*? In a very broad sense, a **gene** is the basic unit of heredity, comprising a unique sequence of amino acids on the DNA molecule that code for the production of a single protein.

One misunderstanding about genes is that there is a one-to-one correspondence between genes and phenotypic traits; that is, one gene equals one trait

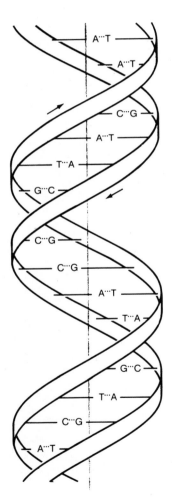

Figure 4-4. The DNA molecule, which looks like a spiral staircase with the base pairs forming the steps. (Reprinted by permission from *Introduction to Child Development* by J. P. Dworetzky, 1987, p. 34. Copyright 1987 by West Publishing. All rights reserved.)

(e.g., a gene for blue eyes or for intelligence). In actuality, single genes typically affect many different traits, and each trait typically reflects the action of many different genes. Moreover, there are so-called master genes that regulate the activity of other genes. The actions of master genes are apparent during the process of **cell differentiation,** in which cells become differentiated and specialized. Cell differentiation develops even though each cell in an organism's body contains a complete set of genetic instructions for constructing the entire organism. For example, some cells become muscle cells, and others become nerve cells or bone cells. This means that only a small part of the genetic code is being acted on in each cell type. It is the master genes that regulate the direction, rate, and extent of cell specialization.

Patterson (1978) probably spoke for many biologists when he said of the genetic code that "the simplicity of this arrangement is surely the most stunning knowledge to ever have come out of biology" (p. 31).

Genetic Mutation

In genetics, **mutation** is defined as any change in the sequence of nucleotides in the DNA molecule. Mutations can be of two types. The first, **a point mutation,** consists of the replacement of a single nucleotide pair. Point mutations result when one amino acid is altered, with the result that the gene codes for a slightly different protein. The second type of mutation consists of the

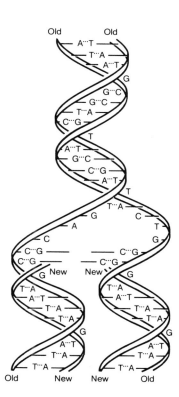

Figure 4-5. Replication of DNA. (Reprinted by permission from *Introduction to Child Development* by J. P. Dworetzky, 1987, p. 35. Copyright 1987 by West Publishing. All rights reserved.)

insertion or deletion of nucleotide pairs and is called a **chromosome mutation.** Chromosome mutations usually cause the DNA to be read out of sequence, and the result is the production of a completely different kind of protein. Point mutations occur during DNA replication (as mentioned above), whereas chromosome mutations occur when the nucleus reproduces itself during cell division, especially meiosis (see below) (Patterson, 1978). Both types of mutations can occur spontaneously or as a function of external agents called **mutagens.** Known mutagens include radiation and some drugs (e.g., mustard gas and hydrogen peroxide).

The transmission of a point mutation to an offspring depends on the (rare) occurrence of a sequence of unlikely events. To be passed on, a point mutation must occur in a gamete, and that gamete must be involved in fertilization. Because all chromosome mutations occur during meiosis and therefore in gametes, their fate depends only on whether they are involved in fertilization. In short, for an offspring to inherit a mutation, (1) the mutation must occur in a gamete of the parent, and (2) that gamete must be involved in fertilization.

Genetic Variation

If a point mutation occurs in a single gene on one of a pair of like-sized (homologous) chromosomes, the code for that gene is altered and the gene will now direct the production of a slightly different protein. The corresponding gene on the other chromosome is unaffected by the mutation. The result is that, at each gene locus (the location of the gene on the chromosome), there may be two or more alternative or variant forms of that gene, called **alleles.** When two alleles at a given locus are identical, the individual is said to be **homozygous** (the same) at that locus, and when the two alleles are different, the individual is said to be **heterozygous.** When an organism is heterozygous for a particular gene, one allele is usually dominant, in the sense that it overrides the other allele and determines the resulting protein and phenotypic trait.

Although Mendel knew nothing of the molecular basis of genes and alleles, he correctly described the facts of homozygotes and heterozygotes and dominance and recessiveness. Eye color in humans provides a good example. Each individual inherits two alleles at a given gene locus that determine eye color. Suppose that a person inherits a brown-eye allele (*B*) and a blue-eye allele (*b*). In humans, brown eye color is dominant over blue, which is recessive. This means

	Parent 1	
	B	b
B	BB (Brown)	Bb (Brown)
b	bB (Brown)	bb (Blue)

Parent 2

Figure 4-6. The possible outcomes of the mating of two parents who are heterozygous for brown eyes. On average, 75% of the offspring will have the brown genotype, which is dominant in humans, and 25% will have the blue genotype, which is recessive.

that an individual needs only one brown allele (e.g., *Bb*) in order to have brown eyes but must have two blue alleles (bb) to have blue eyes. Figure 4-6 shows the possible results of the mating of two parents who are heterozygous for brown eyes.

Without genetic mutation at a given locus, all individuals in a population would be homozygous for the allele at that locus (i.e., they would have the same gene) and there would be no variation in that allele. If all individuals within a population were homozygous for *all* alleles, then there would be no variation in that population and everyone would be identical. Identical twins illustrate this circumstance on a small scale.

Having introduced the concept of genetic mutation and the distinction between genes and alleles, we can now define **genetic variation** as the number of different alleles in a population (e.g., the number of alleles for eye color in humans). Genetic variation is clearly a prerequisite for evolutionary change (Ayala, 1978). Without it, different traits could not arise and be selected.

In addition to mutation, genetic variation results from two other related processes, called *crossing over* and *independent* (or *random*) *assortment*, both of which occur during meiosis. In the first phase of meiosis, chromosomes duplicate and then pair with matching chromosomes (i.e., those of approximately equal size called **homologous chromosomes** (refer to Figure 4-3). In the second phase (called *recombination*, or *crossing over*), each chromosome actually breaks apart, and corresponding segments then **cross over** and rejoin with the other "broken" chromosome. The outcome is that corresponding sections of chromosomes are exchanged, and the result is a new combination of genes on each chromosome. In other words, during crossing over a section of a paternal chromosome (one inherited from the father) joins with a maternal chromosome (one inherited from the mother) and vice versa; consequently, some paternal genes exist along with maternal genes on that maternal chromosome, and some maternal genes lie on the paternal chromosome. Gametes, then, have chromosomes with varying combinations of maternal and paternal segments. In short, crossing over generates new combinations of alleles (maternal and paternal) on the same chromosome,[1] and genetic variation is increased.

During the last stage of meiosis, each cell divides to yield four gametes (Figure 4-3). At this time, the homologous chromosomes are **independently assorted,** which means that they are randomly distributed to each of the four gametes. Thus, any one chromosome has a 1 in 4 chance of ending up in any gamete. The result is a mixture of maternal and paternal chromosomes in each sex cell.

To summarize, crossing over scrambles genes on chromosomes, and independent assortment results in new combinations of chromosomes in the sex cells. Both increase variation in the population. The relative contributions of mutation and recombination were expressed nicely by Ayala (1978):

> Although mutation is the ultimate source of all genetic variation, it is a relatively rare
> event, providing a mere trickle of new alleles into the much larger reservoir of stored

[1]Normally, during crossing over, the chromosome parts manage to line up precisely, gene for gene. Sometimes, however, there is unequal crossing over, in which one chromosome loses some genetic material (a deficiency) and part of the other chromosome becomes duplicated (Futuyma, 1979). In some cases, the resulting chromosomes can cause chromosomal abnormalities. An example is trisomy 21, which leads to the clinical condition called *Down syndrome.*

genetic variation. Indeed, recombination alone is sufficient to enable a population to expose its hidden variation for many generations without the need for new genetic input by mutation. (p. 63)

Evolution in Action

The great diversity of life forms now evident resulted from the accumulation of genetic changes that have continued in populations because they enhanced the reproductive success of organisms possessing them. We described how these genetic changes originated with mutation and are continuously recombined to produce new sources of variation via the processes of crossing over (recombination) and independent assortment. We will now consider an example of evolution at work.

The story begins with the industrial revolution and the burning of coal to fuel the fires of factories. Soot from the burning coal caused environments near industries to become blackened. As a consequence, the British peppered moth, *Biston betularia*, developed "industrial melanism," or blackening (Kettlewell, 1973). Like most moths, the peppered moth flies at night. During the day, it rests on tree trunks and other vertical surfaces. Originally, the common form of the moth was a whitish color with small black marks; on lichen-covered whitish-colored trees, this form was barely visible. Patterson (1978) described what happened to this moth's coloring with the coming of the industrial revolution:

> In all eighteenth- and early nineteenth-century insect collections, the moth had this (i.e., the whitish) coloration. In 1849 a single melanic or black example was caught near Manchester, and by 1900, 98 or 99 per cent of moths collected near Manchester were black. In the 1870s black individuals were still quite uncommon, but in the 1880s they already outnumbered the pale form. In the Manchester district, this change from a pale-colored population of the peppered moth to a 98 per cent dark population took about fifty years, and this period corresponds with the most rapid increase in human population of Manchester, and in the quantity of coal burned there. The same change occurred around other industrial cities, and also in some nearby rural, unpolluted areas. (p. 81)

How did most members of the species change from white to black? First, we may take for granted that, like most organisms, these moths produce more offspring than can possibly survive. The defining difference between the light- and dark-colored moths was the presence in the dark variety of a dominant genetic mutation that made it black. The primary selective force operating on the moths is predation by birds. And those moths that stood out against their background were more likely to be seen and eaten than those that did not stand out. The mutation resulting in black moths presumably arose spontaneously several times over many hundreds of years. Because the mutation was dominant, all first-generation offspring that inherited the mutant allele were black. Against normal light-colored trees these moths would have been easily seen and probably eaten by birds. Thus, the mutation would not have conferred a selective advantage and would not have been transmitted to offspring, and the non-mutant allele resulting in white-colored moths would have predominated. Only when the trees became black from the burning of coal did the mutation for black color have a selective advantage. The moths that survived and produced offspring in this particular environment were the dark-colored ones, which are now common around Manchester.

This example illustrates that natural selection can be envisioned as a creative process, in that it results in species that are well suited to the ecological niche that they occupy. If, however, that niche changes dramatically, disaster can occur. Consider this case:

> Something happened 65 million years ago, at the end of the Cretaceous, something so devastating that it altered the course of life on earth. With seeming abruptness, as geologic time goes, almost half of the genera living throughout the world disappeared, animal life and vegetable, marine and terrestrial, large and small. . . . No species living exclusively on land and weighing more than twenty-five kilograms seem to have survived, and the most conspicuous of the nonsurvivors were the dinosaurs. Although the fossils of a variety of dinosaurs are found in the uppermost Cretaceous rocks, none has ever been unearthed in the Tertiary layer just above. The dinosaurs had vanished, never to be seen again. Extinctions at the close of the Cretaceous rang down the curtain on the Age of Reptiles. (Wilford, 1985, p. 212)

The cause of this great dying is open to debate. One likely possibility, first proposed by the Nobel laureate Luis Alvarez and his son, Walter, is that a sizable extraterrestrial object, perhaps an asteroid, collided with the earth (see Wilford, 1985). The collision spawned earthquakes and tidal waves and hurled into the atmosphere a cloud of dust that darkened the earth. Photosynthesis stopped and temperatures fell. Most species were unprepared for this new and hostile environment—they had evolved in a different and more benign world—and did not survive.

Evolution of Behavior

Although we do not usually realize it, evolution is—in a real, but very general, sense—the cause of all behavior. For instance, the sound of the can opener may cause your cat to run into the kitchen because, in the past, when it has done so it has received food. The most obvious cause of the behavior of running into the kitchen is the sound of the can opener. The fact that your cat can learn to run into the kitchen at sound of the can opener is due, however, to the evolutionary history of cats: their responses to sounds associated with food in the offing presumably had survival value. Moving in the direction of such sounds was frequently followed by obtaining food, and success in procuring food was likely to be directly related to the animal's success in reproducing. Not surprisingly, cats and many other species are genetically equipped to learn to approach sounds correlated with the availability of food.

The Inheritance of Behavior

Any discussion of evolution and behavior must deal with the concept of inheritance. This is a much misunderstood and misused concept. When a trait, behavioral or nonbehavioral, is inherited (i.e., has evolved because of its adaptive value), it simply has a genetic basis different from that of some alternative trait. (Remember that it is genes that are selected by natural selection.) For example, the sharpness of the canine teeth in lions results from alleles that are different from those that produce duller canines. During the evolution of lions, the alleles associated with sharp teeth were selected over those associated with dull ones.

In principle, it should be possible to discover the genetic bases of all traits, including behavioral ones. Although this is still a lofty goal, scientists have made meaningful progress. Scientists who are interested in the genetic bases of behavior are called *behavior geneticists.* **Behavior genetics** is the study of the relation between differences in genotype and differences in behavior in a population. Through several types of experiments, behavior geneticists may conclude that differences between individuals, or variations, in a behavioral trait are correlated with differences in genes. Ideally, the behavior in question is a response or pattern of responding that can be objectively defined and accurately measured. Often, however, this is not the case; behavior geneticists frequently study heterogeneous and poorly defined "traits" like "intelligence." This kind of study can pose obvious problems, for one must meaningfully define and accurately measure a variable to determine whether it is influenced by genotype, or by anything else.

Even when the behavior of interest is adequately defined and measured, it is easy to misinterpret behavior geneticists when they say that a trait is genetically determined or inherited. They do not mean that the specific gene (or combination of genes) has been identified and manipulated and that the effects on behavior have been observed. Rather, they mean that behavioral differences between individuals are correlated with genetic differences between those same individuals (recall from Chapter 3 the problems connected with inferring causation from correlation).

Behavior geneticists generally use three methods of investigation: crossing experiments, selection experiments, and studies of family resemblance (Brown, 1975). Crossing and selection experiments are used with nonhumans, and studies of family resemblance are used with humans.

In **crossing experiments,** organisms that differ with respect to a particular behavior are crossed (mated) while environmental factors are held as constant as possible, and their offspring are then examined. The most convincing evidence for the genetic determination of behavior is obtained by comparing individuals that differ by only a single gene.

One of the most frequently cited examples of a relatively complex behavioral difference resulting from a single gene involves the hygienic behavior of honeybees (Rothenbuhler, 1964). The Van Scoy strain of honeybee is susceptible to a particular type of bacterial infection, whereas the Brown strain is resistant. The Brown strain is resistant because of the cleaning behavior of worker bees, which uncap the infected cells and remove the dead larvae, thus preventing the spread of infection. Van Scoy strain workers do not emit these behaviors. Rothenbuhler crossed members of each strain and showed that each behavior pattern (uncapping and removing) was controlled by separate genes (symbolized by U and R), and, moreover, that the genes determining the hygienic behavior were recessive. Thus, bees homozygous for the recessive allele of each gene (i.e., *uu rr*) would both uncap cells and remove the dead larvae from the hive.

Bees that were either heterozygous or homozygous for the dominant form of each gene (i.e., *Uu Rr*, or *UU RR*) would do neither. In addition to these two groups, Rothenbuhler produced, through crossing experiments, (1) bees with the genotype *Uu rr*, which failed to uncap cells with dead larvae but removed the larvae if Rothenbuhler lifted off the wax cell caps for them; and (2) bees with the genotype *uu Rr*, which uncapped the cells but failed to remove the larvae.

Although studies such as those by Rothenbuhler are informative, few have been conducted, and their appropriate interpretation may be deceptively complex. Alcock (1984) pointed out that "almost certainly single gene effects on behavior occur because one gene's product can play a key role in a complex developmental process that requires the regulated interaction of dozens or thousands of genes" (p. 36). In most cases, behavioral traits are **polygenic;** that is, they result from the integrated action of many genes. When single gene effects cannot be determined, other methods must be used.

In the typical **selection experiment,** individuals from a genetically varied population are tested for a particular behavioral trait. Males and females with extreme scores are then selectively mated over a number of generations, and two distinct behavioral lines are created. Finally, the offspring are compared with randomly mated individuals to reveal any significant divergence between the different groups (Barnard, 1983). The term *selection* is used because these experiments mirror the process of natural selection, although on a much smaller scale. One of the pioneering selection experiments was conducted by Tryon (1940), who attempted to select for maze-running ability in laboratory rats.

Tryon first tested a diverse population of rats for their performance in running a maze. On the basis of the results, he divided the rats into two groups: (1) "maze-bright" rats, which quickly learned to run the maze, and (2) "maze-dull" rats, which slowly learned to run the maze. Tryon then allowed only maze-bright males to breed with maze-bright females and maze-dull females to breed with maze-dull males over several generations. He tested the resulting progeny in the same maze and found that each generation of maze-bright rats learned the maze faster than the preceding generation, and that each generation of maze-dull rats learned the maze more slowly than the preceding generation (see Figure 4-7). Although there is some question about what was actually being selected (see Searle, 1949), Tryon's experiment provided evidence that there were heritable differences related to maze learning among the original population of rats.

Ethical considerations prevent scientists from conducting crossing or selection experiments with humans, so the most persuasive evidence for the heritability of human behavioral characteristics has come from **studies of family resemblance.** In such studies, a behavioral trait is observed in one individual and his or her biological relatives are observed for the same trait. In principle, if the trait is heritable, the trait should appear more often in individuals who are closely related than in those who are not. For example, assume that the ability to sing on key is heritable, and that one of a pair of monozygotic (identical) twins is observed to sing on key at a very young age and in the absence of obvious training. We would then predict the presence of the ability to sing on key in the individual's biological relatives on the basis of the proportion of genes shared with this individual. Thus, the other identical twin, who shares 100% of the genes, would be expected to sing on key; the probability of other relatives' doing so should decline with the percentage of genetic material shared with the proband (i.e., the person in whom the trait was initially observed).

The problem with studies of family resemblance is that biological relatives characteristically share not only genes, but environments as well. Hence, it is difficult to determine what accounts for any observed consistency in behavior. If, for example, sons of fathers who abuse heroin are more likely to abuse heroin than other males, this discovery might mean that (1) genotype contributes to the likelihood of heroin abuse; (2) exposure to certain environments (those in which fathers and sons who abuse heroin live) increases the likelihood of heroin abuse; or (3) genotype and environment interact to determine the likelihood of heroin abuse.

Special circumstances, such as adoption, help researchers to tease apart the contribution of genetic and environmental variables. Adoption reduces the degree to which siblings are exposed to the same environmental variables, making it more probable that any correspondence in observed behavior is the result of genotype. Studies of identical twins reared apart in disparate environments are

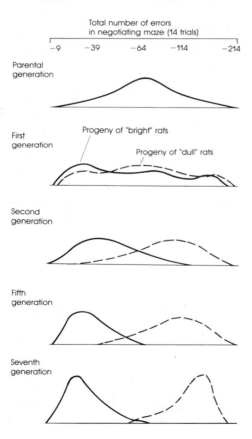

Figure 4-7. The effects of selective breeding of the fastest and slowest learners of a maze. (From *Animal Behavior: An Evolutionary Approach* by J. Alcock, 1984, p. 41. Copyright 1984 by Sinauer. Reproduced by permission.)

especially informative and are "the only really adequate natural experiment for separating genetic from environmental effects in humans" (Gould, 1982, p. 234). Identical twins reared apart in disparate environments are, however, exceedingly rare. Therefore, other strategies are characteristically used to try to disentangle the role of genetics and environment in controlling human behavior. Consider, for example, alcoholism. As Petrakis (1985) noted:

> Separating the effects of environment and heredity is a fundamental problem in studying the genetics of alcoholism, and scientists have used various methods to solve it. One approach to separating these effects is to compare alcoholism rates among identical twins who were separated at an early age, with one brought up in an alcoholic home and the other brought up in a nonalcoholic home. Another is to compare alcoholism rates among identical twins versus fraternal twins. Yet another is to measure the rate of alcoholism among adopted-out children of alcoholics and compare it with the rate in a control group.
>
> All such approaches to varying degrees separate the effects of environment and heredity. For example, if separated identical twins tend to become alcoholic regardless of whether one of them is brought up by nonalcoholic adoptive parents, this favors the existence of hereditary factors in their alcoholism, since identical twins have virtually identical genetic makeup. Similarly, genetic factors are indicated if individuals with diverse genetic backgrounds are brought up in the same environment, as in the case of half-siblings, but show different susceptibility to alcoholism. Heredity is also implicated if people born to alcoholic parents, but removed from that environment at an early age through adoption, show a greater than expected rate of alcoholism. (p. 4)

Clearly, many different tactics are used in an attempt to disentangle genetic and environmental contributions to human behavior. The task is a formidable one, and some have argued that it is neither possible nor valuable (see Kamin, 1974; Lewontin, Rose, & Kamin, 1984). Nonetheless, the available data do suggest that intelligence, schizophrenia, and alcoholism, like most human "traits," are to some degree heritable.

Interpreting Heritability

Heritability refers to "the extent to which genetic differences among individuals in a population make a difference phenotypically" (Plomin, Defries, & McClearn, 1980). Plomin *et al.* stated that

> For any behavior, we are likely to observe a wide range of individual differences. These phenotypic differences may be caused by environmental experiences, as well as genetic differences. One important aspect of behavioral genetics involves partitioning phenotypic variability into parts due to genetic and environmental differences. (p. 225)

It is important to remember that heritability is meaningful with respect to populations (groups of individuals), not individuals. For example, to say that height has a heritability of .60 means that 60% of the variation in height observed in a population at a given time is due to genetic differences in that population. It does not mean that if you are 6 feet tall, then 3.6 feet are the result of genes and 2.4 feet are the result of environment. Scientists cannot partition an individual's phenotype into genetic and environmental causes because they interact to produce that phenotype.

Is behavior primarily learned (that is, a function of nurture) or inherited (that is, a function of nature)? The appropriate answer to the **nature–nurture question** has been a point of historical contention between so-called extreme environmentalists and innateness theorists. It is still occasionally debated, as when sociobiologists[2] make the case that many important human behaviors are inherited. Most biologists and psychologists, however, now agree that behavior is usually the result of the interaction of genotype and individual history. There are, nonetheless, many examples of behaviors that appear to be primarily a function either of genes or of environment.

For example, the calling song in the male cricket does not require and presumably cannot be modified by learning, whereas language behavior in humans won't appear without an extensive learning history. It would be a mistake, however, to describe the cricket's calling song as an exclusive function of instinct and human language as an exclusive function of learning. Although the calling song in the cricket appears perfectly the first time it is emitted, it is emitted only by a mature male cricket with wings developed sufficiently to "sing," and with the appropriate underlying neuronal structure. In addition, the appearance of the song depends on environmental factors such as the time of day and weather conditions (Alcock, 1984). In humans, certain parts of the brain, as well as the vocal apparatus, must be developed before language can be acquired.

Cricket song and human language represent extremes of nature and nurture, although both depend at least to some degree on genetic and environmental variables. Moreover, it is worthwhile to examine the kind and degree of control that the variables exercise. As Dobzhansky (1964) noted:

> The nature–nurture problem is . . . far from meaningless. Asking right questions is, in science, often a large step toward obtaining the right answers. The question about the roles of the genotype and the environment in human development must be posed thus: To what extent are the *differences* observed among people conditioned by the differences of their genotypes and by the differences between the environments in which people were born, grew and were brought up? (p. 55)

Genotype clearly influences behavior, but Barash (1977) observed that

> behavior is not contained somehow within a gene, waiting to leap out like Athena, fully armored, from the head of Zeus. Rather genes are blueprints, codes for a range of potential phenotypes. In some cases the specification may be very precise, leaving little room for modification due to learning or other experiences. In others, the blueprint may be so general as to be almost entirely at the disposal of experience. (p. 41)

---

[2]**Sociobiology** is the discipline concerned with the evolutionary analysis of behavior, especially behavior in a social (i.e., group) setting. In essence, sociobiologists offer plausible accounts of the possible adaptive value of patterns of behavior currently observed in humans or other species. They have, for example, proposed that, in humans, there is a genetic basis for sexual differentiations in behavior, including "male dominance" (e.g., Barash, 1977); for homosexuality (e.g., Wilson, 1978); and for altruism (e.g., Wilson, 1975). An account is offered of how each of these behaviors (phenotypes) may confer adaptive advantage and hence lead to selection of the genotype responsible for it. Although the accounts are interesting and may seem to provide a biological justification for Western cultural patterns, they have been rigorously criticized (e.g., Futuyma, 1979).

Among many other characteristics, organisms inherit the capacity to learn. These Canada geese and mallard ducks have learned to approach people who provide food. (Photo courtesy of Sue Keller.)

Genotype determines behavioral flexibility, that is, the extent to which particular response patterns can be modified by environmental events, as well as the range of events that modify them. On the inflexible end of the continuum of modifiability are "closed behavioral programs" (Mayr, 1974) that are relatively unaffected by individual experience, like the male cricket's calling song. Such behaviors, traditionally referred to as innate or instinctive, require very limited environmental input for normal development. On the flexible end are "open behavioral programs," like language in humans, which are strongly dependent on individual history. These behaviors, traditionally referred to as learned, require greater environmental input for normal development.

Behaviorism and Inherited Behavior

Behaviorists have been frequently characterized as insisting that all human behavior is learned. As Michael (1984) pointed out, neither Watson or Skinner made such an argument. In an attempt to set the record straight, Michael described three types of behavioral characteristics that most behaviorists agree are inherited. First, organisms inherit some fairly specific stimulus–response relations called *reflexes*. Second, some organisms inherit more complex behavior–environment relations called **released behaviors, fixed action patterns,** or **species-specific behavior.** Nest building and courtship displays in birds are examples of such behaviors. Finally, organisms inherit the capacity to learn through interactions with the environment.

The capacity to learn is an especially important characteristic. As Futuyma (1979) put it:

> Whether evolutionary biology is important for understanding human behavior is a highly controversial question. Some authors attribute much of the behavior within and between groups to genetic variation; others point out that there is no unequivocal evidence of substantial genetic variation in human behavior and argue that variation arises from social and cultural conditions. Likewise some view supposedly universal human traits—"human nature"—as genetically canalized, evolved adaptations; others see these traits as common responses to common environmental conditions and point to rapid historical changes and cultural variation among peoples as evidence of the immense behavioral flexibility of which all people are capable. On balance, the evidence for the modifiability of human behavior is so great that genetic constraints on our behavior hardly seem to exist. The dominant factor in recent human evolution has been the evolution of behavioral flexibility, the ability to learn and transmit culture. (p. 491)

Behaviorists emphasize the role of environmental events in behavioral development in large part because it is more feasible to manipulate nurture than nature (see Chapter 6). In addition, the environment can be altered to produce desirable changes in behavior. For example, it is possible to arrange teaching procedures to optimize the acquisition of language. Although it is not now possible to alter genotypes to accomplish similar tasks, it is important to recognize the primacy of evolution by natural selection as the ultimate explanation of behavior. Events that occur within the three-score and 10 years we are allotted affect us as they do only because of the 3.5-billion-year evolutionary history of our ancestors. Old roots run deep.

Human Evolutionary (Phylogenetic) Development

"We are what we are because of history, both our ancestors' history and the history of our own lives" (Carlson, 1984, p. 6). This is another way of saying that our phenotype is the combined result of the interaction between genotype, which reflects our evolutionary history, and individual history. We can trace the origin of an individual's history to conception, when a single sperm fertilizes an ovum. At that precise moment, the fertilized ovum contains all the genetic information needed to form an adult human being, given certain environmental influences. This genetic information represents the accumulation of hundreds of millions of years of evolution by natural selection.

In order to trace human evolutionary history, we would have to go back to the beginning of life on earth about 3.5 billion years ago (Dickerson, 1978). Scientists speculate that the first organic material, in the form of amino acids, was created in the oceans when gases in the atmosphere of the primeval earth were subjected to ultraviolet radiation from the sun. These early amino acids then combined in this "organic soup" to form complex molecules. The most important event in evolution was the formation of a special molecule that could replicate itself (Dawkins, 1976). This self-replicating molecule was the ancestor of DNA.

Once genetic material could be replicated, life was off and running, progressing from single to multicelled organisms (about 1.5 billion years ago), aquatic oxygen-breathing animals (about 1 billion years ago), amphibians (500 million years ago), reptiles (400 million years ago), mammals (100 million years ago), and primates (50 million years ago) (see Table 4-1).

The earliest mammals were small, ratlike insectivores that moved about on the ground. Some of these small creatures began climbing into the trees of the immense forests that covered much of the world. Presumably, they did so because of the fierce competition on the ground and the plentiful supply of fruits, seeds, and insects in the trees. These were the earliest primates, the *prosimians* (premonkeys), from which sprang the present array of prosimians (e.g., lemurs and lorises) and anthropoids (the monkeys, apes, and humans). For 30 million years, these early prosimians were extremely successful in the tropical forests of the world and subsequently evolved into many specialized populations (species).

Life in the forest provided an environment that selected many of the unique characteristics found in today's monkeys, apes, and humans (see Table 4-2). Important changes occurred in those body parts that made direct contact with the world, that is, the limbs and the extremities. The hind legs, which were used

Table 4-1
The Evolution of Life

Number of years ago	Evolutionary event
4.5 billion	Formation of the earth.
4.25 billion	Formation of the oceans and continents.
3.6 billion	Primitive one-called organisms that obtained energy through fermentation.
3 billion	Sulfur bacteria that used hydrogen sulfide to conduct photosynthesis.
	Single-celled organisms that used water in photosynthesis instead of sulfur. These were the ancestors of the blue-green algae and green plants.
2 billion	Oxygen atmosphere.
1.6 billion	Bacteria able to use nonsulfur photosynthesis and oxygen in respiration. These bacteria could extract 19 times more energy from food than could the first primitive bacteria.
1.3 billion	Cells with nuclei.
1 billion	Multicelled organisms; plant and animal kingdoms divide.
500 million	Many marine animals, corals, clams, and fish.
300 million	Amphibians, ferns, spiders, insects, and the first reptiles.
150 million	Dinosaurs and reptiles.
	First birds evolve from smaller dinosaurs.
	Modern insects (bees, moths, flies).
70 million	Dinosaurs extinct.
	Marsupials and primitive mammals.
	Flowering plants, deciduous trees, giant redwoods.
50 million	Modern birds, the early horse (only 1 foot high), the ancestors of the cat, dog, elephant, camel, and other mammals.
	Seed-bearing plants and small primates.
1.5 million	*Homo erectus.*
100,000	*Homosapiens neanderthalensis.*
40,000	*Homo sapiens sapiens* (modern humans).

for jumping through the trees and clinging to branches, became longer; the claws on the front paws, which were unnecessary for moving about in the trees, disappeared; and the paws transformed into grasping organs with longer and more flexible, padded digits. These innovations greatly improved the ability of these "new-model animals" to move rapidly and suddenly in trees, and to grasp branches or catch and hold fast-moving insects or lizards. These developments were accompanied by changes in the sensory apparatus of the prosimians. They developed upright posture and rotating heads, which, in concert with their new lifestyle of leaping, clinging, and catching, made their reliance on seeing more important than their reliance on smelling. As the retinas of the eyes became more sensitive to low levels of illumination and were able to differentiate colors, the eyes became larger, thus increasing the amount of light and detail received. The eyes moved gradually to the front of the head, and vision became binocular (two-eyed, where vision in one eye overlaps that in the other) and stereoscopic (depth-perceiving). At the same time, the head also began to change: the snout became shorter and the skull rounder (Campbell, 1985). At this point, many of the characteristics were similar to those belonging to present-day monkeys, apes, and humans.

After the early primates took to the trees, they began to increase in size,

Table 4-2
Major Characteristics of Primates

A. Characteristics relating to motor adaptations
 1. Retention of ancestral mammalian limb structure, with five digits in hands and feet and free mobility of limbs.
 2. Evolution of mobile, grasping digits, with sensitive friction pads, and nails replacing claws. Palmar surfaces with friction skin.
 3. Retention of tail as an organ of balance (except in apes and a few monkeys) and as a grasping "limb" in some New World monkeys.
 4. Evolution of erect posture in many groups with extensive head rotation.
 5. Evolution of nervous system to give precise and rapid control of musculature.
B. Characteristics relating to sensory adaptations
 1. Enlargement of the eyes, increasing amount of light and detail received.
 2. Evolution of retina to increase sensitivity to low levels of illumination and to different frequencies (that is, to color).
 3. Eyes that look forward with overlapping visual fields that give stereoscopic vision.
 4. Enclosure of eyes in a bony orbit.
 5. Reduction in olfactory apparatus, especially the snout.
C. Dental characteristics
 1. Simple cusp patterns in molar teeth.
 2. In most groups, 32 or 36 teeth; all the Anthropoidea have 32 teeth.
D. General characteristics
 1. Lengthened period of maturation, of infant dependency, and of gestation, compared with most mammals. Relatively long life span.
 2. Low reproductive rate, especially among Hominoidea.
 3. Relatively large and complex brain, especially those parts involved with vision, tactile inputs, muscle coordination and control, and memory and learning.

---

their arms grew longer, and they became more dexterous. These early populations then began to spread out in the forest and to eat novel foods. Some of these primates, the monkeys, became quadrupeds, running along the branches on all fours. Others, whose arms became still longer, moved about by reaching, climbing, hanging, and swinging. These were the apes (Campbell, 1985).

Despite the obvious differences between monkeys, apes, and humans, there are many similarities. For example, the sensory system of all the monkeys, apes, and humans has remained virtually unchanged for perhaps 15 million years: we humans see, hear, smell, taste, and touch very much as monkeys and apes do. Still, monkeys, apes, and humans differ in important ways. Monkeys are quadrupeds, whereas the apes have short, wide, shallow trunks and long arms that swing and rotate at the shoulders. These anatomical changes evolved as the apes became more successful in horizontal arm-over-arm locomotion (brachiation). The African apes, the chimpanzee and the gorilla, unlike the gibbon and the orangutan, adapted to terrestrial quadrupedalism; they walk on the soles of their feet and the knuckles of their hands. Human ancestors took a different route than the African apes—to terrestrial bipedalism, which is walking upright on the ground.

Hominid Evolutionary Development

Hominids are primates of the family Hominidae, of which *Homo sapiens* is the sole surviving species. Our immediate ancestors were of this family. Although there is controversy about the specifics of hominid evolution, the earliest hominids probably emerged from the trees of the great forests of Africa and moved into the savanna about 4–6 million years ago. Once they were there, many of the important features that distinguish humans from apes began to evolve. Early developments included bipedalism; changes in the structure of the teeth, from large to smaller canines; and improvements in manual dexterity—all of which probably resulted from a change in diet as well as from an increase in tool use. These developments were paralleled by an increase in brain size, which, along with hunting and scavenging, was a relatively late development. For example, although *Australopithecus afarensis*, an early hominid that lived approximately 3.5 million years ago (see Figure 4-1), was completely bipedal, it had a brain no bigger than that of a chimpanzee (Campbell, 1985).

Changes in the pelvis that were necessary precursors of upright bipedalism predated changes in the size of the human brain. As the brain became larger, the female's pelvis underwent further modifications as a sort of "compromise—not compact enough for the most efficient walking but large enough for the birth of large-brained infants" (Campbell, 1985, p. 234). Another part of the solution to the "small-pelvis, large-brain problem" was for the female to give birth at an earlier stage in infant development, before the infant's head got too big. This meant a longer period of postbirth infant care. Compared to other primates, human infants enter the world at a much earlier stage of development. For example, at birth, the human brain is 25% its eventual size, whereas the chimpanzee brain is 45% and the baboon brain is 75% its eventual size at birth

(Campbell, 1985). This relatively long period of infant care is associated with many of the important early developmental phenomena considered by psychologists, such as sensorimotor development and interpersonal interactions (e.g., socialization), which we will discuss in Chapter 8.

Study Questions

1. Is it true that we evolved from present-day chimpanzees, or did both humans and chimps evolve from a common ancestor that is now extinct?

2. Explain Lamarck's theory of evolution and why it has fallen into disfavor. In what way is it a teleological explanation?

3. Explain the relation between dominant and recessive genes, and why phenotype is not always an expression of genotype.

4. Discuss natural selection by stating the "two undeniable facts and an inescapable conclusion" suggested by Gould (1977).

5. Are all characteristics necessarily adaptive? How could a characteristic have arisen if it is not adaptive?

6. Diagram a flowchart that depicts the processes of mitosis and meiosis.

7. Describe the two functions of DNA.

8. What are master genes, and what is their function?

9. What are the two kinds of mutations, and how can they arise?

10. Genetic variation can result from three processes. What are they?

11. Be able to give an example of "evolution at work."

12. What is meant when a behavior geneticist suggests that a characteristic is "genetically determined"?

13. Describe the general strategies in crossing experiments, selection experiments, and studies of family resemblance.

14. Behavioral flexibility, which is influenced by genotype, represents a continuum. What are the two ends of the continuum, and what is an example of each?

15. What are the three kinds of behavioral characteristics that are inherited?

16. The last section of the chapter presents some milestones in the evolution of *Homo sapiens*. Be able to (a) state the approximate time at which life on earth began; (b) name some important characteristics of the early primates that evolved when they lived mainly in the forests; and (c) list some characteristics of hominids that evolved after the move to the grasslands.

Recommended Readings

Dawkins, R. (1986). *The Blind Watchmaker*. Harlow, England: Longman.

Evolution can be a difficult topic. Any student would be served well by reading this book. In it, Dawkins debates the proposals of the theologian William Paley.

Futuyma, D. J. (1983). *Science on Trial: The Case for Evolution.* New York: Pantheon.

Futuyma provides a nice introduction to evolution. Also of interest is the summary and critique of scientific creationism.

Gould, S. J. (1977). *Ever Since Darwin: Reflections in Natural History.* New York: Norton.

Gould has brought the concepts of evolution to the general public. Any reader will benefit from his discussions, which are delivered in a fascinating and concise presentation. This is only one of many collections of readings published by Gould.

CHAPTER 5

Physiology and Behavior

As noted in Chapter 1, all behaviors have physiological correlates. Common sense suggests, and experimental evidence confirms, that "for every behavioral event, there is a corresponding physical event or series of physical events taking place within the body" (Schneider & Tarshis, 1975, p. 3). These events are the focus of study of many disciplines, known collectively as the **behavioral neurosciences,** a term that covers "any scientific endeavor designed to elucidate the function of the nervous system in the production of behavior" (Woodruff, 1984, p. 652).

This chapter presents an overview of the structure and function of the human nervous system; most of the discussion also pertains to other vertebrate animals. The nervous system has three major functions. One is detecting environmental stimuli and transforming them into nerve impulses, the "language" of the nervous system. This process is commonly known as sensation. A second function is producing effector action. Effectors are muscles and glands, and their actions produce behavior. The third activity of the nervous system is coordinating the first two functions. Taken together, these three functions comprise, in large part, the physiological basis of behavior. It is for that reason that they are of interest to psychologists.

The human nervous system is remarkably complex, and though knowledge of it has grown remarkably in the past two decades, that knowledge is still far from complete. As Skinner (1974) noted:

> Physiology and, particularly with respect to behavior, neurology have of course made great progress. Electrical and chemical properties of many neural activities are now directly observed and measured. The nervous system is, however, much less accessible than behavior and environment, and the difference takes its toll. We know some of the processes which affect large blocks of behavior—sensory, motor, motivational, and emotional—but we are still far short of knowing precisely what is happening when, say, a child learns to drink from a cup, to call an object by its name, or to find the right piece of a jigsaw puzzle, as we are still far short of making changes in the nervous system as a result of which a child will do these things. It is possible that we shall never directly observe what is happening in the nervous system at the time a response occurs, because something like the Heisenberg principle may apply: any means of observing neural mediation of behavior may disturb the behavior. (pp. 213–214)

Be that as it may, what is known about the relation of physiology to behavior is fascinating.

The environment consists of matter and energy in several forms. To interact effectively with the environment, humans and other animals must be able to detect its properties. Humans can detect, and are potentially affected by, energy in electrical, mechanical, chemical, and radiant form. These forms of energy are detected through specialized sense organs. Located within the sense organs are **receptor cells** (or **receptors**), which are specialized nerve cells whose main function is to transform energy into a neural impulse. In other words, receptors convert environmental energy into a form of energy recognizable by the nervous system, a neural impulse. The process of converting one type of energy into another is known as **transduction.** Receptor cells are therefore biological transducers.

Over time, different receptor types have evolved. Typically, a given receptor is sensitive to only one form of energy. Not all species are equally sensitive to a particular energy form. For instance, dogs are sensitive to high-frequency sounds, sharks can detect changes in electric voltage in the water, and some migratory birds can detect changes in the gravitational field. Humans are insensitive to all of these energy forms but are able to detect a wide range of other energy. In general, "The more diversified an organism's receptors are, the wider the range of environmental stimuli that it can respond to will be and the more varied and flexible its potential for adaptive behavior" (Schneider & Tarshis, 1975, p. 116).

Before we discuss the human sensory systems in detail, the notion of stimulation must be considered. **Stimulus** (the plural form is **stimuli**), one of the most common terms in psychology, can be defined as any form of energy that affects the sensory receptors of an organism. It is important to recognize that a stimulus does not necessarily cause a response but simply provides input into the nervous system.

Energy changes may take place in the external environment (i.e., outside the skin) or in the internal environment (i.e., inside the skin). The former are known as **exteroceptive stimuli,** whereas the latter are known as **interoceptive stimuli.** Exteroceptive stimuli are **public stimuli** in that they are capable of affecting the receptors of more than one person. The roar of Niagara Falls, the smell of a rose, and the sight of a Picasso painting are all public stimuli. Interoceptive stimuli are **private stimuli;** they affect only the receptors of the person in whom they occur. Toothaches, muscle cramps, and the feel of hot coffee traveling down one's esophagus are examples of private stimuli. Although private stimuli are more difficult to quantify accurately than public stimuli, they serve the same behavioral functions. (These functions are discussed in Chapter 6.)

Vision

In humans, vision is an especially important sense. Vision begins when light strikes receptors in the eye. Light is a form of electromagnetic radiation that may be regarded as consisting either of waves or of particles (photons). As waves, light has a specifiable frequency and wavelength. Only wavelengths between approximately 380 and 700 nm can be detected by structures within the human eye and are called light (a nanometer, or nm, is one billionth of a meter). As shown in Figure 5–1, other wavelengths of electromagnetic energy exist, and other species are able to detect some of them. Some insects, for example, can detect ultraviolet light, and some nocturnal predators detect their prey through infrared radiation.

Unlike most mammals, humans have good color vision. The color of an object depends on the wavelengths of light that it reflects. As wavelengths lengthen, the perceived color shifts from violet through blue to green, then to yellow, orange, and red. Objects that appear white reflect all wavelengths, whereas black objects absorb all wavelengths. There are three physical dimensions that can be used to describe most colors: hue, saturation, and brightness. **Hue** refers to the color of light and is determined by wavelength. **Saturation** refers to the purity of color. The more a color contains one wavelength, the greater is its saturation. When a color contains more than one wavelength, it is desaturated. This effect is analogous to mixing two paints to produce an intermediate color. If, for example, red light (saturated) is mixed with white light, pink is produced. Pink is a less saturated version of red (Carlson, 1988). **Brightness** refers to the intensity of a color. It is determined by the amplitude of the light wave or, to emphasize the particlelike nature of light, by the number of photons that strike the visual receptors.

How does light produce its effects on human behavior? The visual system consists of three components: the eye, certain portions of the brain, and pathways that connect the two. The eyes have evolved several important mechanisms to keep them from harm. They are encased within a bony skull, which shelters them from direct physical blows. The eyebrows protect the eyes from sweat on the forehead, and the eyelids and eyelashes protect them from dust and dirt. If foreign material does get in the eye, the eyes reflexively "water" to

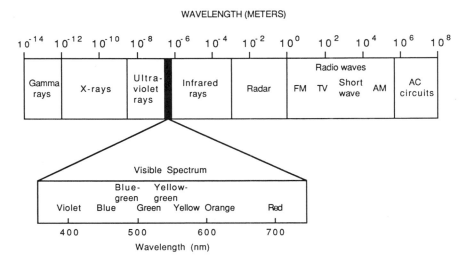

Figure 5-1. The electromagnetic spectrum with wavelengths visible to humans.

wash it out. Finally, rapid movements toward the eyes elicit other reflexive behaviors, including closure of the eyelids and withdrawal of the head (Carlson, 1988).

The structure of the eye has frequently been likened to that of a camera, and the analogy is reasonable. Like a camera, the eye admits light through an adjustable diaphragm and focuses images on a sensitive surface by means of a lens. The eye is, however, far more complicated than any camera. The structure of the human eye is shown in Figure 5–2. As light enters the eye, it first strikes a bulge called the **cornea.** The cornea is transparent and admits light into the eye. Directly behind the cornea is the **aqueous humor,** a fluid that nourishes the eye. Light next passes through the **pupil,** which is a circular opening in the iris. The **iris** is a muscular structure that controls the size of the pupil and hence the amount of light admitted to the eye. When the pupil contracts, as it does in bright sunlight, less light is admitted to the eye; when the pupil dilates, as when one enters a darkened room, more light is admitted. After leaving the pupil, light passes through the lens. The **lens** is transparent and curved. The degree of curvature is controlled by the ciliary muscles and can be varied so as to focus images onto the rear surface of the eye. That area is called the **retina.** The curvature of the lens required to focus an image depends on the distance between the eye and the object reflecting the image. When the object is very close, maximum curvature is required. If for any reason the image cannot be focused on the retina, visual impairment is the result. The impairment is termed *myopia* (nearsightedness) when only images reflected from objects very near the eye can be focused on the retina and therefore be seen clearly. When only objects far from the eye are seen clearly, the impairment is termed *hyperopia* (farsightedness). Fortunately, corrective lenses can easily alleviate both myopia and hyperopia.

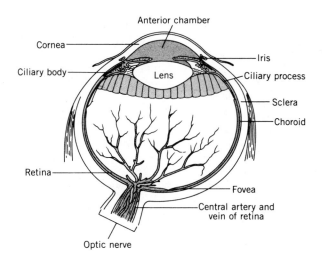

Figure 5-2. Structure of the human eye. (From *The Biology of Behavior and Mind* by Bruce Bridgeman, 1988, p. 105. Copyright 1988 by John Wiley & Sons. Reproduced by permission.)

The **vitreous humor** lies between the lens and the retina. It is a clear fluid that provides nourishment for the interior of the eye. Located within the retina are millions of **photoreceptors.** These specialized cells transduce light into neural impulses.

Figure 5–3 is a simplified diagram of the cells and connections in the retina. As can be seen, light passes first through a layer of ganglion cells, then through the bipolar cell layer, and finally it strikes the photoreceptors. The ganglion and bipolar cells are transparent; light passes easily through them to strike the photoreceptors, which in humans are classified as either **rods** or **cones.** The human eye contains approximately 125 million rods, located primarily in the periphery of the retina. Rods are very sensitive to light and are largely responsible for low-illumination vision. The approximately 6 million cones are densely packed into the center of the retina and are responsible for fine, detailed vision and color vision. The **fovea** is a small area, approximately 1 millimeter (mm) in diameter, which contains only cones. When one looks at an object, the eyes are moved so

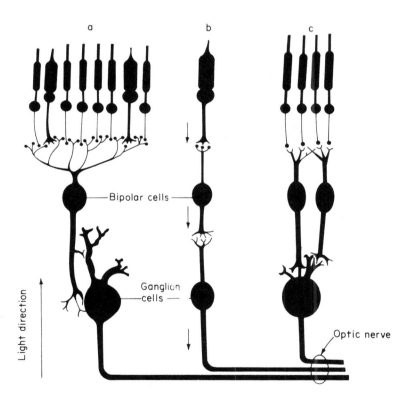

Figure 5-3. Simplified diagram of cells and connections in the human retina. (a) Mixed rod-and-cone system, both types synapsing with one biplar cell and this cell, in turn, with a ganglion cell. (b) Single cone system, found only in the fovea. (c) Multiple rod system, several rods converging on bipolars and these on a ganglion cell. The optic nerve is formed by axons of the ganglion cells. (From *A Primer of Physiological Psychology* by R. L. Isaacson, R. J. Douglas, I. F. Lubar, & L. W. Schmaltz, 1971, p. 118. Copyright 1971 by Harper & Row, Inc. Reprinted by permission of the publisher.)

as to focus an image directly on the fovea. The object is then clearly seen. In contrast, objects lying in the periphery are seen less clearly because the image from the object falls directly on the richly cone-packed fovea; images from objects located in the periphery fall on areas of the retina containing mostly rods and as a result are seen in less detail.

When light strikes a rod or a cone, a chemical and electrical process is begun in which that photoreceptor stimulates the bipolar cells, which in turn stimulate the ganglion cells. Finally, an impulse is conveyed to the brain via the **optic nerve.** The optic nerve exits the eye at the rear. The retina at this point, called the **optic disk** or **blind spot,** contains no photoreceptors. Consequently, images falling on this area cannot be detected. The blind spot in each eye is positioned so that an image falling on it is "picked up" by the other eye; therefore, one is usually unaware of these gaps in the visual field.

On leaving the eye, neural impulses are carried along the optic nerve to several regions at the rear of the brain, known collectively as the *primary visual area*. At these points, the impulses interact with neurons (nerve cells) and may affect behavior.

Audition

Like vision, the sense of audition (or hearing) is very important to humans. Because human language is primarily vocal, the auditory system is especially important in interacting with others. Just as photoreceptors in the eye transduce light into neural impulses, **phonoreceptors** in the ear transduce sound waves into neural impulses. The energy to which the ear is sensitive, sound, consists of rhythmic pressure changes in air (or some other medium) resulting from the vibration of objects. The vibration of an object, such as the bell in a telephone, causes molecules alternately to compress and rarefy (i.e., move together and apart). As the object moves forward, molecules are pressed together (compressed); as it moves backward, they are pulled apart (rarefied). This change in the density of molecules creates a change in air pressure that travels as a wave.

Sound waves are measured along three physical dimensions: frequency, intensity, and complexity (Geldard, 1972). **Frequency,** which is typically measured in Hertz (Hz, which refers to cycles per second), determines perceived pitch. High frequencies produce high-pitched sounds, like that of a smoke alarm, whereas low frequencies produce low-pitched sounds, such as the sound of a bass drum. Humans are capable of detecting sounds ranging from about 16 to 20,000 Hz. Bats, dogs, and porpoises can detect much higher frequency sounds.

Intensity (or *amplitude*) refers to the relative change in air pressure created by a sound wave. It determines perceived loudness. Both loudness and intensity are measured in decibels (db). The decibel scale is a logarithmic scale in which a value of 0 corresponds to either (1) the lowest intensity that can be detected (i.e., the absolute threshold value) or (2) a root mean square pressure of 0.0002 dyne/cm^2. When the former standard is used, the sensation level of a sound is being measured, whereas the latter standard is used to assess the sound-pressure level. In most cases, the result is very similar, because 0.0002 dyne/cm^2 is about the absolute threshold value for most humans. Because the decibel scale is logarithmic, a 10-db sound is 10 times greater than a 1-db sound, but a 20-db sound is 100 times greater than a 1-db sound, and a 30-db sound is 1,000 times greater than a 1-db sound. Table 5-1 shows the sensation level in decibels of some common sounds. Most people report that sounds louder than approximately 120 db are painful. Hearing loss can occur with prolonged exposure to sounds of 70 db or higher.

A third characteristic of sound is complexity. **Complexity** is the degree to which the sound contains waves with a single frequency and amplitude. Psychologically, this is referred to as the **timber** of a tone. Tones with only a single frequency and amplitude are quite rare and are called *pure tones*. The sounds created by tuning forks are often pure tones. Usually, sound contains waves of several different frequencies and amplitudes. These allow us to distinguish, for instance, between a given note played on a guitar and the same note played on a piano. Because each instrument has its own characteristic pattern of vibrating, we can easily learn to discriminate between the sounds they produce.

It is conventional to differentiate the outer, middle, and inner ear. The **outer ear** consists of the auricle, the ear canal, and the eardrum. The first part of the ear that sound strikes is the **pinna** (or auricle). Although it is the most obvious part of the ear and what most people think of when referring to the ear, it plays only a minor role in audition. The auricle serves to funnel sound into the ear canal and aids in determining the direction of sound. If it is removed, however, hearing is not adversely affected. Just inside the auricle is the **ear canal** (or external auditory meatus). This portion of the ear conducts sound inward. Located at the end of the ear canal is the **tympanic membrane,** also known as the *eardrum.* Sound waves striking the ear drum cause it to vibrate. Its vibration matches that of the sound waves in frequency and amplitude.

The major parts of the middle and inner ear are shown in Figure 5–4. The **middle ear** occupies a small space adjacent to the eardrum. Three tiny bones reside there: the **malleus,** the **incus,** and the **stapes.** You have probably heard them referred to by their shapes, as the hammer, the anvil, and the stirrup. These bones form a chain running from the ear drum to a membrane (called the *oval window*) opening into the inner ear. When a sound wave strikes the eardrum, the eardrum vibrates, causing the malleus to move. This movement, in

Table 5-1
Sensation Level in Decibels
of Some Common Sounds[a]

Painful sound, 130 db
Loud thunder, 120 db
Twin-engine propeller airplane, 110 db
Subway train, 100 db
City bus, 90 db
Noisy car, 80 db
Average car, 70 db
Normal conversation, 60 db
Quiet office, 40 db
Whisper, 25 db
Threshold of hearing in a quiet environment, 0 db

[a]Values are as described by Champanis, Garner, and Morgan (1949).

turn, causes the incus to move, which causes the stapes to move. The stapes presses against the oval window, which transmits vibrations into the inner ear.

The **inner ear** consists of three structures: the **cochlea,** the **semicircular canals,** and the **vestibular sacs.** The latter two structures play no role in hearing but are responsible for balance and posture and thus will be considered later. The cochlea is a fluid-filled organ shaped like a snail, which contains the receptors involved in transducing into neural impulses the mechanical vibrations cause by sound waves. Running through the length of the cochlea is the **basilar membrane.** When the stapes pushes against the oval window, waves are created in the fluid inside the cochlea. These waves can occur because there is a mem-

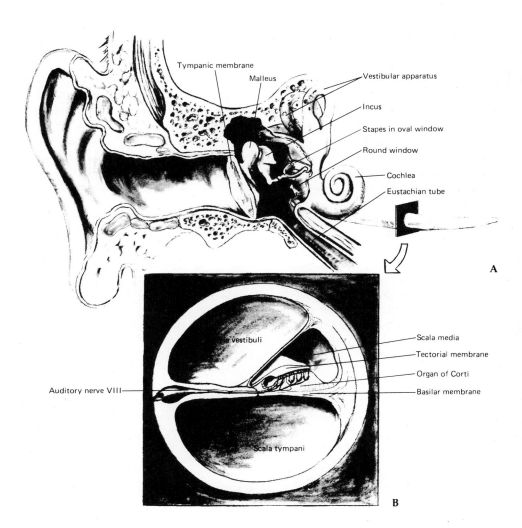

Figure 5-4. (A) Structure of the human ear. The arrow indicates a cross section of an unrolled cochlea, which is shown in (B). (Reprinted by permission of the publisher from *Basic Human Neurophysiology* by D. F. Lindsly & J. E. Holmes, 1984, p. 223. Copyright 1984 by Elsevier Science Publishing Company, Inc.)

brane-covered opening, the **round window,** which allows the fluid in the cochlea to move. These waves cause the basil membrane itself to move in wave-like fashion. This motion bends tiny hair cells, the phonoreceptors, located in the basilar membrane. These phonoreceptors transform the wavelike motion of the basilar membrane into neural impulses. The nerve impulses leave the ear in bundles of nerve fibers called the **auditory nerve.** Most of these impulses are ultimately relayed to the **auditory cortex** of the brain.

Gustation

Vision and audition play crucial roles in controlling human behavior. Gusta-tion (or taste) characteristically plays a smaller, but still significant, role. The sensation of taste is produced by the chemical stimulation of specialized receptor cells, termed **gustatory (or taste) receptors.** They are members of a larger class of receptors, including those that mediate the sense of smell, which are termed **chemoreceptors.** The receptors for taste are commonly referred to as *taste buds.* Actually, the taste buds are not the receptor cells themselves but contain the true receptor cells, the **papillae.** At the ends of the papillae are tiny hairlike struc-tures that extend out of the taste bud and make contact with the saliva and other fluids in the mouth. These fluids contain dissolved molecules, and it is the interaction of these molecules with the tiny hairlike structures that initiates the transduction process.

Gustatory receptors are found on the tongue, on the palate, in the pharnyx, and elsewhere in the mouth and the oral canal. The operation of these receptors is such that four basic qualities of taste can be detected: sweetness, saltiness, bitterness, and sourness. As shown in Figure 5–5, the receptors that detect these qualities are concentrated in particular locations on the tongue. For example, most receptors that detect sweetness lie along the tip of the tongue, whereas those that detect bitterness are most common along its back. Three major nerves carry impulses from taste receptors in the mouth to the brain.

Olfaction

The sense of taste presumably evolved in concert with the sense of smell, or olfaction. The flavor of food illustrates the close ties between the two senses. You

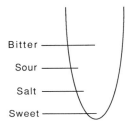

Figure 5-5. The location on the human tongue of gustatory receptors for particular taste qualities.

have probably noticed that food loses much of its flavor when you have a bad cold. This happens because the chemoreceptors located within the nose lose their ability to detect chemical substances when coated with large amounts of mucus. Without the sense of smell, food flavor is greatly reduced.

The receptors for smell are located in the nose and are sensitive to chemicals in the form of gas. Any substance that gives off fat-soluble molecules, called a *volatile substance,* can be detected through olfaction. The **olfactory receptors** lie in 1-inch-square patches of mucous membrane called the **olfactory mucosa,** or *epithelia*. These areas are located deep within the nasal cavity and lie just under the front of the brain. Because of the location of the olfactory receptors, gas molecules do not reach them easily. Sniffing draws molecules into the nasal passage and, as a result, into contact with the olfactory receptors. These receptors initiate nerve impulses, which eventually arrive at a location in the brain called the *olfactory bulb*.

Olfaction is a critical sense for many species. For example, honeybees and a host of other insects communicate by releasing chemicals, called **pheromones,** that influence the behavior of other members of their species. In animals with a well-developed sense of smell, a relatively large part of the brain is devoted to the sense of smell. Rats, for instance, have a very large olfactory bulb. In humans, however, a relatively small part of the brain is directly involved in the sense of smell. Not surprisingly, the sense of smell of humans is crude relative to that of rats.

The Skin Senses

Among the senses referred to as the *skin senses* (or the *somatosenses*) are pressure, temperature, and pain. Like the sense of taste, the skin senses require that the source of stimulation be near.

Pressure

Humans have many occasions daily to detect and respond to pressure, or touch. Pressure is a form of mechanical stimulation; hence, the receptors sensitive to it are called **mechanoreceptors.** There are two forms of mechanoreceptor. The **surface touch receptors** are located near the surface of the skin and transduce mechanical energy into neural impulses. The receptors involved in surface touch are called **Meissner's corpuscles.** These receptors are located throughout the head and the body. The second form of mechanoreceptor is the **deep pressure receptor.** These receptors are known as **Pacinian corpuscles** and are located deep within the body. The sensations produced by a tightly tied shoe or a tap on the shoulder are produced by the stimulation of surface touch receptors. After a large meal, you may have experienced an example of a sensation produced by the stimulation of deep pressure receptors. The pressure exerted by distension of the stomach results in stimulation of these receptors. Nerve impulses initiated by activation of all touch receptors eventually reach the somatosensory area of the brain.

Humans are sensitive to temperature. The receptors that are responsible for this sensitivity are termed, not surprisingly, **thermoreceptors.** There are two types: cold receptors and warm receptors. Interestingly, it is not absolute temperature to which these receptors are primarily sensitive, but changes in temperature. **Cold receptors,** also called **Krause end bulbs,** are activated when the skin temperature falls. **Warm receptors,** the **Ruffini corpuscles,** are activated when the skin temperature rises. Although humans are able to detect slight changes in temperature, adaptation to these changes quickly occurs. For instance, on initial entry, the water in a swimming pool may feel quite cold, but after a time in the water, it feels much less cold. Such adaptation does not, however, occur at extremely high or low temperatures. Nerve impulses that result from the stimulation of thermoreceptors ultimately arrive at the somatosensory area of the brain.

Pain

There are no unique receptors for pain, and any form of energy (e.g., light, sound, pressure, or temperature), if sufficiently intense, can produce the sensation of pain. The one thing that all painful stimuli appear to have in common is the potential for tissue damage. They are called, therefore, **noxious stimuli.** The

Stimuli can affect many receptors at once. What receptors might be affected by the birthday cake in this picture? (Photo courtesy of Tom Kaczor.)

cells that detect noxious stimuli are called **free nerve endings.** They are not true receptor cells, but they are affected by chemicals that are released when tissues are stimulated intensely. These chemicals stimulate the free nerve endings, causing them to transmit electrical impulses to the brain (Zimbardo, 1988). Many variables, including drugs, attitude, sexual arousal, and hypnosis, can influence whether a given stimulus is considered painful (Zimbardo, 1988).

The Body Senses

The body senses are involved in many daily activities. They permit you to detect the position of your limbs in a dark room, as well as to maintain your balance when you are standing or walking. These senses are also involved in reaching for and manipulating objects, and in adjusting your body position when you stumble or bump into another person.

Kinesthesis

People constantly receive information about the movement of their limbs and the position of their body in space. Such **proprioceptive stimuli** occur when you are turning the pages of this book, writing, riding a bike, eating, typing, or making any other movement. The movement of arms or legs results in a change in the angle between adjacent bones. Each time this angle is changed, different receptors are activated. Detecting the change in angles between the bones is called **kinesthesis.** The receptors involved in kinesthesis are sensitive to a form of mechanical energy and are therefore a type of mechanoreceptor. These receptors are located in the muscles and tendons in the limbs. They are sensitive to the length of muscles, the amount of force with which they are contracting, and the angle between bones.

Vestibular Sense

The **vestibular sense** is involved in maintaining balance and posture. The responsible receptors are located in the inner ear within the **semicircular canals** and the **vestibular sacs.** They provide information about the position of the head and its movement. Rotation of the head and, to a smaller extent, the position and acceleration of the head are detected by the three semicircular canals. Each of these canals contains fluid. Tiny hairlike structures called *cilia* extend into the fluid from the **hair cells,** which are the receptors involved in detecting the rotation and acceleration of the head. Whenever the head moves, the fluid bends the cilia and thus activates the receptor cells. Because the hair cells are sensitive to this mechanical stimulation, they are a form of mechanoreceptor. The three canals are nearly perpendicular to one another; therefore, movement of the head in any direction (up or down, forward or backward, left or right, or any combination of directions) can be detected.

The vestibular sacs are involved in sensing the tilt of the head and acceleration in a straight line. These organs are roughly circular in shape and, like the semicircular canals, contain hair cells. The cilia of the hair cells extend into a gelatinous fluid. As the orientation of the head changes, the pressure of the gelatinous mass causes the cilia to bend. This bending, in turn, activates these receptor cells. The result is a nerve impulse that is conveyed to the brain.

Sensation versus Perception

Psychologists have traditionally differentiated sensation from perception (e.g., Boring, 1942). Some use the former term to refer to the action by a receptor when it is stimulated, and the latter to refer to the "meaning" given the sensation (Boring, 1942). *Meaning* here refers to the behavior controlled by a stimulus. Others use the terms *sensation* and *perception* in a different way. Carlson (1984), for example, suggested that

> Most psychologists define *sensation* as the awareness of simple properties of stimuli, such as brightness, color, warmth, or sweetness, and *perception* as the awareness of more complex characteristics of stimuli. According to these definitions, seeing the color red is a *sensation*, but seeing an apple is a *perception*. Psychologists used to believe that perceptions depended heavily on learning, whereas pure sensations involved innate, "prewired" physiological mechanisms. (p. 300)

Carlson went onto explain that recent research has revealed that there is no clear distinction between sensations and perceptions. Several variables determine whether a given stimulus affects behavior and, if so, what effect it has. Among the variables that control perception, in the sense of the responses controlled by a stimulus, are (1) the physical characteristics of the stimulus; (2) the concurrent presence of other stimuli; and (3) the individual's history (experience) with respect to the stimulus. Later in this text, the variables that determine the behavioral function of a stimulus, including how it is "perceived," are described at length. Perception is not, of course, fixed; it varies as a function of historical and current circumstances. This variation is evident in Figure 5–6, which illustrates the **Muller-Lyer illusion.** Line segments a and b are equal in length in this figure (measure them), but segment a appears longer. Another optical illusion is the **moon illusion.** Have you ever noticed that the moon appears larger when it is closer to the horizon than when it is high in the sky? This effect does not reflect a change in the moon's size or the size of the image that reaches the eye; both are constant. Clearly, many variables other than simple stimulation of photoreceptors determine perception.

Neurons

The basic functional unit of the vertebrate nervous system is the nerve cell, or neuron. **Neurons** are specialized cells that interact with receptors, effectors (muscles and glands), and other neurons to control all that a living organism

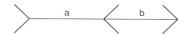

Figure 5-6. The Müller-Lyer illusions. Both lines are actually the same length.

does. These interactions are mediated by chemical and electrical processes that allow cells to communicate with one another in complex ways.

There are many ways to classify neurons. A common mode of classification is according to the kinds of cells with which neurons interact. **Afferent** (or **sensory**) **neurons** receive input from receptors and conduct impulses toward the central nervous system (the brain and the spinal cord). **Efferent** (or **motor**) **neurons** provide input to effectors (muscles and glands) and conduct impulses away from the central nervous system. **Interneurons** conduct impulses between sensory and motor neurons; they may interact with sensory neurons, motor neurons, or other interneurons. About 99% of all neurons in the body are interneurons. Most of them are located in the central nervous system.

Structure and Function of Neurons

Neurons come in many shapes and sizes, but all of them share certain characteristics. Some important structural features of neurons are evident in Figure 5–7, which is a diagram of a typical motor neuron. Anatomically, neurons can be divided into three parts: the cell body, the dendrites, and the axon. The **cell body** (also known as the *soma*, or *perikaryon*) contains DNA and is primarily responsible for controlling cell maintenance and metabolism. **Dendrites** are branchlike structures that extend from the cell body. They are sensitive to chemicals released by other cells and carry nerve impulses toward the cell body. The **axon** carries nerve impulses away from the cell body toward the terminal buttons. Many axons are insulated with a sheath of myelin, which is a whitish, fatty substance. The **terminal** (or **synaptic**) **buttons** are located at the end of the axon. They contain **synaptic vesicles,** which, when stimulated, release chemicals

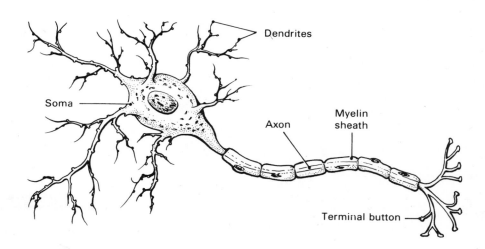

Figure 5-7. Structural features of a typical motor neuron. (From *Physiology of Behavior* by Neil R. Carlson, 1981, p. 19. Copyright 1981 by Allyn & Bacon. Reproduced by permission.)

called *neurotransmitters*. Neurotransmitters alter the activity of other cells and will be discussed below. The terminal buttons of one neuron are in close proximity to the dendrites and/or cell body of adjoining neurons. When two cells are juxtaposed so that they can interact chemically, they are sometimes referred to as *connected*. The terminal buttons of a single neuron typically connect with many other neurons. Likewise, the dendrites and the cell body of a given neuron are often connected to the terminal buttons of many other neurons.

The Nerve Impulse

The **nerve impulse** is a "chemically initiated electric signal conducted along neurons" (Schneider & Tarshis, 1975, p. 121). As this definition indicates, the nerve impulse involves both chemical and electrical processes. The initiation of the impulse is a chemical process, whereas conduction of the impulse along the neuron itself is an electrical process. Because mammalian nerve cells are so small, scientific study of the nerve impulse awaited the discovery, in the 1930s, that squid have thick and long nerve cells. These cells can be kept alive outside the body of the squid, so that study of the chemical and electrical processes underlying neurotransmission is facilitated. Much of what is known today about this process came from the study of nerve cells from squid.

Electricity moves along an electrical wire because of the flow of negatively charged particles (electrons) toward positively charged particles (protons). Similarly, the neural impulse results from the movement of charged particles, or ions. The flow of ions is regulated by the cell (neural) membrane. This membrane allows only certain ions to pass in and out of the cell; that is, it is a semipermeable membrane. In its resting state, the inside of each neuron is negatively charged (about −70 millivolts) with respect to its outside. This negative charge results from the unequal distribution of ions within and outside the neuron. In the resting state, the neuronal membrane is relatively impermeable by sodium, which is positively charged, and is more easily crossed by potassium ions (positively charged) and chloride ions (negatively charged). In addition, the membrane is always impermeable by large, organic anions (negatively charged) that are trapped within the cell. Because of these properties and the action of the "sodium pump," which actively extrudes sodium from within to outside the neuron, in the resting state sodium is found in high concentrations outside, and organic anions in high concentrations inside, the neuron. As a passive consequence of this distribution, potassium ions are in excess within the cell and chloride ions are in excess outside it.

Because oppositely charged ions attract, there is a potential for movement of these ions across the cell membrane during the resting state. This potential is known as the **resting potential** of the cell. If the neuron is perturbed in particular ways, as when an endogenous (naturally occurring) substance combines with receptor material on its membrane, the permeability of the membrane by specific ions may be altered, and its electrical potential may consequently change. This change may involve either an increase in potential or a decrease in potential. If the depolarization is of sufficient magnitude, the membrane becomes very permeable by positively charged sodium ions, which begin to enter the neuron.

As the sodium ions rush in, an action potential, or **nerve impulse,** is generated. This wave of electrical activity, which is approximately 60 millivolts in magnitude and lasts less than 3 milliseconds, passes rapidly and without decrement along the axon to where the cell terminates at the terminal buttons. After the action potential has ended, the permeability of the neuronal membrane by sodium decreases, the sodium that has entered is extruded, and the resting potential is eventually restored.

It is important to recognize that the nerve impulse involves a localized change in membrane permeability, a "window" of increased permeability that moves along the neuron. As the initiation of electrical activity at one location stimulates the adjacent section so that it now becomes depolarized, this depolarization then stimulates the next section, and so on. The impulse may be accurately envisioned as traveling down the length of the axon much as flame travels along a fuse. In myelineated neurons, the membrane can be crossed by ions only when the myelin sheath is interrupted, which occurs at the nodes of Ranvier. Electrical activity in myelineated neurons "jumps" from one node to the next, a process that serves to speed up the conduction of the impulse.

The action potential occurs without decrement and is confined to the axon. Electrical activity in the dendrites and the cell body is graded, and it differs from that which occurs in the axon. In the dendrites and the cell body, the wave of electrical activity decreases in magnitude as it travels away from the point of initiation. Moreover, its strength is directly related to the strength of stimulation. In the axon, only stimulation above a certain level (threshold) initiates an impulse. Stimulation above threshold has no effect on the magnitude of the impulse. In other words, the axonal impulse is an all-or-nothing effect; stimulation below threshold produces no impulse, whereas any amount of stimulation above threshold produces the impulse at its maximum value.

The Synapse

Neurons interact with one another and with other cells, but not through direct physical contact. There is a very small, fluid-filled gap, known as a **synapse,** between the synaptic bulbs of one neuron and the dendrites or cell body of adjoining cells. It is estimated that one nerve cell may share up to 100,000 synapses with other neurons (Zimbardo, 1988) and that the human nervous system may consist of more than 100 trillion synapses (Hubel, 1979).

Neurons interact with other cells at the synapse through a chemical mechanism known as **synaptic transmission.** This process begins when a nerve impulse stimulates the synaptic vessicles, causing them to release a neurotransmitter. Molecules of the neurotransmitter diffuse across the synaptic gap and combine with receptors on the membrane of adjacent cells. Formation of the neurotransmitter–receptor complex influences the activity of these cells. Several chemicals are known to function as neurotransmitters. Among the best studied neurotransmitters are norepinephrine, dopamine, acetylcholine, serotonin, and gamma-aminobutyric acid (GABA). The type and amount of neurotransmitter determines whether or not a neural impulse will be triggered in the next neuron, or whether an effector will be activated. Neurotransmitters are generally classified as excitatory or inhibitory. Both types work by altering the electrical potential of the dendrites and the cell body of the adjacent cell.

Excitatory transmitters alter the permeability of the membrane in the adjoining cell so that the positive ions flow into the neuron. This flow, of course, results in the onset of the nerve impulse in this cell. If the impulse is of sufficient magnitude, it will be conducted to the axon, where it is carried to the terminal bulbs as described above. Inhibitory neurotransmitters serve not to excite the adjacent neuron, but to prevent the neural impulse from being conducted in this cell. This effect is achieved by increasing the potential of the cell, so that a greater than normal amount of excitatory transmitter is required to initiate a nerve impulse. As a result, impulses in the next (postsynaptic) neuron are reduced in frequency or are prevented altogether. Both excitatory and inhibitory transmitters may act on a neuron at a given time. It is the sum of their effects that determines potential and hence whether or not an action potential is generated.

The Peripheral Nervous System

As shown in Figure 5–8, the human nervous system can be divided into two broad categories: the central nervous (CNS) and the peripheral nervous system (PNS). This section describes the PNS, which includes the somatic nervous system and the autonomic nervous system. Together, they serve to (1) transmit nerve impulses from sensory receptors to the CNS and (2) transmit nerve impulses from the CNS to the effectors.

The Somatic Nervous System

In all branches of the PNS, hundreds of neurons are bundled together by bands of connective tissue to form **nerves.** Nerves containing only sensory neurons are called **sensory nerves;** nerves containing only motor neurons are called **motor nerves;** and nerves that contain a combination of sensory and motor neurons are called **mixed nerves.**

The **somatic** (or skeletal) **nervous system** contains sensory neurons that run from the external receptors (e.g., photoreceptors and phonoreceptors) to the central nervous system and motor neurons that run from the central nervous

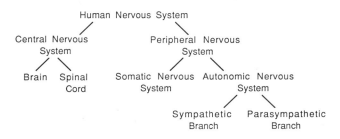

Figure 5-8. Divisions of the human nervous system.

system to the skeletal muscles. Both of these types of neurons typically run uninterrupted from their point of origin to their destination. The skeletal muscles are generally those that operate directly on the external environment. They include the muscles involved in speaking, throwing a ball, walking, eating, and so on. The somatic nervous system plays an obvious and crucial role in detecting environmental stimuli and in producing behavior appropriate to these stimuli.

The Autonomic Nervous System

The autonomic nervous system consists of sensory nerves running from sensory receptors to the central nervous system and motor nerves running from the central nervous system to the heart, to smooth muscles, and to glands. Unlike the motor neurons in the somatic nervous system, which run uninterrupted from the central nervous system to the skeletal muscles, the neurons in the autonomic system synapse just outside the central nervous system (spinal cord) with other neurons that synapse with smooth muscles and glands. In general, the autonomic nervous system functions to regulate the internal environment. For instance, when the body is overheated, the autonomic nervous system cools the body by increasing respiration, producing perspiration, and dilating peripheral blood vessels.

The autonomic nervous system has two branches, the **sympathetic** and the **parasympathetic.** Most smooth muscles and glands receive inputs from both. As shown in Table 5–2, these two branches generally produce opposing effects. For example, input from the sympathetic branch increases heart rate, whereas input from the parasympathetic branch lowers heart rate. As a rule, the parasympathetic branch exercises primary control when an organism is quiescent, that is, when energy is being conserved and stored. The sympathetic branch takes over to prepare an organism for vigorous activity—for "fight or flight." If, for example, a large dog snaps at your face, your blood pressure and heart rate will rise, your rate of respiration will rise, the flow of blood to your skeletal muscles will increase, and glucose will be released into your bloodstream from the liver. All

Table 5-2
Responses of Selected Effector Organs to Autonomic Nerve Impulses

Organ	Parasympathetic impulses	Sympathetic impulses
Adrenal medulla	None	Secrete adrenaline (epinephrine) into bloodstream
Blood vessels	None	Generally constrict, dilate in skeletal muscle
Heart	Decrease rate, force, and volume of constriction	Increase rate, force, and volume of constriction
Lung	Contract bronchial muscle, stimulate bronchial glands	Relax bronchial muscle
Male genitalia	Produce erection	Produce ejaculation
Pupil of eye	Constrict	Dilate
Salivary glands	Secrete thin, watery saliva	Secrete think, viscous saliva

of these physical changes prepare you to use energy effectively and behave vigorously, as might be required to deal effectively with the dog. Their occurrence is the result of the release of adrenaline (epinephrine) from the adrenal glands, which occurs when the sympathetic branch of the autonomic nervous system is activated.

The Central Nervous System

The central nervous system (CNS) includes all neural material within the brain and the spinal cord. More than 99% of all neurons are located in the CNS. Over 10 billion neurons, packed at a density of up to 100 million per cubic inch, are found within the CNS. Obviously, the brain is the most complex part of the human nervous system.

The brain and the spinal cord are cushioned by cerebrospinal fluid and are further protected from external injury by bony structures, the brain by the skull and the spinal cord by the spinal column. The brain is also protected from damage by internal agents by the **blood–brain barrier.** The exact mechanisms underlying its function are complex, but in essence, the blood–brain barrier keeps many chemicals from entering the brain while allowing nutritive substances to enter readily.

Because neurons cannot store the nutrients required for their survival, they depend on a steady flow of blood to bring these substances to them. When this blood supply is interrupted, damage results. Stroke, for example, damages parts of the brain because blood flow to these areas is stopped.

The Spinal Cord

The spinal cord, which is about the diameter of your little finger, is involved in all behavior taking place below the neck. This is where sensory and motor neurons synapse with interneurons running to the brain or other parts of the spinal cord. The spinal cord is also where sensory neurons synapse directly with motor neurons to control spinal reflexes. The **spinal reflex** is among the simplest environment–behavior relations. It occurs when a stimulus elicits a response without the involvement of the brain.

An example of a spinal reflex is a leg jerk that results from a tap to the knee (i.e., the pateller tendon). (Note that the reflex involves the stimulus eliciting the response, not the response or the stimulus alone.) In this case, a tap to the knee (stimulus) excites receptors that in turn stimulate afferent (sensory) neurons. This stimulation leads to the production of neural impulses, which pass along the axon of afferent neurons. The afferent neurons end in the spinal cord, where they synapse with efferent (motor) neurons. When the nerve impulses reach the end of the afferent neurons, they cause molecules of a neurotransmitter to be released. These molecules combine with receptors to produce nerve impulses in descending (motor) neurons. When these nerve impulses reach the terminus of the motor neurons, the process is repeated, but in this case, the neurotransmitter (acetylcholine by name) causes muscles to contract and to produce the leg contraction commonly known as a knee jerk. Figure 5–9 (top panel) schematically diagrams this process, which is known as a *reflex arc.*

The knee-jerk reflex involves only sensory and motor neurons. In most spinal reflexes, interneurons are interposed between sensory and motor neurons (Figure 5–9, bottom panel), allowing for more complex forms of behavior. For instance, stepping on a sharp object with the left foot results in immediate withdrawal of that foot. As this occurs, the opposite leg stiffens and prevents falling. The latter effect is achieved because interneurons connect the sensory neurons from one leg to motor neurons of the other leg.

Although the brain is not directly involved in spinal reflexes, it can modulate their occurrence. If instructed not to allow their leg to move as a result of a tap to the patellar tendon, most humans can keep the response from occurring. Thus, the brain, while not directly involved in each and every response, can modulate even simple reflexive behavior. The brain is connected to the peripheral nervous system and the spinal cord through systems of neurons called *pathways*. The pathways run up and down the spinal cord. It is through thes⸱ pathways that the brain receives sensory input and controls motor responses.

The Brain

The human brain weighs only about 3 pounds, but it contains billions of neurons and trillions of interconnections. Neuroanatomists conventionally divide all mammalian brains into three major sections: the hindbrain, the midbrain, and the forebrain. These areas have different functions and are believed to

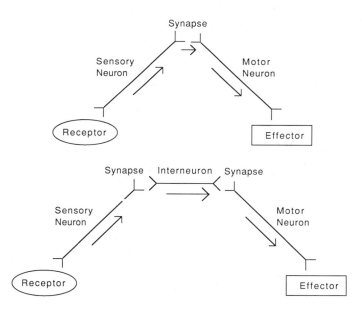

Figure 5-9. Schematic diagram of reflexes arcs that do (bottom panel) and do not (top panel) involve interneurons.

have come about at different times during the course of evolution. Although most mammals have all three divisions, species differ considerably with respect to the size, complexity, and function of each. Snakes and lizards, for example, do not have well-developed forebrains. They also do not engage in many of the complex behaviors characteristic of, say, humans, who have extremely well-developed forebrains.

With respect to evolution, the **hindbrain** is the oldest and most primitive part of the brain. It connects the spinal cord with the brain and consists of three major subdivisions: the medulla, the pons, and the cerebellum. Together, these structures control activities important for basic survival. In humans, for instance, the **medulla** is involved in controlling such critical functions as heartbeat, blood pressure, and respiration. The **pons** is a sort of biological bridge that carries impulses from one side of the cerebellum to the other. The **cerebellum** controls bodily balance, motor coordination, and locomotion.

The **midbrain** was the next part of the brain to evolve. It is relatively small in humans, but in some species, including snakes and reptiles, it is large and controls much of the behavior. A large and complex structure, termed the **reticular formation,** occupies the center of the midbrain. It controls arousal (activation), sleeping and awakening, and many reflexes (e.g., cardiovascular reflexes).

The **forebrain** is the largest part of the human brain and the most recent to evolve. It contains many identifiable structures. One, the **thalamus,** is where incoming sensory impulses are relayed to the cerebral cortex, described below. Located just below the thalamus is the **hypothalamus,** a structure smaller in diameter than a dime. Although small, the hypothalamus serves functions of heroic proportions. It plays a crucial role in regulating the internal environment of the organism by maintaining proper temperature, fluid balance, and food stores. It performs these functions by controlling the pituitary gland (discussed below) and the autonomic nervous system. The hypothalamus is also involved in controlling the species-specific behaviors sometimes jokingly summarized as the "four F's": feeding, fighting, fleeing, and mating.

The role of the hypothalamus in controlling aggressive behavior was demonstrated over 30 years ago by José Delgado (see Delgado, 1969). Delgado implanted electrodes, aimed at the hypothalamus, in the brain of a fighting bull. Then, armed with only a radio transmitter and a cape, he faced the bull in a bullring. When the bull charged, Delgado activated the radio transmitter, which delivered electrical stimulation to the electrodes implanted in the bull's brain. The bull came to a complete stop and turned away. Delgado offered this reaction as proof of the role of the hypothalamus in aggressive behavior. There is, however, some controversy about whether Delgado's electrodes were implanted in the hypothalamus or in motor areas, in which case the stimulation might have impaired locomotion. not aggression. Be that as it may, Delgado's work was an early, and interesting, demonstration of the brain's role in controlling behavior.

The **limbic system** is closely connected with the hypothalamus and the cortical areas lying above it. Part of the limbic system, the **olfactory bulb,** is related to the sense of smell. Other limbic-system structures perform quite different functions. The **hippocampus** is involved in learning and memory. Damage to this area has been linked to memory loss. Also, the hippocampus appears to play a role in movement and spatial organization (Kolb & Whishaw, 1985). The

amygdala is involved in learning and memory. It also plays a role in emotional (e.g., aggressive or fearful) behavior and in maintaining the internal environment. The **septal** area appears to be involved in emotional behavior of another kind. Stimulation to parts of the septal area produce what have been described as pleasurable sensations. In an early demonstration of this phenomenon, Olds and Milner (1954) implanted electrodes in the septal area of rats. The rats could, by pressing a bar, self-administer electrical current to the electrodes. They did so repeatedly, pressing the bar thousands of time per hour, often to the point of exhaustion. When the septal area of humans is electrically stimulated, they report experiencing sensations similar to those preceding orgasm.

In humans, the **cerebrum** is extensively developed. It is the outermost and largest portion of the brain and consists of a right and a left hemisphere. They are connected by several bundles of nerve fiber; the largest and most important is the **corpus callosum.** The cerebrum is covered by a layer of neurons, approximately 2 millimeters thick, called the **cerebral cortex.** The cortex consists largely of cell bodies and unmyelinated nerve fibers. Myelin, you recall, is a whitish fatty insulating substance covering certain axons. Because cells in the cerebral cortex contain no myelin, they appear gray (hence the term *gray matter*). The lack of myelin allows for many more interconnections between neurons than in myelinated cells. The cerebral cortex of humans, which if smoothed and flattened would be about the size of a double sheet of newsprint, consists of more than 10 billion neurons and trillions of interconnections. Some species, such as snakes, have no cortex at all; the cortex of others is small and relatively smooth. In humans, it is large and wrinkled. This wrinkling has the effect of dramatically increasing the surface area. The convoluted nature of the cortex coupled with the vast numbers of neuronal interconnections affords humans the capacity to perform many complex activities. All sensory systems eventually terminate in the cerebral cortex. All responses except the simple reflexes are also controlled by specific areas in the cortex. Finally, the cortex is involved in many other complex activities including those commonly termed *learning, memory, thinking,* and *emotion.* Because of its importance to all human functioning, we will consider the structure of the cerebral cortex in some detail.

Cerebral Structure and Function

As noted above, the cerebral cortex is typically divided into the left and the right hemispheres. The hemispheres are essentially symmetrical, and each can be divided into four **lobes: the frontal, parietal, temporal,** and **occipital.** Figure 5–10 show the location of these lobes. Within each lobe, specific areas of the cerebral cortex have been shown to be associated with specific functions, a phenomenon known as **localization of function.** Among the major areas that have been isolated are the motor, somatosensory, visual, auditory, and association areas.

Located at the rear of the frontal lobe is the **motor area** of the cortex. This area controls the more than 600 skeletal muscles found in the human body. Electrical stimulation at specific points in the motor area produces movement of specific body parts. In all cases, the movement occurs on the side of the body *opposite* the hemisphere to which stimulation was applied. Thus, the right side of the brain controls movement on the left, and vice versa. Muscles in the lower part of the body are controlled by neurons in the upper portion of the motor area, and muscles in the upper part of the body are controlled by neurons in the lower portion. Interestingly, the areas of the body capable of the finest movement (e.g., the fingers), irrespective of size, are influenced by the greatest quantity of neural material.

The **somatosensory** (body-sense) **area** of the cortex is involved in the sensations of pain, temperature, touch, and body position. This area is located within the parietal lobe. The stimulation of neurons in the somatosensory area produces specific sensations. Humans report experiencing pain, heat, cold, touch, or changes of body position when certain somatosensory neurons are stimulated. The somatosensory area receives inputs from the opposite side of the body (e.g., inputs from the left hand arrive at the somatosensory area located in the right hemisphere). Also, as in the motor area, the body is represented in an "upside-down" fashion and the amount of tissue allotted to a given body part is directly related to its sensitivity to stimulation, rather than to its size.

As its name implies, the **visual area** receives inputs from photoreceptors. This area is located at the rear of the occipital lobes. A disproportionate number of neurons in the visual area receive inputs from the fovea, the most sensitive retinal area. Each visual area receives stimulation from both eyes. Stimulation from the left visual field of both eyes is transmitted to the right hemisphere, and stimulation from the right visual field of both eyes is transmitted to the left hemisphere.

The **auditory area** is located in the temporal lobe. Neurons in the auditory area are particularly sensitive to patterns of stimulation that are characteristic of human speech (Atkinson, Atkinson, Smith, & Hilgard, 1987). The auditory area in each hemisphere receives stimulation from both ears.

The areas described above constitute only one quarter of the total area of the cortex; the remaining three quarters is devoted to processes other than those

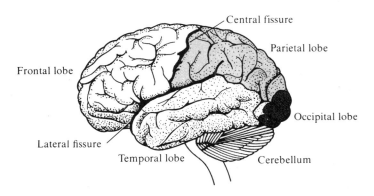

Figure 5-10. Location of the four lobes of the human brain. (From *Psychology* by Henry Gleitman, 1988, p. 29. Copyright 1988 by W. W. Norton. Reproduced by permission.)

involved in direct sensory and motor functions. The **association areas** play a role in the many "higher level" activities engaged in by humans, including complex learning. Evidence of involvement of the association areas in these activities comes primarily from humans who have sustained injury (e.g., tumors or stroke) to certain parts of the cortex. In these individuals, an injury to one part of the cortex disrupts only certain mental processes, leaving others intact. By testing many different individuals with damage to known areas, the areas responsible for specific functions can be mapped.

Hemispheric Specialization

We have noted that the two hemispheres are essentially symmetrical anatomically. This is not so, however, with respect to function. Some functions are lateralized; that is, they are controlled primarily by one side of the brain (Springer & Deutsch, 1984). Much evidence for lateralization of function comes from humans who have incurred some injury to one hemisphere. Injury to a specific area of one hemisphere often produces quite different effects from injury to the identical area in the other hemisphere. For instance, in right-handed individuals, injury to the left hemisphere may interfere with language abilities, whereas similar injury to the right hemisphere leaves language intact (but produces other problems). Such findings led researchers to classify the left hemisphere as dominant over the right hemisphere because of their belief that the right hemisphere was simply a left hemisphere without language capabilities.

More recently, however, evidence has begun to accumulate indicating that the right hemisphere performs its own specialized functions. Much of this evidence comes from patients with **split brains.** The split brain results from a procedure in which the corpus callosum (the neurological bridge connecting one hemisphere to the other) is surgically severed. This procedure is sometimes performed in patients with severe forms of epilepsy that cannot be managed by other treatments. When the corpus callosum is severed, seizure activity cannot spread from one hemisphere to the other. Although successful in reducing seizures, the split-brain procedure leaves the patient with functionally separate hemispheres.

It is now known that the right hemisphere plays a role in detecting a pattern as a whole rather than as its constituent parts. The right hemisphere is also involved in spatial organization, solving simple (two-digit) addition problems, musical and artistic abilities, imagery and dreaming, and emotion and impulsiveness. Moreover, the right side of the brain has been shown to underlie some language capabilities itself.

The left side of the brain has been shown to control most language-related activities (i.e., those that involve words or numbers). In addition, the left hemisphere has been implicated in controlling fine-motor skills in left-handed persons; in right-handers the right side controls them. Finally, analytical skills and high-level mathematical skills are primarily under the control of the left side of the brain.

As discussed in Chapter 2, behavior is not easy to define adequately. It is the case, however, that behavior can be indexed in terms of effector action. **Effectors** are cells that receive inputs from efferent nerves and, when activated, affect the internal or external environment. Different species may have different kinds of effectors. For instance, fireflies have luminescent organs and some eels possess electric organs. Humans can neither glow nor electrify; however, they can affect the environment in a wide variety of ways by using the two kinds of effectors that are available: muscles and glands.

Muscles

The human body contains three kinds of muscles. The **skeletal muscles** are usually attached to bones at both ends by tendons. These muscles move the

Receptors and effectors in action. (Photo courtesy of Neil Rankin.)

bones relative to each other. When placed under a microscope, they have a striped or striated appearance and, for this reason, are also referred to as **striped** (or **striated**) **muscles.** The skeletal muscles allow vertebrate animals to alter their external environments. Not surprisingly, **smooth muscles** have a smooth appearance under the microscope. They generally control movement in internal organs. Cardiac muscles are the third type. **Cardiac muscles** have characteristics similar to those of both smooth and striped muscles. They look somewhat like striped muscles but act like, and are generally thought of as, smooth muscles.

Muscles move by doing one of two things: contracting or relaxing. When contracting, a muscle tightens and becomes shorter. Muscles are attached to the bones of the skeleton in opposing pairs. When one set of muscles contracts, the opposing set relaxes, and the bone is pulled in one direction; when the opposing set of muscles contracts, the first set relaxes, and the bone is moved in the opposite direction. Note the reciprocal interaction between the two sets of muscles. One set contracts while the other relaxes; both cannot contract at the same time.

Like neurons, muscles are activated by chemical molecules. When a nerve impulse passing down the axon of a motor neuron reaches the terminal bulbs, the neurotransmitter acetylcholine is released. This chemical diffuses across the synapse (specifically termed the *neuromuscular junction*) and changes the potential of the cells making up the muscle. This change causes the muscle to move.

Glands

Glands are specialized groups of cells that manufacture and secrete chemicals that affect the function of other parts of the body. You have, for example, no doubt noticed that your eyes "water" when foreign material gets in them. The watering of the eyes is the result of lachrymal gland secretion. Like muscles, glands are activated by neurotransmitter molecules that are released by efferent neurons. There are many glands in the human body. Some, like the lachrymal gland, have ducts that carry secretions to an epithelial surface. Such glands are **exocrine glands.** Unlike exocrine glands, **endocrine glands** do not have ducts. They release chemicals, called **hormones,** directly into the bloodstream.

Perhaps the most influential gland in the endocrine system is the **pituitary gland.** This pea-sized gland is located just below the hypothalamus. It produces and releases a relatively large number of hormones that control the action of other endocrine glands. For this reason, it is often referred to as the *master gland.* One of the major roles of the pituitary gland is to control physical growth. If too much of the growth hormone is released, the person will become a giant; if too little is released, the person will become a midget. Several other endocrine glands and their functions are listed in Table 5–3. Figure 5–11 shows the location of the major endocrine glands.

Neuroscience and Psychology

This chapter has provided only a bare summary of the structure and function of the human nervous system and has ignored completely many important

Table 5-3
Human Endocrine Glands and Their Functions

Gland	Major functions
Adrenal cortex	Regulates carbohydrate metabolism, salt balance, water balance
Adrenal medulla	Affects sympathetic nervous system and increases carbohydrate metabolism
Anterior pituitary	Affects growth, sexual development, skin pigmentation, thyroid function
Pancreas	Regulates carbohydrate metabolism through the secretion of insulin and glucagon
Parathyroid	Regulates calcium and phosphorus metabolism
Posterior pituitary	Affects absorption of water by the kidney, uterine contraction
Testes and ovaries	Affect secondary sexual characteristics
Thyroid	Affects basal metabolism, indirectly affects growth and nutrition

organ systems, for instance, those involved in digestion and reproduction. The human body is remarkably complex and beautifully integrated, and it is impossible to do it justice in a single chapter.

Despite its complexity, the workings of the human body are not beyond comprehension. Scientists now know, for instance, the physiological basis of

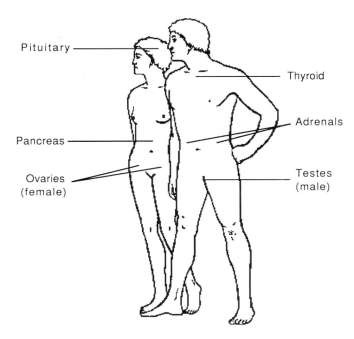

Figure 5-11. Location of the major human endocrine glands. (From *Physiological Psychology* by M. R. Rosenzweig & A. L. Leiman. Copyright 1982 by M. R. Rosenzweig. Adapted by permission.

many disorders that impair behavior. Two such disorders are Parkinson's disease and phenylketonuria. Parkinson's disease is a serious neurological disorder that afflicts approximately 500,000 persons in the United States alone. It results from the loss of dopaminergic neurons (i.e., cells in which the neurotransmitter is dopamine) in the part of the brain known as the *substantia nigra* (Biachine, 1985). These cells are involved in the control of voluntary movements; they work in concert with cells in which the neurotransmitter is acetylcholine. The dopaminergic component of the system is inhibitory, whereas the cholinergic component is excitatory. The death of dopaminergic cells throws the system out of balance and produces the motor disturbances characteristic of Parkinson's disease. Treatment involves using two kinds of drugs: (1) those that increase dopaminergic activity in the cells that remain and (2) those that decrease cholinergic activity.

Phenylketonuria (PKU) is a recessive hereditary disease evident in about 1 in 13,000 to 1 in 20,000 newborn babies (Robinson & Robinson, 1976). The disease involves an accumulation of the amino acid phenylalanine, which causes brain damage and mental retardation (see Chapter 11). Phenylalanine accumulates because a person with PKU lacks an enzyme (phenylalanine oxidase) that oxidizes phenylalanine to tyrosine, another amino acid. The logical and effective treatment for PKU involves a dietary regimen restricting phenylalanine intake. If such a diet is followed early in life, impairment is minimal or absent.

Neuroscientists also know much about the physiological mechanisms through which abused and medicinal drugs produce their effects. For example, neuroleptic drugs (i.e., those used to treat schizophrenia and related forms of mental illness; see Chapter 11) such as chlorpromazine (Thorazine) and thioridazine (Mellaril) appear to produce their antipsychotic effects by blocking receptors that are normally occupied by the neurotransmitter dopamine. Such an action is shown in stylized form in Figure 5–12. Opioid drugs, such as heroin and morphine, also produce their behavioral effects by combining with receptors. These receptors, however, are normally occupied by endogenous (i.e., produced in the body) substances termed **endorphins** (a term coined from *endogeneous morphine*).

Physiology and a Science of Behavior

As Skinner (1978) noted, a science of behavior is a part of biology, and

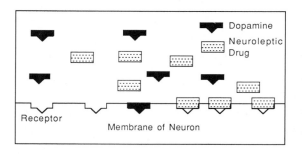

Figure 5-12. A depiction of the action of dopamine and neuroleptic drugs on individual receptors. Note that the neuroleptic drug blocks the receptor normally occupied by dopamine; as a result, dopaminergic activity is diminished.

the organism that behaves is the organism that breathes, digests, conceives, gestates, and so on. As such, the behaving organism will eventually be described and explained by the anatomist and physiologist. As far as behavior is concerned, they will give us an account of the genetic endowment of the species and tell how that endowment changes during the lifetime of the individual and why, as a result, the individual then responds in a given way on a given occasion. Despite remarkable progress, we are still a long way from a satisfactory account in such terms. We know something about the chemical and electrical effects of the nervous system and the location of many of its functions, but the events that actually underlie—a single instance of behavior—as a pigeon picks up a stick to build a nest, or a child a block to complete a tower, or a scientist a pen to write a paper—are still far out of reach. (p. 69)

The future can only bring further advances in our understanding of the physiological events that accompany behavior. But as Carlson (198) explained:

It is not enough to observe behaviors and correlate them with physiological events that occur at the same time. Identical behaviors, under different conditions, may occur for different reasons and thus be initiated by different physiological mechanisms. This means that we must understand "psychologically" why a particular behavior occurs before we can understand what physiological events made it occur. (p. 3)

In the next chapter, some very important "psychological" causes of behavior are explored.

Study Questions

1. Know the three general functions of the nervous system and keep these in mind as you go through this chapter.

2. Refer back to Chapter 1 and review the behavioral view of the importance and role of physiological variables in a science of behavior.

3. Be able to describe what the environment consists of (matter and energy) and the evolutionary role of receptor cells in sensing it. Refer back to the section entitled "Human Evolutionary (Phylogenetic) Development" in Chapter 4 for a brief over-view of the phylogenetic development of human sense organs. As you read this chapter, keep in mind the question of the function of the various sense organs.

4. Describe receptor cells, the process of transduction, and the different classes of stimuli.

5. For each of the human senses (i.e., vision, audition, gustation, olfaction, the skin senses, and the body senses), be able to describe the receptor cells, the process of transduction, and the relevant stimuli.

6. Sensation is usually discussed as a physiological phenomenon, whereas perception is discussed as a psychological phenomenon. What is the difference between the two?

7. Be able to describe the structure and function of neurons (especially the latter), including both afferent and efferent systems and how they are related to sensory input and motor output.

8. Give a general description of the nerve impulse and the synapse.

9. Describe the function of the peripheral nervous system, including the functions and roles of the somatic and autonomic nervous systems.

10. Discuss the function and structure of the central nervous system.

11. Be able to describe (a) the spinal reflex as a simple example of a behavior–environment relation and (b) the role of the brain and the spinal cord in controlling behavior.

12. Be able to describe the major parts of the brain and their functions. Include those parts that mediate sensory input, motor output, innate behavior such as aggressive and reproductive behavior, and learning.

13. To complete the picture, describe the different kinds of effectors and how they fit in to the neurological facts about motor output you have learned.

14. Now, to put this together with the orientation of the book, discuss the role of physiology in a science of behavior.

Recommended Readings

Carlson, N. R. (1981). *Physiology of Behavior.* Boston: Allyn & Bacon.

Carlson provides a comprehensive and detailed coverage of the nervous systems and their relation to behavior.

Kimble, D. P. (1988). *Biological Psychology.* New York: Holt, Rinehart, & Winston.

The author presents a very detailed and advanced treatment of the biology underlying sensation and behavior. Not recommended for the beginning student.

Schneider, A. M., & Tarshis, B. (1975). *Physiological Psychology.* New York: Random House.

Excellent treatment of the cellular and genetic basis of behavior, the nervous system, sensory process, motivation, emotion, and learning and memory.

CHAPTER 6

Learning

As usually defined, **learning** refers to relatively permanent changes in behavior due to experience. Although all mammals and most other animals are capable of learning, no other species learns as readily as *Homo sapiens*. Of all the characteristics we have acquired through evolution, the ability to learn is perhaps the most important. This ability has enabled our species to live successfully from the tropics to the Arctic and to develop sophisticated cultures with social, political, religious, and economic institutions. On a more personal scale, learning accounts for much of what we do each day. The language we speak, the sports we play, and even the thoughts we think depend on learning.

Learning has long been of interest to psychologists for two reasons. First, learning is a powerful determinant of behavior. One cannot understand behavior without understanding learning. Second, understanding learning allows for the development of an effective behavior-change technology. Behavior can be altered greatly through learning, and as described in Chapters 11 and 12, many potent clinical interventions are based on learning principles. The purpose of the present chapter is to consider learning and the variables that control it.

Respondent Conditioning

Words are cheap in psychology. They must be, for psychologists give the same phenomenon many names. For instance, respondent conditioning is the same as classical and Pavlovian conditioning. As the last term implies and Chapter 1 explains, Ivan Pavlov is rightfully famous for his work in this area. You may remember that Pavlov was a Soviet physiologist interested in digestion, which he studied in dogs. Pavlov initially observed that presenting food to a food-deprived dog caused the dog to salivate. This relation is an unconditioned reflex.

Unconditioned Reflexes

Unconditioned reflexes are automatic, stereotyped responses to specific stimuli. Contrary to popular conception, a reflex is the relation between a stim-

Performance and appreciation of dance are both learned. (Photo courtesy of Nina Nelson.)

ulus (S) and a response (R), not just the response. For example, the patellar (knee-jerk) reflex is not just a leg kick, but a leg kick (R) elicited (caused) by a tap on the patellar tendon (S). Unconditioned reflexes are unlearned. They do not require a special ontogenetic history and therefore appear in similar form in most neurologically intact members of a species. If each of 50 people places a hand on a hot stove, the odds are good that every one of them will withdraw it. How rapidly this happens may vary slightly—there are individual differences even in reflexes—but the stimulus provided by the stove (heat) will elicit the same response (hand withdrawal) in every person. This response will occur regardless of whether or not the person has had experience with stoves, or with extreme heat from any other source. Dozens of unconditioned reflexes are evident in humans. A sample of them is provided in Table 6–1. Note that many stimuli elicit a number of different responses.

Unconditioned reflexes are present from birth. In fact, several of them that are present early in life later disappear. Chapter 8 considers the important role that these early reflexes play in child development. Many unconditioned reflexes appear to have adaptive value. For instance, pulling one's hand away from a hot object prevents tissue damage. Closing one's eyes when an object approaches the face often does the same.

In a reflex, an antecedent stimulus elicits a response. An **antecedent stimulus** precedes the response that it controls. A **response** is a defined unit of behavior selected for study. Any stimulus that elicits a response in the absence of a special learning history is termed an **unconditional stimulus** (**US**). The response elicited by the US is termed an **unconditional response** (**UR**). Although the US elicits the UR, this does not mean that their relation is an invariant one in which each US presentation is followed by a response of fixed form and magnitude. Several variables influence unconditioned reflexes. Among them are the intensity of the US and the frequency of its presentation.

Consider this: You're sitting in a boring class, half asleep. You are unaware that a construction worker outside the room is about to start a loud circular saw. The saw starts. What do you do? In all likelihood, you bolt upright, your heart races, and your blood pressure soars (this is the activation response described in Table 6–1). In a word, you're startled. This response is reflexive; most people in the room behaved similarly. The saw runs for 10 seconds—long enough to cut a two-by-four—then silence. A minute or so later, it starts again. This sequence continues throughout the class. What happens? Eventually, the sound of the saw fails to control a response. In the vernacular, you grow used to it. In psychological terms, habituation has occurred. **Habituation** refers to diminished responsiveness to an unconditional stimulus as a result of repeated exposures. It is a general phenomenon that is evident across many reflexes. In an evolutionary

Table 6-1
Some Unconditioned Reflexes Evident in Humans

Stimulus	Response(s)
Food in mouth	Salivation (glands)
Genital tactile stimulation	Penile erection, vaginal lubrication (smooth muscles, glands)
High temperature	Sweating, peripheral vasodilation (smooth muscles, glands)
Irritation to nasal mucosa	Sneezing (smooth and striped muscles)
Irritation to throat	Coughing (smooth and striped muscles)
Light-intensity increase	Pupillary constriction (smooth muscles)
Light-intensity decrease	Pupillary dilation (smooth muscles)
Loud sound	Eyelid closes, eardrum is pulled inward (striped muscles)
Low temperature	Shivering, peripheral vasoconstriction (smooth and striped muscle)
Nipple stimulation	Milk release in lactating woman (glands)
Painful stimulation of hand or foot	Hand or foot withdrawal (striped muscles)
Sudden and intense stimulation (described as painful or frightening)	Activation syndrome: heart rate and blood pressure increase, release of adrenaline and sugar into bloodstream, cessation of visceral muscle activity, vasoconstriction in periphery, vasodilation in skeletal muscles (smooth muscles, glands)
Tap to knee (patellar tendon)	Leg jerk (striped muscles)

sense, habituation is beneficial in that it prevents an organism from wasting time and energy in responding to potentially important but situationally irrelevant stimuli (Fantino & Logan, 1979).

Because it involves a change in behavior due to experience (i.e., repeated US presentations), habituation can be viewed as a rudimentary form of learning. The change is not permanent (let two weeks go without your hearing the circular saw and it will again elicit the startle response), but it is *relatively* enduring, and that is sufficient. Habituation, by the way, does not involve simple fatigue or satiation. If you have heard the saw 30 times and have stopped responding to it, a dynamite blast will still elicit a startle response. Habituation is stimulus-specific and does not involve a general waning of responsiveness.

Simple unconditioned reflexes of the type that have been discussed form the basis of respondent conditioning. Respondent conditioning provides for a degree of behavioral flexibility well beyond that provided by unconditioned reflexes. As Pavlov (1927) noted:

> Under natural circumstances the normal animal must respond not only to stimuli which themselves bring immediate benefit or harm, but also to other physical or chemical agencies . . . which in themselves only signal the approach of these stimuli. . . . The essential feature of the highest activity of the central nervous system . . . consists, not in the fact that innumerable signaling stimuli do initiate reflex reactions in the animal, but in the fact that under different conditions these same stimuli may initiate quite different reflex actions; and, conversely, the same reactions may be initiated by different stimuli. (p. 15)

Stimulus–Stimulus Pairing and Conditioned Reflexes

The essence of respondent conditioning is stimulus–stimulus pairing, that is, an arrangement in which some other stimulus reliably and more-or-less immediately precedes a US. This stimulus is technically termed a **conditional stimulus** (CS). Before being paired with the US, the CS is a **neutral stimulus** (NS) in the sense that it does not elicit a response similar to that elicited by the US, although it may control other responses. After being paired with the US, the CS comes to reliably elicit a response similar to that elicited by the US. The response elicited by the CS is termed the **conditional response** (CR). Respondent conditioning has occurred when a CS comes to elicit a CR reliably.[1] Figure 6–1 provides a schematic representation of respondent conditioning.

Pavlov's work with salivating dogs is the classic example of respondent conditioning. Three steps were involved in his basic demonstration of respondent conditioning with a tone as the CS, food powder as the US, salivation elicited by the tone as the CR, and salivation elicited by the food powder as the UR. First, Pavlov presented the tone alone to verify that it did not elicit salivation as a UR. It did not. The second step was to repeatedly present the tone just

---

[1]Many psychologists use the terms *conditioned* and *unconditioned* instead of *conditional* and *unconditional* when describing stimuli and responses. The latter terms are more accurate Russian-to-English translations of Pavlov's writings, but either usage is appropriate.

before the food was presented. Finally, after several tone–food pairings, the tone was presented alone. Each dog salivated. The tone, previously neutral with respect to salivation, had, by virtue of being paired with the food, acquired the ability to elicit salivation. This is respondent conditioning, and the control of salivation by the tone is an example of a conditioned reflex. A **conditioned reflex** is a learned relation in which a conditional stimulus comes, through respondent conditioning, to control a conditional response. As the preceding example illustrates, three steps are required to demonstrate respondent conditioning:

1. The stimulus to be established as a CS is presented several times to demonstrate that it is a neutral stimulus (i.e., does not elicit a response similar to the UR of interest) before being paired with the US.
2. The neutral stimulus (NS) is paired repeatedly with the US, which establishes the NS as a CS.
3. The CS is presented without the US in a test of whether the CS elicits a CR. If so, respondent conditioning has occurred.

For practice, consider how you would establish the word *blink* as a CS controlling an eye-blink response in a young child.

Higher Order Conditioning

After an NS has been established as a CS (i.e., has acquired an eliciting stimulus function through repeated pairings with a US), it can be paired with other neutral stimuli to make them conditional stimuli. This phenomena is known as **higher order conditioning.** Consider an experiment in which dogs are conditioned to salivate (CR) at the sound of a tone (CS). If a different neutral stimulus—for instance, a light—is paired with the tone, the light alone will eventually elicit salivation. This is second-order conditioning. The process could be extended to third-order conditioning by the pairing of another neutral stimulus, perhaps a touch on the shoulder, with the light. It, too, might eventually come to elicit salivation. But it probably would not, because third-order conditioning is usually impossible with appetitive USs such as food. Even second-order conditioning is relatively weak, although it can be readily demonstrated (Mackintosh, 1974).

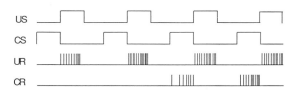

Figure 6-1. Schematic representation of a typical respondent conditioning preparation. Note that, from the onset, each time the unconditional stimulus (US) was presented it elicited the unconditional response (UR), but the conditional stimulus (CS) elicited the conditional response (CR) only after having been paired with the US on a number of occasions.

Quantifying Respondent Behaviors

In Pavlov's early accounts, the CR was assumed to be exactly the same as the UR. We know today that this frequently is not so. In many cases, the CR is not a precise equivalent of the UR. For example, the chemical composition of the saliva elicited by food differs slightly from that of the saliva elicited by a prefood stimulus (Fantino & Logan, 1979). Nonetheless, the responses are similar, and this is typically the case.

Conditional and unconditional responses are known as **respondent behaviors.** Characteristically, respondent behaviors are measured along one or more of four dimensions: magnitude, latency, percentage of occurrence, and duration. **Magnitude** refers to the amount or force of a response, for example, drops of saliva. **Latency** refers to the time that elapses between the onset of some stimulus (e.g., the CS) and the occurrence of a response (e.g., salivation). The **percentage of occurrence** refers to the relative number (percentage) of CS presentations that elicit the CR. **Duration** refers to the time that elapses from the beginning to the end of a response. The measure that is appropriate for quantifying respondent behavior largely depends on the nature of the response (it is, for instance, hard to quantify the duration of a response without a discrete beginning and end) and the question being explored.

Respondent behaviors usually, but not always, involve smooth muscles or glands (see Table 6–1). Nevertheless, it is not possible to determine, on the basis of effector type or topography, if a particular response is a respondent behavior. To make this determination, one must also be aware of the organism's history and the stimuli that control the behavior.

Temporal Relations

For any species, a range of stimuli can be established as effective CSs with a given US, but the rapidity of learning may vary considerably across CSs. In some cases, learning is clearly evident after three or four CS-US pairings; in others, hundreds of pairings are required. With any CS-US pair, learning is influenced by the temporal relation. Figure 6–2 shows five general respondent conditioning procedures that have been explored by researchers. *As a rule, learning occurs (i.e., the CS comes to elicit the CR) under all procedures in which the CS occurs shortly before the US.* Such a relation is arranged in **delayed conditioning,** in which the CS begins before the US and ends either when the US begins (a in Figure 6–2) or when the US ends (b in Figure 6–2).[2] **Trace conditioning** (c in Figure 6–2), in which a measurable period of time (called the *trace interval*) elapses between the end of the CS and the onset of the US, is also effective if the trace interval is short. As a rule, the CS does not come to elicit a CR when the two occur at precisely the same time, which is termed **simultaneous conditioning** (d in Fig-

---

[2]There is no universally accepted set of terms for describing the various temporal relations that can be arranged between a CS and a US. For example, what we term *delayed conditioning* is sometimes termed *simultaneous conditioning* (a sure misnomer) or *forward pairing*.

ure 6–2), or when the CS occurs after the US (e in Figure 6–2). The latter relation is termed **backward conditioning.**

The precise temporal arrangement of CS and US that lends to the most rapid learning depends on many variables, including the nature of the stimuli. With many preparations, including human eye-blink conditioning, a CS presented about 0.5 seconds (sec) before and overlapping the US is very effective. Regardless of exact temporal parameters, for any learning to occur the CS must be predictive of the US. This means in essence that the CS must closely precede the US in time, and the probability that the US will occur must be higher immediately after CS presentation than at any other time. It is not essential that all CS presentations be followed by the US, nor that all US presentations follow the CS. What is essential is that the CS and the US be correlated in time, so that the probability that the US will occur is greatest after the CS occurs. This is the necessary condition for respondent conditioning.

Respondent Extinction

When respondent conditioning does occur, the CS continues to elicit the CR only as long as the CS-US pairing is at least occasionally maintained. If the pairing is not maintained, either by presentation of the CS without the US or by presentation of the two stimuli independently of each other (i.e., in uncorrelated fashion), the CR weakens and eventually ceases to occur. The cessation of responding due to the presentation of a CS not paired with a US is termed **respondent extinction.** If, for instance, Pavlov had stopped giving meat powder to his dogs after sounding the tone, they would eventually have stopped salivating at the sound. Like habituation, respondent extinction serves an organism by preventing it from responding needlessly to once-significant but now unimportant stimuli.

Interestingly, if a considerable period of time (e.g., a day) passes from the end of one series of extinction trials (CS presentations) to the beginning of a second series of trials, response strength increases measurably. This phenomenon is known as **spontaneous recovery.**

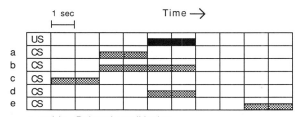

a and b: Delayed conditioning
c: Trace conditioning
d: Simultaneous conditioning
e: Backward conditioning

Figure 6-2. Temporal relations between the CS and the US in respondent conditioning.

Respondent Stimulus Generalization and Discrimination

After a stimulus is established as a CS, stimuli that are physically similar to it may elicit the same CRs, even though these stimuli have never been paired with a US. This phenomenon is termed **respondent stimulus generalization.** Envision a four-year-old child who has been stung by a wasp. The sting is a US; it is painful and elicits crying and a general activation response. The physical characteristics of the wasp (its size, shape, color, pattern of movement, and sound) preceded the US; therefore, they come to serve as a compound CS (a CS with multiple elements). When a wasp approaches, the child cries and is generally aroused. Similar responses are also likely to be engendered by other wasplike insects, such as hornets. The likelihood that a given insect, or other stimulus, will elicit such responses depends on their similarity to the wasp. In general, the greater the similarity between an untrained stimulus and a CS, the greater the likelihood that the untrained stimulus will elicit a response similar to the CR.

The probability that untrained stimuli will elicit responding can be diminished through **respondent discrimination training.** In such training, a CS is repeatedly paired with a US, whereas another stimulus (which differs from the CS along a specifiable dimension) is repeatedly presented without such a pairing. Consider a training procedure in which a dog receives food after each presentation of a 7,000-hertz (Hz) tone, but never after presentation of a 12,000-Hz tone. After several pairings, the 7,000-Hz tone will be established as a CS that elicits salivation. In contrast, the 12,000-Hz tone will not elicit salivation. If, however, the 7,000-Hz tone had simply been paired with food, presenting the 12,000-Hz tone as a novel stimulus probably would have elicited salivation. The general phenomenon of stimulus control will be discussed further later in this chapter.

The Importance of Respondent Behavior

Interest wanes if one thinks of respondent behaviors only in the context of salivating dogs and technical terms. Close reflection reveals, however, that reflexes are of critical importance. We cough when our throat is irritated, cry when something enters our eye, sweat when we are hot, and blink when an object approaches our eyes. These and a multitude of other unconditioned reflexes minimize the adverse effects of potentially harmful environmental variables and help to maintain our normal physiological states. Conditioned reflexes often serve similar functions.

Taste-aversion learning provides an interesting example of an adaptive behavior controlled by stimulus–stimulus pairings, although it is more complex than a simple conditioned reflex. The phenomenon was first demonstrated in the 1950s by John Garcia and his colleagues. In an early study, Garcia, Kimeldorf, and Koelling (1955) allowed rats to drink saccharin-flavored water (saccharin tastes sweet) and then exposed them to gamma radiation, which induced nausea. After a single pairing, the rats preferred tap water alone to saccharin-flavored water, although a strong preference in the opposite direction had been evident at the start of the study. Apparently, by virtue of being paired with the radiation, saccharin-flavored water had acquired nausea-producing characteristics and was therefore avoided.

Taste-aversion learning differs from conventional respondent procedures in three important ways. First, learning occurs after only one pairing of the CS (taste) and the US (radiation), whereas several pairings are usually required. Second, the effective interval between the CS and the US can be minutes or hours in taste-aversion learning, but not in most other preparations. Third, taste-aversion learning involves operant as well as respondent behavior. When such learning occurs, animals avoid contact with stimuli paired with nausea, and as discussed in the next section, avoidance behavior is operant behavior. Because of the complexity of taste-aversion learning and its differences from typical examples of respondent conditioning, many scientists do not consider taste-aversion learning unaugmented respondent behavior. Be that as it may, the phenomenon does involve a pairing of stimuli and is of obvious adaptive value: If an animal eats a food that makes it sick, it is well served to eat no more of the same substance.

One can easily see instances of taste-aversion learning in the wild. A fascinating one involves blue jays (Brower & Brower, 1964). Blue jays eat many insects, including butterflies. Nevertheless, most wild blue jays will not eat monarch butterflies. Beyond being showy and abundant, monarchs have an interesting characteristic: they become poisonous when the larvae eat certain kinds of milkweed. The milkweeds are harmless to the larva, but harmful to birds and mammals. Poison from the milkweed is stored in the body of the larva and is retained as it passes to the butterfly stage. If a blue jay eats a butterfly that has fed on milkweed, the bird grows ill and vomits. Subsequently, it avoids all monarchs, even though some are not poisonous. As Fantino and Logan (1979) noted:

> The adaptive advantage conferred on palatable monarchs by automimicry of unpalatable conspecifics is shared by any species of palatable butterfly sufficiently similar to the monarchs. This . . . constitutes *Batesian mimicry* [wherein a species that is not dangerous or unpalatable mimics or evolves similarly to one that is], and the monarchs are in fact known to have several Batesian mimics. (p. 350)

The viceroy butterfly is a common Batesian mimic of the monarch; the two are very similar in appearance.

Humans don't characteristically ingest butterflies, but we aren't immune to taste-aversion conditioning. Perhaps you've eaten a new food, then got sick to your stomach. If so, you know firsthand the meaning of a learned taste aversion.

A phenomenon similar to taste-aversion learning causes problems for patients with cancer who receive chemotherapy or radiation treatment. The problem is that they become nauseated when they approach the clinic where the treatment is delivered. Some vomit, others report severe distress. This reaction, of course, involves respondent conditioning: the set of stimuli that constitute the clinic are reliably paired with treatment, which elicits nausea, and these stimuli come through respondent conditioning to elicit a similar response.

Respondent conditioning may even play a role in the stimuli that control sexual arousal. Some stimuli do so automatically as USs. Others may do so by being paired with USs or established CSs. In an interesting nonhuman demonstration of this phenomenon, Howard Farris (1967) showed that the courtship of male Japanese quail could be easily conditioned to the sound of a buzzer. The buzzer (CS), a previously neutral stimulus, was sounded for 10 sec, after which a female (US) was placed in the male's cage. She remained in the cage until copulation occurred or 1 minute (min) elapsed from the start of the CS (buzzer), whichever came first. After a few pairings, the males began to display courting behavior at the sound of a buzzer. Within 32 pairings, the buzzer elicited the full courtship display in every male. This display, which is normally elicited by females, involves a series of behaviors in which (1) the posterior is elevated and the neck is thrust forward; (2) the legs straighten and stiffen so that the body bounces; (3) the bird struts on its toes; (4) a subdued, hoarse, vibrating call is emitted; and (5) the body feathers are fluffed. Leather, perfume, whips, or chains may turn some people on, but a buzzer sufficed for the quail. Given the right (or wrong?) history, it might do as much for us.

Rachman and Hodgson (1968) used procedures similar to those used by Farris to condition sexual arousal in male humans to women's knee-length boots. Subjects were first shown a color slide of the boots (CS), then a slide of an attractive naked woman (US). Sexual arousal was measured by assessing penile erection with plethysmograph. Initially, the US controlled erection but the CS failed to do so. After a number of pairings, the CS also controlled erection. When the CS was repeatedly presented alone (i.e., extinction was arranged), it eventually failed to elicit arousal. This study suggests that respondent conditioning may play a role in the development of sexual fetishes, which are abnormal sexual attachments to inanimate objects.

Operant Conditioning

Although survival would be difficult or impossible without them, conditioned and unconditioned reflexes constitute only a small part of the human repertoire. Moreover, respondent conditioning does not produce novel behavior; it only brings reflexive behavior under the control of new stimuli. Novel behavior, including most of the complex things that people do, is operant behavior. **Operant behavior** is behavior that is primarily controlled by its consequences, that is, by the changes in the environment that it produces. The term *operant*, which was coined by B. F. Skinner, emphasizes that behavior operates on the environment and changes it in some way. Operant behavior usually, but not necessarily, involves the action of striped muscles. Operant behavior is also termed *instrumental behavior;* this term emphasizes that responding is instrumental in changing the environment.

Consider a child, Ann, who is learning to write her name under her father's guidance. Certain movements of the pencil produce something approximating letters, and her dad praises the child for producing them. Other movements result in unrecognizable marks; these movements are never praised and sometimes result in reprimands (e.g., the father says, "No, not that way"). After a considerable amount of time, the child learns to write her name. She does so because of the consequences of particular movement patterns: correct movements of the pencil produced one outcome (praise), whereas incorrect movements produced another (reprimands). The child's behavior operated on the environment in the sense of determining what her father did: he praised some

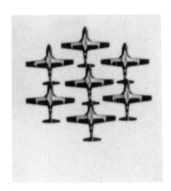

Precision flying is a complex and potentially hazardous collection of behaviors. Such behaviors are a result of specialized learning histories. (Photo courtesy of Sue Keller.)

movements and criticized others. As a result of the different consequences of particular movement patterns, some were strengthened, and others were weakened. Finally, a useful pattern emerged. This is an example of operant conditioning.

There is much for little girls to do beyond writing their names, and no reasonable father would want that response to be the primary one in his daughter's repertoire. Therefore, once the child has acquired the response, her dad is likely to praise it only under special circumstances, as when someone says, "Ann, please write your name." If she does so in this circumstance, praise is forthcoming. If, however, she does so at other times, perhaps when her father is talking on the phone or watching television, he either fails to respond to her writing or responds in a way not valued by his daughter: "Not now, Ann, can't you see I'm busy?" Eventually, the girl writes her name only when asked to do so.

The verbal request "Please write your name" is an antecedent stimulus with respect to the operant response of writing "Ann," and the verbal praise delivered by the father is the consequence of that response. All operant relationships can be described in terms of three components: an antecedent stimulus in the presence of which a response produces certain consequences, a response that produces certain consequences, and the consequences. Schematically, this is an S-R-S (stimulus–response–stimulus) relationship.

Reinforcement

Stimuli produced by a response (i.e., their consequences) can have two effects: the future likelihood of the occurrence of the response under similar circumstances can increase (as did Ann's correct movements), or it can decrease (as did her incorrect movements). We use the term *reinforcement* to refer to the former relation, whereas *punishment* (discussed later) is used to describe the latter. In a technical sense, **reinforcement** is an operant conditioning process (or procedure) in which a response is followed by a stimulus (**reinforcer**) and is thereby strengthened. The response-strengthening effects of reinforcement typically involve an increase in the future **rate** (number of responses per unit of time) or the probability of occurrence of the response, although other changes in behavior (e.g., a decrease in response latency or an increase in response magnitude) may also be indicative of a reinforcement effect. It is important to recognize that reinforcement always strengthens the operant response class that preceded its delivery, although this process may weaken, strengthen, or have no effect on other operant response classes. An **operant response class** is defined as all behaviors, regardless of topography, that produce the same effect on the environment. For instance, a rat might press a bar with its left paw, right paw, chin, or butt. Though very different in form, all of these behaviors are members of the operant response class of lever presses, for each produces the same effect on the lever: depressing it.

Reinforcers may involve adding something to the environment (e.g., presenting food) or taking something away (e.g., turning off a loud noise). When a stimulus strengthens a response class by virtue of being presented (or increased in intensity) following a response from that class, the stimulus is termed a **positive reinforcer,** and the procedure is termed **positive reinforcement.** When a stimulus strengthens a response class by virtue of being terminated (or decreased in intensity) following a member of that response class, the stimulus is termed a **negative reinforcer,** and the procedure is termed **negative reinforcement** (see Figure 6–3).

The only way to determine whether a stimulus is functioning as a reinforcer is to look at its effect on behavior. If, after one arranges for the putative reinforcer to follow a response, the response increases in strength, the stimulus is called a *reinforcer.* If the response is not strengthened, the stimulus is not a reinforcer. For example, a parent, after rocking a baby for 10 minutes, returns the child to its crib. The baby begins to cry. The parent returns and begins to rock the child once more. Has the rocking reinforced the crying? The only way to tell is to determine whether, in the future, the child is more likely to cry under similar circumstances. That may well be the case. If so, this is positive reinforcement in action. Negative reinforcement may also be at work in this scenario. Assume that the child stopped crying when rocking began. If this happened and if the mother's response of rocking the child was strengthened because it terminated the crying, this is an instance of negative reinforcement. It is important to recognize that reinforcers are functionally defined: they are defined in terms of how they affect behavior, not in terms of their subjective effects. Although most positive reinforcers make us "feel good," this reaction is irrelevant. The important thing is that

	Stimulus is Presented	Stimulus is Removed
Behavior is Strengthened	Positive Reinforcement	Negative Reinforcement
Behavior is Weakened	Positive Punishment	Negative Punishment

Figure 6-3. A 2 × 2 matrix defining two types of reinforcers and punishers. Note that reinforcers always strengthen responding, whereas punishers always weaken responding.

they strengthen the behaviors that precede them. Reinforcement does not require or produce a particular subjective state, and humans are often unable to describe the reinforcers that maintain their behavior.

Classifying Reinforcers

A wide variety of environmental changes (i.e., stimuli) can serve as reinforcers. **Unconditioned reinforcers** (also called *primary reinforcers*) strengthen behavior in organisms without any particular history, which is to say in most "normal" members of a particular species. Many unconditioned reinforcers are of direct biological significance. Air, food, water, and sex are examples of positive reinforcers that fit into this category. Unconditioned negative reinforcers, which organisms will **escape** (respond to terminate) or **avoid** (respond to prevent contact with) include high-intensity stimulation in most modalities (e.g., loud sounds, bright lights, or intense cold or heat). Psychologists often use the symbol S^R for an unconditioned reinforcer. They use other symbols to designate stimuli with other behavioral functions. Table 6–2 provides a list of these symbols.

In contrast to unconditioned reinforcers, **conditioned** (or **secondary**) **reinforcers** gain their ability to strengthen behavior through learning. Specifically, conditioned reinforcers are stimuli that are paired with (i.e., precede the delivery of) unconditioned reinforcers or other established conditioned reinforcers. Perhaps you have trained a dog. If so, you have undoubtedly made use of a conditioned reinforcer, probably a phrase like "good dog." Early in puppyhood,

Table 6-2
Symbols Used to Describe Operant
Conditioning

Symbol	Refers to
S^R	Any unconditioned reinforcer
S^{R+}	An unconditioned positive reinforcer
S^{R-}	An unconditioned negative reinforcer
S^r	Any conditioned reinforcer
S^{r+}	A conditioned positive reinforcer
S^{r-}	A conditioned negative reinforcer
S^D	A discriminative stimulus
S^+	A discriminative stimulus
S^Δ	An S delta
S^-	An S minus; same as an S^Δ
S^P	Any unconditioned punisher
S^{P+}	An unconditioned positive punisher
S^{P-}	An unconditioned negative punisher
S^P	Any conditioned punisher
S^{P+}	A conditioned positive punisher
S^{P-}	A conditioned negative punisher
EO	An establishing operation
CSS	A contingency-specifying stimulus

and now and again throughout the dog's life, "good dog" was voiced while you petted him, and when you gave him food. By virtue of being paired with stimuli that were unconditioned reinforcers (tactile stimulation and food), the phrase came to function as a secondary reinforcer. It will strengthen behavior in a dog with a special history, which your dog has, but not in other dogs. Food, in contrast, will strengthen behavior in all healthy dogs.

The stimuli that serve as conditioned reinforcers vary greatly across people because of differences in their conditioning histories. For example, certain kinds of painful stimulation (e.g., being struck with a leather belt) are positively reinforcing for a few people, who are called *masochists*. This response may reflect a history in which such stimulation reliably preceded a powerful positive reinforcer, perhaps sexual stimulation. Being struck with a belt was not initially reinforcing, but it eventually came to be so by virtue of its correlation with sexual stimulation. Like other conditioned reinforcers, it will maintain its reinforcing ability only if it continues to be paired, at least occasionally, with some other reinforcer. Once a conditioned reinforcer is no longer paired with another reinforcer, it loses the capacity to strengthen behavior.

In humans, some conditioned reinforcers are paired with many other reinforcers. Money is a good example of such a generalized conditioned reinforcer. Giving a baby a dollar each time she smiled would probably not increase her smiling, but the same operation would be likely to turn a college freshman into a Cheshire cat. The reason for the disparity of outcome, obviously, is that the freshman, but not the child, has a long history in which dollar bills are paired with (i.e., exchanged for) a great variety of "good things," or positive reinforcers. Attention is another powerful and generalized conditioned reinforcer.

Laboratory studies with nonhumans suggest that the response-strengthening effects of reinforcers diminish rapidly as the delay between the response and the reinforcer increases. Here, consequences delayed by more than a short period—a minute, at most—are essentially ineffectual. As a result, some behavior analysts add a requirement of immediacy to their definition of reinforcement. For example, our definition could be modified to read: Reinforcement is an operant conditioning procedure in which a response is followed immediately by a stimulus (reinforcer) and is thereby strengthened. This definition may be unduly restrictive. *Immediately* means with no delay, and even in laboratory experiments with nonhumans, reinforcers delayed by a few seconds do strengthen behavior. Moreover, long-delayed events are capable of strengthening behavior in humans, although they may do so indirectly. For example, few people would work without pay, even though a paycheck delivered on Friday afternoon probably does not strengthen the responses that occurred throughout the week in the same direct way that food delivered immediately after a bar press reinforces the response in a hungry rat. Verbal responses appear to play a critical role in mediating the effects of long-delayed consequences in humans, and it may be useful to distinguish as special any consequences whose effects are so mediated, and to call them something other than reinforcers. At present, however, this convention has not been established.

Environmental events may reinforce responses that precede them even if the response does not actually produce the reinforcer. A crap shooter who, for unknown reasons, says, "Be there, baby," before rolling the dice is apt to repeat the phrase under similar conditions in the future if the roll is a seven, even though there is no plausible mechanism through which the verbal statement could control the dice. Reinforcement of this type has been termed *superstitious, adventitious,* or *response-independent* and is undoubtedly involved in the control of some human behaviors.

The Opportunity to Behave as a Reinforcer

For any two behaviors that occur with different probabilities (here, *probability* is defined as the amount of time spent engaging in the behavior), the opportunity to engage in the higher probability behavior will reinforce the lower probability behavior. Conversely, forcing an organism to engage in the lower probability behavior contingent on the higher probability behavior will punish the higher probability behavior. These two relations constitute the **Premack principle** (Premack, 1959). Consider two behaviors that a junior-high student can emit: playing basketball and doing algebra problems. When allowed to do either, much time is spent in playing basketball and little in doing algebra problems. Arranging conditions so that the student must do algebra problems (the lower probability behavior) before playing basketball (the higher probability behavior) is a good way to increase the time spent in doing algebra problems.

Reinforcing stimuli often allow an organism to engage in behaviors that otherwise could not occur. For instance, food allows for eating; a mate, for mating. One can often predict whether a particular stimulus will be reinforcing by determining the probability of the response associated with it relative to the probability of the operant response that it follows. All else being equal, a food-deprived rat will spend far more time eating then pressing a bar. Hence, it is not surprising that food delivery (which allows for a higher probability behavior) will reinforce bar pressing (which is a lower probability behavior).

Motivational Variables

The reinforcing effectiveness of a given stimulus is not fixed; it varies as a function of several variables. The degree of deprivation relevant to the reinforcer maintaining behavior and the history of the person in question are obvious and strong determinants of reinforcing effectiveness. Food is a more effective reinforcer if we have not eaten for a day than if we have just finished a five-course meal, and money is a reinforcer only for persons who have learned of its exchange value. Deprivation and history can be considered antecedent, or setting, variables, in that they precede the response that they affect.

Michael (1982) proposed the term **establishing operation (EO)** as a general label for operations such as deprivation that (1) increase (or decrease) the effectiveness of a particular reinforcer and (2) increase (or decrease) the likelihood of occurrence of behavior that has in the past been followed by that reinforcer. Although *drive* and *motivation* have traditionally been used to describe changes in an organism that produce these two effects, both terms implicate an inner state, rather than antecedent environmental change, as the primary determinant of responding. For this reason, *establishing operation* appears the best of the three alternatives.

Establishing operations increase or decrease the strength of *all* behaviors that have been followed by the relevant consequence. For instance, food deprivation will strengthen not only asking for food, but also looking in places where food has previously been found, going to the store for food, and so on. Thus, an EO alters the strength of an entire operant response class, not just one particular response.

Satiation is the term used to describe a momentary reduction in the reinforcing efficacy of a stimulus as a result of repeated presentations. Satiation is common with some unconditioned positive reinforcers (e.g., food, water, and sex), but not with all. For example, satiation does not occur when briefly increasing a low ambient temperature is the reinforcer. Satiation characteristically does not occur with negative reinforcers, or with conditioned reinforcers alone. If, however, the unconditioned positive reinforcer paired with a conditioned reinforcer is presented often enough, satiation may be evident with both the unconditioned and the conditioned reinforcer. Satiation rarely occurs with generalized conditioned reinforcers such as money.

Operant Extinction

If a response is no longer followed by a reinforcer, the response eventually stops occurring. Cessation of responding due to a response occurring without reinforcement is known as **operant extinction.** The same term is also used to refer to the procedure of failing to reinforce an established operant. As an example of operant extinction, consider what happens when you try to buy candy from a machine that is out of order. The money goes in, and you press the button. Nothing happens. You press again. No candy. Eventually, you stop pressing. But the waning of responsiveness is not necessarily smooth. In fact, the rate of responding often goes up on initial exposure to extinction: You hammer the button in a phenomenon known as **extinction-induced bursting.** You may also curse or kick the machine and wiggle the button from side to side. **Emotional responding** and an **increase in the variability of behavior** are also characteristic results of extinction.

Intermittent Reinforcement

Reinforcers need not follow every occurrence of a behavior to determine the rate and pattern of its occurrence; intermittently occurring reinforcers can strengthen behavior. For example, most of the time, the hunting behaviors of a hungry gray fox are not successful in producing a mouse or other food, but the behaviors continue. They continue because they sometimes produce a meal. Our responses, too, are characteristically reinforced intermittently, not continuously. Can you think of anything that you do that is always reinforced? Probably, but intermittent reinforcement is nonetheless the rule, not the exception.

Behavioral psychologists use the term **schedule of reinforcement** to refer to relations among stimuli, responses, and the passage of time that lead to an increase in response strength. In simple terms, "schedules of reinforcement are the rules used to present reinforcing stimuli" (Zeiler, 1977, p. 202). Schedules of reinforcement are important for four reasons:

1. *Schedules of reinforcement are ubiquitous.* They operate throughout the natural environment of humans and other animals, even though it is frequently difficult to determine precisely what schedule is in effect at a given time for a particular response class.

2. *Schedules of reinforcement determine the rate and temporal pattern of behavior.* Some schedules generate high and consistent response rates; others generate very different rates and patterns. Characteristic behaviors under four simple and well-studied schedules are described in Sidebar 6–1.

3. *Schedules of reinforcement determine resistance to extinction.* Responding always approaches near-zero levels if extinction is arranged for a sufficient period, but the rapidity with which it disappears and the pattern of responding evident in extinction depend on the schedule in effect before extinction.

4. *Schedules of reinforcement determine choice.* The time and effort allocated to one particular kind of behavior relative to another (i.e., choice) is determined in part by the schedule in effect for the alternative behaviors.

A moment's reflection reveals the presence of simple schedules in everyday life. If, for example, a second-grade student named Amy always receives a gold star each time she correctly answers an addition problem, that response is reinforced under a fixed-ratio 10 (FR 10) schedule. But if the teacher, being busy, delivers stars depending on the completion of a number of problems that changes irregularly across time but averages out at 10, the schedule approximates a variable-ratio 10 (VR 10) schedule. Assuming that stars are effective

---

Sidebar 6-1
Four Simple Schedules of Reinforcement

Fixed-ratio (FR) and **variable-ratio (VR)** schedules are purely response-based. In the former, a reinforcer follows every *n*th response, for instance, every fifth response in an FR 5 schedule. So-called continuous reinforcement is an FR 1 schedule. In a VR schedule, on average every *n*th response is followed by the reinforcer, although the number of responses required for reinforcement varies irregularly. With protracted exposure, both of these schedules typically engender relatively high rates of responding. Postreinforcement (or preratio) pausing, the cessation of behavior following a reinforcer, is characteristic of performance under FR, but not VR, schedules.

In contrast to FR and VR schedules, fixed-interval (FI) and variable-interval (VI) schedules are both response- and time-based. The FI schedules specifies that the first response emitted after a given period of time has elapsed (e.g., 10 minutes in an FI 10-min schedule) will be reinforced. This interval is usually timed from the delivery of the previous reinforcer. Relatively low overall response rates are typical in FI schedules. In some but not all cases, most responses are emitted toward the end of the interval, a pattern known as *scalloping*. Variable-interval schedules specify that the first response emitted after some average period of time has elapsed will be reinforced; this interval varies irregularly around the mean value. These schedules generally evoke moderately high and very steady rates of responding. Resistance to extinction is great after exposure to a VI schedule.

reinforcers and the student can solve the problems, either the FR 10 or the VR 10 schedule should engender relatively high rates of problem completion.

Now consider a teacher who is both busy and lazy. He checks Amy's performance only at the end of each hour, delivering a star if she completes the problem correctly as the teacher watches. This arrangement would constitute a fixed-interval 60-min schedule and would generate little behavior. Checking at irregular intervals—some short, some long, some of intermediate length—would change the schedule to a variable-interval schedule and would substantially increase Amy's rate of problem completion.

Simple schedules can be combined to form a complex schedule. The concurrent schedule is an important example of a complex schedule. **Concurrent schedules** arrange reinforcement simultaneously for two or more response classes. For example, in a concurrent variable-interval 1-min–variable-interval 5-min (conc VI 1-min–VI 5-min) schedule of food delivery, left-key responses by a pigeon would be reinforced under a VI 1-min schedule, whereas right-key responses would be reinforced under a VI 5-min schedule. Humans are constantly exposed to concurrent schedules. When such schedules are arranged, we make choices. Consider a typical party. Among the response options are talking to any of a number of people, listening to music, dancing, eating, or drinking. For any person at the party, these responses are not equally likely to occur, and there will be sizable differences across people in the amount of time spent in each activity. Cathy may spent 80% of her time talking to K.W. and 5% talking to L.C., but these proportions may be reversed for John. Why? There are several possibilities. One is that, by virtue of their histories, the objects and events that function as reinforcers differ for Cathy and John. K.W. may talk at great length about chess, which reinforces Cathy's listening, but not John's. Another is the L.C. might arrange different schedules for John and Cathy. Perhaps L.C. compliments John often but rarely says anything good to Cathy. Obviously, operant relations control social behavior. That they do so should be evident in your own life: Who do you first approach at a party attended by your friends, and why do you approach that person? Do the consequences of prior interactions influence your choice?

Stimulus Control

It's noon and you're walking along a downtown street. You had breakfast at seven and haven't eaten since. Five hours of deprivation have established food as a powerful reinforcer, and responses that have produced food in the past are at strength. These responses are to a large extent under the control of antecedent stimuli. For example, it is highly unlikely that you'd walk up to the counter in a boutique and say, "I'd like a hamburger, large fries, and a chocolate shake." Change the setting to a fast-food restaurant, however, and the response becomes highly probable. Why? Because in the past the response of asking for food has been reinforced in restaurants, but not in boutiques. In technical terms, being in the restaurant is a discriminative stimulus that controls the response of asking for food.

In essence, a **discriminative stimulus** (S^D or S +) evokes a response because, in the past, that kind of response has been more successful in the presence of that stimulus than in its absence. Discriminative stimuli come to control a particular type of behavior by being present when that behavior is reinforced. Stimuli present when a particular type of behavior is not successful (i.e., is not reinforced) also influence responding. The term S^{delta} (S$^\Delta$), or S −, is used to designate such stimuli. An S$^\Delta$ is a stimulus that (1) weakens a particular type of behavior (2) because, in the past, that type of behavior was extinguished in its presence but reinforced in its absence.

When behavior differs in the presence and absence of a stimulus, **stimulus control** is evident. Stimulus control is not an all-or-none phenomenon; it occurs along a continuum from absent to complete. The degree of stimulus control can be determined by presenting a number of stimuli that differ from the stimulus of interest (e.g., the S^D) along some physical dimension and comparing the rate of responding evoked by them.[3] Envision a situation in which a food-deprived rat receives food pellets when it depresses a bar in the presence of a 10,000-Hz tone, and at no other time. This arrangement may be sufficient to establish the tone as an S^D. To test whether this is the case, we would briefly present test stimuli ranging from 10 to 20,000 Hz and graph the relative response rates evoked by each of them.[4] Such graphs are known as **stimulus-generalization gradients**.

Three possible results of this hypothetical study are shown in Figure 6–4. One set of data depicts complete stimulus control. When stimulus control is complete, a given response occurs when a particular stimulus is present, and at no other time. A second set of data shows a total absence of stimulus control. Here, behavior does not differ as a function of the presence or absence of a particular stimulus. The third set of data in Figure 6–4 demonstrates partial stimulus control. When stimulus control is partial, a response occurs more often when a stimulus is present than when it is absent, but the response also occurs at other times.

As its definition indicates, the development and maintenance of stimulus control requires **differential reinforcement,** in which a response is reinforced in the presence of one stimulus and is extinguished in the presence of one or more other stimuli. These conditions are arranged in operant discrimination training. The degree of stimulus control produced by such training depends on the sim-

[3]*Elicit* and *evoke* are synonyms in the vernacular, but many psychologists restrict the use of *elicit* to respondent relations (e.g., a CS elicits a CR). Some restrict the use of *evoke* to operant relations (e.g., an S^D evokes an operant response), but others use *evoke* in the context of both operant and respondent relations. We have followed the convention of using *elicit* to describe respondent relations and *evoke* to describe operant relations. But the reader should realize that simply designating operant behavior as "evoked" and respondent behavior as "elicited" does not explain how they differ.
[4]The actual test procedure would be a bit more elaborate. It could be arranged by having a variable-interval schedule of food delivery in effect during test sessions in which the 10,00-Hz tone is present. Each test stimulus, which would differ with respect to cycles per second (Hz), would be presented for a brief period (e.g., 10 sec) in which extinction has been arranged. Arranging extinction when test stimuli are presented prevents their being established as S^{D}s in their own right, and using a variable-interval schedule during the rest of the session ensures that responding will continue through the brief extinction periods.

ilarity of the S^Δ to the S^D. In general, the degree of stimulus control (i.e., the sharpness of the generalization gradient) increases as the similarity of the S^Δ to the S^D increases. As an example, consider two pigeons, each exposed to conditions in which key pecking is reinforced with food when the key is illuminated in light of one wavelength, 580 millimicrons (wavelength determines color). This light is the S^D for both birds. Key pecking for each bird is also extinguished when the key is illuminated in light of another wavelength, the S^Δ, which is 480 millimicrons for Bird 1 and 560 millimicrons for Bird 2. After considerable training, each bird is tested with key illumination of 565 millimicrons. This stimulus evokes a considerable amount of responding by Bird 1, but little or no responding by Bird 2. The degree of stimulus control in both cases has been determined by training history.

History plays a similar role in discriminated human operant behavior. Traditional Inuits discriminate over a dozen kinds of snow. Their verbal (and other) responses to snow are controlled by subtle features of frozen precipitation that exercise no control over the behavior of most other North Americans. This difference in verbal behavior reflects a difference in training: young Inuits are reinforced (by their family and other associates and by the physical environment itself) for responding differently to physically dissimilar forms of snow, but most other young people do not have such reinforcement histories, and snow exercises only coarse stimulus control over their behavior. That stimulus control changes if they take up diagonal-stride cross-country skiing on waxed skis. If they do, fine discriminations based on subtle snow characteristics (e.g., age, temperature, and compression) are learned because of differential reinforcement: red klister snow (old, crusted snow at a relatively warm temperature) simply can't be skied effectively on wax designed for polar green snow (new snow at a very low temperature). We learn the discriminations that are relevant to our personal environment.

Obviously, many of these discriminations are based on multiple stimulus dimensions. You recognize your best friend not by virtue of any single physical characteristic (e.g., size, color, or form), but on the basis of a unique combination of characteristics. Discriminations may also be conditional. In a **conditional discrimination,** whether a response is reinforced (and therefore subsequently

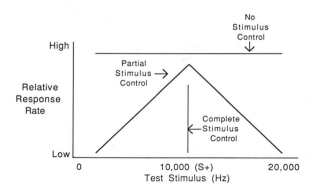

Figure 6-4. Hypothetical generalization gradients showing varying degrees of stimulus control. The dimension along which stimuli are varied (Hz) determines the pitch of a sound.

occurs) in the presence of one stimulus depends on the presence of a second stimulus. For instance, you're sitting in one room, studying, and a friend is in the adjoining room. One room, yours, has a digital clock; the other does not. The numbers *8:17* appear on the clock face, but they exercise no control over your behavior until your friend queries, "What time is it?" You respond, "It's eight seventeen." Here, a sequence of two stimuli—the auditory one provided by your friend and the visual one supplied by the clock—control your behavior.

Conceptual Behavior and Functional Equivalence

Conceptual behavior occurs when, as a result of stimulus generalization, an organism responds in the same fashion to stimuli that share certain features but responds differently to stimuli that do not share these features. In many cases, the response involves identifying novel members of a given class of stimuli, as when a child trained to identify dogs on the basis of experience with springer spaniels, beagles, Irish setters, labradors, and poodles says, "That's a dog," or something to that effect, when shown a bassett hound or a German shepherd. Interestingly, people are often unable to describe the features of a stimulus class that control their behavior. What stimulus characteristics lead you to call an animal a cat?

Members of the same stimulus class are functionally equivalent; that is, they control the same operant response class, although they need not have similar physical characteristics. For instance, you might say, "That's a dog" when presented with the printed word *basenji*, a picture of a German shorthair, or a living malamute. As a rule, variables that affect the ability of one member of a stimulus class to control behavior affect the ability of all members of that class to do so. Consider the following stimuli, all evident to a person driving a car: (1) a stop sign that the driver has never seen before; (2) a passenger yelling, "Stop"; and (3) a police car with flashing lights approaching from behind. For most people, each of these are discriminative stimuli for stopping the car, and encountering each would lead to the car stopping. If, however, the driver were a fugitive escaping the law, there is little likelihood that any of these stimuli would produce this effect. The complex of the events that make a person a fugitive also renders ineffective the reinforcers associated with stopping, and an S^D evokes behavior only when the reinforcer historically correlated with it is momentarily effective.

Stimulus control plays a critical role in the development of complex human behavior. As Fantino and Logan (1979) emphasized, "Whether we are concerned with the behavior of pigeons or monkeys in the laboratory, or humans in applied settings, the adequate specification of stimuli controlling behavior is of fundamental importance for understanding and changing behavior" (p. 167). Establishing operations and discriminative stimuli are one major class of controlling stimuli. They are antecedent stimuli; they precede the responses that they control. Response-dependent and response-independent reinforcers (and punishers) are a second major class of controlling stimuli. They are postcedent[5] stimuli, for they follow the responses that they control. When antecedent and postcedent stimuli are considered together, operant behavior can be represented fully by a slight modification of the S-R-S introduced earlier. For example, unconditioned positive reinforcement can be represented as $EO\text{-}S^D\text{-}R\text{-}S^R$. As discussed previously, some unconditioned reinforcers do not require a specific establishing operation in order to be effective. In this case, the operant relation can be described as $S^D\text{-}R\text{-}S^R$. The relation between discriminative stimulus, operant response, and reinforcing stimulus is known as the **three-term contingency.**

Shaping and Chaining

To this point, no mention has been made of how new operant responses are acquired. The fundamental process of operant response acquisition is called the *reinforcement of successive approximations,* or *shaping.* **Shaping** is a procedure in which a given operant response is achieved by the reinforcement of successively closer approximations to that response. Initially, the response in the existing behavioral repertoire closest to the desired response is reinforced on a few occasions. Then, a new criterion for reinforcement is adopted. This new criterion demands a response more similar in topography to the desired response than the previously reinforced behavior. Hence, if one is teaching a young child to say, "Dad," she or he might first reinforce any vocalization. Then, when babbling was occurring at a high rate, the teacher would selectively reinforce only *da* sounds, or the nearest observed approximation of that sound. Although it is possible that no response meeting the criterion for reinforcement will occur, this is unlikely. By failing to reinforce diffuse babbling, extinction is arranged. The variability of behavior increases in extinction, and this makes it more likely that some *da*-like sound will be emitted. If, however, this does not occur, prompting (telling the child, "Say dad") and modeling the correct response ("Dad, dad, dad") would probably serve to evoke the response. Once *da* had been voiced and reinforced on several occasions, a final criterion for reinforcement, emitting the *dad* sound, would be adopted, and the child would be treated as described above.

To help in understanding shaping, imagine that you are the animal trainer at a marine aquarium. Your first job is to train a dolphin to leap completely out of the water and grab a fish. How would you proceed? One possibility would be to hold a fish several feet above the water and wait for the dolphin to leap for it. If this occurred and the animal grabbed the fish, the response might be reinforced

---

[5]The term *postcedent* is not standard English. It appears, however, to be the best term available for referring in general to stimuli that follow behavior and weaken or strengthen it. *Postcedent* is symmetrical in form with *antecedent,* it emphasizes that the stimuli follow a response, and it includes, without violating linguistic convention, both response-dependent and response-independent events. Although some writers use *consequences* to refer to both response-independent and response-dependent events, *consequence* is used in the vernacular to refer only to events that occur as the result of a prior happening. Thus, it appears that the use of the term *consequences* should be restricted to response-dependent events.

and might recur. But your wait could be a long one; dolphin's don't typically fly through the air pursuing fish. But they do chase and eat fish, and the response of leaping for one could be readily shaped. You might begin by attaching a fish to a rope so that the dolphin could eat the fish while leaving the rope intact. First, the fish would be placed in the water, and the dolphin would be allowed to eat it. This would occur a few times. Next, the fish would be raised to water level. Once the behavior of grabbing the fish at water level was reliably occurring, the fish would be raised above the surface of the water in one-foot increments, and you would make sure the dolphin was successful at each level before moving on to the next. Eventually, it would be flying through the air to delight thousands and secure your position as master trainer.

Shaping is a potent device for producing new responses, although other procedures, such as response chaining, are involved in the development of complex patterns of behavior. In **response chaining,** a sequence of behaviors must be emitted before the unconditioned reinforcer is delivered. Only the terminal (final) response is followed by a unconditioned reinforcer; prior responses in the sequence simply provide an opportunity for subsequent responses to occur. Purchasing soda from a vending machine is a good example of response chaining. A sequence of many different responses is required to produce the drink, but only the final movement of the can to our lips is followed by the reinforcer that ultimately maintains behavior: a drink of pop.

Punishment

At the beginning of the section on operant conditioning, we noted that stimuli that follow behavior can have two effects: The future likelihood of occurrence of the response under similar circumstances can increase, or it can decrease. The term *punishment* is used to describe relations of the latter kind. In a technical sense, **punishment** is an operant conditioning process (or procedure) in which a response is followed by a stimulus (**punisher**) and is thereby weakened. Punishment is defined in exactly the same way as reinforcement, with one critical difference: punishment always *weakens* behavior, whereas reinforcement always *strengthens* it. Although punishment is typically unpleasant, subjective effects are irrelevant in determining whether a particular operation constitutes punishment. Like reinforcement, punishment is defined independently of any subjective feelings concerning it. That being the case, the only way to determine whether a particular stimulus is a punisher is to determine whether presenting that stimulus following a response reduces the future probability that the response will recur. If so, the stimulus is a punisher. If, however, responding increases or does not change, the stimulus is not functioning as a punisher.

Consider a case in which a teacher wants to decrease a child's talking out in class. The teacher decides to say in a stern voice, "Stop that, Dale!" immediately after each occurrence of the undesired behavior. Is this procedure punishment? It's impossible to tell without further information. Surely it is *intended* as punishment, but it functions as punishment only if it reduces the rate (or some other dimension) of talking out.

Like reinforcers, punishers can be unconditioned or conditioned, depending on whether their response-suppressing actions depend on a special learning history. Intense stimuli in any modality (e.g., loud sounds, bright lights, or high temperatures) are likely to function as unconditioned punishers; such stimuli can produce physical damage, and there is obvious survival value in not repeating behaviors that produce them. Conditioned punishers acquire their ability to control behavior through being paired with established punishers, and they continue to have this effect only as long as the pairing is maintained. For example, you may establish the verbal stimulus "No" as an effective conditioned punisher for many of your dog's responses by picking up the dog and shaking it while saying "No" when an undesired response occurs. After a few pairings, "No" alone should serve as a punisher. If, however, it is repeatedly delivered alone, this behavioral function will eventually disappear.

To retain symmetry with the terms used to describe reinforcement, punishment can be classified as positive or negative, depending on whether it involves delivering a stimulus (or increasing its intensity) or terminating a stimulus (or decreasing its intensity).[6] An example of positive punishment is a reduction in the rate of a college student's touching a television switch because of the delivery of electric shock through that switch. A reduction in the rate of putting money in a broken vending machine because of a loss of money is an example of negative punishment (plus extinction). Figure 6–3 distinguishes positive and negative punishment and makes clear their relation to positive and negative reinforcement. Table 6–2 lists the symbols used to designate the different kinds of punishing stimuli.

Timeout, which involves the response-dependent institution of a period of time in which one or more positive reinforcers are unavailable, is a form of punishment commonly used in clinical setting. Making a child go to his or her room because of cursing at supper is an example of time-out: because the response of cursing occurred, the child lost access to the reinforcers available at supper (e.g., food and interaction with family members).

Overcorrection, another clinically useful response-deceleration procedure, makes use of the Premack principle to punish responding. Under overcorrection procedures, a person is forced to engage in a low-probability behavior each time a higher probability, and undesired, response occurs. For instance, a teenager may be required to scrub the classroom floor (a low-probability behavior) when observed to spit on it (a higher probability behavior).

A final punishment operation, **response cost,** involves removing a positive reinforcer that a person has earned whenever misbehavior occurs. An example is fining a child five dollars each time she or he fights with a sibling. Note that this operation, and all others, would be punishment only if it weakened behavior.

Punishment procedures have been widely criticized when used to control human behavior. Surely such procedures can evoke aggression and avoidance

---

[6]The distinction between positive and negative punishers is not always made, and some have argued that it is unnecessary and confusing. Of course, the same argument can be made with respect to positive and negative reinforcement (Michael, 1975). Regardless of terminology, the student needs to be aware that behavior can be changed if something is added to an organism's environment, or if something is taken away.

and can be inhumane if poorly conceived. Punishment is nonetheless a ubiquitous part of life and must be considered in attempts to explain behavior. Why, for instance, don't you habitually walk into objects around you? Because you've been punished (with tissue damage), for doing so in the past. Why don't you talk loudly and fidget at church, or strike everyone who displeases you? The answer is the same: a history of punishment. Adapting to one's environment requires failing to repeat responses with adverse consequences, as well as repeating responses with beneficial consequences. Punishment produces the former outcome, reinforcement the latter.

Laboratory studies have revealed a great deal about the variables that determine the degree of response suppression produced by punishment (e.g., Azrin & Holz, 1966). We know, for example, that maximum response suppression occurs when:

1. The punisher is delivered immediately after the response. As delay in the delivery of the punisher increases, relative response suppression decreases.
2. The punisher follows every occurrence of the response. As a rule, intermittent punishment is less effective than continuous (i.e., FR 1) punishment.
3. The punisher is initially presented at high intensity. Organisms eventually adapt to low-intensity punishers, which lose their ability to suppress responding.
4. An alternative to the punished response is available. Obviously, only responses that occur at some strength can be punished. Typically, these responses are operant behaviors maintained by specifiable reinforcers. If the response to be punished is the only one that is effective in producing this reinforcer, it will be harder to suppress than if some alternative response that produces the same reinforcer is available.

Many attempts to use punishment are ineffective because they involve weak, delayed, and intermittent punishers and offer no alternative to the punished response. Consider, for example, attempts to reduce illegal drug sales through court-imposed fines and jail sentences. Would you expect them to be effective punishers?

Rule-Governed Behavior

Behavior that is controlled by direct exposure to reinforcement (or punishment) is called **contingency-shaped behavior.** This term emphasizes the importance of stimulus–response–stimulus relations (contingencies) in controlling behavior. Operant behavior, as we have discussed it to this point, is contingency-shaped.

Unlike the behavior of other organisms, human behavior can be rule-governed, as well as contingency-shaped (Skinner, 1969). **Rule-governed behavior** is behavior controlled by the description of relations among responses and other events, rather than actual exposure to these contingencies. Envision a situation in which you're visiting a friend who lives on a farm. You're going for a walk and come to a low electric fence around a hog lot. Your friend says, "Don't touch that electric fence; it's hot and will knock your socks off." What do you do? In all likelihood, you avoid the fence. Your friend's statement describes a contingent relation—touch the fence and get a strong shock ("your socks knocked off")—and you behave appropriately by not touching the fence.

Whether a person follows a particular rule depends in large part on her or his prior experience with respect to the rule giver and the accuracy of similar rules provided in the past. We learn through operant conditioning to follow rules, or to refrain from following them. For instance, a parent says to a child, "Don't touch the stove, it's hot and you'll get burned." The child doesn't follow the rule, touches the stove, and gets burned. As a result of the correspondence between real and described contingencies, the future likelihood of rule following increases. If, however, the child touches the stove and does not get burned, the future likelihood of rule following decreases.

Rules can be self-generated as well as provided by others. Assume that you are in an airport in a foreign country, which we'll call Xanadu, and you are hungry. There is a vending machine that's getting lots of use by other travelers, and you have a pocketful of Xanadu change. The only problem is that you can't read Xanadu, and the machine has no pictures, just labels in Xanadu script. You can't tell what kind of food is available or what it costs. One way to learn is through trial and error (i.e., exposure to contingencies): you go to the machine, then put in money and push buttons until something happens. Eventually, if you have enough time and money, appropriate behavior will emerge: you'll learn how to obtain a desired food. This will occur with less effort if a person skilled in the English and Xanadu languages comes along and says, "You can get rice soup, plain tofu, and chicken feet from that machine. Each costs five cellops [a Xanadu coin which she shows you]. Push the top button for soup, the middle for tofu, and the bottom for feet." No problem. Go for the feet.

Unfortunately, there aren't many people conversant in English and Xanadu. That being the case, your best bet is to watch other travelers operate the machine and, on the basis of your observations, formulate your own rule. You see that everyone inserts a particular kind of coin (which you call a little round one), and that the food they receive depends on the button they push. Hence, you generate the rule, "To get soup, put in a little round coin, then push the top button," and you behave accordingly.

Some psychologists, Albert Bandura (e.g., 1977) and other social-learning theorists being among them, regard one person's imitation of another's behavior as involving a special kind of learning. They term it **observation learning.** Observation learning has three important features:

1. The learning occurs in one trial. A person need observe a model only once to behave in the same way.
2. The observer may emit the modeled response long after observing it, and in the absence of the model.
3. Behavior by a model that leads to a positive outcome is more likely than other behavior to be emitted by an observer. "Vicarious reinforcement" is assumed to be responsible for this phenomenon.

Although some social-learning theorists assume that observational learning cannot be accounted for in terms of operant and respondent conditioning principles, this is not the case (Deguchi, 1984). Observational learning appears to involve a complex operant history in which a person is initially reinforced for mimicking a model's actions. You've undoubtably seen parents attempting to get their child to behave as they do (say, "Mama," or shake the rattle). They typically succeed, and generalized imitation develops in most people as operant behavior. Over time, self-generated rules come to play an important role in observational learning. Such learning often serves a person well, for it provides a rapid means of behavior change.

Rule-governed behavior is of crucial importance to humans because it enables us to behave effectively in novel situations, and to learn without exposure to the harmful consequences of our behavior. However, rule-governed and contingency-shaped behaviors are not necessarily identical; a person whose behavior is controlled by exposure to a verbal description of a contingency of reinforcement (or punishment) may not respond in the same way as a person who has actually been exposed to that contingency. Moreover, rules can be faulty, fostering behaviors inappropriate to the situation at hand.

Verbal statements that describe contingencies of reinforcement (or punishment) are termed **contingency-specifying stimuli** (**CSSs**) (Schlinger & Blakely, 1987). A CSS can control behavior as an S^D, or as an EO. In other cases, however, CSSs affect behavior by altering the function of other stimuli and, thus, the strength of the relations among these stimuli and behavior. Assume that you are the subject in an experiment. You sit facing a panel with a green light, a red light, a counter that can be incremented and decremented, and a lever. The experimenter comes in and tells you, "You can earn points only by pressing the lever when the green light is on. You will lose points for pressing at any other time. When the session ends, you will receive a dollar for each point on the counter."

These instructions are contingency-specifying stimuli; they spell out the relation between antecedent stimuli, responses, and consequences. Moreover, in most people, they would control behavior by (1) establishing point gain as a reinforcer; (2) establishing point loss as a punisher; and (3) establishing the green light as a stimulus that evokes lever pressing. The experimenter's instructions in this case serve as function-altering stimuli: they alter the ability of other stimuli to control behavior. They do so, of course, because the person whose behavior they control has a special history with respect to verbal statements and the consequences of behaving in accordance with them.

As our brief discussion of rule-governed behavior indicates, operantly conditioned verbal behavior occupies an important place in the repertoire of most humans. Further discussion of verbal behavior and its unique characteristics is provided in Chapter 7.

The Importance of Operant Conditioning

To an even greater extent than respondent conditioning, operant conditioning allows the behavior of an organism to adapt to its environment. Through operant conditioning, behaviors that produce food, water, sex, a comfortable environment, and a host of other objects and events of obvious biological significance come to be repeated. So, too, are responses that prevent or terminate exposure to harmful stimuli. If the environment is static, the same set of responses will persist, but if the environment changes, behavior will also change. The extent to which behavioral plasticity occurs varies with the species; the sensitivity of most human behavior to operant conditioning is very great. It is this sensitivity that accounts for many of the behavioral differences that we observe in people: They have experienced different behavior–environment interactions and hence have developed different repertoires.

Operant conditioning provides for behavioral plasticity, but it does not automatically ensure that a person will acquire and emit responses that are deemed desirable by other people, or that ensure his or her success in any regard. Some environments foster behaviors that are, in the long run, harmful to an individual, and to society at large. Drug abuse, child abuse, robbery, racism, sexism, and a host of other vexing problems involve operant behaviors, troublesome patterns of responding that are primarily acquired and maintained because of their short-term consequences. Understanding the role of short-term consequences in these problems is a first step toward their treatment and prevention.

Unfortunately, adequately understanding human behavior is no easy task. The basic principles of operant (and respondent) conditioning are relatively simple, and it is easy to see how these principles apply to the behavior of humans and nonhumans alike in controlled laboratory settings. Applying these principles to the behavior of humans in their natural environment is a more difficult task. Practical and ethical considerations make the controlled study of humans difficult. Moreover, within a short time of their birth, humans characteristically have a rich and complicated history of behavior–environment interactions. By virtue of this history, a given stimulus often has more than one behavioral function, and these functions can change across time or situations. Thus, it can be difficult to determine precisely the variables that control a particular behavior in a given individual. Nonetheless, psychologists know, in principle, the kinds of variables that do control human learning and, as explained in the balance of this text, can offer plausible if not proven explanations of a very wide range of human activities.

Study Questions

1. Define learning and discuss the point about the evolution in humans of the capacity to learn.

2. What are the two main reasons that learning is of interest to psychologists? Can you think of any others?

3. Be able to describe unconditioned reflexes using the terms *unconditional stimulus* and *unconditional response*. Provide some common examples.

4. Describe habituation. Should it be considered a form of learning?

5. Be able to describe respondent conditioning (including two other names) as stim-

ulus–stimulus pairing, using the terms *conditioned reflex, conditional stimulus, neutral stimulus,* and *conditional response.*

6. What are the three steps of respondent conditioning?

7. What are higher order conditioning, respondent extinction, and respondent stimulus generalization and discrimination? It might be helpful to incorporate these aspects of respondent conditioning into the same example.

8. State the importance of respondent conditioning, especially in humans.

9. What is operant behavior and how is it different from respondent behavior?

10. Be able to describe reinforcement both as a procedure and as a process (i.e., a procedure and an outcome), and to provide the traditional distinction between positive and negative reinforcement. Provide an example in which both positive and negative reinforcement work on the behavior of two persons.

11. Distinguish between unconditioned and conditioned reinforcers. What is the point about immediacy of reinforcement?

12. What effects do motivational variables produce?

13. Describe operant extinction (procedure and outcome) and the phenomenon of extinction-induced bursting. Give an example of this phenomenon.

14. What is a schedule of reinforcement? What behavioral characteristics are determined by reinforcement schedules? How does behavior reinforced intermittently differ from behavior reinforced continuously?

15. What is stimulus control and why, from an evolutionary perspective, is it important? Describe the process of discrimination (including the operation of differential reinforcement and the outcome).

16. What is operant stimulus generalization (you might want to refer back to respondent stimulus generalization), and how does it contribute to conceptual behavior? What is a concept? Is it behavior or something else? Give an example.

17. Describe the operant three-term contingency. What is meant by the term *contingency?*

18. What is shaping, and how is it used to produce new operants? How is extinction actively used in the shaping procedure? Provide examples.

19. Define and give examples of punishment, and list the four variables that lead to maximum response suppression. Be able to describe time-out as an example of one type of punishment.

20. What is rule-governed behavior? How does it differ from contingency-shaped behavior? Why is it crucial in the chapter on learning? Why is rule-governed behavior crucial for humans?

21. What is observational learning? Is it a third type of learning? (What are the other two?)

22. State the importance of operant conditioning. Consider the concepts of evolution, behavioral plasticity, and the difficulty of studying operant behavior.

Mazur, J. E. (1986). *Learning and Behavior.* Englewood Cliffs, NJ: Prentice–Hall.

Several books provide a clear and careful presentation of basic learning principles, and this is one of them. Two advantages of this text are its relative recency and the level at which it is written, which is suitable for undergraduates.

Reynolds, G. S. (1975). *A Primer of Operant Conditioning.* Glenview, IL: Scott, Foresman.

In his preface, Reynolds states that "this primer presents a concise but detailed account of the theory and principles of operant conditioning" (p. vii). It does exactly that and is a superb source for anyone who wants to learn the essential facts concerning operant conditioning.

CHAPTER 7

Language, Consciousness, and Memory

This chapter provides a behavioral overview of language and of two language-related topics: consciousness and memory. Because these topics have been favorites of cognitive psychologists, a cognitive view of each is also briefly considered.

Language

The term **language** has a wide variety of usages. Traditionally, language has been construed as the use of words and symbols to communicate information, and to represent or express internal events, such as thoughts and feelings. The famous French philosopher René Descartes believed that language provided evidence that humans had self-conscious souls, whereas nonhumans, which gave no evidence of language (a debatable contention, as Sidebar 7-1 indicates) were automata without self-conscious souls. For Descartes, human language was innate, creative, and voluntary and expressed rational thought, but non-human vocal signals communicated only primitive bodily states like hunger or fear (Leahey, 1987). The Cartesian view of language as a vehicle for the expression of internal events, such as thoughts, ideas, needs, wants, or reasons, has persisted to the present. This approach has caused problems, in large part because the internal events have no independent existence and are inferred from the very language that is said to express them.

Fully aware of these problems, Leonard Bloomfield, in his 1933 book entitled *Language*, contended that the facts of language are observable phenomena that one can study profitably without inferring mental factors. Moreover, Bloomfield emphasized that the form of language—that is, the verbal behavior of the speaker—results from interacting with other people, and that the meaning of any utterance is to be found in the circumstances in which it occurs, not inside the speaker. This is of course a functional analysis. In 1957, B. F. Skinner dramatically extended the functional analysis of language with *Verbal Behavior*, a book that views "language" as operant behavior.

Despite the efforts of Bloomfield and Skinner, most attempts to understand language have focused largely on its structure. Noam Chomsky is well known for his structural approach to language. Chomsky, in the Cartesian tradition, has argued steadfastly that language is an innate reflection of the rational human mind. Therefore, much can be learned about the mind by discerning the structure and rules of language (grammar). It is informative to contrast Chomsky's structural theory with the functional approach favored by most behavior analysts.

Chomsky's Analysis of Language

In the 1950s and 1960s, Chomsky (1957, 1965) developed a theory of language acquisition that emphasizes innate factors. He suggested (1) that humans are born with an innate capacity to acquire language, and (2) that, to develop language, children need only exposure to the language of others. The elements of his theory follow.

Linguistic Units

For Chomsky, the essential linguistic unit is the sentence, which can be analyzed on two levels. One is the **deep structure,** which is thought by some to

---

Sidebar 7-1
Language in Apes

Philosophers have long discussed the possibility of teaching language to apes. For example, the French philosopher Julien Offray de la Mettrie (1709–1751) suggested that apes might be taught language and thereby transformed into "little gentlemen" (Leahey, 1987). In one of the first documented efforts, researchers attempted to teach a chimpanzee named Viki to talk (Hayes, 1952). After six years of training, Viki could say only three or four words. Viki would be no "little gentleman" or, in her case, no "little lady." Real progress came when researchers taught apes *American Sign Language* (Ameslan, or ASL), which is used extensively by hearing-impaired people.

In one project, Beatrice T. and R. Allen Gardner acquired a 10-month-old chimpanzee named Washoe (after Washoe County, Nevada, where the research was conducted). The Gardners were primarily interested in showing that chimpanzees could acquire a human language, given the appropriate medium (i.e., ASL), and then in comparing the language skills of the chimpanzee with those of children (Gardner & Gardner, 1978). Washoe lived in a home environment similar to that enjoyed by a normal human child.

Washoe lived in separate quarters, but most of her day was spent interacting with human caretakers. ASL was used for all interactions.

After approximately four years of training, Washoe acquired a 132-sign vocabulary. She learned to ask for rewards and to describe features of the environment, and she also showed generalization of both skills. For example, Washoe would sign "dog" when she saw a dog she had never seen before, or a picture of a dog. Moreover, in some instances, the resulting sign was a novel combination of two previously separate signs. When shown a duck, for which Washoe had not learned a sign, she made the signs for "water" and "bird." Other sequences emerged, such as "open drink" (for water faucet), "listen dog" (at the sound of barking), and "more tickle" (asking her companion to resume tickling her).

Did Washoe acquire language? The question is moot and depends critically on how language is defined and, consequently, on how an organism must behave to demonstrate it. Wahoe's behavior was remarkable in its own right, regardless of how we label it.

exist in the brain (Owens, 1984). A deep structure provides the basic meaning of a sentence. Deep structures are formed according to **phrase structure rules.** For example, any sentence must have at least a noun and a verb; the noun may be accompanied by other words such as adjectives or articles, and the verb by adverbs, prepositional phrases and so on. For instance, "The man hit the ball" comprises a noun phrase ("the man") and a verb phrase ("hit the ball"). The noun phrase consists of a noun and an article, and the verb phrase consists of a verb ("hit") and a noun phrase ("the ball").

The second level is the **surface structure,** or the actual form of a spoken sentence. A surface structure "expresses" the meaning embedded in its corresponding deep structure. Thus, the deep structure "The house fell down—the house was old" might be spoken as "The old house fell down." How does the deep structure become a surface structure? A deep structure is changed into a surface structure according to **transformation rules and operations.** They serve to create different sentence types, to reorder words, to select the correct verb form, and so on (Owens, 1984). According to Chomsky, these rules allow a child to produce sentences from deep structures even though the sentences have never been heard or spoken before.

There is no direct evidence that deep structures exist. They are not physical entities that are measured, but hypothetical entities that are inferred. Moreover, the role of formal rules in language is moot. Although knowledge of the rules of grammar may facilitate language, humans can and clearly do speak appropriately (i.e., formulate good sentences) without knowing (i.e., being able to describe) such rules (Skinner, 1974). Although it might be argued that, in such cases, rules are somehow used "unconsciously," this hypothesis is untestable and hence meaningless.

Development

Chomsky has suggested that innate factors play an important role in language acquisition. He posited that each child is "prewired" with a **language acquisition device** (LAD), which contains a collection of basic information common to all languages. When the LAD is exposed to the language of others, hypotheses and rules are formulated that apply to the child's native language (Figure 7–1). These rules are then used to transform deep structures to appropriate surface structures.

But Chomsky's LAD is not universally accepted. As Owens (1984) noted:

> The notion of a language acquisition device is too simplified and provides an inadequate explanation. To assume that the ability to use language is innate does little to facilitate our understanding of the actual process of language development. (p. 66)

Figure 7-1. The language acquisition device (LAD) hypothesized by Chomsky.

Obviously, the LAD is a hypothetical construct: it is a nonphysical entity inferred from observed behavior. The LAD provides a fundamentally inadequate explanation of language.

Structural approaches to language, like Chomsky's, emphasize topics such as syntax (grammar), phonetics (the study of the constituent sounds of words), and semantics (the study of word meaning). Research and theorizing in these areas has revealed much about *what* patterns of language characteristically occur and *what* grammatical and syntactical rules describe those patterns. Very little has been revealed about *why* certain patterns develop, that is, about the actual variables that produce the complex behaviors subsumed by the term *language*. Such questions are better answered by a functional analysis, which treats language as behavior and searches for its causes in the interaction of empirical variables. A behavioral interpretation of verbal behavior is such an analysis.

A Behavioral Analysis of Language

B. F. Skinner (e.g., 1957) and most other behavior analysts (e.g., Salzinger, 1978) have treated language first of all as *behavior,* to be explained by appealing to environmental influences in concert with physiological and genetic variables. From this perspective, language neither exists apart from behavior (i.e., speaking, writing, listening, reading, and signing), nor represents ideas, concepts, or thoughts. Instead, it is simply a special class of behavior that is controlled by the same kinds of variables as nonverbal behavior. For these reasons, Skinner used the term *verbal behavior* to refer to what is commonly termed *language*. The unique and defining aspect of **verbal behavior** is that it is reinforced through the mediation of other persons who are trained (though not formally) to mediate and reinforce such behavior (Skinner, 1957). Verbal behavior is like nonverbal operant behavior in that it is learned as a result of its effects on the environment. However, verbal behavior differs from nonverbal operant behavior in that its effects on the environment are indirect: they are mediated by other persons. For example, you can get a glass of water by getting up, walking to the sink, and turning the faucet; the reinforcement for these actions is the water-filled glass. Or you can say, "Please bring me a glass of water," which produces the same outcome, but through the actions of another person.

Although the fact is rarely recognized, verbal behavior is first and foremost social behavior: it exists primarily because of its effects on listeners, collectively called the **verbal community.** Listeners perform two functions with respect to the acquisition of verbal behavior. First, they condition verbal behavior in new speakers (i.e., children). Second, they train new speakers to become listeners, that is, to be able to condition verbal behavior in others. In this way, a verbal community, and the linguistic conventions it supports, is transmitted from generation to generation.

Verbal Units

Because verbal behavior is controlled largely by its consequences, it is operant behavior. Like other kinds of operant behavior, verbal behavior can be classified according to (1) the antecedent variables that evoke it and (2) its consequences. Skinner (1957) described five general units of verbal behavior:

Mand. A mand is a verbal response that is evoked by a motivational variable (e.g., food deprivation) because in the past it was reinforced by a type of reinforcer related to that motivational variables. For example, a child who says, "Candy" because he or she "wants" (e.g., is deprived of) candy is emitting a mand. The request "Candy" occurs because the child is hungry, and the request has in the past procured candy from sympathetic adults. In general, mands identify the reinforcer that the person desires; such as "Bring me a beer," "Take the trash out," and "Just let me hear some of that rock-and-roll music."

Note that mands require the presence of a "listener," a person who provides (or mediates) the reinforcer. The relation among motivational variables, the listener, the mand, and the reinforcer is represented in Table 7–1.

Tact. A tact "describes" objects or events in the environment. It is evoked by some physical characteristic of the internal or external environment. For example, a child who is asked, "What is that?" might respond with "Chair" in the presence of a chair or "Dog" in the presence of a dog. A sick child who is asked, "How does your stomach feel?" might say, "It really hurts." The reinforcement for a tact is typically generalized conditioned reinforcement, such as "Thank you" or "Good boy." The tact relationship is described in Table 7–1. (We will return to the tact relation when we discuss how the verbal community teaches us to describe private events.)

Intraverbal. An intraverbal is a verbal response that is evoked by verbal discriminative stimuli. For example, if a speaker hears "red, white, and _____," she might very well say, "Blue." Other examples of intraverbal

Table 7-1
Basic Verbal Operants

Functional unit	Evoked by	Response	Reinforcer
Mand	Motivational variable + listener (Lack of food + mother)	Mand ("Food please!")	S^R (Food)
Tact	Physical characteristic (Car + presence of dad)	Tact ("Car")	S^r ("Good")
Intraverbal	Spoken stimulus (Teacher asks, "What is four plus four?")	Intraverbal ("Eight!")	S^r ("Correct!")
Textual response	Written stimulus (Written word *dog*)	Textual ("Dog")	S^r ("Right!")
Echoic response	Spoken stimulus ("Say, 'Ma-ma.' ")	Echoic ("Ma-ma")	S^r ("Good")

behavior might be saying, "White" to "Black," "Off" to "The opposite of on is
_____," or "Four" to "Two plus two equals _____." Longer sequences of
intraverbal responses are evoked by questions such as, "Tell me about your
vacation" or "What did she say?" Sophisticated intraverbal responding is developed through a long and complex conditioning history.

Textual. A textual response is evoked by the written word (see Table 7–1).
Such behavior is a part of reading (reading also involves many other reactions to
written words). For example, a child is emitting textual behavior when he says,
"Dog" when shown the written word *dog,* or "Candy" when shown the word
candy. Textual behavior may be "out loud" (overt) or "silent" (covert).

Echoic. An echoic response is evoked by an auditory verbal discriminative
stimulus. Unlike intraverbal behavior, the behavior and the discriminative stimulus "match." In other words, echoic behavior is verbal imitation. Echoic behavior
is evident when a child says, "Candy" after an adult says, "Candy." The reinforcement for echoic behavior may come from another listener (e.g., "Good!"), or it
may come "automatically" when the sound of the match between stimulus and
response "sounds good" or "sounds right."

Meaning

The essential element of the behavioral view is that verbal behavior is classified according to its function. A given word of the same form can have many
different functions, depending on the circumstances in which it occurs. Moreover, the function of an utterance is its "meaning." Suppose you hear someone
say, "Fire." What does it mean? The answer depends on the variables responsible for its emission, that is, *on why it was spoken.* For example, if it was shouted by
an army officer to induce his squad to shoot, then "Fire" is a mand. If a child
standing in front of a burning log says, "Fire," then "Fire" is probably a tact. If it
is someone's reply to the question, "What did early humans discover by rubbing
two sticks together?" then "Fire" is an intraverbal. The "meaning" of the response "Fire" cannot be discerned by its form or by the way it sounds. Instead,
its meaning depends on why the speaker said it.

Multiple Causation

It is important to point out that any given verbal response, whether a single
word or a combination of words (e.g., a sentence or paragraph), usually has
multiple functions and is under the control of more than one antecedent stimulus. This means that verbal behavior is not simply a linear sequence of stimuli
and responses. For example, the response "Fire," by Speaker B to the question,
"What is that?" by Speaker A is determined not only by the presence of a fire
(tact) but also by the question (mand) of Speaker A. Moreover, Speaker B's
response is partly influenced by his or her past experience with Speaker A, for
instance, whether Speaker A has always praised Speaker B or has threatened
bad things for incorrect answers. Identifying the complex of variables responsible for verbal behavior is the goal of a functional analysis.

Verbal behavior, like most nonverbal behavior, arises through the interplay of maturation and learning. Consider babbling. Evidence suggests that all children begin babbling at about the same age. Even deaf children with deaf parents babble, even though neither they nor their parents can hear the sounds produced (Lenneberg, Rebelsky, & Nichols, 1965). That babbling occurs at approximately the same age suggests that innate (maturational) factors play a role in language development.

The refinement of babbling into functional verbal behavior depends on operant conditioning, which involves environmental variables. The importance of such variables is illustrated by research showing that social consequences can increase the frequency of vocalizations in infants. For example, Rheingold, Gewirtz, and Ross (1959) reported that the vocalizations of three-month-old infants increased when they were followed by experimenter smiles, "tsk" sounds by the experimenter, and light touches to the infant's abdomen. Whitehurst (1972) showed that two-year-old children learned two-word sequences (of the adjective–noun form) through a combination of imitation and reinforcement. Interestingly, studies have shown that the proper use of syntax can also be trained and, just as important, that the new skills transfer to the child's everyday environment (e.g., Hester & Hendrickson, 1977).

These and other studies indicate that environmental variables, acting through operant conditioning, play a critical role in the development of verbal behavior. This development can be divided into prespeech (prelinguistic) development and speech development, each comprising several stages.

Stages of Prespeech Development

Prespeech development consists primarily of maturational changes in vocal behavior and ends at about one year of age, when formal words are emitted.[1] Language scholars (e.g., Eisenson, Auer, & Irwin, 1963) have described several stages of such development:

Stage 1: Undifferentiated crying. This is reflexive crying and is elicited by a variety of stimuli, including sudden loud noises, strong odors and tastes, discomfort from hunger or pain, and loss of support.

Stage 2: Differentiated crying. In this stage, crying becomes a learned behavior because it produces many reinforcers (e.g., food and termination of pain). The reinforcers vary, and as a result, crying assumes slightly different characteristics, depending on why it occurs. For instance, parents report a difference between "hunger crying" and crying that occurs for other reasons. All of these different "types" of crying can probably be classified as mands. For example, pain-evoked

---

[1]It is important to remember that, from a functional standpoint, verbal behavior may exist before the appearance of recognizable words. For example, if an infant emits a particular form of grunt when it is hungry and has received food in the past for doing so, the grunt is a mand equivalent in function to "Food please!" Nevertheless, the verbal community requires speakers to adopt standard forms (words).

crying occurs because the pain is reliably relieved or terminated. It is as if the infant is saying, "Please stop the pain." From the standpoint of language development, differentiated crying is important because it is perhaps the first step in bringing vocal behavior under the control of consequences provided by the verbal community.

Stage 3: Cooing. At about one month of age, infants begin making vowel sounds. The *oo* sound occurs at especially high frequency.

Stage 4: Babbling. At about three or four months of age, the child begins making sounds that approximate those that occur in speech. The frequency of babbled sounds peaks at between nine and twelve months of age. Babbling resembles speech in that it seems to occur in sentencelike sequences with rising and falling intonation. This resemblance to speech often leads parents to remark that their children are talking in a language all their own. As noted above, babbling is sensitive to its consequences.

Stage 5: Lallation. At about the sixth months, infants begin repeating sounds and syllables that they themselves have made.

Stage 6: Echolalia. When 9 or 10 months old, the infant begins to imitate (echo) sounds made by others. Lallation and echolalia are crucial because they are an important means by which the infant acquires a large repertoire of sounds (Eisenson *et al.*, 1963). Ultimately, these sounds are elements of the more sophisticated language of adults.

Linguistic Development

Structural analyses, which frequently include normative data, are not without merit. For example, it is informative to know the average sequence of development of words and sentences in a given community and the respective ages at which they occur.

Single Words

The first single-word utterances occur at about 10 to 13 months of age. They are often nouns and consist of a single consonant–vowel (CV) unit, or a series of such units (CVCV). The consonants are usually **stops,** which are produced by the lips (e.g., *b* and *p*), or **nasals** produced at the front of the mouth (e.g., *m*). The first vowel voiced is usually the soft *a* sound in *father*. The first word uttered is often *dada, papa,* or *mama.*

Although such words are characteristically involved in asking for (mands) or naming (tacts) objects in the environment, some researchers suggest that single words sometimes have more complex meanings for the child (de Villiers & de Villiers, 1978). Such words are called *holophrases.* For example, *papa* may mean that the child wants her father, or perhaps that some object in the environment belongs to her father. Recognize, however, that inferring what a child "means" when a given word is voiced is difficult and requires a consideration of its function and the context in which it was spoken.

At 18 to 24 months of age, the child begins to speak two-word combinations that consist of nouns, verbs, and adjectives (Sroufe & Cooper, 1988). Words are included that are essential in inferring the meaning of the sentence. The infant's mand "Want milk" is roughly equivalent to (i.e., has the same meaning as) an adult's mand "I want some milk, please;" the child's mand "Where block?" is equivalent to the adult's mand "Where is my block?" Because the economy of words resembles a telegraphed message, these two-word combinations are termed **telegraphic speech.** Two-word combinations are used in a variety of situations. Brown (1973) reported a number of two-word utterances that, in addition to naming or asking for objects, indicated possession ("Mommy car"), specified a location ("Mommy home"), or declared nonexistence ("Dog away"), all tacts.

The two-word stage gives way to more complex sentences. Consider how much there is to acquire. Articles, adverbs, prepositional phrases, possessive nouns, and verb tenses all must be mastered. Verb tenses are particularly difficult for the child learning English, which has many irregular verbs. Subtle but important features of speech, such as stressing particular words and intonation, become more pronounced as utterances grow longer. The **mean length of utterance (MLU)**, which increases as new language skills permit longer and more complex sentences (Brown, 1973), is one useful index of overall language development. For example, Brown reported a collection of stages in multiword development that were associated with increases in MLU.

Children do not progress through the developmental stages described above at the same rate, and the stages can overlap. Most children do, however, pass through these stages in the order described.

Linguistic Input

For theorists who stress innate factors in language development (e.g., Chomsky), the environment is primarily the source of acquired sounds. Language develops automatically, but the specific sounds acquired depend on what the child hears. This theory explains why Chinese children grow up speaking Chinese and French children grow up speaking French. By contrast, a functional approach views the environment as having a far more active role in the acquisition of language. Parents certainly reinforce verbal behavior in language-learning children, and an extensive amount of research shows that they speak very differently to language-learning children than to other people (de Villiers & de Villiers, 1978; Hoff-Ginsburg & Shatz, 1982). Even other children speak differently to language-learning children than to adults (Shatz & Gelman, 1973). In particular, the utterances of adults to young children are short, syntactically and semantically simple, well formed, and repetitive (Brown & Bellugi, 1964). Interestingly, a mother's utterances become even shorter when her child begins to emit words (Phillips, 1973; Lord, 1975.) As a rule, adults' utterances to language-learning children are clearly pronounced, with distinct pauses between them and an exaggerated singsong intonation (deVilliers & deVilliers, 1978). This intonation may partially explain why infants' babbling often has a singsong quality.

The Physiology of Speech

Verbal behavior is not limited to vocal behavior (speech), but producing and responding to speech does play a critical role in human interactions. Speech is produced by a portion of the human anatomy collectively called the **vocal apparatus,** which includes the lips, mouth, tongue, nasal cavity, pharynx, larynx, and diaphragm. Major parts of the vocal apparatus are shown in Figure 7–2. To produce a sound, air expelled from the lungs contacts the larynx. As a result, the vocal folds of the larynx vibrate to form short puffs of air into a tone. This tone is further modified in the vocal tract, which includes the pharynx, the mouth, and the nasal cavity.

The pharynx[2] serves as a combined opening for the windpipe (which goes to the lungs) and the gullet (which goes to the stomach) and is also the anchor for the base of the tongue. During speech, the muscles in the walls of the pharynx and the base of the tongue move continuously, constantly varying the dimensions of the pharynx and the sound produced. The actions of the pharynx are like those of

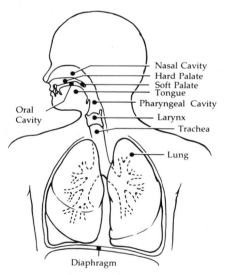

Oral
Cavity

Nasal Cavity
Hard Palate
Soft Palate
Tongue
Pharyngeal Cavity
Larynx
Trachea

Lung

Diaphragm

Figure 7-2. The vocal apparatus. (From *Language Development: An Introduction* by R. E. Owens, 1984, p. 158. Copyright 1984 by Charles E. Merrill. Reproduced with permission.)

[2]Comparisons of adult humans with monkeys, apes, and human infants demonstrate the importance of the human pharnyx (see Figure 7–2). Monkeys and apes have a limited ability to vocalize. They can only vary the shape of their mouths and there is almost no movement of their pharynx. Human infants' ability to vocalize is limited by an undeveloped pharynx in which the larynx sits high in the throat, permitting the infant to swallow and breathe at the same time without choking. By the time infants reach the babbling stage at about three months, the base of the tongue and the larynx have begun to descend into the throat and thus to enlarge the pharyngeal region. It is only then that human infants are able to make speech sounds like those of adults (Campbell, 1985).

a pipe organ with numerous pipes of different lengths and diameters, each making a particular tone (Campbell, 1985). To produce some sounds, such as *m* and *n*, the nasal cavity is closed off from, or opened to, the vocal tract; the mouth (including the tongue, lips, and jaw), too, can be manipulated to produce a variety of sounds.

The Brain

By the early 1900s, scientists had identified several regions of the brain that are implicated in language production and comprehension. Much of this information was obtained through studying people with brain injury. Since then, other methods have been developed to study brain function (e.g., electrical brain stimulation), but study of the effects of brain damage remains important.

Paul Broca, a French scientist of the mid-1800s, demonstrated that certain areas of the brain are associated with language. He discovered that damage to an area on the left side of the frontal lobe, which is now called **Broca's area** (see Figure 7–3), produces speech disorders such as **aphasia** (an impairment of language production or comprehension). The speech of persons with damage to Broca's area (e.g., from stroke) is slow and laborious and is often without articles, adverbs, and adjectives. For this reason, the speech is often described as *telegraphic;* the words used tend to be in the correct order and have clear meaning, but speech is reduced to its rudiments. Hence, the request "I would please like to have some milk" may become instead "Want milk." Broca found that damage to the left side of the brain produced aphasia, but damage to the corresponding part of the right side did not. For some functions, one side of the brain is vastly more important than the other.

A German scientist, Karl Wernicke, identified a particular type of aphasia and, in so doing, linked language to another area of the brain. **Wernicke's aphasia** results from damage to a localized region in the left cortex. This region, called **Wernicke's area,** is located between the primary auditory cortex and a structure called the **angular gyrus** (see Figure 7–3), which probably mediates between the visual and auditory centers of the brain (Geschwind, 1979). Although speech is grammatically correct in patients with Wernicke's aphasia, it is meaningless or inappropriate to current circumstances. Moreover, those afflicted do not comprehend what they hear.

Damage to the angular gyrus results in another type of aphasia, called **anomic aphasia.** In this disorder, language comprehension and production are intact, but nouns are often omitted, substituted, or paraphrased (Beaumont, 1983). In some cases, lesions of the angular gyrus functionally disconnect the systems involved in auditory and written language. The result is patients who speak and understand speech, but who have trouble with written language.

From the study of aphasia, scientists concluded that Broca's area, Wernicke's area, and the angular gyrus, among other areas of the cortex, must be important in the production and comprehension of normal speech. Karl Wernicke first proposed a theoretical model of the brain's role in language production that is, in principle, still accepted today. According to this model, an utterance (actually a neural transmission) arises in Wernicke's area; from there, it

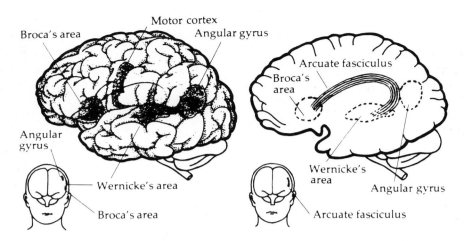

Figure 7-3. Areas of the brain that are involved in speech. (From *Humankind Emerging*, 5th ed. by B. G. Campbell, 1985, p. 356. Copyright 1985 by Bernard G. Campbell. Reprinted by permission of Scott, Foresman & Company.)

moves to Broca's area, which determines its vocal structure; and finally, the adjacent area of the motor cortex is stimulated, which activates the appropriate muscles of the mouth, lips, larynx, and pharynx. Though informative, this model does not describe how or why language develops.

Why Is Language Important?

Verbal behavior is important for phylogenetic as well as ontogenetic reasons. Although we can only speculate about the phylogenetic functions of verbal behavior, its ontogenetic functions are more obvious. Verbal behavior has important and irreplaceable social functions. People involved in business, teaching, science, entertainment, medicine, and politics all rely heavily on spoken and written words to conduct their daily affairs. Imagine how difficult life would be if you were unable to tell a doctor your symptoms, if your teacher could not explain a difficult concept, or if your friend could not give you directions to an important destination.

Language is involved in asking for things ("Please give me that pencil"), describing the environment ("The book by Hemingway is in the store on Main Street"), and reading ("Oranges are high in vitamin C"). The advantages for the speaker are obvious: many important reinforcers, including information about the world, can be obtained through the use of language. Language also has an important function for the listener, and it is this important characteristic that we will now discuss.

Rules

People frequently describe relationships observed in the environment. The relations described may involve only stimuli ("When the resistor is red, it is very hot") or stimuli and responses ("If you arrive on time, you will receive a bonus"). Descriptions of relations between stimuli, or between stimuli and behavior, are termed **rules** (Skinner, 1969). For Skinner, rules involve a speaker's behavior; they are spoken (or written) and thus can be observed and measured. Moreover, they constitute a physical stimulus (usually auditory) for a listener. Contrast these rules with those posited by Chomsky (e.g., transformational rules inherent in a hypothetical LAD), which cannot be directly observed or measured.

The important characteristic of rules is that listeners can learn from (i.e., have their behavior altered by) them. For example, a person can acquire new behavior, with very little effort, through rules such as "Turn the computer off by pushing the green button," "To get to Main Street, turn left on Maple," or "If you touch that wire, you will get a shock." Without the rules, the listener would have to learn the behaviors through direct exposure to the environment (imag-

Communication is an important element in most activities. Here, communication among defensive players has failed, and the opposing team scores in spectacular fashion. (Photo courtesy of Neil Rankin.)

ine how difficult it would be if you had to find Main Street without rules). In a sense, rules mimic the effects of learning through contact with the environment.

The ability to state and be affected by rules is an invaluable characteristic of humans. For example, rules are important in transmitting information across generations. The lessons of life are passed down from mother to son, grandfather to granddaughter, and artisan to apprentice. Without rules, each new generation would have to relearn old lessons. Some rules describe facts about nature, as when scientists report the results of experiments (e.g., "Compound A when combined with compound B will produce compound C"). Others describe the social environment (e.g., "To get along with Mr. Higgins, you have to ask about his garden").

Among other functions, rules can increase the effectiveness of delayed consequences. For example, the consequences of poor study habits—low grades—are often too delayed to improve study behavior. Low grades can, however, be made more effective as behavioral consequences by rules such as "Your low grades are a result of insufficient attention to the study guides." Or consider drug abuse, which often leads to impaired social and vocational functioning. These consequences are delayed and, more often than not, do not decrease drug taking. But rules that describe these consequences, such as "If you want to keep your job, you must stop taking drugs," can be effective.

Rule-governed behavior occurs when an individual's behavior is affected by verbal instructions describing environmental relations that the person has not directly contacted. (Behavior that is affected by directly contacting environmental relations is termed **contingency-governed.**) For example, a motorcyclist's friend may say, "Don't ride in the rain; the road gets slick and its darned easy to wipe out." This rule describes relations among an antecedent stimulus (the presence of rain), the response of riding a cycle, and the probable outcome of that response (an accident). If the biker follows the rule and refrains from riding in the rain—and whether he or she will do so will depend largely on the biker's prior experience with respect to the rule giver and the accuracy of similar rules provided in the past—the behavior is rule-governed. Rules may be provided by others or formulated by the individual whose behavior they are to control. Rule-governed behavior is of crucial importance to humans because it (1) provides for very rapid behavior change and (2) enables us to behave effectively without requiring direct exposure to environmental events that might prove harmful or ineffectual. Rule-governed and contingency-governed behaviors are not, however, necessarily identical; a person whose behavior is controlled by exposure to a verbal description of a response—outcome relation (e.g., "If you eat yellow snow, you'll get sick") may not behave in exactly the same way as a person who has actually been exposed to that relation (e.g., one who has eaten yellow snow and has got sick). Moreover, rules can be faulty (e.g., speakers can lie), fostering behaviors inappropriate to the situation at hand. "All Irish setters are mean and to be avoided" is an example of such a rule.

It is important to recognize that producing and following rules is operant behavior, acquired through a complex interaction with the social and natural environment. From the time that a person is very young, she or he is given rules and is reinforced for following them. For example, a parent may tell a child, "Don't hit the cat, or it will scratch you." If the child complies, playing gently with the cat and not hitting it, the parent may well say something like "That's good; you play so gently with Kitty," thereby strengthening the child's behaving in accordance with the specific rule, and with rule following in general. If, however, the child fails to comply and hits the cat but is not scratched or otherwise exposed to an adverse outcome (e.g., parental disapproval), the tendency to follow rules may be reduced.

Consciousness

The study of consciousness has long occupied an important place in psychology. You may recall from an earlier chapter that psychology was founded as a discipline by Wilhelm Wundt. Wundt was interested in consciousness in a restricted sense. For him, consciousness consisted of an individual's sensory experience at a given moment. Given this orientation, much of the research conducted by Wundt and his immediate successors (e.g., Titchener and the Gestalt psychologists) entailed manipulating the stimuli to which subjects were exposed and then recording their reports of the resulting sensory experience. For example, the experimenter might present a four-row by four-column array of randomly chosen letters for a brief period (e.g., 0.1 second), then immediately ask the subject to recall as many letters as possible. Presumably, the response would reveal "conscious content," the sensations, perceptions, and ideas that consciousness comprised.

Consciousness and Verbal Behavior

Partly because of the criticisms of early behaviorists (e.g., Watson), the term *consciousness* fell into some disrepute through the midpart of the present century, but it has undergone a revival in popularity fostered by cognitive psychologists. Psychologists use *consciousness* and *conscious* in a variety of ways. In humans, the terms usually refer to (1) the verbal description of stimuli impinging on sensory receptors ("We lose consciousness of repetitive events as we get used to them") or (2) the verbal description of our own behavior ("I'm conscious that I lied to her"). (The issue of consciousness in nonhumans is complex and will not be addressed here. Griffin, 1981, and Rollin, 1986, have provided overviews of this topic.) When we say that we are conscious of our surroundings, our behavior, or our feelings, we are reporting the fact that we can talk about them (i.e., our verbal behavior is under their discriminative control). Consider a woman who is looking toward 10 paintings on the wall of a museum; light is reflected from each painting to her eyes and affects the rods and cones (visual receptors) located there. Is she conscious of the small abstract at the lower left of the display? It's impossible to tell from this description. If, however, she says, "I'm looking at that ugly little blue abstract," there is no ambiguity: she is obviously conscious of it. In this case, the woman not only describes the abstract but reports that she is looking at it. As Skinner (1974) put it, we are conscious of a visual stimulus when we see (report to ourselves or to others) that we are seeing it.

Self-Awareness

When we refer to self-awareness, we usually mean that we are able to describe verbally (i.e., are conscious of) our own behavior or of stimuli that originate within our body. In either case, self-awareness involves discriminated operant behavior that is conditioned by a verbal community.

People are taught to be aware of their overt behavior (responses that other people can easily detect) as they are taught to be aware of other objects and events, that is, by discrimination training. From the time children can first tact (describe) objects in the external environment, they are asked to tact their own behavior. A parent might, for example, ask, "Pat, what are you doing, *crawling?*" (with heavy emphasis on the *crawling*) as the child crawls across the floor. In the beginning, Pat cannot know the answer, "Crawling." If, however, the child has learned to imitate or echo words—and this is a perfectly reasonable assumption—Pat is likely to say, "Crawling." When this occurs, the parent says something like, "Good, you're crawling," which serves to increase the likelihood of Pat's responding with "Crawling" in the future if (1) the parent asks, "What are you doing?" and (2) Pat is crawling when the question is asked. Note that, in this example, the verbal response, "Crawling" is conjointly controlled by Pat's behavior and the parent's question.

Through protracted training of this sort, we eventually learn to describe in great detail our actions and the environment in which they occur. Of course, the behaviors and environmental variables that are characteristically described, as well as the words that we use in their description, are determined by the verbal community. A child reared by parents with little interest in birds and no training in recognizing bird species will not describe a small gray-and-black bird in the same way as a child reared by ornithologists. The two sets of parents represent different verbal communities, and they condition different patterns of verbal behavior. The ornithologists' child will learn to call the bird a chickadee, because only that response is reinforced. Similarly, the other child may learn to call it a little snowbird, because that response is adequate to secure reinforcement in her world.

Descriptions of overt behavior and objects and events in the external environment are apt to be consistent within a verbal community, in large part because members of this community can confirm the relations described and respond appropriately. For example, a parent is unlikely to reinforce a child's response of "I'm walking" when the child is crawling, or to reinforce the response of saying, "Table" in the presence of a chair.

In addition to public events, we also learn to describe **private events:** stimuli and responses that occur within our skin. Ironically, we are taught by others to describe our private events. This is ironic because the verbal community has limited access to our private events. The main difference between learning to tact (describe) public and private events is that other people can't directly check to see whether the private events are actually occurring. If, for example, a child says that he has a stomachache and pleads that he can't go to school, how can his mother tell if it's true? At one level, she can't. Only the child knows how he feels. The mother can, however, search for public events that might reasonably occur in conjunction with a stomachache.

Some private events, including stomachaches, may have associated **collateral responses** (Skinner, 1945). These are overt (public) changes in behavior that occur in conjunction with a private event. A child with a stomachache may, for instance, rub his stomach, vomit, fail to eat, and grimace. Experience teaches and the verbal community recognizes that these responses regularly, but not inevitably, occur in conjunction with a stomachache.

Public accompaniments (public nonbehavioral events) may also occur in conjunction with private events. A warm and swollen stomach is likely to be correlated with a stomachache, as is having suffered an injury to the stomach. How the verbal community responds to a description of some private events depends to a large extent on whether the description is supported by collateral responses and public accompaniment. Many private events, however, are not highly correlated with directly observable events. In such cases, it is difficult or impossible to teach people to describe them accurately.

To summarize, awareness of internal events (self-awareness) is taught in the same way as awareness of external events: by reinforcing tacting behavior, that is, descriptive verbal behavior in the presence of particular stimuli. The only difference between tacting behavioral and tacting nonbehavioral events is in the nature of what is described. The only difference between tacting external and internal events is their accessibility.

The Role of Awareness in Learning

Like Freud and contemporary cognitive psychologists, behaviorists recognize that most behavior in humans in unconscious in the sense that the behaver is unaware of (i.e., cannot verbally describe) its causes. But the behavioral explanation of this phenomenon does not rest on unobservable and hypothetical entities. For Skinner and many other behaviorists, "conscious" behavior is characteristically rule-governed, whereas "unconscious" behavior is contingency-governed. As discussed earlier, contingency-governed behavior is controlled by direct exposure to operant contingencies of reinforcement (or punishment), whereas rule-governed behavior is controlled by descriptions of such contingencies. Contingency-governed behavior is no more the result of a hypothetical entity called the unconscious mind than rule-governed behavior is the result of a conscious mind. Both can be fully explained in terms of lawful behavior–environmental interactions.

Interestingly, some cognitive psychologists contend that contingency-governed behavior does not occur in adult humans. Their position, evident in the following quote from Brewer (1974), is that all adult learning requires awareness:

> In human beings, classical conditioning and operant conditioning work according to behaviorist theory in very young children, in the mentally retarded, and normal people who are asleep. In these cases, consciousness and the internal representation of the world outside are undeveloped or turned off; when that is so, people do behave according to stimulus-response theory. (p. 73)

The fallacy of this position is twofold. First, there is no "internal representation of the world" to turn off. Second, several experiments have apparently shown that learning can occur (through both operant and respondent conditioning) without the subjects' being aware of what they were to learn. For example, Carter (1973) told college students that they could earn points by pressing a key but actually delivered points dependent on blinks of their right eye. This relation yielded a high rate of eye blinking, which fell to near-zero levels when blinking no longer produced points. Key pressing, which never produced points, occurred throughout the study.

This is not to say that awareness of the contingencies is never a factor in learning. Parton and DeNike (1966) gave children a task involving marbles and found that learning occurred only in the children who were able to state the contingencies. Moreover, those children who gave incorrect accounts of the contingencies behaved in accordance with their false hypotheses. This and other experiments show that awareness, when defined as statements about contingencies in the world, can strongly influence behavior. Such statements interact with other variables to determine human behavior in a given situation.

Memory

Past events obviously influence current happenings. Your grandmother, for example, may say, "I remember my grandad's old horse, Jasper, a big bay," and then go on to tell a series of stories about it. Here, her experiences with an animal now long dead play a major role in determining what she says to you. How and why does this occur? In asking these questions, we enter the realm of memory. Unfortunately, like most words borrowed from everyday language, the term *memory* has no precise psychological definition.

A Behavioral Perspective

In many cases, what is termed memory is closely related to, if not identical with, learning. Consider an example of operant conditioning in which we teach a pigeon to peck a red Plexiglas disk, but not a green one, by delivering food when the bird pecks red, but not when it pecks green. If, after days of training, the bird, when presented simultaneously with red and green disks, begins pecking the latter, we might be tempted to say that the pigeon "remembered" to peck red. But it would be equally informative to say that it had learned to do so. To take this idea one step further, suppose we teach a child to say the Pledge of Allegiance when he sees a picture of George Bush. We could say that the child remembers to recite the pledge when he sees George Bush's picture. But this is saying nothing more than that he has learned to do so.

In behavioral approaches to what is commonly called memory, the object of inquiry is the persistence of behavior over time in and of itself. Consider a child who is memorizing a math fact. On Monday, Tyler learns to say, "9" when the teacher says, "What is 3 times 3?" To test Tyler's recall, the teacher on Tuesday again asks, "What is 3 times 3?" and Tyler excitedly says, "9". The teacher exclaims, "Very good, you *remembered*." The important thing here is that the behavior learned on Monday persisted over time: Tyler was, 24 hours later, able to say "9" when asked, "What is 3 times 3?" At the level of real observation, *to*

Pictures help us recall events from the distant past. (Photo courtesy of Roger Ulrich.)

remember is to emit a particular behavior appropriate to a set of circumstances, despite the passage of time. Likewise, *to forget* is to be unable to emit a behavior that is appropriate to a circumstance (e.g., "He forgot his manners" or "She forgot the answer to question 4").

Some Memory Phenomena

The variables that determine persistence of behavior over time have been examined at great length. Psychologists who are interested in memory typically study the ability to recall words, syllables, facts, or events and to answer questions like "What word followed *apple* in the list?" or "What was the first and last word in the list?" A series of famous studies of memory were conducted in the late 19th century by Herman Ebbinghaus. Using himself as the only subject, Ebbinghaus identified a number of important phenomena that still provide the empirical underpinnings of many theories. He first devised thousands of nonsense syllables, each of which consisted of a consonant–vowel–consonant combination (e.g., *daz* and *wic*). Such nonsense syllables were used so that the results would not be affected by previous familiarity with words. The basic procedure in most of his experiments was to form a list of nonsense syllables (e.g., 13 syllables), and then to learn to say them in the correct order by going through the list over and over until he could recall all the syllables perfectly. The number of times that he went through the list (or the repetitions) was noted. At a later time, Ebbinghaus relearned the list and compared the number of repetitions required for remastery with the number required for mastery on initial exposure. The data were usually expressed in a percentage-of-savings measure, which was computed by dividing the difference in the repetitions by the initial repetitions. If learning the list required 50 repetitions, and the relearning required 40, then the percentage of savings would be (50 − 40)/50, or 20%. In this example, very little was remembered.

What did Ebbinghaus discover? One important finding was that, as the length of a list increased, the number of repetitions required for mastery of the entire list also increased, as did the number of repetitions per syllable. Moreover, when Ebbinghaus varied the amount of time between the initial learning and the relearning of the list, he found that a large portion of the list was forgotten after 20 minutes (see Figure 7–4). Thereafter, less and less was forgotten, even after a full month. He also reported an **overlearning** phenomenon: after the list was recited perfectly, additional repetitions improved recall at a later date.

Many other memory phenomena have been discovered since Ebbinghaus performed his studies. For example, Glanzer and Cunitz (1966) demonstrated **serial position effects.** Subjects were given a series of words and were then asked to recall as many as possible in any order. The subjects were generally able to recall words at the beginning of the list (a **primacy effect**) and words at the end of the list (a **recency effect**) better than those in the middle of the list.

Other research has shown that learning other material can interfere with recall. **Retroactive interference** occurs when learning new material interferes with recalling previously learned material. For example, learning Spanish grammar in second period might interfere with recalling an English lesson learned in first period. In **proactive interference,** previously learned material interferes with the recall of newly learned material. For instance, if Jayne learns a French

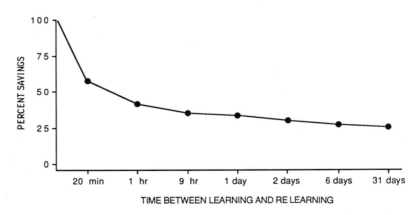

Figure 7-4. Percentage of savings as a function of time between learning and relearning in Ebbinghaus's experiment. (From *Psychology: Themes and Variations* by Wayne Weiten, 1989, p. 253. Copyright 1989 by Brooks/Cole. Redrawn with permission.)

lesson in first period, this material may inhibit her recall of a Latin lesson learned in second period. The research designs for studying retroactive and proactive interference are presented in Figure 7–5.

In both proactive and retroactive interference, the degree of interference often depends on the nature of the task. Kroll, Parks, Parkinson, Bieber, and Johnson (1970) gave subjects a letter of the alphabet to remember, which was either presented visually or spoken aloud. The subjects then recited aloud a list of other letters and, after 10 or 25 seconds, were asked to recall the original letter. There was more interference, or poorer recall, when the memory letter and the interference task were in the same sensory modality (termed **intramodal interference**) than when they were in different sensory modalities (called **intermodal interference**).

A Cognitive Perspective

A unique feature of the cognitive approach to memory (and to psychology in general) is concern with *representations* of stimuli over time. Consider our example of the grandmother and the horse. It is obvious that her experiences with the horse altered her in some way, so that she could talk about it years later. In a sense, some representation of the horse persisted through time. Clearly, there is no little horse in the grandmother's head; the stimulus that endured has somehow been transformed. Presumably, the horse became an **engram,** which is a term coined to label "a persistent protoplasmic alteration hypothesized to occur on stimulation of living neural tissue and to account for memory" (*The American Heritage Dictionary of the English Language,* 1984).

No one has ever found an engram, although physiological psychologists continue to explore the correlation between neurophysiological events and learning. Cognitive psychologists do not work at this level of analysis. Instead, they liken what goes on in the human body to what goes on in some other, better understood, system. The current favorite is the computer, which is the basis of the information-processing model of memory.

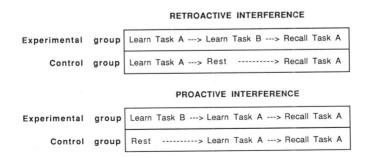

Figure 7-5. Experimental designs for studying retroactive and proactive interference.

Historically, psychologists have conceived of memory metaphorically. For example, memory has in days past been compared to a muscle (it could be strengthened through frequent use), to a system of writing or recording, to electrical pathways, and to a library in which memories are stored, classified in a hierarchical fashion, referenced, and then retrieved just as books would be (Hunt, 1982). The most popular recent model, called **information processing,** reflects current technology and was first suggested by Atkinson and Shiffrin (1968).

The information-processing model attempts to explain memory by referring to mechanisms similar to those in computers. This model posits *structural components*, which are analogous to the hardware (e.g., the central processing unit) of a computer, and *control processes*, which are analogous to the software of a computer. The structural components (e.g., permanent memory stores and temporary registers) "contain" representations of stimuli, and the control processes (e.g., the storage and retrieval processes) govern the form and movement of these representations within the system (see Figure 7–6).

Structural Components

All stimuli first enter **sensory memory (SM)** a temporary store with a rather large capacity. Stimuli in SM exist in the same form as in the environment; for example, a visual image of a visual stimulus or an echo of an auditory stimulus exists in SM. Only a portion of the stimuli in SM are processed further; most are not and are forgotten in a second or less. The cause of forgetting is usually decay (i.e., the passage of time), although displacement by a new stimulus representation also occurs.

The next system, **short-term memory (STM)**, also called **working memory,** presumably holds information to which the person is attending. The form of the stimuli in STM is an encoded, or transformed, version of the stimuli first entered into SM. For example, a written word may be stored in terms of its sound. Short-term memory also differs from SM in that the capacity is limited to between five and nine individual bits of information (Miller, 1956). Forgetting usually results

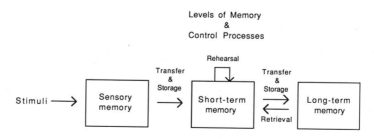

Figure 7-6. A depiction of the information-processing model of memory, including the three levels of memory and the various control processes.

from displacement of old items by new ones, although some forgetting may be caused by decay. Material typically resides in STM for 15 to 30 seconds.

The third memory system is **long-term memory (LTM).** Information in LTM exists as an encoded version of STM information. Important ancillary information is also included. Thus, for the word *peach,* information pertaining to its meaning is stored, as well as a peach's appearance, taste, and smell. The capacity of LTM is unlimited, and forgetting results from interference or from some difficulty in a control process, like retrieval (described below). Unlike SM and STM, LTM can hold material for many years. Some researchers believe that there are different divisions of LTM. Winograd (1975), for example, suggested that we have **declarative memory** (names, dates, and events) and **procedural memory** (information about how to execute tasks or perform skills).

Control Processes

Control processes orchestrate the flow of information through the three levels of memory. In **encoding,** information is transformed into a memory code for subsequent storage in STM or LTM. One encoding process is **pattern recognition** (Klatzky, 1980), in which information in SM is transformed into a meaningful form for subsequent storage in STM (e.g., the visual image of the letter *A* might be given its appropriate name). Once the information is in STM, further encoding can occur to enable storage in LTM. For example, a sequence of words may be encoded according to their meaning.

When material is encoded, it is ready for **storage.** Storage in STM usually involves rehearsal. For example, you can keep a 7-digit number in STM as long as you continue to repeat it. If the number of digits is increased to 12, then even rehearsal will not keep the information to STM. However, some of the individual bits may be grouped into units. Thus, instead of trying to remember 12 individual numbers, one might remember 4 "chunks" of 3 numbers each. This grouping of individual bits into units is called **chunking.**

Some material in STM is transferred to and stored in LTM. This can be accomplished through rehearsal, in which material is repeated over and over. **Mnemonic devices,** which are rules that aid in recall (e.g., "30 days hath September . . ." or "*i* before *e* except after *c*"), are often developed to enhance storage in LTM. Interestingly, particularly meaningful or important information (i.e., "flashbulb memories") may be stored in LTM with little rehearsal. For instance, most people can provide detailed accounts of their activities and whereabouts when they learned that the space shuttle *Challenger* had exploded.

When material is stored in LTM, it can be extracted through **retrieval.** It is thought that many strategies are used for retrieval. One such strategy is using retrieval cues. If Robert is unable to remember a friend's last name, he might repeat the first name a few times in the hope that the last will be remembered. Another strategy involves imagery: retrieval of the score of yesterday's football game might involve imagining what you were doing when you heard the score.

The information-processing model is popular, but its adequacy as an explanation of memory is hard for many people to evaluate. The task is made easier if we ask a simple question: Are the structural components and control processes real?

Computers have real memory stores in the form of disks, cards, and chips. Moreover, information can be compiled and translated ("encoded") for use by the computer, and such information can be stored in and retrieved from its memory. These systems are real and their operation can be observed. In humans, however, such systems cannot be observed and have no physical existence. We humans are not factory-equipped with memory cards, encoders, or internal disk drives. Physiological activities underlie all that we do—including what is termed *remembering* and *forgetting*—but these activities resemble computer processes only by analogy. Analogical models are not completely useless, but they neither describe physiology nor provide an adequate explanation of behavior.

Summary

This chapter has discussed language, consciousness, and memory, three topics of great historical importance in psychology. They are also important in drawing distinctions between the traditional and the behavioral approaches to psychology, which is a goal of this book. Traditional explanations of the phenomena presented in this chapter appeal to hypothetical entities: language develops through the actions of a language acquisition device, overt behavior is determined by a conscious mind, and recall is a function of retrieval from long term memory. Behavioral interpretations reject the existence and relevance of hypothetical entities and emphasize instead (1) the behaviors that lead us to use the terms *language, consciousness,* and *memory* and (2) the empirical variables that control these behaviors.

The behavioral perspective leads to an emphasis on phenomena that are somewhat different from those of concern to other psychologists. For example, the word *memory* fails to appear in the index of many good psychology books written from the behavioral perspective (e.g., Karen, 1974; Lutzker & Martin, 1981; Skinner, 1987). The phenomena of interest to behaviorists are primarily interactions between behavior and environmental—and, to a lesser extent, genetic and physiological—variables. These variables, working together in ways that are often difficult to study and always difficult to understand, control the complex behaviors encompassed by the terms *language, consciousness,* and *memory.*

Study Questions

Language

1. Be able to describe the issue concerning the structure of language (Descartes, Chomsky) versus the function of language (Bloomfield, Skinner).

2. Considering the structural approach to language behavior, describe the essential features of Chomsky's study of language, including the different levels of linguistic analysis (linguistic units) and the development of language.

3. Interpret the following statement: "Language neither exists apart from behavior (i.e.,

speaking, writing, listening, reading, signing) nor represents ideas, concepts, or thought." What is language? Define verbal behavior and contrast it with nonverbal behavior.

4. Describe the essence of meaning from a behavioral perspective. How does this perspective differ from a structural view?

5. In general, how do behaviorists view the development of verbal behavior? In your answer, use the example of babbling. In so doing, list and briefly describe the six stages of prespeech development.

6. In the first sentence of the section "Linguistic Development," what is meant by *normative data?* Why is knowledge of normative data informative and how does this section illustrate this point?

7. Describe the vocal apparatus. What is the point of the section on the role of the brain in speech?

8. Most of this section is devoted to the importance of language for the speaker; the section on "Rules" considers the importance of language for the listener. Define a rule (form and function), and describe how listeners benefit from rules.

Consciousness

9. Be able to say what is meant by the word *consciousness,* perhaps by finishing the sentence, "When we say that we are conscious of our surroundings, our behavior, or our feelings, . . ."

10. What does it mean when one is "self-aware"? How do we learn to become conscious of our overt behavior as well as of covert (private) events (in considering the latter, use the concepts of public accompaniments and collateral responses)?

11. State the central issue in the role of awareness in learning, including the behavioral view and the cognitive view.

Memory

12. Describe the general behavioral view of memory. Why do behaviorists not use the term *memory?* Does this mean that they don't study phenomena we call memory?

13. Describe the general procedure used by Ebbinghaus.

14. Define *overlearning, serial position effects,* and *interference* (all four kinds).

15. What is the unique feature of cognitive approaches to memory, and how does the information-processing model represent it?

16. What is the main point in the evaluation of the information-processing model?

Summary

17. With regard to the topics of language, consciousness, and memory, what two things do behavioral interpretations emphasize?

Owens, R. E. (1984). *Language Development: An Introduction.* Columbus, Ohio: Charles E. Merrill.

Owens provides a thoughtful and concise discussion of language development. Included are the essentials of the major theories in a style appropriate for any student.

Skinner, B. F. (1957). *Verbal Behavior.* Englewood Cliffs, NJ: Prentice-Hall.

Skinner provides the seminal behavioral interpretation of language. Among the highlights is the functional classification of various kinds of language. A must for any serious student of the behavioral perspective, although the book is not for the novice.

Skinner, B. F. (1974). *About Behaviorism.* New York: Knopf.

Skinner presents a behavioral interpretation of many of the topics discussed in this Chapter. Skinner's books are a must for any reader who hopes to appreciate the scientific approach to human behavior.

CHAPTER 8

Child Development

Development refers to change over time. Human development, which involves changes in physical structure and in behavior over time, can be described at two levels: changes in the species across generations (**phylogenetic development**) and changes in individuals during their lifetimes (**ontogenetic development**). The phylogenetic development of humans was explored in Chapter 4. The present chapter is an overview of ontogenetic development, with a special focus on how behavior–environment interactions change during the first few years of life. The coverage is limited to this period because it is the time when the most conspicuous changes in behavior occur and serves well to illustrate how behavior develops.

Conception and Prenatal Development

Stages of Development

Prenatal development is usually described in terms of three stages. In the **germinal stage,** a **zygote** is formed in one of the mother's Fallopian tubes through the union of a sperm (from the father) and an ovum (from the mother). The sperm contains 23 chromosomes, as does the ovum, and the zygote therefore has 46 chromosomes. The single-celled zygote immediately begins a two-week trip down the Fallopian tube toward the uterus; along the way, the zygote begins to divide and redivide, each time producing new cells with a copy of the original 23 pairs of chromosomes. As will become evident, however, the newly formed cells differ from one another in many important ways. Sometimes, two ova are available in the Fallopian tubes and both unite with a sperm; the result is fraternal twins. Fraternal twins have different genetic makeups. On other occasions, a single zygote may split into two separate units, producing identical twins who have the same genetic makeup.

When the zygote finally reaches the uterus, it attaches to the uterine wall via tendril-like extensions. At this time, the **embryonic stage** of prenatal development begins. The tiny cell mass, now referred to as an **embryo**, differentiates during the next six weeks into three layers: (1) the ectoderm, or outer layer,

183

which further differentiates into the hair, the nails, the outer skin, the sensory cells, and the nervous system; (2) the mesoderm, or middle layer, which develops into the muscles, the skeleton, the excretory and circulatory systems, and the inner skin; and (3) the endoderm, or inner layer, which develops into the gastrointestinal track, the trachea, the bronchia, the glands, and the vital organs.

The embryo's three life-support systems—the amniotic sac, the placenta, and the umbilical cord—form after implantation in the uterus. The **amniotic sac,** in which the embryo floats, contains amniotic fluid that serves as a protective buffer against physical shock and temperature changes. The tendrils that attach the embryo to the uterine wall grow into a semipermeable membrane, called the **placenta,** through which nutrients pass to and waste products pass from the developing infant. Semipermeable membranes are so called because some molecules (e.g., oxygen, carbon dioxide, and nutrients), but not all, can cross them. Nutrients and wastes travel to and from the embryo through blood vessels in the **umbilical cord.**

Most spontaneous abortions (i.e., miscarriages), in which the embryo becomes detached from the uterine wall and is expelled, occur during the embryonic stage. It has been estimated that approximately 25% of pregnancies end in spontaneous abortion. The majority of aborted embryos have severe genetic or chromosomal disorders. It is not surprising that a mechanism, spontaneous miscarriage, has evolved to eliminate such embryos early in pregnancy.

The **fetal stage,** characterized by, among other things, the appearance of the first bone cells, begins at about the ninth week and ends at birth. By the time this stage begins, 95% of the major body parts have been differentiated; thus, the bulk of the changes that occur in the fetal stage involve the growth and refinement of these parts. The fetus begins to kick, swallow, and turn his or her head, although such movements typically are not detected by the mother until the fourth or fifth month. Fingers, toes, eyebrows, and eyelashes form in the fetal stage. There are significant increases in body length early in this period, as well as substantial increases in body weight near the time of birth.

Effects of the External Environment on Prenatal Development

The developing embryo is extremely vulnerable to damage from environmental agents. Agents that act during pregnancy to produce abnormal development are called **teratogens.** Known teratogens include alcohol and other drugs, certain maternal diseases (e.g., rubella, or German measles), irradiation, and temperature extremes. The effects of a particular teratogen often depend on the developmental stage of the infant (see Figure 8–1). In general, vulnerability to teratogens is greater during the embryonic period (i.e., during the first three months, or trimester, of pregnancy). This is so because it is at this stage of prenatal development that most of the organs and systems develop.

The effects of the drug thalidomide provide tragic documentation of the sensitivity of the embryo to environmental agents. Thalidomide, developed by a German company, was introduced in 1958 as a safe and effective agent for reducing nausea and inducing sleep. The drug was given to thousands of preg-

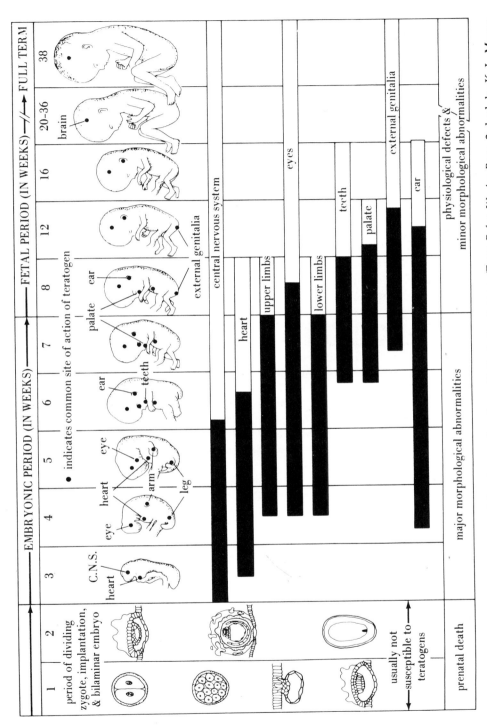

Figure 8-1. Critical periods in prenatal development and sensitivity to teratogens. (From *Before We Are Born*, 3rd ed. by K. L. Moore. Copyright by W. B. Saunders Co., Philadelphia, 1989. Reproduced by permission.)

nant women in Europe, Australia, and Japan; it was not legally available in the United States. It soon became apparent that thalidomide caused severe malformations in some children. The deformities included eye defects, cleft palate, depressed nose bridge, small external ears, fusing of the fingers and toes, dislocated hips, and malformations of the digestive tract and heart. A typical deformity was phocomelia, a condition characterized by missing limbs, with hands and feet attached directly to torsolike flippers. In all, about 8,000 babies in 20 countries were afflicted. As is typically true of a teratogen, the damage was most severe when the drug was taken early in pregnancy.

It might appear that only extremely toxic agents can produce developmental abnormalities. That is not the case. A variety of widely used drugs can harm the developing infant. For example, the incidence of miscarriage, prematurity, low birthweight, and sudden-infant-death syndrome is higher for mothers who smoke and drink than for those who do not. Alcoholic mothers have about a 1-in-3 chance of giving birth to an infant with **fetal alcohol syndrome,** in which the infants have facial, heart, and limb defects and are likely to be mentally retarded and hyperactive. Even moderate drinking or occasional binges can cause damage to the developing infant (Council Report, 1983).

Genetic Abnormalities

A wide range of genetic abnormalities can interfere with development. Examples of such abnormalities are phenylketonuria, Down syndrome, and various sex-linked disorders including fragile-X syndrome.

Phenylketonuria (PKU) is a disorder caused by a single recessive gene. PKU is caused by the inaction or absence of the enzyme phenylalanine hydroxylase, which converts the amino acid phenylalanine (found in most protein sources) into the amino acid tyrosine. The result is that phenylalanine levels in the blood increase and phenylpyruvic acid accumulates in the urine. Although PKU infants appear normal at birth, they show increasing signs of mental retardation, irritability, poor coordination, and convulsions as phenylpyruvic acid builds up in the body. Phenylketonuria well illustrates the effects that a single gene can have, as well as simple Mendelian genetics. If two people who carry a recessive allele for PKU mate, there is a 1-in-4 chance of producing a child who is a homozygous carrier of two PKU alleles and actually has the disorder (see Figure 8–2).

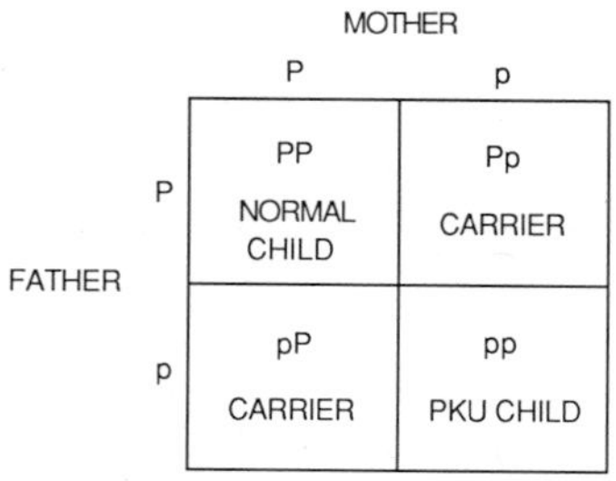

	MOTHER	
	P	p
P	PP NORMAL CHILD	Pp CARRIER
p	pP CARRIER	pp PKU CHILD

FATHER

Figure 8-2. The possible outcomes of the mating of two parents who each have a recessive gene for PKU. On average, 25% of the offspring will have PKU, 25% will be normal, and 50% will be carriers.

Fortunately, infants can be tested before or at birth for PKU, and most states require such testing. If an infant tests positive for the disorder, he or she can be treated with a diet that limits the amount of phenylalanine. If such a diet is continued through middle childhood, much of the damage caused by PKU can be averted.

Down syndrome, also called *trisomy 21,* occurs when there is an extra 21st chromosome. Children with Down syndrome have upward slanting eyelids, small (epicanthal) folds of skin over the inner corners of the eyes, and thick protruding tongues. In addition, they have a higher than average incidence of hearing problems, respiratory infection, heart problems, and leukemia. Perhaps the most striking feature of Down syndrome is the presence of mental retardation, which ranges from moderate to severe (see Chapter 11).

Sex-linked disorders are so named because they result from problems with the 23rd pair of chromosomes, the so-called sex chromosomes. Of the 23 pairs of chromosomes, 22 are possessed equally by males and females. The 23rd chromosome differs in males and females. Females have two X chromosomes (XX), and males have one X and one Y chromosome (XY) (see Figure 8–3). Because the mother is XX, meiosis in her sex cells produces only X chromosomes. In contrast, because the father is XY, meiosis in his sex cells produces an approximately equal number of X and Y chromosomes. As the father can contribute either an X or a Y chromosome, he determines the sex of the zygote.

The X chromosome is about five times longer than the Y chromosome and hence carries more genes. The fact that the X chromosome carries more genes

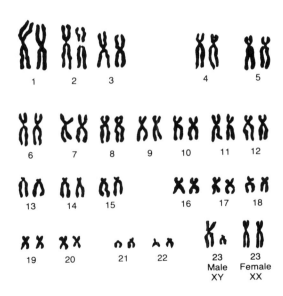

Figure 8-3. A photograph of the chromosomes in a normal human male and female. The first 22 pairs of chromosomes are similar for both sexes, but the 23rd pair in the female contains two X chromosomes, whereas the 23rd pair in the male contains an X and a Y chromosome. (From *Psychology: A Concise Introduction,* 2nd ed., 1989, by T. E. Pettijohn. Reprinted with permission of the Dushkin Publishing Group, Inc., Guilford, CT.)

than the Y chromosome means that some genes on the X chromosome have no counterpart on the Y chromosome. A recessive trait on the X chromosome may therefore be expressed in the phenotype because there is no equivalent dominant allele on the Y chromosome to counteract it. Characteristics that result from this circumstance are called *sex-linked* or *X-linked*. They are not a problem unless the recessive trait codes for developmental defects. There are, unfortunately, many such X-linked characteristics, among the hemophilia, color blindness, and diabetes.

In addition to sex-linked characteristics, there can be deviations in the number of sex chromosomes. These result in individuals with problems in sexual differentiation. Deviations in the sex chromosomes can lead to females with only one X chromosome (XO, or Turner syndrome), females with an extra X chromosome (XXX), males with an extra X chromosome (XXY, called *Klinefelter syndrome*), and males with an extra Y chromosome (XYY). Table 8–1 provides a summary of sex-linked chromosomal abnormalities.

Another sex-linked abnormality is called *fragile-X syndrome*. Fragile-X syndrome is a condition in which the X chromosome appears to be pinched or narrowed in some places. These pinched areas may actually break, so that

Table 8-1
Summary of Chromosomal Anomalies

	Type of anomaly	Incidence of live births	Symptoms
Autosomal anomalies:			
Edward syndrome	Trisomy 18	1 in 5,000	Early death; many congenital problems
D-trisomy syndrome	Trisomy 13	1 in 6,000	Early death; many congenital problems
Cri du chat	Deletion of part of short arm of chromosome 4 or 5	1 in 10,000	High-pitched monotonous cry; severe retardation
Down syndrome	Trisomy 21; 5% involve 15/21 translocation	1 in 700	Congenital problems; retardation
Sex chromosomal anomalies			
Turner syndrome	XO or XX-XO mosaics	1 in 2,500	Some physical stigmata and hormonal problems; specific spatial deficit
Females with extra X chromosomes	XXX XXXX XXXXX	1 in 1,000	For trisomy X, no distinctive physical stigmata; perhaps some retardation
Klinefelter males	XXY XXXY XXXXY XXYY XXXYY	2 in 1,000	For XXY, sexual development problems; tall; perhaps some retardation
Males with extra Y chromosomes	XYY XYYY XYYYY	1 in 1,000	Tall; perhaps some retardation

sections of the chromosome come apart. Males with fragile-X syndrome exhibit a range of clinical symptoms, including mental retardation, abnormal electroencephalograms, seizures, cleft palate, and disorders of the eyes. Because fragile-X syndrome is a sex-linked disorder, women may be carriers without exhibiting any clinical symptoms (Opitz & Sutherland, 1984). Fragile-X syndrome is a frequent cause of mental retardation in males; it ranks second to Down syndrome as a genetic cause of mental retardation (*Report to the National Advisory Child Health and Human Development Council*, 1981).

Birth and Postnatal Development

Birth represents a drastic change in that the infant goes immediately from an existence in which it depends on the mother for respiration, digestion, thermal regulation, and protection to an independent existence in which circulatory relations with the mother are terminated and autonomous respiration begins (Bijou, 1979). But the **neonate,** which is the term applied to infants during the first two weeks of life, is ready for the change. It inherits (1) sensory structures (receptors) that enable it to detect the stimuli that define its environment; (2) motor structures (effectors) with which it acts on that environment and moves about in space; and (3) a central nervous system that coordinates and organizes the sensory input and the motor output (see Chapter 5). The development of these structures follows a plan determined by the individual's genes. But it is a plan that can be fully realized only with extensive input from the environment.

From the time of birth, interactions with the environment, which includes other people, alter an individual's behavior, increasing its diversity and complexity until the remarkable behavioral repertoire characteristic of the adult human is evident. Psychologists refer to this process as **psychological development,** which can be defined as progressive changes over time in behavior–environment interactions. Psychological development results from the interaction of maturational and environmental factors. Psychologists use the term **maturation** to refer to a genetically determined plan of biological development that is relatively independent of experience (i.e., the environment). The word *relatively* is included because it is extremely difficult to disentangle completely the effects of the environment from those of maturation. Nevertheless, maturation (e.g., bone, muscle, and brain growth) generally requires less environmental input than psychological development.

The infant comes into the world largely helpless in terms of organized behavior; it exhibits uncoordinated motor movements and little else. Such behavior has not yet come under the control of environmental stimuli. In fact, most stimuli have no meaning for the neonate; that is, they affect sensory receptors but do not influence behavior either as antecedent or consequent stimuli. But neonates are not completely helpless. Immediately after birth, they are able to respond in specific ways to specific stimuli. These inherited (organized) stimulus–response relations are known as **unconditioned** (or **unlearned**) **reflexes.**

As described in Chapter 6, reflexes are automatic or stereotyped responses to specific stimuli. The fact that reflexes are present in all neurologically healthy neonates is good evidence that these reflexes are inherited. Many of them also appear to have adaptive value; for example, the rooting reflex, in which a touch or stroke on the infant's cheek causes the head to turn in that direction, should help the infant to find the nipple in nursing.

The neonate is a veritable reflex machine. Its behavior resembles the actions of a complex vending machine in which pushing different buttons produces different outcomes. For example, a touch on the palm will cause an infant's fingers to close (palmar or grasp reflex), a stroke up and down the sole of the foot will cause the toes to fan out (Babinski reflex), a sudden loud noise will elicit crying and related autonomic responses such as increased heart rate (startle reflex), and a sudden loss of balance will cause the arms and legs to extend and then be pulled back in (Moro reflex). Table 8–2 lists the major reflexes found in newborns and their developmental course. It is important to recognize that the eliciting stimulus for some reflexes may be internal, and therefore hard to observe, but it is nonetheless present.

Neurological Development

Human infants are developmentally more immature at birth than other primates. The human brain at birth is only about 25% of its eventual size. This means, among other things, that 75% of the development of the human brain occurs while the person is in contact with the external environment. For this reason, two important questions are (1) How do changes in the developing brain influence behavior? And (2) how does contact with the environment influence brain growth?

Neurological development, which includes changes in the shape and size of the brain, the density of the synaptic connections, and the speed of transmission among the neurons, is certainly necessary for behavioral development. If we recognize that, by adulthood, there are approximately 1 trillion neurons, each neuron participating in 100 to 1,000 synaptic contacts with other neurons (Lerner, 1984), then we can begin to appreciate not only the complexity of the central nervous system, but also the difficulty inherent in trying to understand how it mediates behavior.

Until recently, it has been extremely difficult to observe developmental changes in the brain. A device called the PET (position-emission tomography) scanner now makes the task easier. During a PET scan, the patient is injected with a radioactive chemical, 2-deoxyglucose (2-DG), which resembles the glucose that normally fuels the brain. This chemical is absorbed into cells that are metabolically active (i.e., using energy), but unlike glucose, it is not metabolized. Rather, it accumulates within cells, from which it eventually dissipates. After the injection of 2-DG, the patient's head is placed in the scanner, and X-ray beams are passed through. The PET scanner detects which areas of the brain have absorbed the 2-DG (i.e., are using energy) and produces a picture that displays those areas (Carlson, 1986).

Pictures from the PET scan have shown that, in newborns, the deeper (subcortical) brain structures (e.g., the thalamus and the hypothalamus) are more active than the cerebral cortex. The cerebral cortex, which is associated

Table 8-2
Major Newborn Reflexes

Name	Eliciting stimulus	Response	Developmental course	Significance
Blink	Light flash	Closing of both eyelids	Permanent	Protection of eyes from strong stimuli
Biceps reflex	Tap on the tendon of the biceps muscle	Short contraction of the biceps muscle	In the first few days, it is brisker than in later days	Absent in depressed infants or in cases of congenital muscular disease
Knee-jerk or patellar-tendon reflex	Tap on the tendon below the patella or kneecap	Quick extension or kick of the knee	More pronounced in the first 2 days than later	Absent or difficult to obtain in depressed infants with muscular disease; exaggerated in hyperexcitable infants
Babinski reflex	Gentle stroking of the side of the infant's foot from heel to toes	Dorsal flexion of the big toe; extension of the other toes	Usually disappears near the end of the first year; replaced by plantar flexion of big toe as in the normal adult	Absent in defects of the lower spine
Withdrawal reflex	Pinprick is applied to the sole of the infant's foot	Leg flexion	Constantly present during the first 10 days, present but less intense later	Absent with sciatic nerve damage
Plantar or toe grasp	Pressure is applied with finger against the balls of the infant's feet	Plantar flexion of all toes	Disappears between 8 and 12 months	Absent in defects of the lower spinal cord
Palmar or automatic hand grasp	Rod or finger is pressed against the infant's palm	Infant grasps the object	Disappears at 3 to 4 months; increases during the first month and then gradually declines; replaced by voluntary grasp between 4 and 5 months	Response is weak or absent in depressed babies; sucking movement facilitates grasping

(continued)

Table 8-2
(*Continued*)

Name	Eliciting stimulus	Response	Developmental course	Significance
Moro reflex	(1) Sudden loud sound or jarring (for example, bang on the examination table); or (2) head drop—head is dropped a few inches; or (3) baby drop—baby is suspended horizontally, and examiner lowers hands rapidly about 6 inches and stops abruptly	Arms are thrown out in extension and then brought toward each other in a convulsive manner; hands are fanned out at first and then clenched tightly; spine and lower extremities extend	Disappears in 6 to 7 months	Absent or constantly weak Moro indicates serious disturbance of the central nervous system
Stepping	Baby is supported in upright position; examiner moves the infant forward and tilts it slightly to one side	Rythmic stepping movements	Independent walking develops by about 15 months	Absent in depressed infants
Rooting response	Cheek of infant is stimulated by light pressure of the finger	Baby turns head toward finger, opens mouth, and tries to suck finger	Disappears at approximately 3 to 4 months	Absent in depressed infants; appears in adults only in severe cerebral palsy diseases
Sucking response	Index finger is inserted about 3 to 4 centimeters into the mouth	Rhythmical sucking	Sucking is often less intensive and less regular during the first 3 to 4 days	Poor sucking (weak, slow, and short periods) is found in apathetic babies; maternal medication during childbirth may depress sucking
Babkin or palmarmental reflex	Pressure is applied on both of baby's palms when it is lying on its back	Mouth opens, eyes close, and head returns to middle	Disappears in 3 to 4 months	General depression of central nervous system inhibits this response

with sensory and motor control, learning, memory, and speech, shows activity only in the areas that mediate sensation and physical movement; most of the cerebral cortex shows low metabolism (i.e., low energy use). As the infant grows older, activity in the association areas of the cerebral cortex increases and more of the brain becomes active. Scientists interpret the correlational data provided by the PET scan as supporting the belief that brain growth precedes, and is necessary for, behavioral development (e.g., Chugani & Phelps, 1986).

Brain growth obviously influences behavior, but early experience can also affect brain size, biochemistry, and the structure of neurons (Greenough & Green, 1981). For example, Rosenzweig (1966) showed that rats' cerebral cortex increased in weight as a result of their being exposed to an enriched environment (consisting of "toys" such as ladders, wheels, boxes, and platforms), daily 30-minute exploratory sessions, and formal maze-training at 25–30 days of age. In addition, Rosenzweig and Bennet (1970) showed that the activity of two enzymes important in the synaptic transmission of nerve impulses also increased as a function of the enriched environment. The branches that develop from the neuron, called *dendrites,* also increased, thus expanding the number of synapses per neuron, and contributing to the increase in brain size. All of this may lead to smarter rats, that is, rats that learn faster and more efficiently. These effects on brain weight and biochemistry have also been demonstrated in older animals, findings indicating that the brain may be sensitive to environmental factors throughout life, although sensitivity may diminish as the organism ages (Greenough & Green, 1981).

The implications for human infants are obvious. Infants exposed to a stimulating environment—that is, to an environment that is reactive—may be better learners than infants reared in homogeneous, restrictive, and unreactive environments. However, if an infant is neglected or otherwise unstimulated, we may be able to overcome at least some of the damage through intensive remedial training. It is unclear at present how much plasticity there is in the human brain. Maximizing it, and consequently maximizing the behavioral repertoire, is the challenge that faces parents, teachers, and therapists.

We are now in a better position to answer the questions posed at the beginning of this section. As a rule, neurological growth is necessary, but not sufficient, for behavioral development. Conversely, interaction with the environment is generally necessary, but not sufficient, for healthy neurological development. Deficiencies in either will retard the other.

Motor Development

Many developmental psychologists seem primarily interested in the normative aspects of motor and other development. **Normative changes** are those that are correlated with changes in age. An interest in the normative aspects of development leads to different questions than an interest in the functional aspects of development. For example, normative concerns are evident in the following introduction to the section on motor development in a text by Hetherington and Parke (1986):

> What course does the infant's motor development follow? How soon can an infant reach and grasp? How early do infants crawl and walk? (p. 202)

These questions are all about when, on average, certain changes occur in infants. These are important questions. Motor development does indeed follow a maturational plan. But answers to these questions will tell us only "what" develops and "when," not "why" or "how." The alternative to a normative approach is to study the functional aspects of development. A functional approach emphasizes the variables that cause developmental changes; the questions generated by a functional approach emphasize the variables that cause developmental changes; the questions generated by a functional approach are "How?" and "Why?"

As part of a functional approach to motor development, Bijou (1979) suggested that we study motor development "for the purpose of determining the conditions (organismic, physical, and social) that shape and maintain motor behavior" (p. 177). In addition to increasing basic scientific knowledge, an understanding of these conditions offers practical benefits. It could, for example, benefit therapists in helping children who, for unknown reasons, display re-

Successful motor development has its advantages! (Photo courtesy of Neil Rankin.)

tarded motor development, or who are recovering from an injury that has resulted in a loss of motor behavior.

Motor development (like all behavioral development) originates in the interaction between maturing biological structures and the antecedent and consequent stimuli for relevant behaviors (Bijou, 1979). Although mature biological structures (e.g., nerves, muscles, and bones) are prerequisite for all motor development, understanding the effects of interaction with the environment may provide some clue to how early the biological structures are sufficiently developed. For example, White and his associates showed that institutionalized infants whose environments were enriched in various ways displayed visually guided reaching approximately 45 days before control infants (White, 1967; White & Held, 1966; White, Castle, & Held, 1964). Thus, it appears that interactions with a stimulating and reactive environment may speed the development or functioning of the biological structures involved in motor behavior.

Motor development includes body management, such as reaching and grasping (prehension), and mobility, such as walking. The development of motor behavior generally proceeds in two directions: from the upper to the lower body, called **cephalocaudal development** ("head to tail"), and from the arms to the hands and fingers, called **proximodistal development** ("near to far").

Body Management

Soon after birth, the newborn's arms move reflexively. These are uncoordinated movements that have not yet had any effect on the external environment. In infants as young as two months, "attractive" objects, as well as the infant's mother, will evoke stretching of the arms and legs (Brazelton, 1982). Eventually, these arm movements will affect some aspect of the environment. They might, for example, cause a mobile hanging above the crib to move. Typically, any behavior, such as reaching and swatting, that produces these effects will be strengthened.

Prehension skills (grasping) begin to develop at about 16 weeks. By the end of the first year, the child is able to execute a neat pincer grasp of small objects. Table 8–3 and Figure 8–4 show the normative schedule of prehension development beginning at about 16 weeks. The reinforcement for grasping may not be obvious until we consider its immediate effects on the environment. The strongest effect is that the infant successfully manipulates or moves objects. The stimulation that arises from such behavior consists of tactile, proprioceptive, and visual feedback, all of which form the probable reinforcement. Reinforcers that result from the successful manipulation of the environment have been termed **ecological reinforcers** (Bijou, 1979). Because ecological reinforcers appear to be effective in all infants from birth, they can be classified as unconditioned reinforcers.

The development of other kinds of body management is more subtle. For example, an uncomfortable position will cause the baby to move to a more comfortable one; the more comfortable position will reinforce the behavior that produced it. The "discomfort" and "comfort" consist of interoceptive and exteroceptive stimuli that are altered by the infant's moving. But how can we test such a notion? Consider a theoretical experiment in which an infant is placed in an uncomfortable position. She will be moved to a new position if she pushes a large button. Will she learn to push the button? What do you think? Or will an infant learn to pull a string if doing so produces a moving mobile? Although not intending to answer this question, Watson and Ramey (1972) showed that infants would learn to move their heads in a particular way if this movement caused a mobile suspended above them to move.

Gross motor development represents the beginning of the general shaping of the infant's behavior to fit the environment. The more opportunities the infant has to interact with different aspects of the environment, the faster behavioral differentiation and refinement will proceed. The previously mentioned experiments by Watson and Ramey and by White and his colleagues on providing a more reactive environment give general support to this claim (Watson & Ramey, 1972; White, 1967; White & Held, 1966; White *et al.*, 1964).

Mobility

The general class of behavior called *mobility* may be said to begin with the infant's pushing its chest up from the prone position. In addition to the interoceptive stimulus consequences, the immediate effect is an increase in the range of visual stimuli: the infant can see more. The next major step in the development of mobility comes when the infant is able to sit on its own, which occurs between 4 and 10 months of age. The immediate effect of sitting up is again to increase the range of visual stimuli; the child can now see things on the horizontal plane. True mobility occurs when the infant begins to crawl. It is at this point that stimuli previously out of reach become accessible. Finally, walk-

Table 8-3
Normative Schedule of Prehension Development

16 weeks	Scratches with finger on tabletop
	Looks at and swipes at objects
	Retains toys put into hand
	Makes no contact with objects on table
20 weeks	Contacts toys on table
	Grasps block precariously
28 weeks	Bangs, shakes, and transfers toys from hand to hand
	Palmar grasp of block
	Whole-hand contact with raisin
36 weeks	Finger grasp of block
	Scissors grasp of raisin
40 weeks	Holds one block in each hand
	Crude, voluntary release of block
	Index-finger approach to raisin
48–52 weeks	Forefinger grasp of block
	Releases block into cup
	Neat pincer grasp of raisin

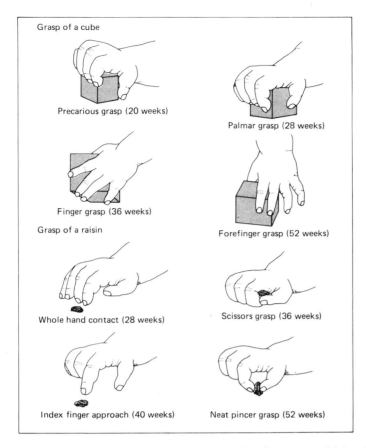

Figure 8-4. The development of prehension during the first year of life. (From *Child Psychology: A Contemporary Viewpoint* by E. M. Hetherington & R. D. Parke, 1986, p. 203. Copyright 1986 by McGraw-Hill. Reproduced by permission.)

ing, which appears from about 10 to 19 months of age, increases dramatically the part of the environment that is accessible to the infant, and it decreases the amount of time required to gain access to it. These are powerful consequences that strengthen the behavior that produces them: walking.

Figure 8–5 shows the normative stages of development of posture control and locomotion. Although it is possible, as Shirley (1933) did, to average and plot normatively various aspects of behavioral development in a certain population, we mustn't misinterpret these data. Although they reveal something about the development of underlying biological structures, they also probably reflect environmental variables, both nonsocial and cultural. For example, Dworetzky (1987) pointed out that children today typically walk a few months earlier than the 15 months indicated by Shirley. He wrote that the generally earlier development

> might be due to parents who are eager to see their children walk. Such parents might encourage their children to try just as soon as they are able. On the other hand, parents

during the 1930s, who often had larger families, might have been considerably less excited by the first steps of their fourth, fifth, and sixth children and so have encouraged them less. (p. 107)

Dworetzky emphasized that general training practices may have changed over time, and the result may be earlier walking on average. Surely, the time at which a particular child walks is determined in part by the antecedent and consequent stimuli related to the behavior. Several studies have shown that early training can facilitate walking in infants. For instance, researchers have taken advantage of the neonate's unlearned walking (or stepping) (see Table 8–2) to facilitate

Figure 8-5. Milestones in a child's motor development. (From *Life-Span Human Development* by D. Goldhaber, 1986, p. 116. Copyright 1986 by Harcourt Brace Jovanovich, Inc. Reproduced by permission.)

nonreflexive walking. If a neonate is held by the hands in an upright position with the soles of the feet barely touching the ground, the infant will walk forward in the direction in which she or he is led. The walking reflex is transitory and usually disappears at about 3 months.

If, however, infants are made to practice reflexive walking during four three-minute sessions each day, the walking reflex lasts longer than usual, and normal, nonreflexive walking begins much sooner (Zelazo, Zelazo, & Kolb, 1972). Moreover, when infants 6 to 10 months of age are placed in walkers (i.e., devices that support infants on wheels so that their feet just touch the ground), their behavior or propelling the walker is consequated by most of the same events as walking infants (e.g., contact with more stimulating objects and people). As a result, they appear precocious and resemble walking infants more than their nonlocomoting peers (Gustafson, 1984). Eventually, the differences between infants exposed to walkers and those not so exposed disappear as nonlocomoting infants begin to walk and contact the same environmental events. Practice and exposure to walkers may well lead to walking at a relatively early age, but it is unclear whether the child derives any real benefit from these practices. Studies such as those discussed above show that, by maximizing the efficacy of environmental variables, it may be possible to lower the average age associated with various behavioral accomplishments.

Visual Development

If scientists want to assess the sensory capacities of verbal humans, they simply manipulate stimuli and ask the subjects whether they can detect (e.g., see, hear, or smell) the relevant environmental change. Such methods cannot be used with infants. (The word *infant* comes from the Latin for "without speech.") Researchers must examine nonverbal behavior in order to measure this type of stimulus control in infants. The three most common methods used for this purpose are (1) the single-stimulus procedure, in which a single stimulus is presented and the infant's reactions (e.g., eye movements, vocalization, or reaching) are measured; (2) the preference method, in which two stimuli are presented and the amount of behavior directed to each stimulus is measured; and (3) the habituation method, in which a stimulus that elicits a response (e.g., sucking, heart rate, or visual fixation) is presented until responding diminishes. The examiner then presents a second stimulus to see if responding recurs (Dworetzky, 1987). Although all of the senses are important, vision and audition are especially so for humans. We will discuss the infant's basic visual abilities in the remainder of this section.

Basic Visual Abilities of Infants

By measuring changes in reflexive sucking rates and heart rates as objects are passed through the infant's visual field, researchers have determined that the infant's visual system is sensitive to movement as early as two or three days after birth (Finlay & Ivinkis, 1984; Haith, 1966). Visual acuity is not, however, good; very young infants have a visual acuity of about 20/150 (Dayton, Jones, Aiu, Rawson, Steele, & Rose, 1964). This means that the infant sees an object at 20 feet with the same clarity as a visually normal adult sees the same object at 150 feet. This determination resulted from measuring in the newborn a reflex called **optokinetic nystagmus,** a kind of reflexive focusing in which a lateral movement of the eyes is elicited by passing of a series of fine vertical stripes past the infant's eyes. The black lines are gradually made finer until the reflex is no longer elicited. In this way, the neonate's vision can be tested.

By one to three months, focused (vs. nonfocused) visual events function as reinforcement for behavior that produces the focusing. Kalnins and Bruner (1973) demonstrated this effect in a clever experiment by connecting a nipple directly to a focusing device. Infants were placed in front of a screen on which various forms were displayed. The infants learned to suck at rates that maintained a focused picture.

One dimension of visual behavior that is measurable and also appears to be sensitive to various environmental manipulations is the amount of time an infant looks at an object, called **fixation time.** Two techniques have been developed for the study of fixation time. One involves the preferences method described above. In this technique, the infant lies on its back a few inches beneath a plywood screen on which various stimuli are placed (e.g., Fantz, 1961). The experimenter can observe the infant through a small window in the top of the apparatus. Usually, two different stimuli are placed side by side, and the experimenter measures the amount of time the infant spends looking at each. Longer time of fixation on one of the stimuli indicates a greater preference for that stimulus. Researchers have found that infants prefer visual stimuli that are heterogeneous and elicit eye movements (Carlson, 1986; Kagan, 1970). Infants will, for example, spend more time looking at (1) patterns with a high degree of black–white contrast (e.g., a checkerboard) than at solid colors (Fantz, 1961) and (2) moving or intermittent lights than at a continuous light source (Haith, 1966).

The general finding that infants orient toward stimuli that provide considerable visual stimulation has been reproduced by means of a variant of the single-stimulus method and a technologically more sophisticated technique (Haith, 1969, 1976; Salapatek, 1975). In this technique, a harmless spot of infrared light is projected onto the infant's eyes. A television camera, specially designed to be sensitive to infrared light, records the spot and superimposes on it an image of the display at which the infant is looking. The procedure allows a precise determination of which parts of the stimulus array the eyes are scanning. Salapateck (1975) reported that one-month-old infants spend more time looking at the edge of a figure than at its inside. By two months, however, the infant scans across the border and looks at the interior.

Perception of Depth

Humans perceive depth primarily through stereoscopic cues, which occur because each eye receives a slightly different picture when we look at an object.

The use of stereoscopic cues became possible when, through evolution, the eyes of our forebears moved to the front of the head. The ability to be affected by stereoscopic cues conferred on our ancestors a far greater ability to react to distances than the cues that result when the eyes are located on the side of the head, as in, for example, rabbits. Being able to react accurately to distances was critical for early primates.

Developmental psychologists have explored the age at which infants are able to react to depth (distance) cues. To test this, Gibson and Walk (1960) devised an apparatus called the **visual cliff** (see Figure 8–6). The visual cliff consists of two sides covered by a glass surface. On one side (the shallow side) is a checkerboard-patterned platform directly beneath the glass; on the other side (the deep side) is a similar pattern, but it is located a considerable distance below the glass.

When placed on the visual cliff, newborn chicks, kittens, and baby mountain goats did not venture over to the deep end. This response suggests that, in these species, the ability to react to depth cues is innate in the sense of requiring little interaction with the environment. Human infants generally showed the same tendency. However, it is difficult to compare humans and nonhumans on this task because nonhumans are able to move on their own soon after birth and can be tested then. Human infants do not begin to self-propel until about six

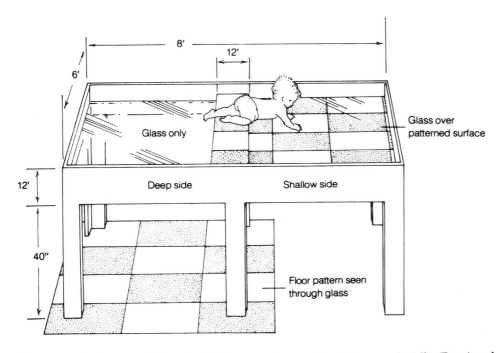

Figure 8-6. A diagram of the visual cliff apparatus used by Gibson and Walk. (Reprinted by permission from *Introduction to Child Development* by J. P. Dworetzky. Copyright 1987 by West Publishing. All rights reserved.)

months. By that time, they have had ample opportunity to learn about depth cues. To determine whether depth perception in humans is "innate," investigators obviously had to find a dependent variable that was sensitive to depth cues and could also be measured before infants became mobile.

Campos and his colleagues decided to measure infants' heart rates on the visual cliff. Interestingly, they found that when infants as young as 1.5 months were placed on the deep side, their heart rates decreased (Campos, Langer, & Krowitz, 1970). Only when infants were able to crawl did they show heart-rate increases. If we view heart-rate decreases as indicative of "interest" and heart-rate increases as indicative of "fear" (Hetherington & Parke, 1986), then these results may tell us something about infants' depth perception. Because any consistent change in heart rate can be interpreted as reacting to depth cues, the heart-rate decreases found in the Campos *et al.* (1970) study showed that young infants (e.g., one month old) are able to react to depth cues, although they have not yet learned a fear of heights. The heart-rate increases found in older infants suggest that, by the time infants become mobile, they have learned to "fear" (i.e., show heart-rate increases) in high places.

Hetherington and Parke (1986) suggested that self-produced locomotion is important in the development of a fear of heights. They cited other evidence by Campos and his associates indicating that, when infants who had not yet learned to crawl and exhibited heart-rate decreases on heights were given walkers, they began to show fear (i.e., heart-rate increases) in high places (Campos, Svejda, Bertenthal, Benson, & Schmid, 1981). This finding, too, "suggests that human infants are biologically prepared to learn to fear heights, but that the interaction with the environment that results from locomotion is necessary for the learning to occur" (Hetherington & Parke, 1986, p. 170).

Cognitive Behavioral Development:
Piaget's Analysis

According to Hetherington and Parke (1986), "**Cognition** refers to mental activity and behavior through which knowledge of the world is attained and processed, including learning, perception, memory and thinking." Consequently, "The study of cognitive development is concerned with describing and understanding the ways in which children's intellectual abilities and their knowledge of the world . . . change throughout the course of development" (p. 337). Although a number of theories of cognitive development have been advanced, the most popular one and the only one we will consider is that associated with Jean Piaget (1896–1980).

Although initially trained as a biologist, Piaget was quite interested in the development of intelligence in children. He worked for a while in Alfred Binet's Paris laboratory on the standardized intelligence tests developed by Binet. Unlike his colleagues, who were interested in children's ability to answer standardized questions correctly, Piaget was interested in the similarity of the incorrect answers given by children of the same age and in how those answers differed from those given by children of different ages. To Piaget, these consistencies seemed to reveal a developmental sequence of thinking processes. His goal was to understand these processes; he wanted to understand not just *what* children think or know, but more importantly, *how* they think and acquire knowledge. Piaget's strategy was to construct "thinking" problems and then to observe children as they solved the problems. His subjects consisted primarily of his own children, although he later extended his observations to other children as well.

As a biologist, Piaget understood that humans, like other animals, adapt to their environment. Piaget's theory of cognitive development (e.g., 1952) attempted to explain how the child adapts to the world around it. In short, Piaget argued that a child adapts to its environment through the use of innate cognitive processes that produce modifications in cognitive structures and, then, behavior.

Cognitive Structures and Processes

Piaget argued that children develop behaviorally and adapt to their surroundings by changing their cognitive structures. For Piaget, observations of behavior revealed these structures, which develop through a fixed series of stages, becoming ever more complex and allowing for more effective adaptation to the environment. The general term for these cognitive structures is *schemata* (singular, *schema*). **Schemata** are different mental activities that are used by children to organize and to respond to experiences. Although it is tempting to view schemata as part of the brain, Hetherington and Parke (1986) suggested that they are "an interrelated and organized group of memories, thoughts, actions, and strategies that the child uses in an attempt to understand the world" (p. 341), where *understand* refers to adapting to the environment. Cognitive structures allow the infant to interact with (i.e., adapt to) the environment. These interactions alter the cognitive structures, which typically become more complex as a result of experience with the environment and biological maturation. Increasingly complex cognitive structures allow for more complex ways of adapting to the environment.

In infants, schemata consist of unlearned sensorimotor relations such as reflexes. Infants are said to have various reflexive schemata, for example, a sucking schema, a kicking schema, and a grasping schema, which are manifested in organized sensorimotor activities (stimulus–response relations). As the infant's interactions with the environment expand, his or her schemata are quickly modified, and new cognitive structures emerge. These new cognitive structures, called **operations,** are internalized, symbolically represented schemata—the "mental equivalents of behavioral schemata"—which can be viewed as a set of rules, or as plans of problem solving and classification (Hetherington & Parke, 1986, p. 341). The cognitive development of children involves a gradual shift from schemata to operations.

According to Piaget, intellectual or cognitive development—the modification of cognitive structures—involves two inherited methods of processing environmental experience: organization and adaptation. **Organization** refers to the infant's tendency to integrate and coordinate behaviors and mental events into more complex systems. For example, an infant first has looking, reaching, and touching schemata that are independent of one another. As development proceeds, these schemata become organized into a higher order system of coordinated actions that can function as an independent unit: a looking–reaching–touching unit.

Adaptation refers to the tendency of humans to change because of experience, and it involves two processes: assimilation and accommodation. In **assimilation,** a new experience is interpreted in terms of existing knowledge (cognitive structures), and behavior in the new circumstance is similar to behavior in similar circumstances in the past. If, however, this behavior is unsuccessful in the new circumstances, cognitive structures are altered and behavior changes. Piaget called this process **accommodation.** Accommodation and assimilation work together to produce a state of cognitive equilibrium and to adapt behavior to a changing environment.

Assimilation and accommodation are typically illustrated with examples like the following: When a child first learns the word *daddy,* she has a tendency to call everyone, or at least all adult males, daddy. It is said that the child is assimilating any new person into her schema, or cognitive structure, of daddy. Gradually, as people stop reacting to the cuteness of being called daddy, and only the real father reacts to the name, the child will say, "Daddy" only when the father is present or is being referred to. At that point, the child has accommodated her concept of *daddy* to these circumstances.[1]

Periods of Cognitive Development

Piaget viewed cognitive development in terms of progressive changes in cognitive structures. Because these changes in children's intellectual development are qualitative and are correlated with changes in age, Piaget classified them according to a series of stages or periods. All children go through the same stages in the same order, but not necessarily at exactly the same rate. The four main stages of cognitive development described by Piaget are the sensorimotor period, the preoperational period, the concrete operational period, and the formal operational period, which are summarized in Table 8–4.

Evaluation of Piaget's Theory

Piaget's theory is based on accurate observations of behavior: The stages that he described generally capture the changes in behavior that occur as a child

---

[1]The reader should recognize that changes in the stimuli that evoke the response "Daddy" can readily by explained in terms of operant conditioning. Initially, people reinforce saying, "Daddy" regardless of whether the father is present. Over time, they establish tight stimulus control by reinforcing the response "daddy" only in the presence of the father. The result is that the child says, "Daddy" only when the father is present. This account is superior to a Piagetian analysis in that it explains the changes in behavior in terms of observable relations, whereas the Piagetian analysis appeals to hypothetical cognitive structures.

ages. Moreover, his explanations of cognitive development are widely accepted. But Piaget's theory is scientifically unsatisfactory. The primary reason is that the cognitive structures and processes on which the theory rests are hypothetical entities. They cannot be observed directly, and they have no physical status. As discussed in Chapter 2, behavior cannot be explained adequately in terms of such hypothetical entities. Although Piaget's theory has some predictive validity, it affords no control over the subject matter. For example, Piaget's system cannot account for individual differences between children of the same age or between children of different ages except by assuming differences in unobservable cognitive structures. Appealing to changes in cognitive structures as explanations of behavior without the ability to observe, measure, and control those changes makes such explanations circular: the only evidence for the explanations is the behavior changes they attempt to explain. Moreover, simply assigning a label to a child on the basis of age and behavior does not explain anything, but this nominal fallacy is not obvious at first glance.

Because Piaget's theory is a normative one, its main value lies in predicting the average age when certain behavioral changes will be observed. Unfortunately, the complete lack of experimental control has diminished his theory's predictive value. Moreover, some studies have tested the central assumption of Piaget's theory (that development is a maturational process) by attempting to teach intellectual skills to children who, according to Piaget, would be too young to learn these particular skills. These studies have shown that some of the more important developmental changes described by Piaget can be taught through

Table 8-4
Piagetian Stages of Cognitive Development[a]

1. Sensorimotor stage (birth to 2 years)	Children begin to distinguish between themselves and the rest of the world. Begin to organize their experiences, fitting them into schemata—first steps toward intentional behavior. Learn object permanence, and that actions have consequences (cause and effect).
2. Preoperational stage (2–7 years)	Children have a growing ability both to remember and to anticipate. Begin to use symbols to represent external world internally. Egocentric—cannot put themselves in someone else's place. Tend to focus on one aspect or dimension of an object and ignore all others, cannot mentally retrace steps to reach a conclusion (irreversibility).
3. Concrete operational stage (7–11 years)	Children learn to retrace thoughts, correct themselves; can consider more than one aspect or dimension at a time. Able to look at a problem in different ways and see other people's points of view. Develop concepts of conservation: number, mass, etc.
4. Formal oerational stage (12 years and up)	Children can think in abstract terms; formulate and test hypotheses through logic. Can think through various solutions to a problem or the possible consequences of an action. No longer tied to concrete testing of ideas in external world: can test them internally through logic.

[a]Adapted from *The Psychology of the Child* by J. Piaget and B. Inhelder. Copyright 1969 by Basic Books, Inc. Reprinted by permission of Basic Books, Inc., Publishers.

relatively simple and explicit training (e.g., Gelman, 1969; Watson & Ramey, 1972). In fact, one of Piaget's most popular notions, that of conservation, can be trained much earlier than Piaget suggested (see Sidebar 8-1).

The Development of Social Behavior

Many species, *Homo sapiens* among them, are social in the sense that the behavior of individual members of a group is affected by, and in turn affects, the behavior of other members of that group. The ways in which humans interact with other members of their culture are determined in large part by early interactions with parents or other caretakers. As discussed in Chapter 4, the period of childhood dependency in humans is prolonged and allows the child to acquire a rich repertoire of social relations.

Social behavior occurs when an individual's actions are determined by stimuli arising from other people. These stimuli are called **social stimuli.** Social stimuli do not differ from other stimuli in their dimensions; that is, they affect visual, auditory, olfactory, and tactile receptors. They also do not differ in function from other stimuli; that is, they are eliciting, reinforcing, discriminative, and motivational (Keller & Schoenfeld, 1950). The difference is in their origin. Social stimuli are unique in that they arise from the behavior of other people. The actual behavior determined by social stimuli is likely to vary somewhat from person to person, but in general, it is fairly consistent within a culture.

Development of Attachment

Social behavior begins very early in life and contributes to what is called *attachment*. Attachment is a metaphor that psychologists use to describe special kinds of parent–child interactions, specifically those that indicate that the child seeks to be close to and in other ways prefers the parent over other people. Many behaviors of the child are indicative of attachment. Among the most important are crying, cuddling, and smiling. In general, these behaviors follow a similar progression in development. Early in life, the infant's behavior is nonselectively engendered by a variety of social stimuli. Next, the social stimuli associated with familiar people come to exercise discriminated control over behavior. Finally, specific attachment behaviors appear: the infant acts selectively to increase contact with specific people (e.g., the parents) and may "protest" (e.g., cry) when they depart. This sequence is further described with respect to two important infant behaviors.

Crying

Crying typically has multiple causes. From birth, crying can be elicited unconditionally by diverse stimuli, including sudden loud sounds and bright lights, loss of support, and objects or events associated with discomfort (e.g., food deprivation, pain, or cold).

Initially, crying is elicited by stimuli associated with hunger or discomfort,

Sidebar 8-1
Conservation: Cognitive Process or Learned Behavior?

According to Piagetians, perhaps the single most important intellectual achievement of children in the concrete operational period is conservation. **Conservation** occurs when a person responds to an object as unchanged despite transformations performed on that object. Consider the following test. Two glasses of water that are the same size, shape, height, and width are filled with equal amounts of water. Then the contents of one glass are poured into a taller, narrower glass. If a person says that the amount of water in the tall, narrow glass is the same as that in the short, wide glass, convervation (of volume) is evident. According to Piaget, not until a child reaches the concrete operational stage (at about seven years of age) will she or he be able to say that the amounts are the same. In another typical Piagetian test for conservation, a child is presented with two equal-sized lumps of clay and, when asked if they are the same size, will report that they are. If the experimenter then stretches one of the lumps into an elongated form and asks the child if they are still the same size, the preoperational child will report that they are not. In contrast, the concrete operational child will say that they are still the same size. Piaget's explanation for the preoperational child's lack of conservation in both of the above examples was that the child lacked the necessary cognitive structures.

There are several dimensions along which objects can change, including position, shape, space, and volume. And there are several tests that can be used to judge conservation when these dimensions are altered. Cognitive developmental psychologists have determined that the average age at which children demonstrate conservation varies for different stimulus characteristics: conservation of number usually occurs by about six years of age, conservation of mass by seven, and conservation of weight around nine.

But must we wait for hypothetical cognitive structures to "develop" before a child can give the appropriate responses in these circumstances? Can a child under seven years of age be taught these skills? And why don't children under seven typically conserve?

These questions have been partially answered by several studies demonstrating that conservation can be accelerated simply by arrangement of the environment to facilitate learning (e.g., Gelman, 1969; Sigel, Roeper, & Hooper, 1966). Moreover, Gelman (1969) suggested that the reason that children fail tests of conservation is simply that they are not attending to the cue that the experimenters deem critical. Consider the liquid conservation test (described above). In that test, "the stimulus complex of each glass with water can be thought of as a multidimensional pattern with at least six attributes; these being size, shape, height, width, water level, and actual amount of water" (Gelman, 1969, p. 168). Gelman reminded us that the child is likely to react to relations and dimensions other than those specified by the experimenter (E):

> From the E's point of view only one cue is relevant, i.e., related to the solution of the conservation problem, and this is amount of water. All others are irrelevant. However, from the viewpoint of a young S [subject] all cues are potentially relevant to his definition of amount. When he is asked to judge amount, he may do so on the basis of any or all cues in the complex. (p. 169)

If the subject is attending to an irrelevant cue, conservation will not occur. In her study, Gelman used a discrimination-training procedure with a large number of conservation problems containing many stimuli that differed along several dimensions except for one common one. The subjects (children whose median age was five years and four months) were asked questions about the stimuli (e.g., "Do these have the same or different amounts of clay?"). When the children gave correct responses to the common element, they were told, "Yes, that is right," and were given a prize. When incorrect answers were given, they were told, "No, that is not right." The results showed clearly that children who were given explicit discrimination training learned to conserve with much greater accuracy than control subjects.

but it quickly comes under the control of the social environment. In fact, evolutionarily speaking, crying exists only because it affects other humans: ancestral infants who cried when hungry or in discomfort were more likely to be attended to by parents than those who did not. Some have even argued that adults are genetically predisposed to react to an infant's crying. Presumably, ancestral adults who did so ensured that their children would survive and transmit their genes to future generations.

Although crying begins as one of the unconditioned reflexes, it soon becomes both respondently and operantly conditioned. Operant conditioning is especially important in the development of attachment. Not only does the parent's reaction strengthen the infant's crying under certain circumstances, but the cessation of the infant's crying also strengthens the parent's behavior that produced it. This sequence often results in a vicious circle between the parent and child. Moreover, other relations are conditioned in the process. For example, when a child is hungry and cries, the parent picks up, talks to, and feeds the child. The parent's behavior is reinforced at least by the cessation of the crying, if not by other signs of "contentment" in the child (e.g., cooing, smiling, or sleeping). And the child's behavior of crying under similar circumstances is reinforced. Additionally, the effects of the sight and sound of the parent are altered by these interactions and become conditioned reinforcers. The important aspect of crying for attachment, however, is that it results in frequent contact with the parent.

Cuddling

Cuddling is related to feeding in that the infant must be cuddled in order to be breast-fed. But there are other consequences of cuddling: it results in warmth and gentle tactile stimulation, and it keeps the infant close to the parent for protection.

The human newborn does not cling to its mother, but it does have two reflexes (the Moro reflex, in which loud sounds or loss of support elicits extension of the arms and feet, and the palmar reflex, in which a touch on the palm elicits grasping) that may be vestiges of the clinging reflex that is evident in other primates. Moreover, the posture of human infants when cuddled adjusts to the contours of the parent's body. This adjustment may serve to reinforce the parent's behavior.

Theories of Attachment

Several theories of attachment have been popular. An early theory, based on learning principles, asserted that, by virtue of being associated with food and the reduction of hunger, the mother acquires conditioned reinforcing properties (e.g., Sear, Maccoby, & Levin, 1957). Consequently, behavior that results in contact with the mother is reinforced by that contact. In short, the child becomes attached to the mother because she fulfills a biological need for food. A variety of findings logically contradict the notion that attachment is based solely on the mother's meeting the biological needs of the child. First, infants display attachment behavior in situations in which they have not received food. Second, attachment behaviors continue after biological needs have been met. Third, as shown in a famous series of studies by Harry Harlow (e.g., Harlow, 1958; Harlow & Suomi, 1970), attachment behaviors may be directed toward individuals and objects that never provide nourishment.

To test the hypothesis that attachment depends on the mother's meeting biological needs of the infant, Harlow separated infant rhesus monkeys from their mothers at an early age and placed them in a room with two surrogate (substitute) "mothers." The mothers were identical except that one was constructed of wire mesh and the other was covered with soft terry cloth. Both were heated and had in the center of the chest a nipple that the infants could suckle. In one experiment, the infants were allowed to feed on the wire mother but not on the cloth mother. The dependent variable was the amount of time the infants spent clinging to each mother. The results showed quite clearly that, except for feeding time, the infants spent a majority of their time clinging to the cloth mother (see Figure 8–7). From these and other results, Harlow concluded that, even though the infants received all of their nourishment from the wire mother,

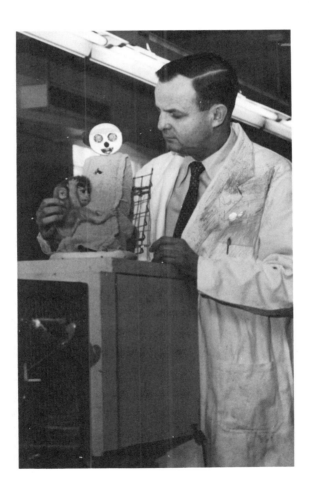

Harry Harlow with a cloth monkey and one of his subjects. (Photo courtesy of Roger Ulrich.)

they developed attachment behavior only to the cloth mother. Attachment did not appear to result from food delivery.

Harlow clearly showed that feeding is not the critical or only variable in the development of attachment in rhesus monkeys. Whether this finding generalizes to humans is unclear, for infant rhesus monkeys differ from infant humans in many ways (e.g., they are mobile, have the upper-body strength to cling, and have more fully developed brains). Regardless of the generality of Harlow's findings, few contemporary theoreticians hold to the old, simpleminded view that feeding is the ultimate source of attachment.

Many behaviorists accept a theory of attachment that incorporates aspects of behavior analysis and ethology. In general, an ethological analysis suggests that infants and mothers are genetically predisposed to behave in certain ways with respect to each other. For example, infants smile, cry, and suck under specific circumstances, and the stimuli arising from these behaviors elicit specific behaviors in the mother. The evolutionary view is that such reciprocal mother–child interactions facilitated survival; hence, the genotype that permitted them became prominent. It is important to understand that this genotype leads not to the inheritance of specific behaviors, but to a tendency to acquire certain behavioral relations.

An early proponent of the ethological view of attachment was Konrad Lorenz. By 1940, researchers had shown that newly hatched chicks, ducklings, and goslings follow the first moving object they see, which is usually their mother. Because all hatchlings were observed to do this, it appeared that the following response was innate. Lorenz provided a dramatic demonstration of innate following by ensuring that he was the first moving object seen by ducklings and goslings. Thereafter, they followed him everywhere, just as they normally would their mothers. Lorenz called this phenomenon **imprinting,** and he soon

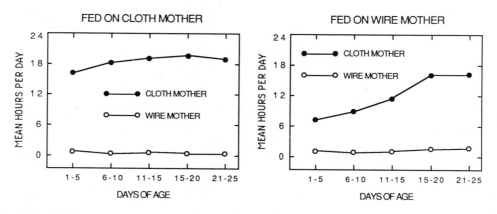

Figure 8-7. Time spent by infant rhesus monkeys on cloth and wire mother surrogates. (From "The Nature of Love" by H. F. Harlow. *American Psychologist, 13,* 673–685. Copyright 1958 by the American Psychological Association. Redrawn by permission.)

discovered that it occurred only during a **sensitive period**[2] lasting for about two days from the time of hatching. The possible survival value of imprinting is obvious: the first moving object a hatchling sees is likely to be its mother, and following her may provide increased access to food or safety from predators. Precocial birds (those able to move about from birth) with a genotype that favors following may, on that basis, be more apt to survive than those without it. Hence, the genotype will become predominant.

Although imprinting is rigidly controlled by innate factors (Fantino & Logan, 1979), there is good evidence that the response of following a moving object is learned. The importance of learning in imprinting was first demonstrated in a clever experiment conducted by Neil Peterson (1960). Peterson arranged conditions so that a yellow cylinder (10 by 20 centimeters) was the first moving object seen by black and Peking ducklings. He then arranged conditions so that the ducklings could view the cylinder if they pecked a Plexiglas disk. Under these conditions, pecking occurred reliably: Peterson demonstrated operantly conditioned pecking with the sight of the imprinted object as the reinforcer. There are two points of interest in this demonstration. First, imprinting established the imprinted object as an unconditioned reinforcer. Second, the imprinted object served to reinforce a response other than, and in fact incompatible with, following. These findings suggest that following behavior is not inherited directly in imprinting. What is inherited is the capacity to be reinforced by the sight of, or proximity to, the imprinted object. In precocial birds, following is the behavior most likely to achieve this reinforcement.

A similar analysis might be extended to Harlow's findings with infant monkeys. They probably directly inherit not clinging behavior, but the tendency to be reinforced by warmth, softness, or even the sight of another monkey. In rhesus monkeys, clinging is the behavior most likely to achieve this reinforcement. This surmise could be tested by selecting some arbitrary response such as button pushing and assessing the reinforcing functions of these stimulus dimensions. Although such a test has not been done systematically, Harlow did arrange conditions so that when infant monkeys pressed a lever, they were allowed to view either the wire mother, the cloth mother, or another infant monkey. They pressed much more when they could see either the cloth surrogate or the other infant monkey, a response that indicates that the sight of either would reinforce the behavior that produced it. Other work by Harlow indicated that visual, tactile, or thermal contact with the surrogate mother reinforced running and clinging to her. The question remains why those events function as

---

[2]Although the terms are sometimes used as approximate synonyms, *sensitive, optimal,* and *critical periods* are distinguished by ethologists (see Fantino & Logan, 1979). A sensitive period is one in which an individual is exceptionally susceptible to the effects of a particular experience; such periods can often be defined only loosely. An optimal period is that portion of a sensitive period in which a particular experience produces the greatest effect. For example, the strongest imprinting in ducks is produced when the moving stimulus is presented 13 to 16 hours after hatching (Hess, 1958). A critical period is evident if (1) susceptibility to an experience is limited to a very brief period of time, and (2) absence of the experience during this time produces permanent behavioral abnormality.

reinforcement and whether the same events function as reinforcement for human infants. The English ethologist John Bowlby (e.g., 1973) suggested that human infants have a predisposition to learn behaviors that maximize contact with the mother, and that mothers are predisposed to be affected by infant's behaviors, including smiling, crying, and looking. From a behavioral perspective, the stimuli arising from these infant behaviors may be eliciting, motivational, or reinforcing, depending on their temporal relation to and effect on behaviors in the mother. After extensive interactions between the mother and the child, it seems clear that the mother acquires conditioned reinforcing functions so that the child will continue to behave in ways that bring her closer. Although the association with food may be important, it is naive to think that it is the sole basis of the conditioned reinforcement. The mother is a source of much more than just food.

As an aside, studies of imprinting are important in revealing the existence of sensitive periods for the acquisition of certain behaviors, and in showing that organisms inherit the capacity to be reinforced by ecologically relevant stimuli. These studies are also noteworthy in revealing that early experiences can have delayed, enduring, and counterintuitive effects. All of these outcomes are evident in research on cross-fostering, in which young birds of one species are raised by and imprinted on foster parents of another species. If, for example, mallard ducks are reared by another species, the males at sexual maturity attempt to mate with females of the species that reared them, not with female mallards. Female mallards, in contrast, typically mate with male mallards, regardless of how the females were reared (Schultz, 1971). In this case, the effects of imprinting are (1) delayed by several months; (2) persistent across years even with exposure to appropriate mates; (3) evident in responses (sexual behavior) that are not an obvious part of imprinting; and (4) different for males and females.

Although imprinting as we have discussed it occurs only in birds, it is clear that the early experiences of primates, including humans, powerfully influence subsequent behavior–environment interactions. One way in which they do so is by narrowing the range of stimuli with reinforcing properties.

Emotional Development

As her grandparents look on, a one-year-old girl is sitting in a stroller gnawing on a plastic rattle. The rattle slips from her grasp and falls to the floor. A rapid sequence of events ensures: She reaches for the rattle, can't get it, turns red in the face, screams and cries, and flails her arms. Grandmother laughs, saying, "She's mad as a hornet." Grandfather retrieves the rattle, wipes it off, and returns it to the baby. This action terminates the screaming and crying; the rattle goes back in the mouth, to be sucked with accompanying grins and coos. "That's one happy kid," the old man observes. The terms *mad* and *happy* refer to what are commonly called *emotions*.

But what are emotions? The word *emotion* comes from the Latin *emovere*, meaning "to move out, stir up, or agitate." Current vernacular definitions of emotion approximate the following:

Emotion. 1. Agitation of the passions or sensibilities often involving physiological changes. 2. Any strong feeling, as of joy, sorrow, reverence, hate, or love, arising subjectively rather than through conscious mental effort. (*American Heritage Dictionary*, 1984, p. 428)

Such definitions raise problems for a science of behavior because they refer to unobservable events (passions, sensibilities, feelings) and do not indicate how, or even if, emotion is related to behavior. Unfortunately, the definitions of emotion characteristically offered by psychologists are little better. Consider the following examples, all taken from introductory psychology books:

Emotions are strong, relatively uncontrollable feelings that are accompanied by physiological changes and often affect our behavior. (Houston, Bee, Hatfield, & Rimm, 1979, p. 316)

[Emotion is] an aroused state within an organism which may occur in response to internal and external stimuli. (Lefton, 1979, p. 563)

[Emotion is an] internal state usually produced by an external stimulus—[it] can result in many different sorts of behavior. (Darley, Glucksberg, Kamin, & Kinchla, 1981, p. 605)

Reading such definitions tempts one to reify emotion, that is, to construe it as a material object or state. This is a misconception. *Emotion* is only a word used as a shorthand description of certain kinds of behavior–environment interactions. These interactions may have overt and covert components. In general, we describe a person as emotional when we directly observe, or the person verbally reports, that she or he is physiologically aroused and is highly motivated (i.e., quite likely) to perform some response.

Physiological Arousal

Most emotions involve activation of the sympathetic branch of the autonomic nervous system, which results in increases in heart rate, pupil size, blood pressure, and skin temperature. We refer, at least in part, to these physiological changes when we say that we "feel" anger, anxiety, or elation. Interestingly, many different emotions are accompanied by similar kinds of physiological changes; sympathetic arousal is likely to be evident in a person who self-reports being angry, fearful, or excited. We are trained to label specific emotions in ourselves and others on the basis of (1) the stimuli that evoke them and (2) the behaviors they control, not on the basis of physiological changes alone. The labeling is, however, apt to be imprecise. There are hundreds of words that describe emotions; they integrate and overlap in complex and confusing ways. What, for example, is the difference between anger and rage, sadness and despair, joy and pleasure? Very little. So little, in fact, that the differentiation is forced and makes no contribution to understanding behavior.

Motivation

Motivational operations alter (increase or decrease) the reinforcing or punishing capacity of particular stimuli. They also alter the likelihood of the occurrence of behaviors that have been relevant to (e.g., have produced or have allowed one to avoid) those stimuli in the past (see Chapter 6). We infer that a stimulus has motivational effects in other people when they emit behavior relevant to the stimulus.

Emotion is only a term used to describe certain kinds of behaviors; it is not the cause of anything. Nonetheless, many psychologists and most laypeople believe that emotions cause bodily reactions, both physiological and behavioral. As Keller and Schoenfeld (1950) explained:

> In this classic picture, the sequence of events is (1) stimulation, (2) subjectively "felt" emotion, and (3) bodily "expression"—behavior. This same sequence, with differences in content, would be characteristic of joy, sorrow, anger, and other time-honored categories. (p. 332)

This conception has a commonsensical appeal. You walk into a friend's room just as she tears the tape from a Michael Jackson cassette and hurls it against the wall. "Why did you do that?" you query. "Because I'm mad" is her answer. Reasonable enough, or so it seems: most laypeople are willing to ascribe a causal status to anger. A moment's reflection reveals, however, that your friend's answer raises another question: "Why are you mad?" "I'm mad," she retorts, "because the damned thing wouldn't rewind." Now we approach the cause of the throwing, which is a real event: the failure of the tape to rewind. That event, by virtue of your friend's history and the current circumstances, may make damaging the tape a reinforcer and may cause her to rip and throw it. It also produces the autonomic arousal and other detectable changes, including overt verbalizations, that cause her to say, "I'm mad."

According to this analysis of emotion, certain environmental conditions (stimuli) alter both physiological and behavioral activity; these responses can interact. Verbal humans have been taught to describe either or both types of activity in themselves and others as different emotions, depending on the context in which they occur. Emotion is not in any simple sense the cause of behavior or its result. It is, however, a label for a wide and fascinating range of behavior–environment interactions, which begin to emerge at an early age.

The behaviors of infants that psychologists refer to as emotional include smiling, laughing, frowning, and crying. These behaviors develop through the elaboration of basic reflexive relations (Bijou, 1979; Dworetzky, 1987). This development involves the intermingling of respondent and operant conditioning and the biological maturation of the infant. The result is not only more differentiated forms of behavior, but behavior under the control of a wider range of stimuli (Bijou, 1979).

Consider the development of smiling and laughter. Smiling involves observable changes in the mouth and lips that result from a contraction of muscles in the face. Although the facial musculature of the infant is fully developed and functional at or before birth (Ekman & Oster, 1979), the infant can smile only slightly. It does so as a reflexive response to a stroking of the lips or the cheek. Smiling in infants is also common during periods of REM (rapid-eye-movement) sleep. Contrary to popular opinion, intestinal distress (i.e., gas) does not cause newborns to smile.

Although initially reflexive, the infant's smiling soon comes under the control of a range of environmental stimuli. Initially, these stimuli are primarily nonsocial. But over time, social stimuli, particularly the parents' faces and voices, begin to evoke smiling. This response reflects operant conditioning and discrimination. In the presence of the parent's face or voice, smiling is reinforced by the parent (i.e., by cuddling, tickling, cooing, etc.). Moreover, the parent's behavior is reinforced by the smile. This reciprocally reinforcing interaction is an important step in the development of attachment.

Laughter begins to occur at around four months of age. As is true of smiling, the number of stimuli that elicit laughter increases with age. Whereas tactile stimulation (e.g., tickling) will elicit laughter in a five-month-old, older infants will laugh when exposed to social games such as peek-a-boo, and to relatively complex visual events such as covering and uncovering the mother's face. Finally, situations in which the infant's behavior changes the environment in particular ways come to evoke smiling and laughing. For example, Watson (1973) reported that children who learned to move their heads because doing so caused a mobile to turn smiled as soon as the mobile turned. Watson surmised that parents and infants play what he called the "contingency game," in which parents set up contingencies (cause-and-effect relations between two events) between their children's behaviors and their own. For example, each time the baby opens her mouth the parent tickles her feet; whenever the baby laughs, the parent touches her nose. During the contingency game, infants smile and laugh, responses that reinforce the parents' behaviors of playing the game. Conversely, the parents reinforce a wide range of social behaviors in the infant, all of which probably lead to stronger attachment and a more socially responsive infant.

In addition to smiling and laughter, infants show other behaviors that lead us to infer emotion. For example, many stimuli cause infants to cry, whimper, or turn away. We have previously discussed how these behaviors can be reflexively elicited by unconditional stimuli such as loud noises, strong odors, and bad tastes. Developmental psychologists, however, have been especially interested in situations in which these behaviors are evoked by other people. If, for instance, an infant is in a room with his mother and she leaves and an unfamiliar woman enters the room, the infant will often whimper or cry and show other signs of distress. Some psychologists refer to these reactions as "fear of strangers" or "stranger anxiety" and have devoted a considerable amount of research to them. Most researchers now agree that the likelihood and intensity of "stranger anxiety" depend on many factors, among them the behavior of the stranger (e.g., whether the stranger smiles and is friendly or is quiet and passive) and the setting (e.g., whether the infant sits on the mother's lap or alone a few feet away when a stranger enters) (Rheingold & Eckerman, 1973).

To account fully for fear of strangers, or for any other emotional behavior, one must be aware of the current setting and the history of the child with respect to variables present in that setting. By early childhood, most humans exhibit a full range of emotional behavior. The conditions under which these emotions are manifested and their intensity depend to a considerable extent on conditioning. Some children cry often and easily, perhaps because crying is richly reinforced in a variety of situations. Others seldom cry; the response has not "paid off" for them. The behavior–environment interactions that constitute emotions are not, however, endlessly modifiable. By virtue of the phylogenetic history of humans, certain kinds of stimuli produce a limited range of subjective and overt reactions. These reactions may, in turn, tend to affect the behavior of other people in particular ways; smiles, for example, often serve as positive reinforcers. All of the behavior of humans has a biological basis, and the effects of events that occur within the course of a person's life are inevitably constrained to some extent by genetic endowment.

Intelligence and Its Development

As infants develop new and more complex ways of interacting with the environment, it can be said that their intelligence develops. Few words are used more often, or in more different ways, than *intelligence*. The term itself comes from the Latin *intellegere*, meaning "to perceive or understand." As characteristically used today, **intelligence** refers to the ability of an individual to learn, to remember information and use it appropriately, to solve problems, to acquire and use language, to exercise good judgment, to find similarities and differences, and generally to behave in ways deemed desirable by the culture (cf. Grossman, 1983). Intelligence is not a thing; it is an abstraction (i.e., a term) based entirely on observations of behavior. A person is intelligent to the degree that she or he exhibits certain behaviors, and that is the extent of it. Intelligence has no material status and cannot be used to explain behavior.

Intelligence is typically measured through the use of standardized tests. The first such scale was developed in France by Alfred Binet. Binet, whose initial test appeared in 1904, had one goal: to devise an instrument appropriate for detecting schoolchildren likely to need special services (i.e., mentally retarded chil-

Emotions are often difficult to label accurately without information about the current environment. What emotion is this child feeling? You might have a better idea if you knew what had just occurred in her environment. (Photo courtesy of Roger Ulrich.)

dren). With the help of his student Theophile Simon, Binet published three versions of the scale before his death in 1911. In each version, the child was required to perform a large series of short tasks, each related to everyday problems of life. As Stephen Jay Gould (1981) explained:

> Binet decided to assign an age level to each task, defined as the youngest age at which a child of normal intelligence should be able to complete the task successfully. A child began the Binet test with tasks for the youngest age and proceeded in sequence until he could no longer complete the tasks. The age associated with the last tasks he could perform became his "mental age," and his general intellectual level was calculated by subtracting this mental age from his true chronological age. Children whose mental ages were sufficiently behind their chronological ages could then be identified for special educational problems. . . . In 1912 the German psychologist W. Stern argued that mental age should be divided by chronological age, not subtracted from it, and the intelligence *quotient*, or IQ, was born. (pp. 149–150)

As Gould (1981) further noted, Binet insisted on three cardinal principles for using his tests:

1. The scores are a practical device; they do not buttress any theory of intellect. They do not define anything innate or permanent. We may not designate what they measure as "intelligence" or any other reified entity.
2. The scale is a rough, empirical guide for identifying mildly retarded and learning-disabled children who need special help. It is not a device for ranking children.
3. Whatever the cause of difficulty in children identified for help, emphasis shall be placed upon improvement through special training. Low scores shall not be used to mark children as innately incapable. (p. 155)

Many school boards now use intelligence tests in a way consistent with these principles, that is, to help identify children with special needs. However, for decades following Binet's death, the use of intelligence tests in schools violated all three of Binet's principles. The tests were also used to support social policies that discriminated against groups and individuals on the basis of supposedly inferior intelligence (see Gould, 1981).

Dozens of intelligence scales are available. Their specifics differ, but most include tests of discrimination, generalization, motor behavior, general information, vocabulary, induction, comprehension, sequencing, detail recognition, analogies, abstract reasoning, memory, and pattern completion (Salvia & Ysseldyke, 1981). Table 8–5 lists areas of emphasis for the Stanford-Binet and the Wechsler scales (i.e., the Wechsler Adult Intelligence Scale and the Wechsler Intelligence Scale for Children—Revised), which are widely used.

All intelligence tests are **norm-referenced.** That is, an individual's performance is compared to that of a reference group (the normative, or norm, population). A quantitative measure, usually referred to as the **intelligence quotient (IQ)**, results. As mentioned previously, the IQ is determined by dividing the mental age by the chronological age, then multiplying by 100 (i.e., $IQ = MA/CA \times 100$). It may come as a surprise, but "No major, reputable test today uses an actual IQ score; that is a score based on the ratio of mental age to chronological age, multiplied by 100. Yet, test descriptions in basic texts continue to report the IQ concept" (Reschly, 1981, p. 1096).

Contemporary intelligence scales are constructed with known psychometric properties. They are designed to yield a normal distribution of scores, with a specifiable mean (typically 100) and standard deviation (often 15). Knowing these values allows for meaningful interpretation of the score earned by an individual. If, for example, a student earns a score of 130 on a scale with a mean of 100 and a standard deviation of 15, that score is at about the 98th percentile. Hence the child's performance is exceptional; few would be expected to do as well.

Intelligence tests are controversial for a number of reasons. Psychologists, educators, philosophers, and laypeople have all failed to generate a universally accepted definition and explanation of intelligence, although theories of intelligence abound. Thus, it is not clear exactly what intelligence tests measure. Moreover, most intelligence tests are recognized as being culturally biased. As Reschly (1979) contended:

> IQ tests measure only a portion of the competencies involved with human intelligence. The IQ results are best seen as predicting performance in school, and reflecting the degree to which children have mastered middle class cultural symbols and values. This is useful information, but it is also limited. Further cautions—IQ tests do not measure innate-genetic capacity and the scores are not fixed. Some persons do exhibit significant increases or decreases in their measured IQ. (p. 224)

The foregoing should not be construed to mean that intelligence is a meaningless construct, or that intelligence scales are devoid of worth. People surely differ with respect to the kinds of behaviors that are subsumed under the label of intelligence, and these differences are of practical as well as theoretical importance. Moreover, intelligence tests provide a useful summary of a person's behavioral repertoire in certain domains compared to that of others of his or her age. This is potentially useful information; as Binet recognized, it helps professionals identify children with special needs. The problem with intelligence is that it is too often reified, then used to explain behavior. In actuality, intelligence has no real causal status. Intelligence is inferred on the basis of what a person does; it does not determine her or his actions.

Table 8-5
Areas of Emphasis on the Stanford-Binet
and the Wechsler Scales

Stanford-Binet Scale	Wechsler Scale
Verbal	Verbal
Vocabulary	Information
Comprehension	Comprehension
Absurdities	Arithmetic
Verbal relations	Similarities
Pattern analysis	Vocabulary
Copying	Performance
Matrices	Digit span
Paper folding and cutting	Picture comprehension
Quantitative	Picture arrangement
Number series	Block design
Equation building	Object assembly
Bead memory	Digit
Memory for sentences	
Memory for digits	
Memory for objects	

Like other behaviors, those subsumed under the label of intelligence are controlled by genotype, maturation, and behavior–environment interactions. Over the years, there has been considerable debate about the heritability of intelligence. In the late 1800s and early 1900s, it was rather widely believed that genotype determined intelligence in a fixed and invariant manner. In those days, support for the heritability of intelligence came primarily from pedigree studies. One such study, conducted by Henry Goddard (1912), merits description. In it, Goddard reported on the progeny of "Martin Kallikak." Kallikak, a name fabricated by Goddard from Grecian words meaning "good" and "evil," was a Revolutionary War soldier who fathered an illegitimate son by a feebleminded girl. Goddard claimed to have identified 480 descendants by way of this son. Of them, 143 supposedly were mentally retarded. There was also a high incidence of alcoholism, criminality, and promiscuity among descendants of Martin Kallikak's son and the feebleminded girl. In contrast, these problems were not evident in the descendants of Kallikak and the woman of normal intelligence whom he married.

Goddard's study was seriously flawed (see Gould, 1981), but its results and the findings of other inadequate studies (e.g., those allegedly showing that southern European immigrants to America tested at Ellis Island performed poorly on intelligence tests, providing evidence of their innate stupidity) were taken to indicate that feeblemindedness was inherited and could not be improved by environmental manipulations. This position was stated forcefully by Goddard in 1920:

> Stated in its boldest form, our thesis is that the chief determiner of human conduct is a unitary mental process which we call intelligence; that this process is conditioned by a nervous mechanism which is inborn; that the degree of efficiency to be attained by that nervous mechanism and the consequent grade of intellectual or mental level for each individual is determined by the kind of chromosomes that come together with the union of the germ cells; that it is but little affected by any later influences except such serious accidents as may destroy part of the mechanism. (Quoted in Tuddenham, 1962, p. 491.)

The *our* to whom Goddard referred were those people who supported **eugenics,** an effort to improve humanity through selective breeding. The eugenicists feared the "menace of the feebleminded." From their perspective, morons (people with an IQ of approximately 50 to 70) were immoral, unproductive, and dangerous to society. Moreover, their behavior was considered genetically determined and unmodifiable. This being the case, the only way to protect society was to prevent feebleminded people (and other "inferiors") from procreating. This prevention could be accomplished by segregating them in institutions, or by sterilizing them, and both occurred.

The eugenics movement did not long endure in the United States. By 1928, Goddard had realized that the behavior of morons was influenced by environmental variables, and in that year, he concluded: "Feeble-mindedness is not incurable [and] the feeble-minded do not generally need to be segregated in institutions" (p. 225). He argued in the same article that morons benefit from training and education, which can enable most of them to live relatively independent lives.

The fact that the behaviors considered indicative of intelligence are influenced by environmental variables does not indicate that intelligence is not heritable. It undoubtedly is to some extent. The problem is that too many people misunderstand the meaning of heritability and base social policy on their misunderstanding. Stephen Jay Gould (1981) provided a sterling analysis of what he termed "the hereditarian fallacy." In essence:

> The hereditarian fallacy is not the simple claim that IQ is to some degree "heritable." I have no doubt that it is, though the degree has clearly been exaggerated by the most avid hereditarians. It is hard to find any broad aspect of human performance or anatomy that has no heritable component at all. The hereditarian fallacy resides in two false implications drawn from this basic fact:
>
> 1. The equation of "heritable" with "inevitable." To a biologist, heritability refers to the passage of traits or tendencies along family lines as a result of genetic transmission. It says little about the range of environmental modification to which these traits are subject. In our vernacular, "inherited" often means "inevitable." But not to a biologist. Genes do not make specific bits and pieces of a body; they code for a range of forms under an array of environmental conditions. Moreover, even when a trait has been built and set, environmental intervention may still modify inherited defects. Millions of Americans see normally through lenses that correct innate deficiencies of vision. The claim that IQ is so-many percent "heritable" does not conflict with the belief that enriched education can increase what we call, also in the vernacular, "intelligence." A partially inherited low IQ might be subject to extensive improvement through proper education. And it might not. The mere fact of its heritability permits no conclusion.
>
> 2. The confusion of within- and between-group heredity. The major political impact of hereditarian theories does not arise from the inferred heritability of tests, but from a logically invalid extension. Studies of the heritability of IQ, performed by such traditional methods as comparing scores of relatives, or contrasting scores of adopted children with both their biological and legal parents, are all of the "within-group" type—that is, they permit an estimate of heritability *within* a single, coherent population (white Americans, for example). The common fallacy consists in assuming that if heredity explains a certain percentage of variation among individuals within a group, it must also explain a similar percentage of the difference in average IQ between groups—whites and blacks, for example. But variation among individuals within a group and differences in mean values between groups are entirely separate phenomena. One item provides no license for speculation about the other.
>
> A hypothetical and noncontroversial example will suffice. Human height has a higher heritability than any value ever proposed for IQ. Take two separate groups of males. The first, with an average height of 5 feet 10 inches, live in a prosperous American town. The second, with an average height of 5 feet 6 inches, are starving in a third-world village. Heritability is 95 percent or so in each place—meaning only that relatively tall fathers tend to have tall sons and relatively short fathers short sons. This high within-group heritability argues neither for nor against the possibility that better nutrition in the next generation might raise the average height of third-world villages above that of prosperous Americans. Likewise, IQ could be highly heritable within groups, and the average difference between whites and blacks in American might still only record the environmental disadvantages of blacks. (pp. 155–157, reproduced by permission of W. W. Norton)

It appears that most people who understand the genetic basis of behavior would agree with Gould's conclusions. Some, however, do not. For instance, in a highly controversial article, Arthur Jensen (1969) presented data showing that, on average, blacks score about 15 points lower than whites on IQ tests, and he explained this difference in terms of genotype: "Genetic factors are strongly implicated in the average negro-white intelligence difference" (p. 82). This interpretation is erroneous, in part because it is based on a confusion of within- and between-group hereditability. Moreover, (1) environmental variables differ across groups (blacks, for example, are more often culturally disadvantaged than whites); and (2) intelligence tests are known to be culturally biased (as noted earlier, they primarily assess behaviors characteristic of middle-class white Americans). Either of these variables could account for observed racial differences in IQ. Finally, categorizing people as "black" or "white" implies a genetic homogeneity within the groups that does not exist; there is no single "black" or "white" genotype that controls intelligence, or anything else.

The extent to which intelligence is inherited and differs as a function of group cannot be determined by correlational studies, and these are the only kind of studies that can be performed ethically (see Kamin, 1974; Kempthorne, 1978). Fortunately, these issues are of little or no practical importance. It is abundantly clear that environmental variables can and do influence the development of behaviors taken to be indicative of intelligence. The optimistic—and behavioral—approach to intelligence is to configure the environment so that intelligence develops to the fullest extent possible in every human infant.

Study Questions

1. Describe the (three) stages of prenatal development, with an emphasis on the period of the embryo. Why is the embryo especially vulnerable to damage from environmental events, and what are such events called? Give some examples.

2. Be able to describe the three types of genetic abnormalities and how they differ in terms of the problems they produce. (Refer back to Chapter 4 if necessary.)

3. Distinguish between psychological development and maturation.

4. Be able to describe how the infant at birth (called a *neonate*) is equipped. What is meant by *organized behavior*? What is meant by the statement, "The neonate is a veritable reflex machine"? List some of the important reflexes in Table 8–2.

5. What is the main point in the first paragraph of the section entitled "Neurological Development"? Recognize the two questions raised and provide a general answer for each.

6. What is the normative approach? It is important because it is how most developmental psychologists approach the field. Also, contrast a normative approach with the functional one taken in this book. What are the advantages and shortcomings of each?

7. What does the following statement mean: "Understanding the effects of interaction with the environment may provide some clue to how early the biological structures are sufficiently developed." How is the research by White and his associates related to this statement?

8. What are ecological reinforcers, why are they classified as unconditioned reinforcers, and how are they important in the development of prehension skills?

9. What is meant by "behavioral differentiation and refinement"?

10. Using the comments by Dworetzsky, describe how the "normative stages of development of posture control and locomotion" (as described by Shirley) reflect environmental variables in addition to maturational ones?

11. Briefly describe the different methods of studying the sensory capacities of infants, and then illustrate each with something from the sections "Basic Visual Abilities of Infants" and "Perception of Depth."

12. Be able to describe the visual cliff experiment, including what it was designed to test. Using the reported data, tell what it actually showed about human infants in terms of perception of depth versus fear of heights?

13. What is meant by *cognition* and *cognitive development*? Describe the major aspects of Piaget's approach in terms of cognitive structures and processes, as well as the periods of cognitive development.

14. State the main points in the evaluation of Piaget's theory. (It would be helpful to use concepts you have learned, such as normative development, maturation, functional analysis, and scientific explanation.)

15. What is the point of Sidebar 8-1, and what is its implication for Piaget's theory?

16. Define social behavior.

17. What is attachment, and why is it a metaphor? Describe some of the causes of crying and cuddling.

18. Be able to describe Harlow's classic experiment, including its rationale and results.

19. What are the main aspects of the ethological view of attachment, how does the phenomenon of imprinting illustrate it, and what does the study by Peterson imply for this view?

20. What is wrong with most definitions of emotion? What does it mean to say that these definitions tempt us to reify emotion?

21. Be able to describe emotion in terms of physiological arousal and motivation.

22. List the behaviors we label as emotions in infants. Using smiling, laughter, and crying as examples, describe how these behaviors (emotions) "develop through the elaboration of basic reflexive relations" (i.e., by respondent and operant conditioning).

23. How is the word *intelligence* used? Is it a thing? How is it measured? Describe the test by Alfred Binet and his three cardinal principles as described by Gould. Have these principles always been maintained throughout the development of intelligence tests?

24. Why have intelligence tests been controversial? Is intelligence a meaningless construct? How is intelligence (like emotion, above) reified?

25. Be able to make the points about the heritability of intelligence. What is the role of environmental factors?

Recommended Readings

Bijou, S., & Baer, D. (1965). *Child Development: Universal Stage of Infancy* (Vol. 2). New York: Appleton-Century-Crofts.

The authors, two well-known behavioral psychologists, present a coherent discussion of development from a behavioral perspective. Particularly interesting are the behavioral interpretations of traditional concepts in developmental psychology, and the compelling explanations of many developmental phenomena.

Schiamberg, L. B. (1988). *Child and Adolescent Development.* New York: Macmillan.

This is one of many excellent books on development. The book presents popular theories and then takes the reader through the developmental process from conception to adolescence. The author offers comprehensive coverage; thus, the book will also serve as a reference text.

CHAPTER 9

Personality

The ancients proposed many explanations of behavior. One noteworthy proposal was made over 2 millennia ago by Hippocrates, the famous Greek physician. Hippocrates proposed that body fluids determined general behavioral patterns. According to him, the body contains four humors, or fluids: yellow bile, black bile, phlegm, and blood. Behavior was thought to result from the relative quantities of these substances. For example, those who possessed an abundance of yellow bile were aggressive, excitable, and impulsive; Hippocrates termed these individuals *choleric.* When there was an overabundance of phlegm, the individual, called *phlegmatic,* was passive and thoughtful. Hippocrates' theory was one of the first personality theories.

What is personality? This question is not readily answered; 50 years ago there were as many as 50 definitions of the term (Allport, 1937), and no consensus has yet been reached. In general, when psychologists study personality, they are attempting to identify consistencies in behavior across time and situations, and to explain those consistencies. This chapter considers the essential elements of four traditional and important personality theories: the psychoanalytic theory of Sigmund Freud, the humanistic theory of Carl Rogers, the constitutional theory of William Sheldon, and the trait theory of Raymond Cattell. A behavioral interpretation of personality that borrows heavily from the work of B. F. Skinner is also provided. Although this chapter by no means covers personality exhaustively—there are literally dozens of theories of personality and many are complex—it will provide the reader with an appreciation of the divergent approaches to personality. Each theory is discussed generally, with special emphasis on (1) motivation; (2) personality structure; (3) personality development; and (4) assessment. The extent to which each theory provides an adequate scientific explanation of behavior is also examined.

A Psychoanalytic Theory

The first and most famous psychoanalyst was Sigmund Freud (1856–1939), a physician with an interest in the causes and treatment of hysteria (a condition in which the patient believes that some sensory or motor function is lost when it actually is not) and other "nervous" disorders. On the basis of his clinical interactions with patients, Freud fashioned an elaborate theory to explain his patients' symptoms. The theory was eventually extended to account for the behavior of normal individuals. It is important to recognize that Freud developed clinical strategies as well as a theory of personality; psychoanalysis is, on the one hand, a unique set of clinical procedures and, on the other, a novel explanation of behavior. Sidebar 9-1 introduces the clinical component of psychoanalysis.

Motivation

Freud believed that behavior is motivated by energy arising from two classes of instincts, or needs. One, called the **life instincts,** includes thirst, hunger, and sex; he termed the energy arising from these instincts **libido** (libido is now commonly associated only with sexual energy). As we will see, sexual energy is particularly important in Freud's theory. As their name implies, the function of the life instincts is to promote survival and reproduction. Freud suggested that the second class of instincts, the **death instincts,** represents the inherent desire of all humans to die. This class of instincts can include aggression, which, in response to the survival instinct, is turned away from the person and out toward others. Obviously, life and death instincts often conflict.

Freud contended that energy in the form of tension arises from both classes of instincts, and that the function of all behavior is to reduce that tension. It is for this reason that Freud's explanation of behavior is a **tension-reduction** model. For example, sexual behavior reduces tension arising from unfulfilled sexual needs, food-seeking behavior reduces tension arising from hunger. The tension arising from the instincts is inescapable and must be managed. It is for this reason that Freud's motivational theory is a **hydraulic model:** energy is pro-

---

Sidebar 9-1
Freud's Psychoanalytic Therapy

Freud's psychoanalysis required many sessions over months or even years. In the initial sessions, the patient recounted the details of the illness that had prompted the request for help, and Freud informed the clients of the basic tenets of psychoanalysis. Then, efforts were made to discover the repressed impulses, desires, and conflicts that were producing tension and anxiety. To accomplish this, Freud conducted dream analyses and free-association exercises (see text), the results of which were interpreted and discussed with the patient. Early-childhood experiences were also explored. By uncovering unconscious material, the patient could gain insight into his or her behavior and ultimately deal with this material in a more appropriate manner.

Unfortunately, the treatment process was frought with problems, one being **resistance.** When resistance occurred, patients often avoided revealing discomfiting unconscious wishes and desires by changing the subject, developing "mental blocks," or postponing therapy sessions. In an effort to decrease resistances, Freud explained why they were irrational and maladaptive. By the end of therapy, after identifying repressed wishes, working through resistances, and dealing with repressed material, the patient emerged with a stronger ego that was able to achieve tension reduction more effectively.

duced in a closed system and must be released to preserve the system. In Freud's view, how such energy is managed depends on the structure of the personality.

Structure

Freud suggested that the personality is composed of three elements, or structures of the mind: the id, the ego, and the superego. The **id** is where life and death instincts dwell and is the source of all tensions. The id's only role is to seek gratification, through tension reduction, and it does so according to the **pleasure principle,** obtaining pleasure and avoiding pain (Freud, 1963). But unbridled pursuit of pleasure is not practical; many basic needs cannot always be satisfied in the real world. For example, sexual activity may be impossible for much of the day, or perhaps food cannot be obtained for a period of time. The **ego,** which grows out of the id, "decides" how a particular need can be gratified, given the requirements of the real world. Thus, the ego operates under the **reality principle:**

> According to the reality principle, the energy of the id may be blocked, diverted, or released gradually, all in accordance with the demands of reality. . . . Such an operation is not in contradiction to the pleasure principle but, rather, represents a temporary suspension of it. (Pervin, 1984, p. 7)

But we are not merely a cauldron of needs and desires satisfied by whatever works in the real world. Society's standards, values, and morals are also important. Freud suggested that, as young children develop, they adopt the standards of their parents, and that these standards reside in the **superego.** The superego, which grows from the ego, ensures that the needs will be gratified in socially acceptable ways, a function commonly associated with the "conscience." Thus, the superego considers what activities of the ego are "right" or "wrong," "good" or "bad," "moral" or "immoral," and, like our parents, rewards and punishes us accordingly.

Although the id, the ego, and the superego have separate functions, the functions interact. The id seeks gratification of the basic needs: it determines what needs *must* be met and does so in a demanding, selfish, tyrannical way (Pervin, 1984). The ego decides how those needs may be satisfied in the real world; it selects what *can* be done. The superego monitors the ego's decisions to ensure that they will be consistent with the ethical and moral standards of society: it determines what *should* be done. For instance, when the id desires gratification of sexual needs, the ego considers the available options (e.g., possible sexual partners or masturbation). The superego then requires that the ego choose socially acceptable sexual activities. In a sense, the ego considers the id's demand for gratification and the superego's demand for "morality." It is this interaction, among the id, ego, and superego, which some call *negotiation* (Rychlak, 1981), that accounts for observed behavior.

It should be noted that, in Freud's discussion of personality, the three elements seem to be living, acting autonomous beings. But this is not the case. They are not "homunculi" (small people) within the body, even though they seem to have human qualities. Nor are they brain mechanisms with material status. Instead, they are hypothetical entities inferred from observed behavior.

Another important Freudian concept is **layers of consciousness,** or different levels of awareness. Freud posited three such layers. The **unconscious** contains those primitive impulses and needs that are associated with the id, as well as material "pushed" into it, or repressed, by the ego. We are unaware of the contents of the unconscious, even though these impulses and needs affect our behavior. A second layer is the **conscious.** Conscious mental activity is activity of which we are aware and is usually associated with the ego (Rychlak, 1981). If this material is unpleasant or otherwise inappropriate, it may be forced into the unconscious, which is assumed to be by far the largest layer. To illustrate their relative size, an iceberg analogy is often used (e.g., Hall & Lindzey, 1985). In it, the tip of the iceberg, which is evident but relatively small, is likened to the conscious layer of personality. Most of the remaining part of the iceberg, below the water line and out of sight, represents the unconscious instincts, needs, repressed feelings, and so on that motivate conscious behavior. The third layer, the **preconscious,** includes material of which we are not aware, but that can be easily brought into consciousness. It is not easily incorporated in the iceberg analogy but might be thought of as the area around a fluctuating waterline.

Defense Mechanisms

If all goes well, the interaction among the id, the ego, and the superego result in a well-adjusted person. The unconscious needs arising from the id foster many options, one of which is chosen by the ego with the help of the superego. But things do not always go smoothly. Freud believed that unacceptable impulses from the id or an overzealous superego can produce anxiety, resulting in an indecisive, vacillating, or weakened ego. In a sense, the demands of the id and the superego become too strong, and the ego is unable to "decide." Anxiety and tension increase as the ego is overpowered and unable to gratify the basic needs through tension reduction. As the ego weakens, the psychological "health" of the individual is threatened.

But the ego has defense mechanisms that protect it. The ego may **repress** into the id unacceptable impulses that produce anxiety.[1] For example, we often "forget" unpleasant desires, such as wanting to injure a close friend who offends us. Or the ego may **displace** unacceptable impulses into more acceptable outlets. Hatred of one's parents may, for instance, be displaced to other authority figures (e.g., police officers or teachers). In **projection,** unacceptable feelings are assigned to another person. When we have strong sexual desires that are unacceptable, we may accuse others of having those desires. These and other defense mechanisms are a sign of a weakened ego. Their appearance indicates that the ego is unable to resolve the conflicting demands of the id and the superego and must therefore "defend" itself. But the defense mechanisms are only temporary stopgaps for the anxiety produced by conflict. Anxiety can be

---

[1]Many personality theories were influenced by current social conditions. In Freud's day, pleasures, especially sexual pleasures, were to be resisted whenever possible. Thus, Freud's notion of repressing unwanted desires is a natural outgrowth of this "Victorian" approach to life. Freud believed, however, that the road to good health is not to repress the unwanted desires, but to face them directly and "conquer them through reason" (Leahey, 1987, p. 213).

most effectively dealt with by a strong ego that gratifies basic needs without being overwhelmed by the id impulses or paralyzed by the superego. Developing a strong ego is an important goal of psychoanalytic therapy.

Personality Development

Recall that, of the basic instincts, the sexual urges are particularly important in motivating behavior. Freud suggested that the anatomical focus of the sexual urges (i.e., the **erogenous zone**) shifts during childhood, and that each shift is associated with a new **psychosexual stage** of personality development. The core of the personality develops in the first three stages, during which the child encounters important problems and conflicts.

In the **oral stage** (during the first year of life), the primary focus of pleasure and tension reduction is the mouth. In this stage, oral activities, such as biting, sucking, and eating, occupy most of the infant's time. A high degree of dependency is also typical of this stage.

In the **anal stage** (ages one to two years), the focus is on the anus and the expulsion of feces. Aggressive impulses also are important. It is during this stage that parents begin toilet training, in which the child is required to withhold feces. Freud suggested that children sometimes rebel against this training and become "retentive," later manifesting this tendency in stubbornness and stinginess. Other children may be angry and hostile during the training and, as a result, become cruel or destructive later in life (Hall & Lindzey, 1985).

In the **phallic stage** (ages two to five years), the genital organs become important in gratifying sexual needs. Touching and stroking the genitals are frequent activities. During this stage, sexual attraction to the parent of the opposite sex develops in both boys (the **Oedipus complex**) and girls (the **Electra complex**). As a result, a difficult stage in the child's life begins, in which there is intense resentment of the parent of the same sex. These complexes are resolved only after much effort.

In the **latency stage** (ages six to twelve years), sexual urges are subdued through repression, and most activities are nonsexual in nature. This period of relative calm follows the tumultuous phallic stage and its conflicts and anxieties.

In the **genital stage** (ages twelve years to adulthood), the focus of pleasure returns to the genitals. But the method of procuring pleasure is sexual intercourse with a partner, not self-stimulation. Ideally, as this occurs the individual begins to develop altruistic (selfless) concern for the partner, and a fully socialized adult emerges.

The psychosexual stages do not necessarily proceed systematically, one at a time. They can be shortened, lengthened, or overlapped. Moreover, although the child should emerge from the sequence of stages with a strong, effective ego, the process can and often does go awry. Some children become **fixated** at a particular stage. In these cases, the focus of pleasure remains at one the early erogenous zones, and personality development ceases. For example, adults who smoke, drink excessively, or chew gum may be fixated at the oral stage, whereas those who are overly concerned with cleanliness may be fixated at the anal stage. Psychoanalysts believe that serious personality disorders can arise from fixations. Freud also suggested that adults may **regress** to earlier stages of sexual development when they are unable to cope with reality, or when there is insufficient genital activity. When, for instance, a sexual partner is lost, the jilted lover may regress to the oral stage and engage in smoking, drinking, nail biting, or thumb sucking.

Personality Assessment

Freud collected most of his information through direct interactions with his patients. Such information was an essential part of therapy. One technique he favored was **free association,** the classic technique depicted in scenes in which a patient lies on a couch and a therapist listens intently and takes notes. In free association, the client is instructed to say whatever "comes to mind," no matter how trivial or inappropriate the material seems. The goal of this technique is to reveal the patient's unconscious. A second technique for recovering unconscious material is **dream analysis.** In this procedure, the client recounts dreams, which in Freud's view are expressions of unconscious motives. The dreams require interpretation because the motives are expressed symbolically, not literally. For

Figure 9-1. An inkblot similar to a Rorschach Inkblot.

example, if a patient unconsciously wants to harm his mother, he might dream of a battle in which a female authority figure is killed. Freud believed that unconscious wishes and desires had to become conscious, perhaps through free association or dream analysis, before they could be effectively dealt with during therapy.

More recently, psychoanalysts have used tests such as the **Rorschach ink-blot test** (see Figure 9-1) to reveal the unconscious. In this test, the patient is asked to look at 10 cards, each with an inkblot on it, and then to tell the therapist what she or he "sees." The form of the inkblots is rather vague and the variety of responses almost limitless. Psychoanalysts assert that the way a patient responds to the inkblot reveals unconscious motives and desires, which may become a focal point of therapy.

Note that all of the assessment devices described above are inferential. Although the patient's behavior is directly observed, these observations are used as a basis for inferences about the unconscious. Such inferences may be expected to differ from therapist to therapist, depending on how the observations are interpreted.

Are Freudian Explanations of Behavior Adequate?

Freud's theory was a radically new enterprise in his day. He assumed that behavior is determined (e.g., by the unconscious), which was a controversial assumption at that time. Nonetheless, Freud's general approach was accepted by many psychologists and remains popular today. Many of its technical terms (e.g., *ego* and *libido*) have been incorporated into everyday language, and most people have at least heard of psychoanalysis. But can we, on this basis, assume that Freud's theory is consistent with a scientific approach to behavior? Not really, as is apparent if we ask three questions concerning it.

Is the Subject Matter a Quantifiable Characteristic of Behavior?

Undoubtedly, Freud was strongly interested in behavior in its own right. Many of his patients exhibited behavior (e.g., hysterical paralysis of an arm) that caused them a great deal of anguish, and he attempted to find ways to change it. But he often used behavior only as an index of the unconscious, as in free association or dream analysis. Unfortunately, the focus here was on the "behavior" of the hypothetical constructs, as when the ego "represses" or the superego "evaluates." This appeal to the actions of hypothetical entities should not be construed as studying behavior. Hypothetical constructs cannot, in any sense, exhibit behavior. In addition, quantitative measurement was not a hallmark of his theory. For the most part, Freud's notions were based on global clinical impressions, which do not allow for a fine-grained functional analysis. In fairness, however, most other personality theories of Freud's day were no more quantitative.

*Are the Causes of Behavior Observable,
Quantifiable Phenomena?*

The major causes of behavior in Freud's theory are hypothetical constructs, namely, the id, the ego, and the superego. Although the constructs are not real, they are used in ways that seem to imply that they are: the id "seeks gratification," the ego "represses desires," or the superego "demands perfection." Because they have no physical existence, the id, the ego, and the superego are reifications.

Using reifications as explanations is inconsistent with a scientific approach to behavior and also has two adverse consequences. First, the proposed causes of behavior cannot be manipulated directly to effect desired changes in what people do. Instead, observable variables must be manipulated. As a case in point, imagine that some undesirable behavior is attributed to a "weak ego." Directly strengthening the ego is obviously impossible because the ego does not really exist. A therapist may nonetheless attempt to strengthen it, perhaps by prompting the patient to talk about desires, thoughts, and feelings. Suppose this is done and the maladaptive behavior decreases. What has happened? All we really know is that the "talking therapy" changed the patient's behavior; the technique has been successful apart from any supposed effect on the patient's ego. Any effect on the "ego" must be inferred, and such speculation seems unnecessary. Second, reified causes divert attention from empirical phenomena. In the example above, the patient's ego is the primary concern. Therefore, the direct value of talking about desires, thoughts, and feelings may not receive due attention.

*Did Freud Seek Functional Relations
among Empirical Variables?*

In a very broad sense, Freud attempted to identify functional relations. He suggested, for example, that certain kinds of childhood experiences could strongly influence subsequent sexual and nonsexual behavior. But generally, Freud did not isolate the functional relations between empirical variables. His theoretical postulations involved hypothetical entities that were formulated on the basis of uncontrolled studies of his patients. As a result, direct effects of environmental events on behavior may have escaped notice. Although psychoanalysis sometimes benefits patients, the reasons for changes in behavior are obscured by an appeal to changes in nonexistent structures.

A Humanistic Theory

Humanistic psychologists believe that humans are inherently good, and that our lives are characterized by choices, creativity, and growth.[2] Moreover,

[2]Rogers's theory, like Freud's, was a logical outgrowth of his times. The 1950s and 1960s saw a new-found emphasis on personal freedom accompanied by a tolerance of nonconformity. Thus, the emphasis of Rogers's theory was not on an adjustment to society's norms, but on the discovery of one's real needs and how to meet them.

we strive for personal fulfillment, and if our choices are not overly restricted, we will achieve that goal. One of the most influential humanists was Carl R. Rogers (1902–1987). Rogers, whose father was an Illinois businessman, was raised in a strict, religious family. His early interests included agriculture, philosophy, and theology. In fact, it was in seminary that he first became interested in psychology. His initial experience was with Freudian psychoanalysis, but his work with a young pyromaniac resulted in disillusionment with the psychoanalytic perspective and led him to develop an alternative to it. Like Freud, Rogers endeavored to treat as well as explain troublesome behavior. Consequently, Rogerian psychology involves both clinical and theoretical components.

Motivation

Rogers believed that the **actualization tendency** is the one overriding motivator of behavior. This tendency promotes behavior that results in physiological maintenance, growth, maturation, and fulfillment of potentials. Thus, we ensure our physical well-being through eating, drinking, and avoiding injury. We also seek new experiences and learn new skills to grow, enhance our life, and move toward "self-government, self-regulation, and autonomy, and away from . . . control by external forces" (Rogers, 1951, p. 488). Because Rogers's theory holds that behavior is directed toward maintenance and enhancement, it can be characterized as teleological (i.e., behavior is controlled by future events or goals; see Chapter 2).

Rogers's theory of motivation, like Freud's, is a tension-reduction model:

> All needs . . . spring from and have reference to, the basic tendency to maintain and enhance the organism. These needs occur as physiological tensions which, when experienced, form the basis of behavior which appears functionally designed to reduce the tension (Rogers, 1951, p. 491)

The needs are not always conscious. Some, such as hunger, can affect behavior without awareness. At other times, we may be fully aware of a particular need and its effect on our behavior.

Do the needs directly express themselves in behavior? Not typically. Rogers believed that a person's perceptions and the value attached to the perceptions are important. He suggested that our perceptions and experiences, or **phenomenal field** (the phenomenal field is the sum of everything that is experienced, both conscious and unconscious), determine behavior. In other words, how we behave depends on how we perceive the world. For example, a thirsty man will react to a hallucination of a water fountain much as he would to a real fountain; in both cases, his perception of a source of water prompts rapid approach behavior.

Personality Development and Structure

Rogers's theory of development is not a stage theory. In Rogers's view, we are constantly developing and growing in our efforts toward actualization. But some exceptionally important changes do occur in early childhood. Infants, like adults, have a phenomenal field consisting of conscious and unconscious experiences. Each experience is evaluated, according to its contribution to actualization, in the **organismic valuing process:** "Experiences which are perceived as maintaining or enhancing the organism are valued positively. Those which are perceived as negating such maintenance or enhancement are valued negatively" (Rogers, 1959, p. 222). The child tends to repeat only those behaviors that result in positively valued experiences, which are those that promote actualization. This innate process is depicted in Figure 9-2. Note in this figure the emphasis that Rogers placed on "perceptions" and "value."

As the child interacts with significant others in the environment, a sense of **self** emerges. This occurs when the individual acts in a consistent manner and perceives this consistency as characteristic of "I," or "me." A person might, for example, observe his or her interactions with others and on that basis make statements such as "I am outgoing," "I am a loving person," or "I make friends easily." The "self" is inferred from a collection of such statements regarding one's own behavior. Although it is cohesive, the self is not insensitive to experience. Rather, it may change as the person pursues actualization. Often, the self is not what we would like; perhaps one is unhappy with "being temperamental" or "being greedy." Thus, we may strive to improve our lot, or to be our **ideal self.**

As the self develops, the person acquires a need for **positive regard** from others and, as a result, strives for their approval and respect. Thus, the values of other people are "introjected," or accepted by the person as her or his own. The person alone no longer determines what is "good" or "bad"; instead, these evaluations are influenced by what others say is "good" or "bad." For instance, parents may say to their child, "Always love other people" or "Your education is very valuable." Over time, the child takes these values as his or her own, and

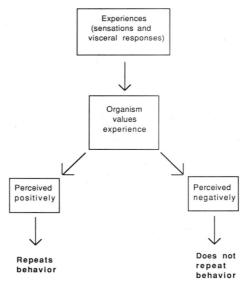

Figure 9-2. The organismic valuing process in infants.

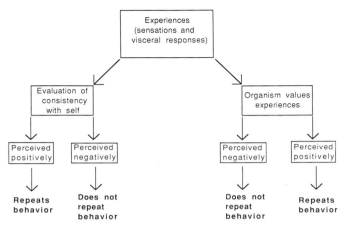

Figure 9-3. The organismic valuing and self-evaluative process in adults. Note the two independent systems, one for the self and one for basic experiences that predominates in childhood.

they then become "I love other people" and "My education is very valuable." To feel good about oneself, or to obtain **self-regard,** a child must behave in ways that are consistent with the introjected values, such as being a good friend or using educational opportunities.

The developing self has its own interests, and for this reason, Rogers spoke of **self-actualization.** The self-actualization tendency, an outgrowth of the actualizing tendency and therefore another kind of motivation, involves the capacity of many activities to maintain and enhance the self. In self-actualization, a person tends to engage in activities consistent with his or her self-perception. For example, if the self includes a perception that "I am nonviolent," then the person will strive to behave in nonviolent ways. Violent behavior, on the other hand, will be rejected as inconsistent with "who I am." Comparing what one actually does (experiences) with self-perceptions constitutes a second evaluative system, which functions in parallel with the organismic evaluative system described above. Although the two evaluation processes coexist, as shown in Figure 9-3, they do not always evaluate an experience in the same way.

Although self-actualization was for Rogers the cornerstone of a healthy personality, Abraham Maslow, another influential humanistic psychologist, proposed that the need for self-actualization is evident only if other, more basic needs are met. Maslow's hierarchy of needs (1970) is the topic of Sidebar 9-2.

Incongruence

With the development of the self and its evaluation system comes the potential for trouble. After we accept self-concepts such as "I am a peace-loving person," "I love my brother," or "I am very intelligent," we often have experiences that are inconsistent with them. Thus, the basic organismic evaluation of the experiences is different from the evaluation with respect to the self. For example, assume that a girl's brother hits her repeatedly during an argument and that, in a rage, the girl strikes back in an effort to protect herself. The basic organismic evaluation process tells her that this action is "good" because it is protective. But the action is inconsistent with the self-concept of "I love my brother" and is evaluated negatively. Such a conflict, called **incongruence,** is threatening and results in anxiety.

Rogers suggested that two defenses, **denial** and **distortion,** deal with incongruence. In the former, the experience is denied, and the self-concept is thus preserved. In the example above, the girl may deny being angry with and hitting her brother and may actually be unaware of such feelings. In distortion, she may misrepresent the experience by saying, "I am not really angry with my brother; I'm really angry with myself for hitting him." Rogers believed that both denial and distortion are signs of maladjustment. When the actual experiences of a person are at odds with the self, tension and lack of growth are the result. But when the self and the organismic experiences are congruent, psychological adjustment and actualization are maximized. Sometimes, a self-concept must change if congruence is to be achieved. In the preceding example, the self-concept might be changed to "I love my brother, but when he hits me, I sometimes hate him." Thus, feelings of hate are accepted as part of the girl's experience. Such congruence between the self-concept and experience permits less anxiety and continued actualization. Achieving congruence between the self-concept and experience is a common goal of Rogerian therapy, which is overviewed in Sidebar 9-3.

Personality Assessment

Rogers and his colleagues have used many traditional personality tests, including the Rorschach inkblot test previously described, as well as ratings by observers or self-ratings by clients. Because the "self" and the "self-concept" are important in Rogers's theory of personality, he also used assessment devices

Sidebar 9-2
Maslow's Hierarchy of Needs

Abraham Maslow (1970) identified a variety of needs arranged in a hierarchy. The important feature of this hierarchy is that the most basic needs must be met first, and only then can the higher order needs affect behavior. First, **physiological needs** (e.g., hunger, thirst, and fatigue) motivate behavior, and if these are satisfied, then **safety needs** (e.g., such as security, stability, or freedom from fear) can become important. When physiological and safety needs are met, then the person can seek relationships with other people that provide love, affection, and companionship and satisfy the **need for love and belongingness.** Next are the **esteem needs,** which refer to the desire for competence, prestige, and self-confidence. Finally, when all of the above needs are satisfied, the person will strive for **self-actualization.** This need involves "growth" and the attainment of what the person is best equipped to do. For example, a writer will write, an athlete will participate in sports, or a chef will cook. The self-actualization needs are unsatisfied more than the others. Why? Maslow suggested that aspirations of greatness, or of being "all that you can be," make a person uneasy, anxious, or awed. Moreover, lofty aspirations are overshadowed by the perceived shortcomings and lack of confidence that many of us share.

designed to measure these constructs. One such technique involves recording and analyzing the patient's verbalizations during therapy. For example, references to the self can be classified as positive or approving, negative or disapproving, ambivalent, and so on (Raimy, 1948).

Another popular test used by Rogerian therapists is the Q-sort. In this technique, the patient is given a stack of cards, each with a description such as "makes friends easily" or "has trouble expressing anger." The patient then sorts them into piles according to the extent to which the description accurately reflects that person's self-concept. The subject may also evaluate each description as it pertains to the "ideal" self-concept.

Are Rogerian Explanations of Behavior Adequate?

Therapeutic techniques have evolved from Rogers's theory, and many patients have benefited from his brand of treatment. But is his approach to personality scientific? Consider the three questions asked of psychoanalysis.

Is the Subject Matter a Quantifiable Characteristic of Behavior?

Rogers was interested in behavior presented in therapeutic situations. He was particularly concerned about promoting behavior that was consistent with the self-actualizing tendency. But Rogers's primary interest was in the self. From Rogers's perspective, the self is active and, in a manner of speaking, "behaves." Rogers talked, for instance, of the self's becoming "organized to maintain itself." Such statements are misleading. The self as conceived of by Rogers is a hypothetical entity, and behavior is not a characteristic of such entities. Rogers also appealed to valuing processes; such processes are not directly observable but are inferred on the basis of behavior. In addition, Rogers's measurement systems

---

Sidebar 9-3
Rogers's Client-Centered Therapy

Rogers developed his own brand of therapy, which is called *client-centered therapy* or, more recently, *person-centered therapy*. A client-centered therapist is generally warm, caring, noncoercive, and nonevaluative. Three specific characteristics are particularly important (Pervin, 1984). First, therapists should be **genuine,** or open, trusting, and able to express themselves freely about the client's behavior. Second, they should provide **unconditional positive regard;** that is, the therapist must show a strong acceptance of and caring for the client, no matter what the client does or says. And third, the therapists should be able to show **empathic understanding** by attempting to understand and relate to the experiences of the client on a very personal level.

In the warm, caring environment provided by the therapist, the goal is to promote **congruence.** Specifically, the client examines his or her self-concept and basic experiences in an effort to resolve conflicts. As a result, the self-concept becomes more consistent with real-life experiences. Moreover, it is hoped that the client will become more realistic and accepting of who he or she really is. If all goes well, the client will be better able to see his or her potential and the road to fulfilling that potential.

lack precision. Information gathered from patients' verbalizations and self-reports may be subject to bias and misinterpretation. Moreover, Q-sort data, presumably a reflection of the "self-concept," require inferences about a hypothetical entity, the self. A focus on behavior is lost when such inferences are made: what a person actually does (in this case, responses on the Q-sort) is not important in its own right, but only to the extent that it characterizes the self.

Are the Causes of Behavior Observable, Quantifiable Phenomena?

Rogers's theory holds that contact with the environment is important, although he did not quantify behavior–environment relations. He did, however, suggest that perceptions and valuing processes can strongly influence behavior. Although private activity that cannot be observed by others obviously can influence behavior, such activity is difficult to quantify accurately or to manipulate.

Another important cause of behavior in Rogers's model, the self, presents even more difficult problems. The reader should recognize that the Rogerian "self" is a reification, inferred from observable behavior. It has no real existence and, therefore, cannot be treated as a bona fide cause of behavior. Moreover, the self-actualization tendency, in which the person strives for enhancement of the self, is a teleological explanation of behavior (see Chapter 2): enhancement of the self, a future event, cannot possibly influence present behavior. Such teleological explanations divert attention from the genuine causes of behavior. For example, *descriptions* of future events (e.g., "Work hard and you will make lots of money") may affect behavior, a fact easily ignored if a teleological explanation (e.g., "She is working hard to make lots of money") is accepted.

Did Rogers Seek Functional Relations among Empirical Variables?

Rogers conducted many studies in an effort to identify cause-and-effect relations. Unfortunately, the relations he reported characteristically did not directly involve empirical phenomena. Phenomena such as valuing processes, perceptions, and the self cannot be directly observed; instead, researchers interested in them must rely on self-reports, which are of questionable accuracy. Moreover, appropriately controlled conditions were often lacking in Rogers's work. For example, he sometimes recorded therapy sessions and then interpreted patient–therapist interactions recorded on the tapes. He also relied heavily on patients' self-reports to support his theory (Ford & Urban, 1963). These techniques, although defensible in clinical practice, are weak methods for discerning functional relations.

A Constitutional Theory

It has long been believed that a person's physical characteristics are related to behavior. For instance, constitutional psychologists, the best known being William Sheldon (1898–1977), have systematically studied this purported relation. Sheldon's father was a Rhode Island farmer, a part-time breeder of poultry and dogs. As a boy, Sheldon learned to judge the physical characteristics of animals; later in life, he obtained advanced degrees in both medicine and psychology. This background served him well in his attempt to describe in detail the human physique and its relation to behavior. The theory he developed is a structural one: it focuses on **morphology** (structural characteristics of the body) and its relation to behavior, not on motivation or development.

Structure

Sheldon did not discount the role of the environment in determining behavior, but he attempted to assess the relation only between physique and behavior, a relation that he believed to be important and largely neglected. Over many years, Sheldon studied the physical characteristics of thousands of men and women. He first took a number of pictures of each subject. By examining these photographs, he evaluated the physical structure of each subject according to the relative presence of three classes of characteristics, termed *endomorphy, mesomorphy,* and *ectomorphy* (Sheldon, 1942).

When **endomorphy** dominates, the digestive apparatus is well developed. Endomorphs are rounded and spherical in appearance, with well-endowed abdomens. These characteristics develop from the inner layer of embryonic cells, or the endoderm.

When **mesomorphy** prevails, there is a prevalence of bone, muscle, and connective tissue. The mesomorph is upright, sturdy, and rectangular, with large blood vessels and thick skin. The upper chest area is more developed than

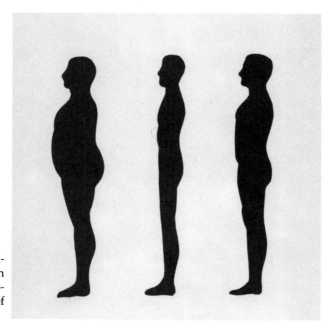

This picture shows a silhouette of an endomorph, an ectomorph, and a mesomorph. (Photo courtesy of Sue Keller.)

that of endomorphs. The mesoderm, or second layer of embryonic cells, develops into these features.

Ectomorphy is associated with large quantities of skin and sense organs. Ectomorphs are thin, with long appendages and fine bone structures. The outer layer of embryonic cells, the ectoderm, gives rise to ectomorphic characteristics.

After careful observation and study of the photographs, Sheldon assigned a number from 1 to 7 that reflected the presence of each of the three components; the higher the number, the more that component was represented in the person's physique. The resultant three-digit scores represent the person's **somatotype** (*soma* is the Greek word for "body"), with the first number coding endomorphy, the second mesomorphy, and the third ectomorphy. For example, 711 (read "seven, one, one") describes an endomorphic physique with all of the accompanying characteristics. A 171 and a 117 describe, respectively, a mesomorphic and an ectomorphic body. These extreme scores are rarely found; most of us have some combination of the three components in the moderate range, such as 533, 453, or 354. To lend meaning to the scores, Sheldon selected an animal or an insect, the physique of which closely matched the physique of a given score. For example, persons with a score of 352 were described as "little horses, ponies, burrows. Sturdy, sure-footed hayburners, built close to the ground" (Sheldon, 1954, p. 162).

Sheldon also evaluated secondary characteristics. For example, subjects were rated on gynandromorphy (the extent to which there were characteristics of the opposite sex), dysplasia (which reflected whether different regions of the body had different somatotypes), and the *t* component (a measure of physical beauty). Together, the secondary and primary ratings provided a fairly complete assessment of each subject's physique from head to toe.

Behavior

Somatotypes were only one half of the picture. Sheldon was interested in whether personality could be predicted from somatotype; therefore, he assessed the behavioral characteristics of his subjects. Sheldon reviewed studies on personality assessment and identified 650 traits that could be used to describe human behavior. After condensing these to a series of 50, Sheldon interviewed 33 men. From these interviews and subsequent refinements, he identified three clusters of behavioral characteristics, or traits. Each cluster had 20 traits. The traits within a cluster were often found together in one person, whereas traits from different clusters were not. He named the three clusters *viscerotonia*, *somatotonia*, and *cerebrotonia*.

Viscerotonia characteristics included love of physical comfort and eating, pleasure in digestion, relaxed posture, love of being with other people and love of their approval, and complacency. **Somatotonia** is typified by assertiveness in posture, a love of physical adventure, pleasure in exercise, a love of power and domination, and combativeness. **Cerebrotonia** features include restraint in posture, love of privacy, emotional restraint, and lack of self-confidence. Sheldon designed a procedure for assessing the presence of each of the three clusters of traits; like the scale for the physique, a number from 1 to 7 indicated the presence of each component. For example, 711 represented a high degree of viserotonia and a minimum of somatotonia and cerebrotonia; 171 and 117 represented a high degree of somatotonia and cerebrotonia, respectively.

Somatotype–Behavior Relations

Having devised a way to assess body type and behavioral characteristics (he called the latter "temperament"), Sheldon examined the extent to which somatotypes and behavior were associated. The results of his efforts suggested that the presence of endomorphy was usually associated with viscerotonia, mesomorphy with somatotonia, and ectomorphy with cerebrotonia. Thus, many popular conceptions of body–behavior relations were confirmed. Fat people were indeed good-natured, whereas thin people were withdrawn and restrained. These findings were important for constitutional psychologists. They showed a relation between physique and behavioral characteristics, which might prove helpful in understanding and predicting behavior throughout a person's life.

As a case in point, Sheldon found a relation between somatotype and antisocial behavior. From 1939 to 1946, he observed 200 juvenile delinquents who were referred to a Boston social agency called Hayden Goodwill Inn. The results showed that the delinquents had more mesomorphic characteristics than a collection of nondelinquent subjects. Moreover, Sheldon suggested that there was a relation between particular somatotypes and specific psychiatric disturbances. He posited, for instance, that manic-depressive patients (who experience wild swings of emotion) suffer from a lack of restraint and control, a characteristic typical of an absence of ectomorphic characteristics.

Does a correlation between physique and behavior mean that the former "causes" the latter, or vice versa? Sheldon believed that both were an expression of the genetic endowment (Hall & Lindzey, 1985), which creates potentials that may be fulfilled in concert with environmental influences. A particular physique, though, might also set limitations. Sheldon wrote of a young man with an ectomorphic physique who was pushed by his parents to play sports. His inability to succeed resulted in psychological problems. Frank discussion with the boy and his parents concerning his physical limitations brought about a more realistic set of goals that were consistent with the boy's somatotype. In fact, this approach was advocated for the treatment of antisocial behavior: "A boy who grasps who he really is constitutionally, and what his potential for achievement is, can, armed with that knowledge, proceed to a sound readjustment of his life" (Hartl, Monnelly, & Elderkin, 1982, p. 558).

Although constitutional psychology still has its advocates, the approach never enjoyed great popularity, perhaps because Sheldon never saw constitutional psychology as a replacement for general psychology; he only attempted to find relations between physique and behavior, associations that he felt had been neglected. Presumably, such information could be used as an adjunct to any therapeutic effort.

Sheldon designed very specific procedures for assessing a person's somatotype. Using standardized camera equipment and lighting, he first obtained three photographs of each subject, one each from the front, the back, and the side. The subjects were photographed naked to permit a clear view of the entire body. Sheldon used many different procedures for deriving the somatotype from the pictures, all of which were refined over time. In his early work, Sheldon rated each subject's physique according to the presence of the three components. Later methods were more precise. One such method considered three measures: the subject's height, trunk index, and ponderal index. The trunk index was the ratio of the chest and abdomen areas, and the ponderal index was the maximal height divided by the cube root of the maximal weight. To score dysplasia (the extent to which areas of the body had different somatotypes), different areas of the body were also rated individually.

Behavioral assessments were conducted with the Scale for Temperament. To gather information on the traits of the three clusters, Sheldon and his associates conducted in-depth interviews with each subject. From this information, a three-digit score was derived that reflected the relative dominance of each of the components.

Does Sheldon's Theory Provide Adequate Explanations of Behavior?

As previously mentioned, Sheldon did not provide a complete account of behavior. He attempted only to show a relation between body type and behavior. Nevertheless, what he did accomplish may be examined in light of scientific principles.

Was the Subject Matter a Quantifiable Characteristic of Behavior?

Behavioral assessments (i.e., the Scale of Temperament) were conducted in a series of interviews in which the subject was rated on each of 60 traits. Although a numerical score was obtained for each temperament component (viscerotonia, somatotonia, and cerebrotonia), the scores were generated from ratings by the interviewers. Such ratings may have been biased, particularly because Sheldon himself conducted the interviews in some studies. We should point out, though, that he was studying observable behavior.

Were Quantifiable Features of the Physique Studied?

As previously mentioned, Sheldon's first methods involved ratings, which were perhaps subject to bias. These subjective measures were later refined into more precise measures (e.g., the subject's height, trunk index, and ponderal index). This kind of measurement is probably more accurate and reliable.

Sheldon took great pains to make his observations under controlled conditions. For example, when taking photographs of each subject in order to determine somatotype, Sheldon specified the size of the room, the camera type, and the lighting requirements. But his work did not identify functional relations. Instead, he showed only that physique and behavior were correlated. He did not show that one caused the other nor explain the mechanism through which they covaried.

But if there is a relation between physique and behavior, what might account for it? Perhaps physique influences behavior but does so indirectly. For example, those with mesomorphic characteristics will be more successful in athletics and may, therefore, "love exercise" and be "competitive." Perhaps behavior influences physique. A child encouraged by her parents to engage in athletics may, as a result, develop the mesomorphic characteristics of a well-muscled body. Or perhaps both are a product of heredity, environmental factors, or a combination of the two (see Hall & Lindzey, 1985). The point is that a correlation between two variables does not imply a particular causal relation between them.

A Trait Theory

Behavior is often thought to reflect a particular trait. Fighters are said to have a trait for aggressiveness; geniuses, a trait for intelligence; or writers, a trait for thoughtfulness. Many psychologists have devoted their careers to studying traits. Raymond B. Cattell (1905–) is one of these dedicated researchers. Cattell, whose father was an English factory owner, became interested in psychology in the 1920s. He later traveled to the United States, where he worked with such researchers as E. L. Thorndike, Gordon Allport (also a trait theorist), and William H. Sheldon. Cattell's efforts have culminated in a complex theory of personality that rests primarily on traits. As we will see, his theory reflects a strong concern with the measurement and categorization of behavior. We will first briefly consider traits in general; then, we will examine the details of Cattell's theory of personality.

What Are Traits?

The term *trait* is used in many ways. In physiology, *trait* often refers to a physical characteristic such as eye color or hair color. In psychology, *trait* usually refers to a behavioral characteristic that appears in many situations. For Cattell, a trait is a "collection of reactions or responses bound by some kind of unity which permits the responses to be gathered under one term" (1946, p. 61). In his theory, traits are abstractions that are inferred from observed behavior. For example, one might suggest that a person who writes, paints, and sculpts has a trait for "creativity." Or one who enjoys boxing, football, and rugby might have a trait for "aggression." When used as descriptions of consistencies in what a person does, traits can be convenient and useful summaries of behavior.

Other definitions of traits go beyond observed behavior. For example, a trait has been defined as an underlying mental structure (Hall & Lindzey, 1985) or "neuropsychic structure" (Allport, 1961, p. 347). Such "structures" have not been and cannot be observed and are not real entities. Instead, they are inferred from observations of behavior. The risks of making such inferences will be discussed later, after an overview of Cattell's theory.

Structure

The fundamental element of Cattell's theory of personality is the trait. In his theory, there are many kinds of traits. Some relate to particular abilities or emotional predispositions; others, to motivation. One important distinction is between surface and source traits. **Surface traits** can be identified through direct observations of behavior. Let us say that Bob is popular and cheerful and frequently attends parties. He might, therefore, score high on the surface trait of "sociability." If, instead, Bob is a "loner" who is gloomy, unpopular, and reclusive, he would score low on "sociability." A particular surface trait reflects the interaction of two or more source traits.

Source traits are the fundamental characteristics of personality. For example, one such trait is dominance versus submissiveness (note that for Cattell, a trait is actually a continuum). A person who scores high on this factor would be assertive, aggressive, and competitive, whereas a low scorer would be humble and docile (Cattell & Kline, 1977). Source traits can reflect different kinds of influences. Source traits can be **constitutional traits,** which originate from "within the organism"; some are innate, and others are related to physiological conditions. Source traits can also be **environmental-mold traits,** which develop as a result of interactions with the social and physical environment. Source traits, are identified through an examination of the consistencies among surface traits and are quantified through a complex statistical procedure called *factor analysis,* to be explained later.

Motivation

Motivation is loosely associated with three kinds of **dynamic traits:** ergs, sentiments, and attitudes. **Ergs** are innate biological instincts such as hunger, sex, fear, gregariousness, and pugnacity (similar to aggressiveness), many of which are characteristic of nonhumans. Ergs are the "source of all response action and energy" (Cattell, 1979). Cattell's conception of erg-generated motivation is a tension-reduction model and in this way has a similarity to Freud's and Rogers's theories of motivation. Tension arises from ergs, which can be reduced only by particular behaviors. Moreover, ergs involve action directed toward biological goals. Although how the goals are met may vary across cultures, the basic goals remain the same.

Sentiments, the second class of motives, are learned. Goals that are associated with social institutions (e.g., job and church), people (e.g., spouse and parents), or broad interests (e.g., literature and sports) reflect sentiments. Sentiments may be expressed by statements such as "I want a job in electronics," "I want a large family," or "I want to play sports." Unlike ergs, sentiments may change in kind and number throughout a person's life. **Attitudes,** like sentiments, are learned but involve more specific goals. They are particular courses of action involving particular objects. For example, a person may express an attitude by saying, "I want to see a football game" or "I want to study psychology."

Ergs, sentiments, and attitudes are interrelated: achieving the goal expressed in an attitude may help achieve the goal expressed in a sentiment, which may help achieve the goal expressed in an erg. For examples, the attitude "I want to study psychology" may be tied to a sentiment of "I want a job with a large corporation that pays well," which, in turn, may be tied to the erg of hunger. Cattell suggested that the three classes of motivations may be interconnected in many ways; for example, one attitude may be tied to more than one sentiment, or one sentiment may be tied to more than one erg. He calls the interplay of attitudes, sentiments, and ergs the **dynamic lattice,** an example of which is shown in Figure 9-4.

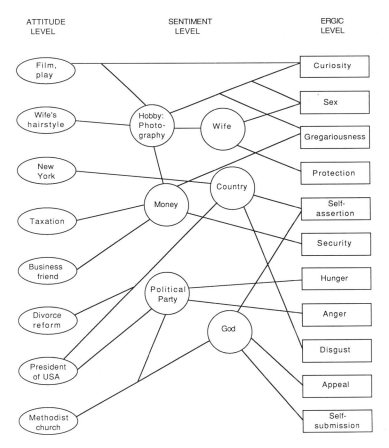

Figure 9-4. An example of a dynamic lattice. (From *The Scientific Analysis of Personality and Motivation* by R. B. Cattell & P. Kline, 1977, p. 177. Copyright 1977 by Academic Press. Adapted by permission.)

Cattell (1965) discussed three types of learning that influence personality development. One is akin to respondent conditioning (see Chapter 6), in which learning involves associations or correlations among environmental events. For example, let us assume that a loud sonic boom elicits a startle response. If the sound consistently occurs in conjunction with the sight of an airplane, the sight of the airplane alone will elicit the startle response. Cattell termed the second kind of learning **reward learning,** which is similar to operant conditioning (see Chapter 6). For example, a baby may learn to cry when hungry because the result, the mother's providing the food, satisfies the ergic goal of food. In **integration learning,** the child learns to act on the goals that will provide the greatest satisfaction to the "personality as a whole" (Cattell, 1965, p. 30). For example, a child may learn to suppress her fear of the unknown and explore a wooded area to satisfy her curiosity.

Most traits develop through the interaction of heredity ("nature") and environment ("nurture"). Using a procedure called *multiple abstract variance analysis (MAVA),* Cattell attempted to identify how much influence each exerts on a particular trait. To accomplish this, he gave personality tests to many families. Many analyses were conducted, including comparisons of natural siblings, adoptive siblings, and twins. Not surprisingly, some traits seemed to be influenced more by heredity, and others were more a function of environment. Cattell also attempted to track the development of personality traits by studying subjects in different age groups. In this research, traits that characterize children, adolescents, and adults were identified. The results showed that most of the important traits appear in childhood.

Personality Assessment

Cattell collected three general types of data in his efforts to identify personality traits (Cattell, 1957). **L-data** are based on life records, consisting of direct observations of behavior involving counting procedures (e.g., the number of social interactions or aggressive acts), ratings by trained judges, and life event statistics (e.g., the number of accidents or job changes). **Q-data** are obtained from a subject's responses to a questionnaire. In these tests, subjects are usually asked to rate themselves on several characteristics. For example, questions such as "Are you afraid of heights?" or "Is blue a depressing color?" may be asked. The third kind of data are **T-data.** They consist of responses (e.g., verbal or physiological) to particular stimuli (e.g., verbal or pictorial). For example, Cattell has measured the time needed to complete a paper-and-pencil maze, heart-rate changes when the subject is startled, and reaction times to various stimuli.

Using all three kinds of data, Cattell distilled what he believes is a collection of traits (source traits) that are the fundamental traits underlying personality. His method for identifying these traits is **factor analysis,** a complex statistical procedure. In factor analysis, scores on many tests are examined, and correlations among them are computed. Let us say that scores on Tests 1, 2, and 3 seem to "move together." In other words, a person's relative scores on the three tests are similar, regardless of whether they are all high, low, or in the middle range. The fact that performance on the three tests covaries highly suggests a common trait responsible for the performance on all three. For instance,

> if such tests as vocabulary, analogies, opposites, and sentence completion have high correlations with each other and low correlations with all other tests, we could tentatively infer the presence of verbal comprehension factors. (Anastasi, 1976, p. 153)

The technique of factor analysis, which Cattell used in an effort to identify basic traits from massive quantities of data, remains popular among many trait theorists.

Are Trait Theories Adequate Explanations of Behavior?

Cattell's measurement techniques are quite sophisticated; he developed many methods of collecting and analyzing data. But is his theory scientifically adequate?

Is the Subject Matter a Quantifiable Characteristic of Behavior?

The primary focus of Cattell's work is on consistencies in behavior. He was interested in behavior in its own right, although he also focused on identifying traits. As previously mentioned, Cattell developed many ways of collecting data, some of which involved gathering information on observable behavior (e.g., life records and responses to particular stimuli). These methods are commendable. In the questionnaire method, the test takers rated themselves on various characteristics. The results of these tests should be viewed with caution. First, a test taker who rates herself or himself may not be aware of her or his own characteristics. Second, even if aware, the test taker may not respond honestly (Cattell, 1957).

Are the Causes of Behavior Empirical Phenomena?

Cattell was primarily interested in identifying particular traits, so that behavior could be predicted in a given situation. He blended his trait theory with three kinds of learning that could, in part, account for the development of traits. Thus, one might say that learning, in combination with heredity, produces consistencies in behavior, or traits.

But the reader should realize that the term *trait* is often used inappropriately. A common error, circular reasoning, occurs when a trait is inferred from behavior and is then used to explain that same behavior. For example, suppose that Susan is able to paint, sculpt, and draw, so we infer in Susan a trait for creativity. When asked to explain Susan's skill in artistic endeavors, we conclude that it must result from her "trait" for creativity. This is circular reasoning. We have inferred a trait (i.e., creativity) from observed behavior (painting, sculpting, and drawing), and then, we have used the trait to explain the behavior ("creativity causes the creative behavior"). Why is this explanation inadequate? Because the trait has no physical existence; it is only a shorthand description of observed behavior. A description of behavior cannot be the cause of that same behavior; rather, the cause must be some other empirical phenomenon.

A second and related error is reification. Recall that some have defined traits as "structures." Because they are assumed to exist and are given names, these posited structures are assumed to be real causes of behavior. The alleged structures are hypothetical constructs, not material entities, and hypothetical entities cannot be legitimate causes of behavior.

Cattell's trait theory also involves teleological explanations of behavior. The motivational traits—ergs, sentiments, and attitudes—involve goals or incentives (Cattell, 1950), and behavior is, or at least appears to be, "goal-directed" (e.g., "I want to study psychology" or "I want to worship God"). But recall that future events cannot directly influence today's behavior; only current or historical variables can do so. Cattell appears to have recognized this and has suggested that ultimate explanations of behavior will involve variables that precede the behavior under study.

Has Cattell Sought Functional Relations
among Empirical Variables?

Through the use of techniques such as factor analysis, Cattell studied many variables simultaneously. Conclusions from such research necessarily involve correlational relations, not functional relations. Although correlational relations may enable one to predict behavior, they typically fail to suggest strategies for changing behavior in desired ways.

A Behavioral Theory

The principles of behavior discussed in Chapter 6 should adequately account for personality, assuming that consistency of behavior is tantamount to personality. Thus, a brief overview of the most influential behavioral psychologist, B. F. Skinner (1904–   ), should suffice. Skinner, a Harvard psychologist, has studied behavior and its environmental determinants for many years; moreover, he has attempted to translate many concepts of traditional personality theories into behavioral terms. In so doing, he has emphasized empirical phenomena, not hypothetical constructs.

Motivation

The theories discussed thus far assign an important role to "needs," "instincts," or "tendencies." Skinner's view of motivation differs. In an effort to deal only with empirical phenomena, he suggested that motivation refers to **procedures** or **operations** with specifiable behavioral effects. For example, withholding fluids for a period of time is a way to motivate (i.e., strengthen) fluid-procuring behavior. A similar effect on behavior may be obtained by salt ingestion or loss of blood. As a further example, food deprivation will motivate food-procuring behavior, or deprivation of sexual stimulation, sexual behavior. Collectively, these **motivational operations,** also called *establishing operations* (see Chapter 6), change the reinforcing capacity of some event and strengthen behavior that has in the past been followed by the event.

Skinner's explanation of motivation does not appeal to inner states. Motivation operations do not affect a "drive" or "need," which in turn affects behavior; drives and needs have no physical existence and are at best inferred from behavior or knowledge of some motivational operation. Rather, motivational operations have direct and measurable effects on behavior, as well as on bodily processes. But no particular behavior is strengthened in all people by a given motivational operation. For example, the yuppie, when deprived of social attention, might go to a restaurant or a disco, but the hippie might attend a "love-in." The behaviors that appear are those that have successfully produced social attention in the past.

Structure

Skinner (1974) suggested that "A self or personality is at best a repertoire of behavior imparted by an organized set of contingencies" (p. 164). For Skinner, personality is neither an explanatory concept nor a thing; a woman does not have a personality as she has an arm or a leg, and she does not behave in a particular way because of personality. Instead, the term *personality* refers to behaviors that consistently occur in particular situations. To say that one has an aggressive personality is only to observe that the person *behaves aggressively* in many situations.

That there are consistencies in behavior across situations reflects similar conditioning histories in those situations. When a woman behaves aggressively in many situations, such behavior has probably been reinforced in many situations in the past. Explanations such as "She has an aggressive personality" or a "trait for aggression" are rejected because the explanatory variables, which are usually inferred from behavior, have no physical existence.

Personality Development

Development is an important component of Skinner's model, but what develops is behavior, not hypothetical constructs such as traits, egos, ids, or selves. Skinner (1978) suggested, "As the contingencies become more complex, they shape and maintain more complex behavior. It is the environment that develops, not a mental or cognitive possession" (p. 99).

Let us consider the development of "sociability," or behaviors involved in getting along with other people. Sociability does not magically appear as a child matures, nor does some mental apparatus develop that somehow spawns such behavior. As the child grows, the parents begin to encourage the child to interact positively with his or her peers. They may even provide incentives (e.g., praise). Antisocial behavior, on the other hand, is penalized in various ways (e.g., by scolding). Thus, the child *learns* to get along with his or her peers and elders. Undoubtedly, people differ in terms of sociability—we are all acquainted with both the recluse and the gadabout—but the primary cause of such differences is learning history, not an inner trait or tendency.

This is not to say that personality development is totally determined by environmental influences. Genetic endowment influences all behavior, and as Skinner (1974) noted, "Species differ in the speeds with which they can be conditioned and in the nature and size of the repertoires they can maintain, and it is probable that people show similar inherited differences" (p. 244). Moreover, there are "sensitive periods" in which the environment can have maximum effects (see Chapter 8). Thus, it is a mistake to assume an unending plasticity of behavior. But the effects of environmental variables must not be ignored, and their effects should not be attributed to hypothesized forces within the person.

Personality Assessment

Behavioral approaches to personality, as implied by the name, consider behavior their subject matter. Doing so takes much of the inference and guess-work out of assessment. Behavior itself is observed and quantified, and an appropriate analysis and evaluation follows, based on the observations. We should note that the results are not used as an "index" of some hypothesized entity: behavior is not said to reflect ego strength or some trait. Instead, the assessment of what is commonly termed *personality* is purely a *behavioral assessment*.

Although there are many ways to assess behavior, behaviorists often gather information through **direct observations.** For example, let us say that a psychologist is interested in how often a man makes negative statements about himself. One method of assessment would be to observe the man and to count the number of such statements. The observations could then be quantified by a computation of the **rate of response,** which is the number of responses per unit of time (e.g., the number of negative statements made per day). Skinner (e.g., 1950) has strongly favored the rate of response as a primary measure of behavior, and it has proved a sensitive and useful index. The observations might be quantified in other ways, such as calculating the **percentage of situations** in which negative statements occurred, or the **latency** to the first negative statement in a particular situation.

Sometimes, direct observations are not feasible. In such cases, behavioral psychologists may collect information from **interviews,** in which a person, or his or her associates, are asked about his or her behavior. In the example above, the man, his family, or his friends might be asked how often he makes negative statements. The man could also complete a **questionnaire** that is designed to estimate the incidence of the behavior in question. A questionnaire might have questions such as "How often do you find yourself making negative state-ments?" or "In what situations do you make negative statements?"

Checklists and **ratings scales** are also used. For example, the Teacher Rating Scale (Conners, 1973) is used to measure hyperactivity. In it, an observer rates the presence of many behaviors, among them the extent to which the person being rated is restless, excitable, inattentive, and demanding. This scale may also be used to measure changes in behavior when a treatment has been implemented. The information gathered with rating scales, as well as with questionnaires and interviews, must be interpreted cautiously because the person providing the information may be unable or unwilling to give accurate information.

A psychologist might also ask a person to **observe and record his or her own behavior.** For example, using a device such as a golf counter, a student might record every time she completes an assignment on time. Self-recording has one advantage: the recorder can "observe" behaviors that are inaccessible to others. A woman can count the number of times she has the urge to smoke a cigarette, but no one else can do so because the "behavior" is private. Unfortunately, self-recording may not yield accurate data. A person may intentionally distort what is reported or may simply fail to accurately monitor the response of interest.

The foregoing is only a sample of the many behavioral assessment techniques. Many texts (e.g., Ciminero, Calhoun, & Adams, 1977; Hersen & Bellack, 1976) provide a good overview of behavioral assessment. But all share an important feature, that is, the focus on behavior as the object of interest.

Role of the Individual

Does Skinner's conception of personality neglect the individual? Not at all. As Skinner (1974) explained:

> It is often said that a science of behavior studies the human organism but neglects the person or self. What it neglects is a vestige of animism, a doctrine which in its crudest form held that the body was moved by one or more indwelling spirits. . . . In a behavioral analysis a person is an organism, a member of the human species, which has acquired a repertoire of behavior. It remains an organism to the anatomist and physiologist, but it is a person to those to whom its behavior is important. Complex contingencies of reinforcement create complex repertoires, and, as we have seen, different contingencies create different persons in the same skin, of which so-called multiple personalities are only an extreme manifestation.
>
> A person is not an originating agent; he is a locus, a point at which many genetic and environmental conditions come together in a joint effort. As such, he remains unquestionably unique. No one else (unless he has an identical twin) has his genetic endowment, and without exception no one else has his personal history. Hence no one else will behave in precisely the same way. (pp. 167–168)

As Skinner noted, genetic endowment and personal history make us unique. By producing consistencies in our behavior, these same variables may be said to determine our own "unique personality."

Is Skinner's Theory an Adequate Explanation of Behavior?

Using Skinner's approach to study behavior, researchers have discovered many important and useful facts about behavior and its causes. Nevertheless, many have criticized his approach for a number of reasons (see Skinner, 1974).

But our concern in this chapter is whether his approach is scientific and provides adequate explanations of behavior.

Is the Subject Matter a Quantifiable Characteristic of Behavior?

Skinner adamantly opposes studying hypothetical entities; instead, he focuses on behavior as the subject of inquiry. He does not reject investigations of "private" behavior, such as feelings, thoughts, and emotions, but he does recognize the problems in accurately recording such behavior.

Are the Causes of Behavior Empirical Phenomena?

As is evident in the foregoing discussion, Skinner rejects hypothetical entities as causes of behavior and instead appeals to environmental variables in concert with inherited factors. Although he is at odds with many other theorists, his approach has practical advantages. When behavior is conceptualized as a function of environmental variables, such variables, because they have a physical existence, can be directly managed to effect socially important changes (see Chapter 12). If, for instance, a child's temper tantrums occur because they have historically gained his parents' attention, the parents can reduce the frequency of his tantrums by withholding attention when such behavior occurs. When a

Some people are participants, others are observers. Can any theory of personality adequately explain why some fly balloons while others merely watch from the ground? (Photo courtesy of Sue Keller.)

juvenile delinquent's behavior results from a particular style of parenting, perhaps her parents can learn more effective child-rearing practices. These lessons can also be passed on to other would-be parents.

But if delinquent behavior is said to result from a low "self-concept," how can the self-concept be manipulated if it has no physical existence? Perhaps a therapist, in attempting to indirectly manipulate the self-concept, might devise a plan that successfully changes behavior; the environmental variables that produced the change would therefore be of interest. But explaining the change in terms of the self-concept seems an unnecessary detour from the variables that actually produced the change in behavior.

*Has Skinner Sought Functional Relations
among Empirical Variables?*

One of Skinner's most important contributions is a methodology for studying behavior. He has proposed investigating the effects of environmental variables on the behavior of individual organisms. These relations are the core of Skinner's analysis. The importance of functional relations to a science and technology of behavior is discussed in Chapter 2.

Summary and Conclusions

The five personality theories we have considered are somewhat complex. To help you differentiate them, Table 9-1 lists some of the important features of each. Note that the theories account for behavior in very different ways. Freud's,

Table 9-1
Summary of Personal Theories

Theory	Structure	Motivation	Development	Assessment
Psychoanalytic (Freud)	id, ego, superego	Life and death instincts	Psychosexual stages in childhood	Interaction with patients, dream analysis, free association
Humanistic (Rogers)	Self	Actualization tendency	Continual-valuing systems guide	Interviews, tests (Q-sort)
Constitutional (Sheldon)	Physical structure	—	Somatotypes do not change	Ratings, measurements
Trait (Cattell)	Source traits	Ergs, sentiments, attitudes	Traits develop from learning and genetic factors	Tests, observations
Behavioral (Skinner)	No structure—just different repertoires of behavior	Operations and procedures (e.g., deprivation)	Behavior develops from learning and genetic factors	Behavior is measured most often by direct observations

Rogers's, Sheldon's, and Cattell's approaches to personality have not directly contributed to the development of a science of behavior and, in the context of the present text, are primarily of historical interest. Skinner's theory has been an important constituent in the development of a scientific approach to behavior. Although our understanding of behavior remains incomplete, his approach offers a useful methodology for studying behavior and its relation to the environment.

Personality, in the simple descriptive sense of consistencies in behavior across time and place, is certainly important. For example, attempts to classify topographically unlike behaviors into categories (traits) whose members are logically related and covary may be of practical value. As a case in point, personality inventories such as the Minnesota Multiphasic Personality Inventory (MMPI—Hathaway & McKinley, 1951) can be used (although imprecisely) to predict clinically significant problem behaviors. It must be recognized, however, that responses to MMPI questions and the labels assigned on the basis of those responses do not in any sense cause or explain the problem behaviors and do not suggest strategies for preventing or treating them.

The five theories described in this chapter are only representatives of a large and diverse array. Personality is an old and large area of psychological investigation, and interest in the area continues. Old theories are regularly refined and extended; for instance, Freud's work laid the groundwork for theories by such notables as Alfred Adler, Carl Jung, Karen Horney, Eric Fromm, and Eric Erikson. New theories are also occasionally proffered, some with surprising applications. Friedman and Rosenman (1974), for example, suggested that people with **Type A** personalities (competitive, aggressive, and time-urgent individuals) are at risk for coronary problems; others without these characteristics, **Type B** personalities (easygoing and slow to anger), have a lower risk. The cause of the Type A personality? The authors suggest a combination of heredity—they call it a trait for Type A—and environmental influences. The latter may be a cultural phenomenon, as these authors argue that the American scene encourages an unrelenting quest for more and more material goods.

Unfortunately, with each new theory and each revision of an old one, the temptation to use fundamentally inadequate explanations of behavior arises. Reification, circular reasoning, and teleology have historically damned the vast majority of personality theories. The astute student of behavior will recognize these errors and will insist on explanations of behavior that involve real phenomena of practical importance.

Study Questions

1. What are psychologists doing when they study personality?

2. According to Freud, when do defense mechanisms arise? Give an example of a defense mechanism.

3. What is incongruence, according to Rogers, and how does a person deal with it?

4. According to Cattell, what is a trait, and how does his usage of the term differ from its use in reference to physical traits?

5. Name and describe three kinds of behavior assessments.

6. In Skinner's theory, describe how the individual is "unique."

7. For each theory, state whether the subject matter is a quantifiable characteristic of behavior and whether the causes of behavior are empirical phenomena.

8. Be able to reproduce Table 9-1, and to define the terms used in it.

Recommended Readings

Hall, C. S., Lindzey, G., Loehlin, J. C., & Manosevitz, M. (1985). *Introduction to Theories of Personality.* New York: Wiley.

The authors present an excellent description and evaluation of the major personality theories. The book is well written and appropriate for the beginning student.

Nye, R. (1981). *Three Psychologies: Perspectives from Freud, Skinner, and Rogers.* Monterey, CA: Brooks/ Cole.

Nye discusses the theories of Freud, Skinner, and Rogers, undeniably three of the giants in psychology. The essentials of each theory are presented in a concise, easy-to-understand manner. Particularly helpful is the final chapter, in which each theory is given a critique, as well as compared to and contrasted with the other theories.

CHAPTER 10

Social Psychology

We are social beings. From cradle to grave, humans spend much of their time together. Consider your daily activities. You probably live with someone, you may have your meals in a cafeteria or restaurant surrounded by diners, you attend classes with fellow students, and you engage in recreational and social activities with friends. It should come as no surprise that other people powerfully influence your behavior. If fact, social isolation early in life can be devastating to the development of a child. Jean Itard's "Wild Boy of Aveyron," Victor, is a case in point. Victor, who will be discussed in Chapter 11, had apparently been abandoned by his family many years before he was captured by hunters in the Cauned Woods near Aveyron, France. When captured in 1799, Victor was about 11 years old and in behavior more closely resembled a wild animal than a typical human child. Although Itard made dramatic progress in training Victor, the boy was never fully socialized and did not develop functional speech.

Fortunately, for most people lack of social interaction is not a problem: Our behaviors are constantly molded by the actions of others around us. How this occurs is the subject matter of **social psychology,** which encompasses the study of the effects of other people on the behavior of the individual. Social psychology deals with the structure of all human interactions and is therefore one of the most diverse fields within psychology. Virtually all social situations have been subjected to scrutiny by social psychologists.

Research and theorizing in social psychology can be divided into three broad categories: social cognition, social influence, and social relations. This chapter is organized around these categories. Social cognition, which involves the relation between attitudes and behavior and the processes by which we generally determine the causes of our own and other people's behavior, is considered first. This is followed by an overview of social influence focusing on conformity, compliance, obedience, persuasion, social facilitation, and social loafing. Finally, social relations such as aggression, altruism, and attraction are considered. Because social psychology is a large and diverse area, in-depth coverage is not provided in any area. Instead, a wide range of topics of interest to social psychologists—and, we hope to readers—is introduced.

Social psychology studies how a person's behavior is influenced by the actions of others. In this picture, consider how each child's behavior could be influenced by the actions of the other children. (Photo courtesy of Sue Keller.)

Social Cognition: Attitudes and Behavior

Historically, the question "How do attitudes affect behavior?" has been of considerable interest to many psychologists. The question seems to be reasonable, but it assumes that attitudes have a real existence apart from behavior. As Bandura (1969) explained:

> In many respects, the question of whether attitudes regulate overt behavior might be considered a pseudo-issue created by arbitrary distinctions between different types of response. . . . Like most implicit tendencies, attitudes are characteristically inferred from various forms of overt behavior rather than identified by some independent criterion. Consequently, if self-ratings were treated as a class of behavior rather than assigned special status as indicants of an internal mediator which is given substance and endowed with influential regulatory powers, then the issue of the relationship of attitude to behavior might be more meaningfully conceptualized as a problem of correlation between different response systems. From this point of view, there exists no intrinsic relationship between these two sets of responses, since they can be either highly correlated or dissociated depending upon their respective contingencies of reinforcement.
>
> The differentiation between attitudes and overt actions disappears completely when the former are primarily inferred from nonverbal behavior. For example, a person who displays antagonistic responses or actively avoids members of a given ethnic group is believed to have a negative attitude, whereas he is assumed to possess a positive attitude if he exhibits approving amicable reactions. In such circumstances, the issue of whether attitudes influence behavior reduces to the meaningless question of whether a particular response pattern determines itself! (pp. 597–598)

Bandura made a number of important points. One is that attitudes are always inferred on the basis of overt behavior, characteristically verbal self-

WMU BOOKSTORE
BERNHARD CENTER
LAST DAY FOR FALL TEXTBOOK
REFUNDS IS SEPTEMBER 13, 1994
=======================================
    RG#00001-00006 RC#14400 16:19
  T# 30130 CS# 666 SV# 101 09-01-94
  DUPLICATE   DUPLICATE   1 TAX 1
PLU   2881592112 N00 DEPT   8.70
GENERAL PSYCHOL   1@   8.70   1 TAX 1
PLU   0306434326 U00 DEPT   24.40
PSYCHOLOGY (HAR   1@ 24.40
                                 33.10
                                  1.99
                               ==========
NET DUE
TAX   35.09
                                 35.09

TOTAL DUE
      FINANCIAL AID VOUCHE
      ACCOUNT # 1-00-01793367457210
      NAME [SUMNER, GREGORY M]
      ACCOUNT TYPE [AWARD]
      NEW BALANCE [8.69]
      FUNDS AVAIL [8.69]
      _____

   X_____
     AUTHORIZED SIGNATURE

          THANK YOU
       KEEP YOUR RECEIPT
    TRADE AND REFERENCE BOOKS NONREFUNDABLE
            (616) 387-3929

reports; they are never observed directly. For example, a subject is asked to report how he or she might respond in a given situation. The answers are taken to indicate an underlying attitude. The self-report is then compared with how the subject actually behaves in the situation of interest. If there is correspondence, the attitude is assumed to cause the overt behavior. If not, no causal status is assigned.

This research strategy is exemplified in a study by LaPiere (1934). In his study, a Chinese couple visited more than 200 motels and restaurants throughout the United States. Even though there was considerable prejudice against Asians in the 1920s, only one facility refused service to the couple. When these same motels and restaurants were sent a questionnaire asking whether they would serve the couple, 92% of the respondents said that they would not. Although this study might be construed as evaluating whether attitudes toward Asians controlled overt behavior, it actually examined the correspondence between saying and doing: Was overt behavior toward Asians correlated with, and hence predictable on the basis of, verbal behavior concerning them?

From the behavioral perspective, saying and doing represent separate response categories that are shaped and maintained by different contingencies and do not necessarily affect one another. Therefore, it is not surprising that research and common experience suggest that there is not necessarily a high degree of correspondence between saying and doing (e.g., Bandura, 1969). The entire field of social psychology underwent dramatic changes in the 1960s when researchers found that only a small proportion of behavior could be reliably predicted from self-reports. Once this was apparent, attention turned to finding the variables that determined the correspondence between verbal and nonverbal behavior.

Correspondence between Verbal and Nonverbal Behavior

An attitude can be considered a subject's verbal report of her or his tendency to behave in a particular way with respect to some person, place, or thing. Several variables are known to affect the degree of correspondence between saying and doing or, in the terms favored by many social psychologists, between attitudes and behavior.

One variable that affects correspondence is the amount of experience with the situation of interest. In general, verbal responses by individuals with direct experience in a given situation are more likely to reflect behavior in that situation than are verbal responses by individuals without such experience. Imagine two people who say, "I don't like watching professional football." One grew up on Long Island and has seen several Jets and Giants games. The other grew up in Sioux Falls and has never seen a game; her attitude (verbal statement) reflects variables other than actual exposure to professional football. That being the case, it is likely (although not assured) that she would, if given the option, be more apt than the New Yorker to attend a game, and to enjoy it (i.e., laugh and cheer).

As you might anticipate, the probability that correspondence will occur can be increased by providing reinforcement when what is done is consistent with what is said. Such a relation was demonstrated by Isreal and Brown (1977), who asked a group of children to state which play activity they intended to engage in at a later time (e.g., "I am going to play with dinosaurs"). First, the children received a snack for making such statements. As a result, the number of children who promised to play with a particular toy increased, but the number of children who actually played with the toy did not. The experimenters then provided snacks for correspondence; that is, each child received a snack when she or he promised to play with a toy and then played with it at the appropriate time. Under this condition, correspondence increased.

Although the relation is imperfect, it is abundantly clear that verbal behavior sometimes allows us to predict other behavior. This does not, however, mean that the verbal behavior *causes* the other behavior in any simple sense. Each reflects, in large part, the conditioning history of the individual and must be explained in terms of that history. Our attitudes, like the rest of our behavior, are learned. Hence, they can be changed.

One variable that influences reported attitudes is the activities in which one engages. For example, Lieberman (1956) found that industrial workers who were promoted to supervisory positions became more sympathetic to management's position. Two theories have been advanced by social psychologists to explain such phenomena. **Cognitive dissonance theory** (Festinger, 1957) holds that a sort of psychological tension arises in situations where one of a person's attitudes is inconsistent with another attitude, or with overt behavior. Cognitive dissonance would occur if, for instance, a person who regularly asserted, "I'm a confirmed heterosexual" had just engaged in a homosexual act. The tension is unpleasant, and people act to reduce it. They do so by changing their attitude; it is too late to change their overt behavior. In the above example, the person might change her or his attitude (descriptive self-statement) from "I'm a confirmed heterosexual" to "I'm a confirmed heterosexual, but I'm liberal and willing to experiment."

In a famous demonstration of cognitive dissonance, Festinger and Carlsmith (1959) had college students engage in the repetitive and boring task of placing empty spools on a tray, dumping them out, sorting them again, and repeating the process. After a hour of this activity, the subjects were asked to lie by telling the person who was to take over the task (a confederate of the experimenters) that the experiment was very interesting. One group of subjects was paid 1 dollar to lie, and another group was paid 20 dollars to lie. A control group was not asked to lie and received no money. All subjects were asked to rate how much they actually liked the spool-sorting task. The group that was paid 1 dollar to lie rated the experiment as much more enjoyable than did the group paid 20 dollars. The control group liked it even less than the other two groups. Festinger and Carlsmith explained these findings by saying that lying is generally unacceptable to most people and therefore creates a state of dissonance. The 1-dollar group had less justification for lying and thus experienced more discomfort than did the subjects in the 20-dollar group. Therefore, to reduce the dissonance, they changed their attitude about the experiment to a greater degree.

The cognitive dissonance theory has been extended to account for many phenomena, with varying degrees of success. The behavioral mechanisms responsible for the reduction of dissonance are difficult to specify. One possibility with some empirical support is that people become aroused physiologically when they have to say or write something that is inconsistent with their attitudes (Croyle & Cooper, 1983). Engaging in behaviors that reduce this arousal, which include providing verbal descriptions consistent with the behavior, are strengthened through negative reinforcement. Why these behaviors reduce arousal is a difficult question. The answer appears to reside in a complex conditioning history, in which the verbal community supports, in some situations, a correspondence between verbal and nonverbal behavior.

An alternative to cognitive dissonance theory, termed **self-perception theory** (Bem, 1967), has been advanced to explain attitude change in general and Festinger and Carlsmith's results in particular. According to this theory, we attribute causes to our own behavior much as we do when explaining others' behavior. Specifically, self-perception theory holds that we check external events and then infer attitudes, feelings, or beliefs. For example, if asked whether or not we are hungry, we are likely to check the time since we last ate or to check our own behavior (perhaps we are eating voraciously) and then to decide how hungry we are. According to self-perception theory, the subjects in the spool-sorting experiment inferred their attitude only after looking at their behavior of lying and the amount of money they received. Subjects who saw themselves lying for 20 dollars may have believed that they lied for the money. Subjects who received only 1 dollar, however, may have believed that, because they were willing to lie for such a small amount, they must really have liked the experiment. The variables responsible for the difference in belief (i.e., verbal statements about alleged causes of behavior) are moot.

Both the cognitive dissonance and the self-perception theories are viable in social psychology today, and a considerable amount of research is directed toward resolving which provides the better explanation of empirical findings. Both theories are mentalistic, and neither emphasizes environmental variables as causes of behavior.

Attribution

Determining the causes of others' behavior may help us to behave more effectively. Like psychologists, laypeople are concerned with why the people around them behave as they do. Unlike psychologists, most laypeople's statements about the causes of others' behavior are not the result of scientific inquiry. **Attribution theory** (Heider, 1958; Kelly, 1967) was developed in an attempt to explain the nonscientific processes by which humans ascribe causes to others' behavior.

There are two sets of variables to which behavior is commonly attributed: dispositional and situational. **Dispositional** (or **personal** or **internal**) **variables** are personal characteristics assumed to be responsible for some behavior. **Situational** (or **environmental** or **external**) **variables** are aspects of the environment (other than the behaver) assumed to be responsible for some behavior. For instance, in explaining a person's disheveled appearance, we could attribute it either (1) to his being slovenly (a dispositional variable) or (2) to his being awake all night cramming for final exams (a situational variable). From a behavioral perspective, dividing variables into dispositional or situational is a false dichotomy: Both dispositional and situational variables typically reflect environmental influences. For example, the behaviors that lead us to call someone slovenly are in all likelihood shaped and maintained by the verbal community.

On what are attributes commonly based? Suppose that you are trying to explain the fact that your friend Vicky earned an A in a modern religion course in which all other students received Cs or below. You know that Vicky gets As in all her other classes as well. According to Kelly (1967), the three variables of consensus, distinctiveness, and consistency are likely to determine whether you attribute her success to dispositional or situational causes. **Consensus** is based on the way others have behaved in the same situation. If they have behaved similarly, consensus is high, indicating situational causes; if they have behaved differently, consensus is low, indicating dispositional causes. In the present example, consensus is low because only Vicky received a high grade. Hence, you are likely to attribute her good grade to a dispositional variable.

Distinctiveness is based on the way the person behaves under different circumstances. If the person behaves similarly in many different situations, distinctiveness is low, indicating dispositional causes; if the person behaves differently in different situations, distinctiveness is high, indicating situational causes. In our example, Vicky gets As in all her classes. Distinctiveness is therefore low, and a dispositional cause is indicated.

Consistency is related to distinctiveness. **Consistency** involves a similarity of behavior across time and situations. If someone behaves similarly across time and situations, consistency is high, indicating dispositional causes; if he or she behaves differently, consistency is low, indicating situational causes. Because Vicky gets As in other classes, at different times, consistency is high. In our example, you would probably attribute Vicky's receiving an A to dispositional causes such as being intelligent. From a behavioral perspective we would, however, attribute Vicky's exemplary performance not to a personal characteristic such as being "intelligent," but to the interaction of genetic and environmental variables.

Attributional Errors

Attribution is not always a rational or accurate process. Biases (systematic errors) and unsystematic errors, as well as lack of knowledge, frequently prevent people from determining the real causes of behavior. The bias that has received the most attention is the **fundamental attribution error** (Ross, 1977), which involves the tendency to attribute others' behavior to dispositional causes rather than to situational causes. That many people tend to discard the role of the environment in explaining others' behavior was demonstrated by Jones and Harris (1967). College students were asked to read debaters' speeches that took either a pro-Castro or an anti-Castro position. When told that the debater chose the position, the students assumed that the position reflected the debater's attitude. Interestingly, when told that the debater's position had been chosen by the debating coach, the students also assumed that the remarks reflected the debater's pro- or anti-Castro attitude.

Although dispositional variables are characteristically favored over situational ones in explaining others' behavior, the opposite is generally true when explaining one's own behavior. In an interesting example, Nisbett, Caputo, Legant, and Mareck (1973) asked college students to describe their reasons for choosing their particular majors. They were also asked to describe the reasons behind their best friend's choice of major. The students gave far greater emphasis to dispositional variables in explaining their friends' choices than in explaining their own.

A third source of attributional error is salience. Social psychologists report that we often attribute behavior to the most salient (conspicuous) feature of the situation we are observing. For example, Taylor and Fiske (1978) showed that, when a single person in a group is made more salient, that person is described as causing whatever happens (Meyers, 1983).

Social Influence

Social influence generally subsumes the topics of conformity, compliance, obedience, persuasion, social facilitation, and social loafing.

Conformity

Look at the two sets of lines in Figure 10-1. Which of the three comparison lines is most like the standard line? Chances are quite good that you can make the right choice. Now imagine that you are seated alongside four other people, who, like you, are participating in an experiment. The first time the group is asked which line matches the standard line, all of you give the correct answer. The second time everyone again answers correctly. The third time, however, the first person gives an answer inconsistent with the one you think is correct. The second, third, and fourth persons all give the same answer as the first person. It is now your turn. Do you give the answer that the four others gave or the one that you believe is correct? If you are like most people, you are much less likely to answer correctly in this situation than if you were asked the question with no

 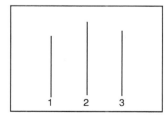

Figure 10-1. In the study by Asch (1956), subjects were shown two cards similar to those in the figure. The subject's task was to choose the line in the group of three that was the same length as the single line on the other card.

one else around. Solomon Asch (1956) performed this classic experiment and found that persons who answered alone gave correct answers 99% of the time. When seated in a group of others who were answering incorrectly, the correct answers dropped to 63%. Thus, even though the subjects "knew" the correct answer, they often behaved as others in the group had behaved. This phenomenon has been termed *conformity* by social psychologists.

Conformity is traditionally defined as a change in behavior as a result of implicit group pressure. Behavior is viewed as being an example of conformity only if it differs from what it would be if one were alone. For instance, cheering for your favorite team in a crowded bar provides no evidence of conformity, but cheering for a team you dislike does so.

Conformity is a part of all of our lives. Even groups that expressly emphasize nonconformity may foster conformity. For example, the hippies of the 1960s were nonconformists with respect to the general culture or "establishment," but they obviously conformed to their own "counterculture" in terms of dress, language, drug use, and sexual practices. Each fall, conformity may be observed on college campuses as the behavior of newly arriving freshmen changes to resemble (i.e., conform with) that of other students.

Four major factors affecting conformity have been identified: the size of the group, ambiguity with respect to appropriate behavior, the perceived expertise

Social conformity? It's hard to tell, but surely the group is affecting the student "onstage." (Photo courtesy of Susan Allen.)

of the group members, and the presence of an ally. In small groups, the greater the number of people, the greater the degree of conformity. After group size reaches six or seven, however, further increases in size have little effect on conformity (Roediger, Rushton, Capaldi, & Paris, 1984).

As a rule, the degree of conformity increases when it is difficult to formulate clear rules about appropriate behavior, that is, when the situation is ambiguous. It also increases when members of the group are perceived to be experts. A fourth factor shown to affect conformity is the presence or absence of another person who resists pressure to conform. One is less likely to conform when there is another person present who also resists conformity (Roediger *et al.*, 1984).

Why does conformity occur? One reason is that most people have a history in which behaving as others behave has been more successful in many situations than behaving differently. A second is that most people also have a history that favors generating and following rules consistent with conformity. "When in Rome, do as the Romans do" is not idle advice; typically, we are more successful in novel situations if we mimic the behaviors that occur around us.

Obviously, conformity does not occur in all situations. Most of us have experienced occasions on which conformity has been counterproductive. In such cases, the probability of conforming in similar circumstances weakens. For example, an adolescent who engages in vandalism in the presence of friends is less likely to repeat the act if caught and immediately punished. Moreover, many people have histories that foster behaviors inconsistent with conformity in certain situations. For instance, some drug-naive adolescents do not try drugs even though they are in the presence of drug users. This response reflects in large part a history that fosters rule-governed behavior incompatible with drug use.

Compliance

Whereas conformity involves behavior change as a result of indirect pressure to behave in a certain manner, **compliance** involves behaving in a way consistent with a direct request for a certain form of behavior. For example, if someone asks to go ahead of you in a checkout line and you agree, your behavior demonstrates compliance. One learns to comply with requests because (1) doing so, at least occasionally, yields a positive outcome and (2) failing to do so, at least occasionally, yields a negative outcome.

Although the mechanisms responsible for compliance are simple at one level, the variables that determine whether it will occur are complex. For example, Freedman and Fraser (1966) found that, once someone complies with a relatively small request, that person is much more likely to comply with a larger request. In this study, California women were approached and asked to place a small sign in their window or to sign a petition to keep California beautiful. Later, the women were asked to place in their yards a very large billboard promoting safe driving. Seventy-six percent of the women agreed. In contrast, only 17% of the members of a control group who were asked only to place the billboard in their yard agreed to do so. Freedman and Fraser called this method of obtaining compliance the "foot-in-the-door technique."

Cialdini, Vincent, Lewis, Catalan, Wheeler, and Darby (1975) developed a different technique for inducing compliance. They called theirs the "door-in-the-face technique." In this approach, the subjects were first asked to comply with a request that required a considerable expenditure of money, time, or effort. Most refused. The subjects were then asked to comply with a much less costly request. Most complied. For example, Cialdini *et al.* first asked college students if they would commit two years to counseling delinquent children (the large request). All refused. The researchers then asked whether the students would agree to take a delinquent child to the zoo. Fifty-six percent of them agreed to the smaller request. Only 32% of a control group, who were asked only to take children to the zoo, agreed. These data suggest that asking for something very large and then "settling" for something smaller is one method of obtaining compliance.

Obedience

Although there is no unambiguous distinction between the two, social psychologists often differentiate compliance and obedience. As usually conceived, compliance involves doing as requested by any other person, and **obedience** involves doing as ordered by a person of some authority. Although obedience may be necessary for the survival of a culture, the results of blind obedience can be most unfortunate. One of the most devastating examples of obedience was the extermination by the Nazis of 6 million Jews. During the Holocaust, hundreds of German citizens routinely tortured and killed Jews and other alleged "inferiors." When questioned at the Nuremburg war crime trials, these people characteristically argued that they were "only following orders." Why did they do so? Could such a thing happen in other cultures? Would most people knowingly inflict injury on another person simply because they are ordered to do so?

In perhaps the most famous of all social psychology experiments, Stanley Milgram (1963) sought to investigate obedience to authority. Specifically, he was interested in determining whether people would injure others simply because they were told to do so. Milgram advertised in local papers and through direct mail for subjects to participate in a study ostensibly involving the effects of punishment on learning. The subjects were 40 males who responded to these advertisements and believed that the study was being sponsored by Yale University. The subjects and another person, who was actually a confederate of the experimenter, were brought into a room and were "randomly" assigned to play the role of either the teacher or the learner. Actually, the selection process was rigged so that the subjects were always assigned the role of teacher.

When the roles had been assigned, the subject was shown an imposing shock generator and was given a sample shock to show that it was operating. The subject then witnessed the learner being strapped into a chair with electrodes placed on his wrist. Next, the teacher (subject) was taken to another room and seated before a console. On the console were 30 switches. Above each switch was a label indicating a single shock voltage. The labeled voltages ranged from 15 to 450 volts, in increasing order across the row of switches. Beneath each set of four consecutive switches were descriptive labels. They read: Slight Shock,

Moderate Shock, Strong Shock, Very Strong Shock, Intense Shock, Extreme Intensity Shock, and Danger: Severe Shock. The last two switches were designated simply "XXX."

The "teacher" was instructed to read a list of questions to the "learner" through a microphone. The learner supposedly responded through a microphone placed in his room. Each time the learner made a mistake, the teacher was told to administer a shock to him. The lowest intensity shock was to follow the first mistake, the second-lowest intensity shock was to follow the second mistake, and so on. Actually, the answers were standardized on tape and no shocks were delivered; the learner behaved, however, as if shocked. At 75 volts, he began to grunt and moan. At 150 volts, the learner demanded to be let out of the experiment. At 180 volts, he cried that he could not stand the pain. At 300 volts, he pounded on the wall. At 330 volts, he became silent (and the taped answers stopped). At this point, the subject was instructed to treat no answer as an incorrect answer and to administer the shock. If at any point the subject began to hesitate or question giving the shock, he was told that he had no choice in the matter and that he must continue.

Milgram was interested primarily in how far the subjects would go before refusing to administer any more shocks. His results are summarized in Figure 10-2. Of his subjects, 100% gave shocks through the "intense shock" level, and 63% delivered the full range of shocks. These findings show clearly that ordinary people will, in some cases, knowingly inflict injury on another when ordered to do so. Another finding of interest is that many of the subjects were obviously in considerable distress but nevertheless continued delivering shocks:

> I observed a mature and initially poised businessman enter the laboratory smiling and confident. Within 20 minutes he was reduced to a twitching, stuttering wreck, who

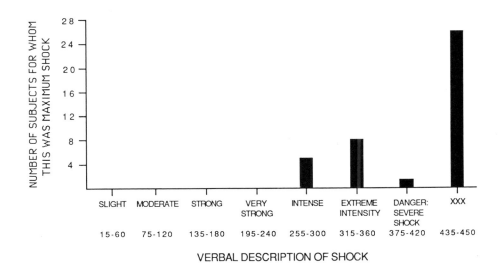

Figure 10-2. The number of subjects in Milgram's study (1963) for whom the listed value was the maximum shock intensity delivered. This figure was prepared from data presented in tabular form by Milgram.

was rapidly approaching a point of nervous collapse. He constantly pulled on his earlobe, and twisted his hands. At one point he pushed his fist into his forehead and muttered: "Oh God, let's stop it." And yet he continued to respond to every word of the experimenter, and obeyed to the end. (Milgram, 1963, p. 377)

Subsequent research by Milgram and others has revealed several variables that affect obedience. Having the learner within sight of the subject reduced the number of persons completing the entire sequence of shocks to approximately 40%. Requiring the subject to hold the learner's arm on the shock plate further reduced obedience to 30%. In another study, in which the experimenter left the room and communicated with the subject via the phone, obedience was approximately 23%. The prestige associated with Yale University in contributing to the obtained effects was shown in another experiment. Here, the location of the experiment was moved to a run-down neighborhood, and only 48% of subjects delivered the entire range of shocks (65% did so at Yale). Finally, the presence of two nonobedient allies decreased the obedience to approximately 10%. Gender and country of citizenship were unrelated to probability of obedience.

Milgram's studies raise important ethical issues. Should researchers be allowed to conduct investigations in which subjects experience strong emotional distress? Should all aspects of the experiment be revealed beforehand to the subjects? Milgram argued that his experiment was ethical because all of the subjects were debriefed and the experiment was explained in full after their participation. They were told that no shocks had actually been delivered and were allowed to meet the learner to see that he was unhurt. Eighty-four percent of the subjects reported that they were happy to have participated in the study. Nevertheless, it is unlikely that studies similar to Milgram's could be conducted today. Human-subjects review boards, which characteristically evaluate all institutional (e.g., university or government) research with respect to costs and benefits to subjects, would undoubtedly find the Milgram protocol unacceptable. Moreover, contemporary researchers are characteristically required to obtain informed consent from all subjects. Securing informed consent involves apprising subjects of the purpose of, and any potentially harmful effects that may result from, a study. Milgram's procedure relied on subterfuge: had the subjects been informed that they weren't really delivering shocks, the results would have been meaningless. And subterfuge is inconsistent with informed consent.

As noted, compliance and conformity are very similar: each involves one person's emitting behavior that has been specified verbally by someone else. Because this is the case, the behavioral analysis of compliance can be readily extended to conformity: we do or do not conform in a given situation largely because of our operant history.

Persuasion

In everyday usage, **persuade** means "cause someone to do something by means of argument, reasoning, or entreaty" (*American Heritage Dictionary*, 1984). Argument, reasoning, and entreaty involve verbal behavior, whether written or spoken. Therefore, persuasion, like compliance and conformity, can be envisioned as a process in which one person emits verbal behavior that causes another person to behave in a particular way. If, for example, an environmental group distributes on campus handbills requesting students to recycle aluminum cans and by so doing increases the number of cans recycled by one or more students, persuasion has occurred. As traditionally conceived of, persuasion involves a communicator, a message, and an audience. In our example, the communicator is the environmental group, the message is whatever is written on the handbills, and the audience is whoever reads the message.

Many social psychologists assume that persuasion, when successful, is a two-step process: first, the message changes the attitude of the audience, and then overt behavior is altered because of the change in attitude. In actuality, the message (i.e., verbal behavior by the communicator) determines both the attitude (verbal behavior) *and* the overt behavior of the audience. For instance, a child given a long lecture concerning the vile characteristics of bats may agree with negative statements concerning bats, indicating a critical attitude toward them. The child may also avoid bats. But the "attitude" does not cause the avoidance; both are the result of hearing the lecture.

Social psychologists, and advertisers as well, have expended considerable effort in isolating the variables that determine the likelihood that persuasion will occur. Three important ones, discussed below, are the source of the message, the message, and the audience.

Source

The person(s) delivering a message can greatly influence its persuasiveness. Among the characteristics of the source that affect persuasiveness are his or her credibility, attractiveness, and similarity to the target audience. Research shows that persons who are perceived as credible are much more effective in producing behavior change than less credible persons. Credibility is often correlated with fame, or with expert status. For instance, Bochner and Insko (1966) demonstrated that subjects were more likely to believe farfetched statements about the amount of sleep needed by a "normal" person when those statements were allegedly made by a Nobel Prize–winning physiologist than when they were made by the director of a YMCA. Interestingly, people tend to forget the source of a message; hence, the effects of communicator credibility often diminish with time.

Dion and Stein (1978) reported that the more physically attractive a person is, the more persuasive he or she is, although not in all situations. Finally, the greater the degree of similarity (with respect to, e.g., age, sex, and occupation) between the person delivering the message and the intended audience, the greater the amount of persuasion (Brock, 1965).

Message

The characteristics of the message strongly affect its potency. Two main methods of presenting the message have been investigated: the emotional and the rational approaches. The efficacy of messages that are intended to produce emotional reactions in the audience differ, depending upon whether the intended reaction is negative or positive. Negative emotional messages, such as those using fear to decrease cigarette smoking or drunk driving, usually produce immediate compliance that weakens significantly as time passes (Weinmann, 1982). Positive appeals tend to produce stronger long-term effects (Beck, 1979).

The rationality, or balance, of a verbal statement also influences persuasiveness. Research shows that forceful one-sided messages are often most effective when the audience initially agrees with the message or when the audience is unintelligent, uneducated, or uninformed (Krebs & Blackman, 1988). Two-sided arguments are more effective when the audience initially opposes the position or when the audience is intelligent, educated, or informed (Krebs & Blackman, 1988). In general, the two-sided argument appears to be the most effective (Deaux & Wrightsman, 1984; Hoveland, Lumsdaine, & Sheffield, 1949).

Although early research indicated that live and video communications were more persuasive that other forms (e.g., written), recent research does not provide unambiguous support for this finding (Roediger et al., 1984). In all likelihood, the most effective medium is determined in part by the type of message. For example, a written argument may be more compelling than a spoken message when complex issues are involved.

Given that the average American spends a considerable amount of time watching television, it may come as a surprise that research indicates that there is only a modest relation between television commercials and television watchers' behavior. Moreover, when commercials do have an effect, it is characteristically quite small (Krebs & Blackman, 1988; Maccoby & Alexander, 1980).

Audience

Of course, we are not all equally susceptible to influence by persuasive arguments. Two major characteristics of the audience, gender and self-esteem, have received the most attention as possible determinants of susceptibility to persuasion. Gender seems to play little role in determining the persuasiveness of messages. Block (1976) reviewed over 150 studies and found that the majority of them showed no differences between males and females. When differences were reported, females were more susceptible to influence than were males (e.g., Block, 1976). Although self-esteem is notoriously difficult to measure, persons with very high or very low self-esteem are resistant to persuasion, whereas persons with moderate self-esteem are more susceptible (Krebs & Blackman, 1988).

Social Facilitation

As we have seen repeatedly, the behavior of others has a profound effect on our behavior. Some studies have shown that the mere presence of other people can influence what we do. For example, individuals often perform better on simple tasks when others are watching. This phenomenon, referred to as **social facilitation,** is evident in an early study by Triplett (1897). Triplett had children wind fishing line on a reel and found that they completed the task faster when others were present than when they were alone. Several other researchers replicated these findings. Some, however, found that the presence of other people interferes with the performance of complex behaviors. For example, the student new to typing may have difficulty finding the correct keys when the instructor monitors performance.

That the presence of others sometimes facilitates and sometimes disrupts performance has caused trouble for researchers in the area of social facilitation. Perhaps as a result, interest lay dormant from early in the present century until the 1960s, when Zajonc offered an explanation of the disparate results. Zajonc (1965) proposed that the presence of others often creates a state of arousal that increases the probability of occurrence of the response that is most likely to occur (i.e., dominant) in a given situation. If the dominant response is the one desired and measured (e.g., winding line in Triplett's study), the presence of others facilitates performance. (If, however, the desired response is not the dominant one, the presence of others impairs performance.) Zajonc's theory is hard to evaluate empirically, but several studies have shown that the presence of others can increase arousal as measured by autonomic nervous system activity (e.g., Geen, 1980; Martens, 1969; Moore & Baron, 1983).

Social Loafing

As we have just said, under certain circumstances, the mere presence of others can facilitate performance. When those others are working with a person toward the same goal, however, that person may perform less effectively than when alone. This phenomenon has been called **social loafing.** One way in which social loafing is investigated in the laboratory is through the use of a tug-of-war apparatus. This apparatus is a long rope attached at one end to a device that can measure force. Along the rope are places for one or more persons to sit and pull on the rope. A subject is brought into the lab and asked to pull on the rope "as hard as you can," and the amount of force generated is measured. Later, the subject and one or more confederates of the experimenter are brought into the lab and seated at the apparatus. The subject is given the first position; the confederates sit behind. All are instructed to pull as hard as possible. Unbeknownst to the subject, the confederates do not pull the rope, and the amount of force expended by the subject is measured. Generally, subjects pull harder when alone than when others are present.

Two factors affecting the likelihood of social loafing have been proposed: identifiability and responsibility. In a group, the contributions of any one person often cannot be easily identified. Consequently, the probability of the individual's receiving social reinforcement for exemplary behavior decreases. Moreover, the likelihood of social disapproval for poor performance is decreased. The result is that the person performs at less than optimal levels. As a rule, making the efforts of the individual more readily identifiable reduces social loafing.

A second variable affecting the occurrence of social loafing is redundancy of responsibility. Research has shown that when responsibility is duplicated—that is, when two or more people perform (are responsible for) the same task—performance suffers. For example, Harkins and Petty (1982) had subjects watch for and report when a dot appeared in one quadrant of a video screen. In one condition, the subjects were each responsible for one quadrant. In another condition, all the subjects watched the same quadrant. In the latter condition, where responsibility was shared, social loafing occurred. Loafing did not occur in the former condition, where there was a clear division of responsibility.

Social Relations

Social relations are characteristically categorized according to (1) the form of the behaviors involved and (2) the consequences of these behaviors for the people involved. Three general social relations of special importance to social psychologists involve aggression, altruism, and personal attraction.

Aggression

No single definition of aggression is generally accepted; the term is applied to a wide and varied range of behavioral interactions. In most cases, the term **aggression** is used to describe situations in which one organism emits behavior directed toward harming another (e.g., Hinde & Stevenson-Hinde, 1973). The harm may be direct or indirect, physiological or psychological, but it must not be "accidental."

Consider the following scenarios:

1. A red-tailed hawk kills and eats a bluejay.
2. A baseball player crashes into the catcher on a close play at home plate.
3. A youth strikes an elderly woman in the face, grabs her purse, and runs away.
4. Two bighorn rams in rut repeatedly slam into one another.
5. A U.S. navy pilot fires a missile, downing a Libyan warplane and killing all aboard.

Each statement describes a behavior that might be used as an example of aggression. But the behaviors in question are very different in form and in cause. The variables that control behaviors labeled as aggressive are many and complex; there is no single cause of aggression. Moreover, and importantly, "aggression" is not a cause of anything. A bully who beats people does not do so because she or he is aggressive; rather, she or he is aggressive (and a bully) by virtue of beating people. Aggression has no legitimate status as a causal variable.

For the most part, psychologists have focused on within-species aggression, with a particular interest in our own species. Several variables are known to affect the likelihood that one person will act so as to harm another. One is exposure to an aversive stimulus. As Hutchinson (1977) noted, "Numerous studies have shown that the delivery of an intense aversive, noxious, or unpleasant stimulus will produce, in a variety of species, movement toward, contact with, and possibly destruction of, animate or inanimate objects in the environment" (p. 418). If, for example, two rats are placed on a metal floor through

Aggression behavior is found
in many species. Because of
such behavior's deleterious
effects, understanding it is
important. (Photo courtesy of
Roger Ulrich.)

which electric shock is delivered, the rats will fight. This reaction is termed **pain-elicited aggression.** In a human demonstration of the phenomenon, Berkowitz and Frodi (1977) had experimental subjects put a hand in ice water for 7 minutes (the ice water was painful but caused no tissue damage). The control group placed their hands in cool (i.e., not painful) water. Members of both groups were then allowed either to reinforce or to punish (with shock) the behavior of a (nonexistent) person waiting in the next room. Subjects in the experimental group delivered more shocks than persons in the control group. Moreover, they also reported more feelings of annoyance and anger. You may have observed pain-elicited aggression in your own repertoire: Have you ever harmed something (or someone) just after it has injured you?

The hypothesis that aggression occurs as a result of frustration has also been explored by social psychologists. First proposed by Dollard, Doob, Miller, Mowrer, and Sears (1939), this hypothesis assumes that frustration results from interference with the occurrence of an instigated goal-response at its proper time in the behavior sequence. Proponents of the frustration–aggression hypothesis assume that frustration causes a buildup of energy within the person that, when it reaches a certain point, must find a release in aggression or some other behavior. An alternative explanation that has empirical support (e.g., Azrin, Hutchinson, & Hake, 1966; Rilling & Caplan, 1973), and that does not ascribe causal status to an unobserved state, is that aggression can be **extinction-induced.** A person who strikes a vending machine that fails to deliver either a snack or a refund is engaging in extinction-induced aggression.

In many cases, aggressive behavior is learned through operant conditioning. When this learning occurs, the consequences of behavior labeled as aggressive serve to increase its future probability. As Skinner (1974) stated:

> Aggressive behavior may be innate and released by specific circumstances in which survival value is plausible. An infant or child may bite, scratch, or strike if physically restrained when it could not have learned to do so. Or the behavior may be shaped and maintained because people are susceptible to reinforcement by signs of damage to others. The capacity to be reinforced when an opponent cries out or runs away would have survival value because a person so endowed would quickly learn to defend himself. Or, third, the behavior may be reinforced by consequences not explicitly related to aggression. Food and sexual contact, reinforcing for other reasons, may reinforce an attack on a competitor if food or a sexual partner is thus obtained. (p. 43)

Interestingly, in some situations, stimuli that elicit or evoke aggressive behavior serve as positive reinforcers. For example, laboratory mice will run mazes for the opportunity to fight with other mice (Lagerspetz, 1964). And male Siamese fighting fish and gamecocks will emit responses (e.g., presses of a paddle) that produce visual access to a male conspecific, to which they will aggressively display (Thompson, 1963, 1964). How these findings relate to human behavior is uncertain, but it is clear that, in some situations, harming another person is reinforcing.

Altruism

Unlike aggression, **altruism** involves behavior that is of some cost to the behaver but of some benefit to one or more others. A reveler dressed to party who stops to help a fellow motorist extricate a car from a muddy ditch is behaving altruistically. So is the good citizen who intercedes to stop a rapist or halt a mugger. In extreme form, altruism becomes heroism and martyrdom.

Social psychologists have identified several factors that influence the likelihood of one person's helping another. One of the strongest variables affecting altruism is the number of bystanders. When one or more others are present, the tendency of a person to provide aid usually decreases. The Kitty Genovese tragedy provides a possible example. Kitty Genovese, a young woman living in New York City, was returning from work at 3 A.M. when a man attacked her outside her apartment in Kew Gardens. Thirty-eight neighbors heard her cries for help, but during the 30 minutes it took him to kill her, no one so much as called the police. Each neighbor apparently waited for someone else to do something. Perhaps, had fewer been aware of the tragedy, someone would have come to her aid.

Laboratory studies offer direct demonstrations of the effects on altruism of the number of others present. Darley and Latane (1968), for example, placed people in separate rooms and allowed them to communicate only through microphones, purportedly for the purpose of preserving confidentiality. During the course of the discussion, the subjects heard one person, a confederate of the experimenter, have an epileptic seizure (which was simulated) and cry for help. Of the subjects who were led to believe that they were the only ones hearing the pleas, 85% sought help. Of the subjects who were led to believe that four others were also hearing the pleas, only 31% sought help.

Observing another person behave altruistically has been shown to increase altruistic behavior. For instance, Bryan and Test (1967) found that drivers who had just seen another motorist giving aid were more likely to stop and help a stranded female motorist than were drivers who had not seen the behavior modeled.

It should come as no surprise that persons who are in a hurry are less likely to come to the aid of another than are persons not in a hurry. In a scientific study of this phenomenon, Darley and Batson (1973) had subjects move from one building to another in order to give a brief presentation. Half of the subjects were told they had plenty of time but that they "might as well head on over." The other half were told that they were late and that they should hurry. Just outside the door, a confederate of the experimenters was slumped in a doorway, coughing and groaning. Of the subjects in the group that had been led to believe that they had ample time, 67% stopped to help the man in the doorway. In contrast, only 10% of the subjects in the other group stopped.

Characteristics of the person in need of aid have also been shown to affect the probability of altruistic behavior. Women are more likely to receive offers of aid than men (Deaux, 1976). And men are more likely to help an attractive woman than a woman they describe as unattractive (Mims, Hartnett, & Nay, 1975; West & Brown, 1975). People are also more likely to help someone who is similar to them than someone who dresses differently or espouses different political opinions (Emswiller, Deaux, & Willits, 1971; Karabenick, Lerner, & Beecher, 1973).

Attraction

Why do we like some persons and dislike others? What causes us to fall in love? Philosophers and psychologists have attempted to answer questions such as these for centuries. Only recently have these questions been subjected to scientific inquiry. And that inquiry is, if nothing else, controversial: Wisconsin Senator William Proxmire has blasted the National Science Foundation for awarding an $84,000 grant for the study of human love:

> I object to this not only because no one—not even the National Science Foundation—can argue that falling in love is a science; not only because I'm sure that even if they spend $84 million or $84 billion they wouldn't get an answer that anyone would believe. I'm also against it because I don't want the answer. (Quoted in Meyers, 1983, p. 464)

Proxmire clearly missed the point; simply because something can be studied scientifically doesn't imply that it is therefore a science. Moreover, scientific understanding of the whys and wherefores of **attraction** might help to solve some of the problems associated with love gone bad—spouse abuse, divorce, and child abuse, to name only three.

Liking

Several variables have been implicated in affecting our choice of friends. Physical proximity is one obvious predictor of friendship. A person's friends and the individual he or she eventually marries typically live or work within walking distance of that person (Meyers, 1983). Physical proximity is one determinant of interaction, and several studies have shown that we see persons with whom we interact frequently, even by chance meetings, as more likable than other people. For example, Insko and Wilson (1977) had three subjects sit in a triangle facing one another. Pairs of subjects were allowed to converse with one another while the third subject observed. The subjects that interacted with one another rated each other as more likable than they rated the observer, with whom no interaction had occurred. Mere exposure to another person can also affect the degree of liking. In general, liking increases with exposure; the more we are exposed to a stranger, the more we tend to like him or her (e.g., Goldberg & Gorn, 1979; Saegert, Swap, & Zajonc, 1973; Swap, 1977).

Physical attractiveness is another powerful predictor of whom we tend to choose as friends and lovers. Many studies have shown that physically attractive persons are seen as more desirable as dates and are guessed to be happier, more intelligent, more sociable, more successful, and more competent (Cash, Begley, McGown, & Weise, 1975; Dion, Berscheid, & Walster, 1972; Landy & Sigall, 1974; Maruyama & Miller, 1980). Similarity also influences the likability of others. As a rule, we tend to like those who are most like us. For example, the greater the similarity of attitudes and beliefs among married couples, the more likely they are to be happily married and the less likely they are to divorce (Byrne, 1971). Finally, we tend to like those who like us. This phenomenon, called *mutual admiration*, has been demonstrated in a number of studies (e.g., Berscheid & Walster, 1978; Kenny & Nasby, 1980).

Loving

There has been considerable controversy over the question of whether loving differs from liking in degree or in nature. In other words, is loving simply intense liking, or are they qualitatively different? Most psychologists now agree that they are qualitatively different. Although there are many different types of love, the one in which psychologists have been most interested is **romantic love.** To study romantic love we must be able to define and measure it. Rubin (1970, 1973) has developed a *love scale* that consists of 13 statements about one's loved one (e.g., "I would do almost anything for _____"). The subject rates the truth of each of the statements from 1 to 9. The total number of points from the 13 statements gives the researcher a numerical value indicating the strength of love. This value can then be compared with other behavioral measures, and the comparison yields a correlation coefficient. For example, Rubin (1970) found that persons scoring higher on the love scale were more likely to report plans to marry and to spend more time gazing into the eyes of their lover.

One rather popular theory of romantic love was proposed by Berscheid and Walster (1978). This theory is a derivative of Schachter and Singer's theory of emotion (1962). Schachter and Singer held that all emotions consist of two components, one physiological and the other cognitive. In determining whether we are in a state of emotion and, if so, in naming the emotion, we first detect changes in our physiological responding. We then look at the situation around us and label the emotion based on this information. One may, for instance, find that his heart is racing, his palms are sweating, and he is breathing rapidly. He is likely to label these responses as indicative of anger if he has just seen a driver back into his new car in the parking lot. In contrast, these same physiological responses may be labeled as being indicative of fear if he has just missed being bitten by a large dog. According to Berscheid and Walster's theory of romantic love (1978), we experience increased autonomic arousal (increased heart rate, sweating, and fast breathing) and sexual excitement when in the presence of a loved one. We then attribute these emotional responses to the other person and call the whole *love*.

To test this theory, several experimenters have arranged for their subjects to become physiologically aroused and then asked them to rate their attraction to another person. To produce arousal, subjects have been asked to walk across a wobbly bridge over a deep gorge (Dutton & Aron, 1974), read or view erotic material (Carducci, Cosby, & Ward, 1978; Dermer & Pyszczynski, 1978), run in place, listen to Steven Martin comedy, or listen to a tape of human mutilation (White, Fishbein, & Rutsein, 1981). The subjects in all these experiments reported greater attraction than did unaroused subjects.

The studies just described do not unambiguously support Berscheid and Walster's theory of love. As Kenrick and Cialdini (1977) noted, the subjects in these studies were probably aware of the source of their arousal; that is, they did not attribute it to the nearby person. Kenrick and Cialdini argued that the presence of another person is reinforcing, perhaps because that person somehow helps to allay anxiety, and the person is liked for that reason. In any case, increased liking is not tantamount to loving. Moreover, and perhaps more importantly, "love" has no existence apart from the behaviors that lead us to use the term. Attempting to clarify the range of behaviors to which the term is characteristically applied, as well as the variables responsible for those behaviors, is potentially within the realm of scientific analysis. Attempting to explain a thing called *love* is not.

Social Psychology and Behavior Analysis

The social interactions of humans are wondrously diverse. Some are hideous, others beautiful. Most are complex. In their attempts to understand these relations, social psychologists have conducted a wealth of interesting research; a tiny fraction of it has been cited in this chapter. The findings have added much to our understanding of the variables that control how we treat one another. But in interpreting these findings, it is important to recognize that social behavior is primarily learned behavior and can be analyzed in terms of the same principles of operant and respondent conditioning that explain nonsocial responding. We learn to obey authority, to comply with requests, to conform, and to behave altruistically. We also learn attitudes and attributions. The specifics of how this learning occurs in a given person are very hard to determine. Experimental analyses of the environmental variables that control social interactions are difficult to conduct, although some have appeared. Notable in this area is the work of Don Hake and his associates in the areas of trust, competition, and cooperation. One of their studies is described in Sidebar 10-1. In most cases, however,

An Experimental Study of Cooperation

Researchers have clearly shown that cooperation can be influenced by environmental variables. For example, Azrin and Lindsley (1956) gave pairs of children a cooperative task. Members of each pair were seated at a table across from one another. Three holes were on each side of the table, and the task for each child was to put a stylus (i.e., a small stick) into one of the holes (see Figure 10-3). A "cooperative response" was judged to have occurred when both styli were placed in opposite holes within 0.04 seconds. The results showed that cooperative responses occurred more often when a snack followed each response than when snacks were not given. Each pair of children usually divided up the snack in some way. In two pairs, however, one of the members always took the snack until the other member refused to cooperate, after which the snack was more equitably shared.

More recent research has shown that cooperation and sharing may depend on the amount of effort in a task. In a study by Hake, Olvera, and Bell (1975), pairs of subjects earned money for correctly completing a discrimination task. To determine which member would attempt the task on a given trial, each pulled one of two levers. If Lever A (the "take" lever) was pulled 10 times by one of the subjects, that subject "took" the opportunity to attempt the task and earn the money. If Lever B (the "give" lever) was pulled 10 times by one of the subjects, the task would be "given" to the other subject to complete. Each of the subjects could pull his or her own lever; thus, whoever first pulled a lever 10 times determined who would receive the task. Under this condition, the two subjects usually competed for the task; that is, they both responded on Lever A in an attempt to procure

the task for themselves. When the number of lever pulls was increased (e.g., to 120), sharing and cooperation both increased. For this study, the authors defined sharing as taking turns in responding on the "take" lever, and they defined cooperation as responding on the "give" lever. Why did the subjects switch to noncompetitive forms of responding as the number of lever pulls increased? The authors concluded that, as competition required more and more effort, sharing and cooperation reduced the amount of effort while still offering a moderate amount of money.

The authors also noted that their results have a parallel in the real world:

> the phenomenon may be operating in academic situations where a small response requirement such as, "Read and be prepared to discuss this article for our next class," generates competition in the form of individual work. When the response requirement is then increased to, "Read and be prepared to discuss these six articles by our next class," students have been observed to divide the response requirement. This might take the form of, "You outline three articles and I'll outline the other three." (p. 353)

These and similar studies on cooperation illustrate two important points: (1) Concepts such as *cooperation, competition,* and *sharing* refer to behaviors, not to hypothetical traits, and (2) environmental variables that affect such behaviors can be studied. As a result, social environments can be designed to encourage desired social behaviors and to provide an optimal social milieu that is satisfactory to the greatest number of people.

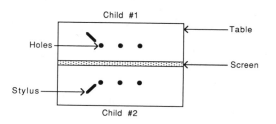

Figure 10-3. An overhead view of the apparatus used in the Azrin and Lindsley (1956) study.

research in social psychology is correlational in nature, so that it is difficult to discern functional (causal) relations.

Is it therefore impossible to specify why a given person consistently behaves in ways that lead others to label her or him as aggressive, altruistic, compliant, or obedient? No. The answer undoubtedly rests in part with this person's unique history: What were the consequences of these actions in the past, and what rules has she or he learned to follow with respect to them? These variables are not the only ones that determine social behavior (genotype and physical pathology, to name only two, are other determinants), but they are surely important. Emphasizing them has two important consequences: (1) It focuses attention on real events in the environment as causes of behavior, and (2) these events are, in principle, capable of being altered to improve social interactions. To build, for instance, the kinder and gentler America that President Bush desires, we must determine what causes people to treat each other kindly and gently, then arrange conditions so that these behaviors occur. Obviously, no one has accomplished this goal on a broad front.

As Skinner has long contended, cultures that are humane and egalitarian do not emerge automatically; they must be planned. He has proposed that the principles of behavior analysis can be used to build such cultures, and in *Walden Two* (1948), he described a utopian behavioral community. Small-scale communities, patterned in some respects after Skinner's fictional *Walden Two*, are in existence: Twin Oaks in the United States and Los Horcones in Mexico are two notable examples. But the development of isolated behavioral communities does not appear to be a feasible solution to the problems of humanity. Indeed, as Sigrid Glenn (1986) noted. "A more likely solution to achieving a better world may lie in arranging better contingencies in our current environments to move us toward that goal. We may as well begin now and where we are" (p. 2).

Sound advice, that.

Study Questions

1. Simply, what is social psychology? What is meant by the following statement: "Social psychology deals with the structure of all human interactions."

2. List and briefly describe the three broad categories of social psychology.

3. Why does Bandura believe that the question "How do attitudes affect behavior" might be a pseudoissue?

4. In general, what is the evidence that attitudes cause (i.e., are related to) overt behavior? (Hint: The correspondence between self-report and behavior.)

5. What is the behavioral perspective on saying and doing? What did research on the two show? And what happened to the entire field of social psychology in the 1960s and why?

6. What do we mean when we refer to *attitude?* Describe some of the variables that affect the correspondence between saying and doing. Note how the cognitive-dissonance and self-perception theories attempt to explain the facts about attitude.

7. What does attribution theory attempt to explain, and what are the two sets of variables to which behavior is commonly attributed? Provide some examples.

8. What specific topics are included under the more general topic of social influence? Be able to describe these topics by providing definitions and examples.

9. How are social relations usually classified? What are the three general relations of special importance to social psychologists?

10. What is the term *aggression* usually used to describe? Be able to make the points in the second paragraph in this section.

11. What type of aggression have psychologists focused on? Why, do you think? Identify and describe some of the variables that affect aggressive behavior.

12. What is altruism? What are some of the variables that affect altruistic behavior? Do any of these "explain" altruistic behavior? Using what you have learned about the causes of behavior (i.e., genetic variables and operant and respondent conditioning), answer the question, "Why do people behave altruistically in some circumstances?"

13. What is meant by *attraction, liking, loving?* What behaviors are involved?

14. What is the main point in the last two paragraphs of this chapter about emphasizing environmental variables in social behavior, the two consequences of doing so, and the development of a "kinder and gentler America"?

Recommended Readings

Cialdini, R. B. (1988). *Influence.* Glenview, IL: Scott, Foresman/Little.

Cialdini discusses the literature on compliance. The presentation is scientific, but makes for enjoyable reading.

Meyers, D. G. (1983). *Social Psychology.* New York: McGraw-Hill.

An overview of the field of social psychology, including social cognition, social influence, and social relations.

CHAPTER 11

Abnormal Behavior

The adjective *abnormal* designates any departure from the typical; therefore "abnormal behavior" is any pattern of responding that is rare or unusual. Psychologists, however, usually restrict the term to patterns of responding that constitute a problem for the person who emits them, or for other people with a justifiable interest in his or her behavior. When the term is used in this sense, **abnormal behavior** is troublesome behavior. The purpose of this chapter is to consider the classification, causes, and treatment of abnormal behavior. The chapter examines the behavioral problems associated with mental retardation and drug abuse, as well as those associated with mental illness.

What Makes Behavior Troublesome?

Troublesome behavior can be classified into three general categories:

1. *Behavior that is troublesome because of its topography (form).* A child's eating glass is an example; this behavior is a problem whenever or wherever it occurs.
2. *Behavior that is troublesome because of its rate.* A second-grader's asking to go to the bathroom is an example; this is no problem if it occurs occasionally, but most teachers would be understandably vexed if the request were repeated every five minutes. Behavior that fails to occur or that occurs rarely can also be a problem, as when a child consistently fails to comply with a parent's commands.
3. *Behavior that is troublesome because of an absence of stimulus control.* Masturbating is an example; it is no problem in private, but undesirable in public.

In some cases, much if not most of an individual's behavior is abnormal. In others, most of the repertoire is acceptable, but some response or set of responses is troublesome. Abnormal behavior varies across individuals in severity as well as in ubiquity, and it can range from mildly irritating to severely life-threatening.

In view of the incredible range of problems encompassed by the term, one would not expect abnormal behavior to have a single cause, and it does not. Causes of human behavior can be appropriately considered at three interrelated levels of analysis: (1) environmental variables; (2) physiological variables; and (3) genetic variables. Many behavioral problems result from exposure to environments that foster inappropriate responses or that fail to engender and maintain appropriate responses. Disease or physical damage can also result in behavioral problems. Finally, genotype contributes to some kinds of abnormal behavior. It is perfectly reasonable to explore the contribution of environmental, physiological, and genetic variables to abnormal behavior and, if the evidence dictates, to explain abnormal behavior in terms of such variables. It is not, however, reasonable to explain abnormal behavior as an "illness of the mind," though much abnormal behavior is categorized as "mental illness."

Mental Illness

There is no absolute scale for determining when behavior is abnormal. Each society determines the range of behavior it considers troublesome and worthy of change. Nonetheless, people severely handicapped by virtue of their behavioral characteristics have long been recognized as unique. The Bible and other ancient texts make reference to people who, if they were alive today, would in all

Abnormal behavior? Although certainly unusual, carrying a rat on her shoulder is no problem for this student, who is participating in a "rat olympics." (Photo courtesy of Mariane Pelletier.)

likelihood be diagnosed as being mentally ill or mentally retarded. In antiquity, these people, along with those seriously disabled in other ways, were frequently given special treatment—special, but not necessarily humane. For example, some ancient Greeks and Romans destroyed handicapped children, and members of the feudal courts of Europe employed handicapped people as a source of entertainment, that is, as jesters (Kanner, 1964).

Mental illness and mental retardation were not clearly distinguished for millennia. One of the first clear distinctions was drawn by John Locke (1623–1704), who wrote:

> In short, herein seems to lie the difference between idiots and madmen, that madmen put wrong ideas together, and so make wrong propositions, but argue and reason right from them; but idiots make very few or no propositions, and reason scarce at all. (Quote in St. John, 1905, p. 277)

Mental illness and mental retardation were not further distinguished until the middle of the 19th century, when it became clear that "idiocy" and "insanity" were fundamentally different (MacMillan, 1982). Jean Esquirol (1772–1840), for example, emphasized that idiocy (mental retardation) was present at birth, whereas dementia (mental illness) appeared later in life:

> Dementia and idiocy differ essentially; otherwise the principles of every classification are illusion. . . . A man in a state of dementia is deprived of advantages which he formerly enjoyed; he was a rich man, who has become poor. The idiot, on the contrary, has always been in a state of want or misery. The condition of a man in a state of dementia may change; that of the idiot is ever the same. (1845, p. 447)

At the present time, the term **mental illness** is used to refer to a wide range of behavioral problems. According to a popular medical dictionary, mental illness is "any disorder which affects the mind or behavior" (Thomas, 1981, p. 879). Although the distinction is no longer favored by some clinicians, the various forms of mental illness have for decades been divided on the basis of severity into psychoses and neuroses. **Psychoses** are severe and pervasive behavioral problems. They are marked by severe functional impairment and often involve **thought disorders** (speaking and thinking illogically), **hallucinations** (reporting stimuli not actually present), and **delusions** (making statements obviously contrary to the facts). **Unusual affect** (emotion) is also common. Thought disorders, hallucinations, delusions, and unusual affect are, of course, inferred on the basis of actual behavior. When psychosis is present, a person does not appear to be well controlled by environmental stimuli and, on that basis, is said to "lose contact with reality." Such a person might (1) report hearing voices; (2) express beliefs inconsistent with current and past events; (3) speak illogically; and (4) exhibit no response to significant personal loss (e.g., the death of a parent). These actions would form the basis for assuming the presence of (1) hallucinations; (2) delusions; (3) thought disorders; and (4) unusual (blunted) affect.

Neuroses are less pervasive and less debilitating than psychoses, although they may cause great suffering. Neuroses do not involve substantial loss of behavioral control by environmental stimuli (i.e., "contact with reality" is maintained) and often appear to be exaggerations of normal reactions. Like psychoses, neuroses are "mental illnesses" only in the sense that a part of their symptomatology involves reporting a world within the skin that differs from that familiar to most people. The "mind" has no physical status, it does not control behavior, and it cannot become ill. The central nervous system is real and does control behavior, and meaningful biological hypotheses of mental illness have been advanced. Nevertheless, at the present time, it is not possible to relate most behavioral problems to pathophysiological processes.

Mental disorder is an approximate synonym of *mental illness*. The American Psychiatric Association favors the former term and uses it in the *Diagnostic and Statistical Manual of Mental Disorders*. The current version, published in 1987, is the third edition, revised; it is known as the DSM-III-R (APA, 1987). The DSM-III-R provides a widely used nosological system (**nosology** is the branch of medicine that deals with the classification of diseases). Sidebar 11-1 considers the meaning of the term *mental disorder* as used in that volume.

The diagnostic system presented in the DSM-III-R is complex. It requires that each case be assessed on a number of dimensions, or axes. These are (1) clinical syndromes; (2) developmental disorders and personality disorders; (3) physical disorders and conditions; (4) severity of psychosocial stressors; and (5) global assessment of functioning. The first three axes determine the official DSM-III-R diagnosis; the last two provide supplemental information. Table 11-1 lists the major Axis I and II categories; each of these categories includes a number of subcategories.

To provide some notion of how the DSM-III-R categories are applied, we will consider the diagnostic criteria for schizophrenia. (Only the general catego-

---

Sidebar 11-1
What Are Mental Disorders?

In [the *Diagnostic and Statistical Manual of Mental Disorders*, 3rd ed., revised] each of the mental disorders is conceptualized as a clinically significant behavioral or psychological syndrome or pattern that occurs in a person and that is associated with present distress (a painful symptom) or disability (impairment in one or more important areas of functioning), or with a significantly increased risk of suffering death, pain, disability, or an important loss of freedom. In addition, this syndrome or pattern must not be merely an expectable response to a particular event, e.g., the death of a loved one. Whatever its original cause, it must currently be considered a manifestation of a behavioral, psychological, or biological dysfunction in the person. Neither deviant behavior, e.g., political, religious, or sexual, nor conflicts that are primarily between the individual and society are mental disorders unless the deviance or conflict is a symptom of a dysfunction in the person, as described above.

There is no assumption that each mental disorder is a discrete entity with sharp boundaries (discon-

tinuity) between it and other mental disorders, or between it and no mental disorder. For example, there has been a continuing controversy concerning whether severe depressive disorder and mild depressive disorder differ from each other qualitatively (discontinuity between diagnostic entities) or quantitatively (a difference on a severity continuum). . . .

A common misconception is that a classification of mental disorders classifies people, when actually what are being classified are disorders that people have. . . . Another misconception is that all people described as having the same mental disorder are alike in all important ways. Although all the people described as having the same mental disorder have at least the defining features of the disorder, they may well differ in other important respects that may affect clinical management and outcome.

From *Diagnostic and Statistical Manual of Mental Disorders*, 3rd ed., revised (DSM-III-R) (1987), pp. xxii–xxiii. Copyright 1987 by the American Psychiatric Association. Reproduced by permission.

Table 11-1
DSM-III-R Major Categories[a]

Axis II: Clinical Syndromes
Disorders usually first evident in infancy, childhood, or adolescence
  Development disorders
  Disruptive behavior disorders
  Anxiety disorders of childhood or adolescence
  Eating disorders
  Gender-identity disorders
  Tic disorders
  Elimination disorders
  Speech disorders not elsewhere classified
  Other disorders of infancy, childhood, or adolescence
Organic mental disorders
  Dementias arising in the senium and the presenium
  Psychoactive-substance-induced organic mental disorders
  Organic mental disorders associated with physical disorders or con-
    ditions, or whose etiology is unknown
Psychoactive-substance-use disorders
Schizophrenia
Delusional (paranoid) disorders
Psychotic disorders not elsewhere classified
Mood disorders
  Bipolar disorders
  Depressive disorders
Anxiety disorders
Somatoform disorders
Dissociative disorders
Sexual disorders
  Paraphilias
  Sexual dysfunctions
  Other sexual disorders
Sleep disorders
  Dyssomnias
  Parasomnias
Factitious disorders
Impulse control disorders not elsewhere classified
Adjustment disorder

Axis II: Developmental and Personality Disorders
Developmental disorders
  Mental retardation
  Pervasive developmental disorders
  Specific developmental disorders
Personality disorders
  Cluster A (paranoid, schizoid, schizotypal)
  Cluster B (antisocial, borderline, histrionic, narcissistic)

[a]From *DSM-III-R* (1987), pp. 3–10. Copyright 1987 by the American Psychiatric
Association. Adapted by permission.

ry of schizophrenia will be considered, although the DSM-III-R deals with a number of subcategories.) The manual lists six diagnostic criteria for schizophrenia; each must be present for the diagnosis to be assigned. These criteria are listed in Table 11-2. Although these criteria are further described in the DSM-III-R, even with book in hand they are vague. As Lickey and Gordon (1983) emphasized:

> A reliable system of diagnosis will achieve at least two goals. First, it will clearly define each illness by specifying its symptoms. Second, it will specify the methods for determining whether a patient has a particular symptom. (p. 39)

The DSM-III-R falls short on both counts. The DSM-III-R (and its predecessor, the DSM-III) is better than earlier editions in that it presents specific diagnostic criteria. Unfortunately, the manner in which these criteria are to be applied—that is, what exactly a person must do to be given a particular diagnostic label—is usually vague. At present, the diagnosis of mental illness is imprecise at best. Expert testimony in the bizarre court case of John Hinckley, President Reagan's would-be assassin, exemplifies this imprecision. Psychiatrists for the defense testified (and convinced the jury) that the accused suffered from schizophrenia and had been driven to attempted murder by the delusion that killing the president would earn him the love an actress, Jodie Foster. As might be expected, psychiatrists for the prosecution argued otherwise. In their opinion, John Hinckley was perfectly rational, a man capable of premeditated murder and free of delusions.

Less newsworthy but perhaps more compelling demonstrations of the vag-

Table 11-2
Diagnostic Criteria for Schizophrenia[a]

I. Presence of characteristic psychotic symptoms as indicated by 1, 2, or 3 below:
  1. Two of the following:
    a. Delusions.
    b. Prominent hallucinations.
    c. Incoherence or marked loosening of associations.
    d. Catatonic behavior.
    e. Flat or grossly inappropriate affect.
  2. Bizarre delusions.
  3. Prominent hallucinations of a voice with content having no apparent relation to depression or elation, or commenting on the person's behavior, or two or more voices conversing with each other.
II. Deterioration from previous level of functioning in such areas as work, social relations, and self-care.
III. Other conditions (schizoaffective disorder and mood disorder with psychotic features) have been ruled out.
IV. Duration of at least six months. Prodromal and residual phases are also described.
V. Not due to an organic mental disorder.
VI. If a history of autistic disorder is present, schizophrenia is diagnosed only if prominent delusions or hallucinations occur.

---

[a]From *DSM-III-R* (1987), pp. 194–195. Copyright 1987 by the American Psychiatric Association. Adapted by permission.

aries of psychiatric diagnosis have been provided in a number of empirical studies (Kanfer & Saslow, 1969; Lickey & Gordon, 1983). These studies indicate that (1) clinicians who assign patients to diagnostic categories often disagree on the appropriate placement (e.g., psychiatrists in the United States seem to favor schizophrenia, whereas their British counterparts seem to favor personality disorder; see Lickey & Gordon, 1983, p. 39) and (2) there are significant differences in the actions of persons given the same diagnosis, as well as very similar behaviors in individuals given different diagnoses.

Perhaps clinicians cannot even tell a normal person from a mentally ill one. A study by Rosenhan (1973) suggests that this may be so. Rosenhan had volunteers determined to be in no way psychotic seek admission to psychiatric hospitals by complaining of a single symptom. The symptom was hearing a voice that said, "empty," "hollow," and "thud." With the exception of reporting this symptom, the volunteers behaved normally. Most of them were diagnosed as psychotic (schizophrenic) and were hospitalized. Once in the hospital, they stopped reporting hearing voices (hallucinations), behaved well, and even took public notes on ongoing events. Nonetheless, mental health professionals failed to realize that the volunteers were not mentally ill. Treatment was provided, and when the volunteers were released, they were usually given the diagnosis of "schizophrenia in remission." Interestingly, some mentally ill patients did recognize the volunteers as normal. One patient observed, "You're not crazy. You're a journalist or a professor. You're checking up on the hospital" (Rosenhan, 1973, p. 252).

Does it follow from Rosenhan's study that clinicians cannot differentiate schizophrenics from normal people and that psychiatric diagnosis is therefore absurd? Not really. Rosenhan did not require clinicians to distinguish between schizophrenics and normal people. Instead, he required them to detect normal people pretending to suffer from schizophrenia. This detection is not a part of conventional diagnostic procedures and says nothing about the adequacy of those procedures. Moreover, as Spitzer (1975) argued, the clinicians in Rosenhan's study behaved reasonably, given the data available to them. Each of the volunteers had requested admission to a hospital, and such a request is in and of itself reason for clinical concern. Finally, the pseudopatients were quite passive after admission. They never told the clinicians, "There's nothing wrong with me; I just pretended to hear voices. Let me go." A patient who was normal would be expected to say so.

Psychiatric diagnosis is not meaningless. The DSM-III-R nosological system is adequate to allow for meaningful communication among researchers and clinicians and to aid in clinical practice. For example, psychiatric diagnosis is related to the likelihood that a patient will benefit from treatment from a particular drug class. A diagnosis of schizophrenia, for instance, suggests that an antipsychotic drug such as thioridazine (Mellaril) might be useful, whereas an antidepressant, perhaps amitriptyline (Elavil), would be more likely to produce the desired effect in treating depression.

There is, however, considerable latitude in the range of conditions that respond to a given drug. As Baldessarini (1985) noted:

> Antipsychotic drugs exert beneficial effects in virtually all classes of psychotic illness, and, contrary to a common misconception, are not selective for schizophrenia. More-

over, antidepressant drugs that are especially beneficial in severe depression can also exert useful effects on less severe depressive syndromes and on conditions that are not obviously depressive in nature (e.g., panic attacks, eating disorders, chronic pain, obsessive-compulsive disorders). Thus, in general, psychotropic drugs are not disease specific; they provide clinical benefit from specific syndromes or complexes of symptoms. (p. 389)

Detailed nosological systems are of little or no value in planning nonpharmacological interventions, and they do not explain abnormal behavior. As Craighead, Kazdin, and Mahoney (1981) put it:

Psychological or psychiatric diagnosis seems to provide little information about behavior beyond that which was known when the diagnosis was made. Specifically, little information is given about the etiology, treatment of choice, and prognosis. (p. 102)

Given these shortcomings, a sizable degree of skepticism regarding psychiatric diagnosis seems appropriate. It is especially important to recognize that assigning a diagnostic label does not explain a set of abnormal behaviors. For instance, to diagnose a narcissistic personality disorder (a DSM-III-R category) is only to assert that a person's behavior meets the general criteria associated with that label. It tells us nothing about why the person behaves as she or he does, or about how the problem behaviors should be treated. Psychiatric diagnosis is a *descriptive* process; it is *not* prescriptive or explanatory. To introduce psychiatric diagnosis, we will further consider schizophrenia, then briefly examine mood disorders and anxiety disorders.

Schizophrenia

Schizophrenia is the most common form of psychotic disorder; the lifelong prevalence is estimated at 0.2–1% (APA, 1987). It is equally common in women and men. The diagnostic criteria for the disorder appear in Table 11-2, and an individual who might be diagnosed as schizophrenic is described in Chapter 1. Clinicians commonly differentiate several subtypes of schizophrenia, including:

1. **Catatonic schizophrenia,** which is characterized by motor disturbances. These disturbances range from wild and excessive activity to complete immobility.
2. **Disorganized schizophrenia,** in which incoherence, inappropriate emotion, and grossly disorganized behavior are prevalent. Speech is loosely organized and nonsensical; some have aptly described it as word salad.
3. **Paranoid schizophrenia,** which is characterized by preoccupation with systematic delusions. *Paranoid* is used in the vernacular to mean unreasonably suspicious, but the term is not so restricted in paranoid schizophrenia. A person so diagnosed may, for instance, believe that he is Julius Caesar but may feel neither persecuted nor suspicious.

Etiology

The term *schizophrenia* comes from two Greek words, *schizein* ("to split") and *phren* ("mind"). The scientist who coined the term, Paul Eugen Bleuler (1857–1939), believed that the disorder resulted from a splitting, or disorganization, of mental functions, and that the result was disturbed thoughts, feelings, and overt behavior. This analysis, like all analyses that assign a causal status to the mind, is inadequate.

The actual cause of schizophrenia is unknown. Drugs that are effective in treating the disorder act by blocking one type of (i.e., D_2) dopamine receptors. Moreover, drugs that increase dopaminergic activity (e.g., amphetamine) can, with prolonged exposure, produce behaviors that closely resemble those characteristic of schizophrenia. These findings have led to the speculation that schizophrenia results from either (1) overactivity of dopamine in the limbic system or cortex or (2) the production of an endogenous amphetaminelike compound (Baldessarini, 1985). These dopamine models of schizophrenia continue to be popular. But attempts to document metabolic differences in humans diagnosed as schizophrenic (or as otherwise mentally ill) have yielded inconclusive results (Baldessarini, 1985). Moreover, as discussed below, genetic studies have provided evidence that inheritance can account for only a portion of the causation of schizophrenia. At present, genetically determined inborn errors of metabolism do not provide an adequate explanation of the disorder.

Schizophrenia does appear to be weakly heritable. For example, a Danish study (Kety, Rosenthal, Wender, & Schulsinger, 1968) looked at the adoptive and biological parents of two groups of adopted children: those who became schizophrenic and those who did not. There was an elevated incidence of schizophrenia only in the biological parents of the children who were diagnosed as schizophrenic. This finding suggests that the disorder is, to some extent, heritable. Precisely what is inherited is unknown; differences in neurochemistry or susceptibility to brain infection are reasonable possibilities. In any case, the vast majority of people with schizophrenic relatives do not develop the disorder.

Environmental variables appear to play a role in the development and maintenance of the problem behaviors characteristic of schizophrenia. Bleuler distinguished two forms of schizophrenia, **reactive** and **process,** based on whether the onset of the disorder was obviously correlated with an important environmental event, such as the loss of a loved one. If such an event occurred, the disorder was reactive.

Momentous environmental events can trigger psychotic reactions. More mundane events appear to play a role in determining the specific behaviors involved in such reactions. For example, delusions typically involve objects and events with which the patient has some familiarity, although they are described in a way that does not correspond to objective reality. Moreover, contingencies of reinforcement and punishment exercise control over much of the bizarre behavior of psychotic individuals. Although the contingencies that operate to engender abnormal behavior in a particular patient are rarely evident, such behavior can, in most cases, be altered by a change in its consequences. This finding indicates that the behavior is operant. Behavioral treatments of schizophrenia and other psychoses rest on this assumption.

Treatment

The treatment of mental illness has a long and fascinating history. For millennia, psychoses were assumed to be caused by evil spirits; therefore, the treatment involved attempts to drive the spirits from the body. Evidence of trephining (drilling holes in the skull) has been found in prehistoric skulls; perhaps the intent was to allow malevolent spirits to escape and thus treat mental illness.

Initially, the spread of Christianity had a beneficial effect on the treatment of mentally ill (and mentally retarded) people. Early Christians sometimes perceived the babbling of behaviorally impaired children and adults as *glossolalia* ("speaking in tongues"), a gift from God to be much appreciated, and therefore treated them kindly. This practice continued into the 1500s, and it is reported that Tycho Brahe (1545–1601), an influential astronomer, kept a handicapped man as a close companion and listened closely to his largely nonsensical verbalizations.

An interesting attempt at treatment had its beginning around the year 1250, when mentally ill and mentally retarded people were first brought to Geel, in what is now Belgium, to seek cures from St. Dympna. St. Dympna was, according to legend, the daughter of an Irish king. When the king's wife (her mother) died, her father developed an incestuous desire for his daughter (Roosens, 1979). She fled with her confessor to Geel (also spelled *Gheel*) in an attempt to escape her father, but she was found. Given the choice of death or incest, St. Dympna chose death and was decapitated as a martyr. She soon "became the patron of the mentally ill and their cure because, by her heroic death, she defeated the evil spirit that had entered into her father to drive him into a rage and madness. As madness was attributed to possession by some evil spirit, the cult of St. Dympna became clear" (Roosens, 1979, p. 28).

The treatment at Geel involved exorcism through prayer and other religious rites. Interestingly, many who came to Geel seeking help from St. Dympna were invited to live with local residents, from whom they received care and friendship in return for the services they could provide. This system of family care persisted long after the church closed.

Attempts to drive out demons at Geel were benign. By the time of the Protestant Reformation, however, many attempted exorcisms involved scourging and torture, and behaviorally impaired people met hatred as often as sympathy. Around 1650, St. Vincent de Paul and the Sisters of Charity established a facility called the Bicêtre near Paris to house the mentally and physically infirm who could not manage by themselves. The Bicêtre provided only custodial care, and conditions in the facility deteriorated over time, so that by the end of the 19th century,

> the buildings were untenable, the cells were narrow, cold and dripping, unlit and unventilated, and furnished with a litter of straw, which was rarely changed and often infested with vermin. . . . The insane, imprisoned here, were at the mercy of brutal keepers, who were often malefactors from the prisons. The patients were loaded with chains and tied with ropes like unruly convicts. This unjust treatment did not quiet them, but rather it filled them with wrath, rage, and indignation, aggravating their mental instability, and making the terrible clanking of their chains still more dreadful by their howls and shrieks. (Nowrey, 1945, p. 343)

By the early 20th century, psychology had emerged as a viable discipline, and attempts were made to use psychological principles in treating mentally ill individuals. Freudian psychoanalysis formed the basis of many early treatments, which were for the most part unsuccessful.

The treatment of psychotic individuals was literally revolutionized in the 1950s with the introduction of a new drug, chlorpromazine (Thorazine). The drug was developed by a French pharmaceutical firm following observations indicating that promethazine, a drug of the phenothiazine class being tested as an antihistaminic, produced a calming effect in surgical patients. This action was recognized as potentially valuable, and other phenothiazines were tested for it. One, chlorpromazine, produced the desired calming without inducing gross sedation. The drug's beneficial effects on psychiatric patients were first described in print in 1952. By 1954, chlorpromazine was being used in the United States, first to prevent vomiting, but soon thereafter as an antipsychotic, the application that made it famous and revolutionized psychiatric practice.

Chlorpromazine revolutionized psychiatry for a single reason: It reduced the undesirable behaviors of most psychotic patients. A sizable number of well-controlled studies has shown that chlorpromazine is generally useful in managing schizophrenia and other psychoses, although not all psychotic individuals benefit from the drug, some improve without it, and all who receive it are at risk of developing motor dysfunctions and other deleterious side effects (Berger, 1978).

Many drugs other than chlorpromazine have antipsychotic (or neuroleptic) effects. According to Baldessarini (1985):

> The use of antipsychotic agents is extremely widespread, as is evident from the fact that hundreds of millions of patients have been treated with them since their introduction in the 1950s. While the antipsychotic drugs have had a revolutionary, beneficial impact on medical and psychiatric practice, their liabilities, especially their almost relentless association with extrapyramidal neurological effects, must also be emphasized. (p. 391)

The neuroleptics firmly established drugs as a major weapon in the psychiatrists' armamentarium. But they are by no means the only drugs of value in managing behavior. Table 11-3 lists a variety of antianxiety, antidepressant, antimania, and antipsychotic drugs. All of the drugs in this table are **psychotropic drugs,** that is, drugs that are used to manage behavior.

The pharmacological management of behavioral problems is a complex area of obvious importance to clinical psychologists. But the role of psychologists in prescribing medications is an indirect one: they may be involved in the assessment process and in evaluating the patient's response to treatment, but decisions concerning medications are ultimately made by psychiatrists or other physicians. In contrast, decisions concerning nonpharmacological interventions are the direct responsibility of psychologists. Many options are available.

As a general rule, the intervention that a psychologist uses in a given situation depends on four variables:

1. *The professional training and experience of the clinician.* A psychologist's professional history determines how she or he construes a behavioral problem and the interventions that will be deemed appropriate. For example, a clinician trained in the client-centered therapy developed by Carl Rogers will favor different treatment strategies from one trained in behavior analysis. The former is likely to try to achieve correspondence between the ideal self and the real self and to provide the client with unconditional positive regard. The latter is apt to change what the client says and does by arranging appropriate consequences.

Table 11-3
Selected Psychotropic Drugs

Generic name	Trade name
Antianxiety agents	
alprozolam	Xanax
buspirone	BuSpar
clorazepate	Tranxene
chlordiazepoxide	Librium
diazepam	Valium
flurazepam	Dalmane
halazepam	Paxipam
hydroxyzine	Atarax, Vistaril
lorazepam	Ativan
meprobamate	Equanil, Miltown
oxazepam	Serax
prazepam	Centrax
temazepam	Restoril
triazolam	Halcion
Antidepressants	
amitriptyline	Elavil, Endep
amoxapine	Asendin
desipramine	Norpramin, Pertofrane
doxepin	Adapin, Sinequan
imipramine	Janimine, SK-Pramine, Tofranil
isocarboxazid	Marplan
maprotiline	Ludiomil
nomifensine	Merital
nortriptyline	Aventyl, Pamelor
phenelzine	Nardil
protriptyline	Vivactil
tranylcypromine	Parnate
trazodone	Desyrel
trimipramine	Surmontil
Antimania agents	
lithium carbonate	Eskalith, Lithane, Lithobid
Neuroleptics (antipsychotics)	
acetophenazine	Tindal
amoxapine	Asendin
chlorpromazine	Thorazine
chlorprothixene	Taractan
fluphenazine	Prolixin, Permitil
haloperidol	Haldol
loxapine	Loxitane
mesoridazine	Serentil
molindone	Moban
perphenazine	Trilafon
pimozide	Orap
piperacetazine	Quide
prochlorperazine	Compazine
thioridazine	Mellaril
thiothixene	Navane
trifluoperazine	Stelazine

2. *The nature of the problem.* The treatment used obviously depends on the desired changes in a patient's repertoire. Among the variables to be considered in selecting an intervention are the kind and number of behaviors to be changed, the direction and magnitude of the desired changes, and the apparent cause of the problem.

3. *Legal and ethical considerations.* Interventions must be instituted with the patient's well-being held foremost. As a rule, therapists begin with the least restrictive alternative treatment likely to prove beneficial (*restrictive* here means "harmful") and then proceed to progressively more restrictive interventions if necessary. *Primum non nocere* ("First of all, do no harm") is an ancient precept of the medical profession, and it is good advice for psychologists.

4. *Practical considerations.* All interventions use resources: time, money, personnel, and equipment. The therapist must consider what is feasible in the situation at hand.

One intervention that has proved ethical, practical, and effective in treating psychotic inpatients is the token economy. In a **token economy,** generalized conditioned reinforcers (tokens) are delivered when the appropriate behaviors are performed. In most systems, inappropriate behaviors result in token loss. Accumulated tokens can be exchanged at predetermined times for backup reinforcers, which usually include preferred objects (e.g., foods, clothing, or cosmetics) and the opportunity to perform preferred behaviors (e.g., watch television or bowl). A token economy requires three ingredients (Kazdin, 1981):

1. *Tokens.* These consist of objects (e.g., poker chips, stars, or cards) that are delivered for appropriate performance. Tokens should not be easily counterfeited, lest patients make their own.

2. *Backup reinforcers.* These are reinforcing objects or activities for which tokens are exchanged; they are responsible for the reinforcing efficacy of the tokens. To maximize the possibility of maintaining behavior, a wide range of backup reinforcers is typically available. If necessary, these reinforcers are individualized for particular patients.

3. *Rules describing the relation between behavior and tokens and between tokens and backup reinforcers.* An effective token economy depends on rules that clearly specify how and when tokens can be earned, lost, and spent. These rules specify schedules of reinforcement and punishment, and it is important that these schedules be appropriate for the patients and behaviors of concern. Different schedules may be required for individual patients. Clients are usually informed verbally of the rules of the token system; the rules may also be listed in a manual available to the clients or posted in a public place. Simply presenting the rules of the token system may engender appropriate behavior. This rule-governed behavior brings the patient's behavior into contact with the contingencies of the token economy, and these contingencies serve to control the behavior further.

Token economies have been used successfully in many studies on psychiatric inpatients. Early and noteworthy successes were reported at Anna State Hospital (e.g., Ayllon & Azrin, 1968), Palo Alto Veterans Administration Hospital (Atthowe & Krasner, 1968), and Patton State Hospital (e.g., Gericke, 1965). Subsequent studies have also documented the value of token economies. For example, Nelson and Cone (1979) used a token system to improve 12 behaviors in each of 16 chronic psychiatric inpatients, 13 of whom had been diagnosed as psychotic, the remainder as mentally retarded. The behaviors were grouped into four classes (personal hygiene, personal management, ward work, and social skills), and a multiple-baseline design was used to evaluate the intervention.

Reinforcing appropriate behaviors with tokens resulted in "abrupt and substantial increases in performance of most target behaviors, significant improvements in global individual functioning, positive changes in general ward behavior, and increases in social interaction during off-ward activities" (Nelson & Cone, 1979, p. 255). Some of the data collected by Nelson and Cone are shown in Figure 11-1.

Token economies and other behavioral strategies can, of course, be combined with pharmacological interventions, and such combined treatments may be especially effective. For example, Hersen, Turner, Edelstein, and Pinkston (1975) reported the case of a schizophrenic who did not respond well to a social-skills training program until a neuroleptic drug was prescribed. After the drug

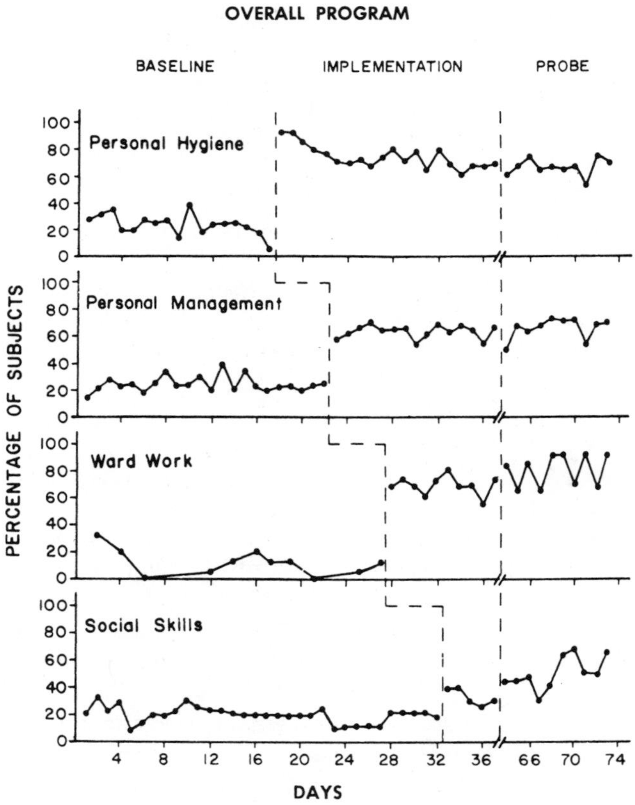

Figure 11-1. Overall mean percentages of subjects performing personal-hygiene, personal-management, ward-work, and social-skills behaviors. The procedure used to change behavior was a token economy. (From "Multiple-Baseline Analysis of a Token Economy for Psychiatric Inpatients" by G. L. Nelson & J. D. Cone, 1979, *Journal of Applied Behavior Analysis*, *12*, 268. Copyright 1979 by the Society for the Experimental Analysis of Behavior. Reproduced by permission.)

was administered, the behavioral intervention was quite effective. Behavioral interventions are not always a viable alternative to pharmacological interventions in the management of psychoses. Instead, they are valuable adjuncts.

In recent years, there has been a major move toward deinstitutionalizing mentally ill (and mentally retarded) people. Therapeutic procedures based on behavioral principles are no less effective outside institutions than inside them, but they can be difficult to arrange when placements are relatively unstructured. Nevertheless, procedures based on operant conditioning have proved useful in community mental-health centers (e.g., Liberman, King, & DeRisi, 1976).

Mood Disorders

Mood disorders are also known as *affective disorders;* they are disorders of emotion, primarily elation or depression. Emotion is inferred on the basis of self-report and overt behavior; a person who makes self-deprecating statements, says that he or she is unhappy, and rarely, if ever, interacts with other people is depressed.

Three important mood disorders are **major depression, bipolar disorder, and mania.** Major depression and bipolar disorder are relatively common; the incidence of the former is about 5%, that of the latter, 1% (Robbins, Helzer, Weissman, Orvaschel, Gruenberg, Burke, & Regier, 1984). Major depression, but not bipolar disorder, is more common in females than in males.

The DSM-III-R criteria for a major depressive episode are listed in Table 11-4. A person experiencing a major depressive episode reports feeling sad and guilty. Objects and events that were once reinforcing control little behavior during a major depressive episode; therefore, operant behavior is generally suppressed. For example, a depressed person may rarely, if ever, go out, have sex, or call friends, even though these activities were enjoyed and often per-

Table 11-4
Diagnostic Criteria for Major Depressive Episode[a]

A. Five of the following characteristics, including (1) and (2) must have been present during the same two-week period and represent a change from previous functioning:
  1. Depressed mood nearly all day, every day.
  2. Markedly diminished interest or pleasure in all or nearly all activities.
  3. Weight change without dieting.
  4. Sleep disturbances (insomnia or hypersomnia).
  5. Change in motor activity.
  6. Fatigue or loss of energy.
  7. Self-reported feelings of worthlessness or guilt.
  8. Diminshed ability to think, indecisiveness.
  9. Recurrent thoughts of death.
B. Not due to an organic factor or the death of a loved one.
C. No delusions or hallucinations.
D. Not superimposed on another condition (schizophrenia, etc.).

[a]From *DSM-III-R* (1987), pp. 222–223. Copyright 1987 by the American Psychiatric Association. Adapted by permission.

formed before the depressive episode. A major depressive episode is severe, disruptive, and even life-threatening: Guze and Robins (1970) estimated that 15% of people with the disorder commit suicide.

A milder, but nonetheless clinically significant, form of depression is termed **dysthymic disorder.** In days past, reactive depression (precipitated by environmental events) and endogenous depression (not precipitated by environmental events) were distinguished, but this dichotomy is no longer widely accepted.

It is convenient to think of mania as the opposite of depression. During **manic episodes,** mood is abnormally elevated and the person is active and frequently irritable, overestimates personal ability, and behaves irresponsibly. From a behavioral perspective, she or he seems to be relatively insensitive to punishing consequences and acts to maximize momentary reinforcement without regard to delayed consequences. For example, during a manic episode, the person may take drugs, have sex, and spend money without regard to the eventual consequences.

Bipolar disorder involves alternation between mania and depression. The time course of the alternation varies; periods of relatively normal affect are relatively common in this disorder. A milder form of bipolar disorder is termed **cyclothymia.**

Etiology

Several theories have been developed in an attempt to explain the development of mood disorders; none are fully adequate. As in schizophrenia, there appears to be a weak inherited susceptibility to mood disorders (e.g., Allen, 1976), but what exactly is inherited is unknown. Based on the neuropharmacological actions of clinically effective drugs, scientists have hypothesized that depression results from underactivity of noradrenergic or serotonergic neurons, whereas mania results from overactivity in these neurons. But direct confirmation of these actions is lacking (Baldessarini, 1985). A link between mood disorders and the brain mechanisms that control sleep cycles has also been proposed (Goodwin, Wirz-Justice & Wehr, 1982) but not yet proved.

We will focus here on major depression. Beginning with Charles Ferster (1965), a number of behaviorists have proposed that insufficient positive reinforcement plays a major role in the development of depression. The notion appears plausible: A major symptom of depression is suppression of operant behavior, and one way to suppress operant behavior is by failing to provide adequate reinforcement. Moreover, the absence or loss of significant reinforcers—for instance, those associated with a good job or a lover—produces feelings and statements indicative of depression: "I'm no good, I can't even keep a job. What will I do for money? Everybody laughs at me." When they first occur, such statements are likely to be reinforced, albeit inadvertently, by a sympathetic audience. Over time, however, associates may come to avoid contact with the depressed person, who isn't much fun to be around. This avoidance decreases the available reinforcers for appropriate as well as inappropriate behavior, and it strengthens the depression (Lewinsohn, 1975).

The insufficient-reinforcement hypothesis has been extended in several directions. Moss and Boren (1972) speculated that depression does not result from insufficient positive reinforcement alone but also requires "aversive control" (exposure to escape, avoidance, or punishment contingencies). Costello (1972) proposed that depression occurs because objects and events that were once reinforcing lose their ability to maintain behavior. These stimuli continue to be available but are not reinforcing, perhaps because of endogenous biochemical or neurophysiological events. This analysis appears to be generally consistent with clinical evidence.

Martin Seligman and his colleagues have proposed an alternative to the insufficient-reinforcement analysis of depression. It is termed the **learned-helplessness model.** Learned helplessness involves learning that a stimulus cannot be escaped or avoided. This phenomenon was first demonstrated in dogs exposed to inescapable and unavoidable electric shocks, then tested in an escape–avoidance procedure (Overmeier & Seligman, 1967). This and many similar studies unequivocally demonstrated that exposure to uncontrollable shocks interferes with the acquisition of avoidance responding (Seligman, Klein, & Miller, 1976). Seligman and his colleagues (Seligman *et al.*, 1976) proposed that learning that shocks are uncontrollable has three effects: (1) the operant behavior relevant to the shocks is weakened and the organism appears passive (a motivational effect); (2) the acquisition of responses that escape or avoid shocks is impaired (a cognitive effect); and (3) responses indicative of fear and anxiety are exhibited (an affective or emotional effect).

These processes may be involved in the genesis of human depression. As Seligman *et al.* (1976) observed:

> Some of the events which typically produce depression are: failure in work or school; death, loss, rejection or separation from loved ones; physical disease; and growing old. We believe that the depressed patient has learned that he cannot control those elements of his life which relieve suffering or bring him gratification. In short, he believes that he is helpless. (p. 196)

Over time, Seligman, in response to critics, modified and refined his notions about the relation of learned helplessness to human depression. Unfortunately, the refinements made the model more mentalistic. For example, Abramson, Seligman, and Teasdale (1978) proposed that a history of exposure to uncontrollable events causes a person to ask, "Why am I helpless?" This question leads to an attribution about the cause, which in turn determines one's expectancies about the outcome of subsequent behavior. These expectancies influence behavior: "Nothing I can do has any effect, so why do anything?" Eventually, this process deflates self-esteem, and full-blown depression ensues.

This analysis is wanting if attributions and expectancies are construed as mental events that control behavior. If they are considered overt or covert verbal responses, the analysis is more appealing. The covert verbal behavior of depressed individuals (i.e., what they say to themselves), like their overt behavior, differs from that of other people. On the basis of these differences in verbal behavior, Aaron Beck (e.g., 1976) argued that depression is a cognitive disorder, and he developed a **cognitive-distortion theory** of depression. According to it, four cognitive distortions, or errors, cause depression: **arbitrary inference** (drawing unwarranted conclusions); **selective abstraction** (not considering all aspects of a situation); **magnification/minimization** (over- or underestimating the significance of events and behavior); and **overgeneralization** (reaching conclusions on the basis of inadequate information).

Treatment

Although behaviors indicative of cognitive distortions are often evident in depression, they may in actuality be a part of the disorder, not its cause. Nonetheless, studies have demonstrated that treatments designed to alter a patient's "cognitions" (covert verbal statements, especially those relevant to self-worth and ability to control the environment) can be effective in treating depression (e.g., Beck, 1976).

Other kinds of interventions have also proved useful, including treatment with **antidepressant drugs** (Table 11-3) and **electroconvulsive therapy (ECT).** ECT involves electrically inducing a seizure and is used primarily to treat depression insensitive to other interventions. Many behavioral interventions have been used to treat depression, and most are relatively complex (see Chapter 12). According to Hersen and Bellack (1982), good nonpharmacological treatments of depression have four characteristics:

1. Therapy should begin with an elaborated, well-planned rationale.
2. Therapy should provide training in skills that the patient can utilize to feel more effective in handling his/her daily life.
3. Therapy should emphasize independent use of these skills by the patient outside of the therapy context and must provide enough structure so that the attainment of independent skill is possible for the patient.
4. Therapy should encourage the patient's attribution that improvement in mood is caused by the patient's increased skillfulness, not by the therapist's skillfulness. (p. 102)

Behavioral therapy and pharmacotherapy each appear to be generally effective in managing depression, and there is emerging evidence that the two can, in some cases, be combined to produce effects superior to either alone (Hollon, Spoden, & Chastek, 1986).

Anxiety Disorders

The behavioral problems discussed thus far in this chapter tend to be diffuse, involving many aspects of a person's repertoire. They significantly and generally interfere with the ability to function appropriately. Some behavioral problems, among them anxiety disorders, are more specific and less debilitating.

Under the general category of anxiety disorders, the DSM-III-R lists following conditions: panic disorder (with and without agoraphobia), agoraphobia (fear of being alone in, and avoidance of, public places) without history of panic disorder, social phobia, simple phobia, obsessive-compulsive disorder, post-traumatic stress disorder, and generalized anxiety disorder. All of these disorders involve "anxiety," although they differ with respect to the conditions that evoke it and the patterns of behavior taken to be indicative of its occurrence.

Anxiety is difficult to define. In general, **anxiety** involves an unpleasant subjective state aptly described as "fearful," physiological arousal, and troublesome overt behavior that minimizes contact with a stimulus. That stimulus may be publicly accessible (e.g., a spider) or the private response of the anxious person (e.g., the thought of a spider). Anxiety as defined above has three components: a self-reported component (e.g., saying, "I'm scared to death of spiders"), a physiological arousal component (e.g., increases in heart rate and blood pressure when a spider is sighted), and a motor component (e.g., screaming and running away when a spider appears). Interestingly, these three measures of anxiety do not always correlate well (Nietzel & Bernstein, 1981). For instance, a person may report being deathly afraid of ordering from a restaurant menu but nevertheless may do so regularly and may exhibit only minimal physiological arousal when doing so. The component of anxiety that is of primary interest to a clinician is the one that causes trouble for the patient.

You will recognize that anxiety is not a thing, but only a label (verbal response) used to describe certain kinds of behavioral and physiological responses emitted under the control of certain kinds of stimuli. The same is true of phobia, obsessive-compulsive disorder, and all related terms. Think of a quiet autumn day at school. You're listening to a lecture when a horse fly buzzes in through an open window. Suddenly, the person to your left screams, "God, bees," and runs wildly from the room. A bid odd; perhaps a bee phobia? Enough to make you wonder. Now consider the same student hiking through the woods and accidentally stepping on a hornet's nest. Same verbal response, "God, bees," same wild running. No phobia there, just simple and reasonable fear. Clinicians, like laypeople, assign diagnostic labels on the basis of what people do and the conditions under which they do them.

Anxiety disorders *are* behavioral problems; they do not *cause* behavioral problems. In fact, from a behavioral perspective:

> We have to deal not with . . . anxiety, but with the conditions giving rise to anxiety. . . . The concept of anxiety is superfluous in dealing directly with people rather than with theories. In a clinical intervention we deal with what is being avoided, with what a person needs to learn or unlearn or relearn. . . . [Accepting the concept of anxiety] makes us think we know something when we do not and should be looking harder. (Krasner & Ullmann, 1973, pp. 98–99)

Etiology

There is no single specifiable cause of anxiety disorders in general or of any subtype. There is no evidence for the heritability of simple or social phobias (Goodwin, 1983), but some researchers have reported a genetic link in panic disorders and agoraphobia (Harris, Noyes, Crowe, & Chaundry, 1983). If there is an inherited propensity toward these disorders (which is not certain), the mechanism through which it works is unknown.

Environmental variables play a significant role in the development of anxiety disorders. The stimuli that produce anxiety disorders are a part of the person's environment; these stimuli are avoided by actions that are troublesome and produce a subjective state that is unpleasant. How the stimuli control these responses is not as simple as it might seem. A temptingly simple analysis is based on the proposition that stimuli evoke anxiety by being paired with other, unpleasant objects or events. You may recall from Chapter 1 that Watson and

Rayner (1920) successfully produced "fear" in a child through a process of respondent conditioning. In that study, a tame white rat (which initially elicited no adverse responses) was paired with a loud noise, which aroused the boy and caused him to cry. After a few pairings, the rat alone did the same. Objects and events that induce crying often serve as negative reinforcers. Hence, it is likely that the child would have responded to escape or avoid the rat. If this occurred, and the avoidance responses, physiological arousal, and emotional responses produced by visual contact with the rat were strong and continued over many exposures, a rat phobia would be evident.

Could this be a model for all phobias? Perhaps. But you will recall that a conditional stimulus (e.g., the rat) controls behavior only by virtue of being at least occasionally paired with an unconditional stimulus (e.g., the loud noise). We know, however, that clinical phobias endure for long periods even when the feared stimulus is not correlated with an external object or event with aversive properties. For example, an adult may have been bitten by a spider only once, long ago, but may still exhibit a serious spider phobia. Why? One possibility is that, after being bitten, the person rarely, if ever, encountered a spider. That is, he was quite successful in avoiding them; hence, there was no opportunity for respondent extinction to occur. Another possibility is that, although simple respondent conditioning is important in producing a phobia, other processes are involved in maintaining it. For example, the adult described above may have seen many spiders and was never bitten; nonetheless, he repeatedly verbalized to himself and other people how hideous spiders are, and how important it is to avoid them. It is possible that the overt verbal responses, like the behavior intended to avoid spiders, was reinforced by a sympathetic audience. Moreover, both overt and covert verbal responses may have helped to maintain the phobia as a form of rule-governed, although undesirable, behavior. For instance, the person with the spider phobia might have regularly stated to himself, "I must stay out of places where spiders live so they won't bite me." This rule states a behavior (staying out of places where spiders live) and a consequences for this behavior (avoiding being bitten). The rules that one generates and follows depend on historical and current variables, and these variables are, in principle, subject to analysis. They are likely to be complex and interactive and therefore difficult to discern retrospectively.

Treatment

In most cases, the cause(s) of a phobia, or some other kind of anxiety disorder, cannot be determined precisely. Therefore, it is fortunate that effective treatment does not require knowing the etiology (cause). Pharmacological and behavioral treatments for anxiety disorders have been carefully studied, in part because some of these disorders are relatively common. For instance, the incidence of panic disorders is 1%–2% in the general population; it is about twice as common in women as in men. The incidence of obsessive-compulsive disorder is similar; this condition is slightly more common in women than in men (Robbins et al., 1984).

Systematic desensitization, a treatment developed by Joseph Wolpe (1958), is one procedure widely used in the treatment of phobias. It is based on the reciprocal-inhibition principle, the essence of which is captured in the statement by Wolpe (1958) that

> if a response antagonistic to anxiety can be made to occur in the presence of anxiety-evoking stimuli so that it is accompanied by a complete or partial suppression of the anxiety responses, the bond between these stimuli and the anxiety responses will be weakened. (p. 71)

In essence, systematic desensitization teaches a person to relax in the presence of stimuli that once produced anxiety. As described by Leitenberg (1976):

> The three major components of systematic desensitization are: (1) construction of a graduated hierarchy of anxiety-provoking scenes, and arrangement of these in an order such that the first scene elicits minimal anxiety and the last scene evokes considerable anxiety; (2) training the patient in deep muscle relaxation usually via the Jacobsen (1938) technique, although hypnotic induction techniques, drugs, and biofeedback have also been employed for this purpose; (3) having the patient visualize each of the scenes while in the relaxed state. (pp. 127–128)

After the client can envision each of the scenes in the hierarchy without feeling anxious, he or she may be required to actually participate in the activities represented in those scenes. For instance, a person with a dog phobia might first be trained until she or he is able to relax while envisioning close contact with a large dog. When this relaxation occurs, the client is introduced to a small (and friendly) living dog at ever-decreasing distances. If anxiety is reported, the distance increases; if not, the dog is brought closer. When the client can pet the dog without feeling anxiety, a larger dog is brought in. Eventually, the client should show no fear of any friendly dog, and treatment would be considered a success.

Many other behavioral procedures are useful in treating phobias and other anxiety disorders. They include **modeling,** a therapeutic technique made popular by Albert Bandura (e.g., 1969), in which the client observes another person responding appropriately in a situation in which the client fails to do so (e.g., one in which an anxiety-arousing stimulus is present). Modeling is effective to the extent that the client has a history in which behaving as others (models) behave has been reinforced. When they have such a history, modeling is a simple and cost-effective intervention.

Mental Retardation

Mental retardation has been defined in many ways, and even at present, there is disagreement over diagnostic criteria. The most widely accepted definition is that of the American Association on Mental Deficiency (AAMD). According to the AAMD (Grossman, 1983):

> Mental retardation refers to significantly subaverage general intellectual functioning existing concurrently with deficits in adaptive behavior and manifested during the developmental period. (p. 11)

"Significantly subaverage general intellectual functioning" is marked by an intelligence quotient (IQ) of 70 or below as assessed by a standardized and individually administered intelligence test, although this upper limit may be extended to 75 or more, depending on the test used and the conditions of assessment. "Deficits in adaptive behavior" are significant limitations in an individual's effectiveness in meeting the standards of maturation, learning, personal independence, or social responsibility that are expected for his or her age level or cultural group. Several standardized tests that assess adaptive behavior are available. Onset "during the developmental period" refers to the period between birth and the 18th birthday.

Note that each of these characteristics must be present for a person to be considered mentally retarded; mental retardation cannot be diagnosed on the basis of IQ or adaptive behavior alone. Moreover, mental retardation is not, in principle, irreversible: it is possible for someone's behavior to change so that she or he does not meet the diagnostic criteria.

The prevalence of mental retardation—that is, the number of existing cases in the population during a given period of time—is unknown, but most estimates place it somewhere between 1% and 3% (Gadow & Poling, 1988). People diagnosed as mentally retarded are a remarkably heterogeneous group; one obvious difference is the degree of impairment in adaptive behavior and IQ test scores. Mental retardation is typically classified according to severity, although other modes of classification (e.g., by clinical symptoms or by etiology) are sometimes used. For instance, the terms *idiot* (IQ 0 to 30), *imbecile* (IQ 30 to 50), and *moron* (IQ 50 to 70), which were widely used as recently as the early 1900s, were not terms of derision; rather, they referred with some precision to severity of mental retardation. The system used most often today is that of the AAMD, which classifies mental retardation as **mild, moderate, severe,** or **profound,** based on an individually administered IQ test score in conjunction with present level of adaptive behavior. Table 11-5 describes these categories.

In school systems, the designations **educable mentally retarded (EMR), trainable mentally retarded (TMR),** and **severely and profoundly mentally retarded (SPMR)** are often used. These terms have no precise definition, but in

Table 11-5
Classification of Mental Retardation by Severity[a]

1. *Mild mental retardation* is a term used to describe the degree of mental retardation present when intelligence test scores are 50 or 55 to approximately 70; many mildly retarded (educable) individuals who function at this level can usually master basic academic skills whereas adults at this level may maintain themselves independently or semi-independently in the community. Most (about 90% of) mentally retarded people are in this category.
2. *Moderate mental retardation* is a term used to describe the degree of retardation when intelligence test scores range from 35 or 40 to 50 or 55; many trainable individuals function at this level; such persons usually can learn self-help, communication, social, and simple occupational skills but only limited academic or vocational skills.
3. *Severe mental retardation* is a term used to describe the degree of retardation when intelligence test scores range from 20 or 25 to 35 or 40; such persons require continuing and close supervision; sometimes called *dependent retardation*.
4. *Profound mental retardation* is a term used to describe the degree of retardation when intelligence test scores are below 20 or 25; such persons require continuing and close supervision, but some may be able to perform simple self-help tasks; profoundly retarded people often have other handicaps and require total life-support systems for maintenance.

[a]From *Classification in Mental Retardation* by H. J. Grossman (1983), p. 1984. Copyright 1983 by the American Association on Mental Retardation. Reproduced by permission.

general, EMR students are those who can be taught basic academic subjects, TMR students typically concentrate on functional academics with emphasis on self-help and vocational skills, and SPMR students require special care (often within an institution). Until recently, SPMR students were not educated within the public school system.

Developmental disability is sometimes used as a synonym for mental retardation, but this usage is inaccurate. The term **developmental disability** covers a range of handicapping conditions and is defined as follows (Grossman, 1983):

> A severe, chronic disability which is attributable to a mental or physical impairment or combination of mental and physical impairments; is manifested before age 22; is likely to continue indefinitely; and results in substantial functional limitations in three or more areas of major life activity. (p. 168)

The concept of *developmental disability* was introduced in the early 1970s to emphasize that other handicapped individuals may require services similar to those typically provided for mentally retarded people. Although all mentally retarded people are developmentally disabled, not all developmentally disabled people are mentally retarded.

Etiology

Over 250 conditions are known to cause mental retardation, but the etiological mechanisms are unknown in most cases because mild mental retardation (the most prevalent form) is often determined by the same complex maze of variables that influences ability and performance in nonretarded people (MacMillan, 1982). Causal factors are more readily apparent in cases of severe mental retardation. For example, about one third of TMR students have Down syndrome, and another one third have some form of brain damage. Detailed coverage of the causes of mental retardation is provided elsewhere (e.g., Grossman, 1983; MacMillan, 1982; Matson & Mulick, 1983). They include:

1. Chromosomal aberrations.
2. Metabolic and nutritional disorders.
3. Gross brain disease.
4. Unknown prenatal influences resulting in conditions such as microcephaly (very small head and brain) or macrocephaly (very large head and brain).
5. Trauma or physical insult resulting in brain damage.
6. Environmental influences, including psychosocial disadvantage and sensory deprivation.

Treatment

Teachers, social workers, occupational and physical therapists, physicians, and other professionals work with psychologists to enhance the behavioral repertoire of mentally retarded people. Although psychologists use a variety of interventions with mentally retarded people, procedures based on the principles of behavior analysis are especially popular and successful. As John Scibak (1983) noted in a chapter reviewing behavioral treatments:

> In the last 20 years, a technology has emerged that focused on a behavioral approach to treatment with the mentally retarded. Through the monitoring and systematic manipulation of antecedents and consequents, it has been possible to develop rudimentary self-help skills and complex vocational assembly tasks while controlling inappropriate responses such as aggression and self-injurious behavior. . . . Over 400 studies have appeared in the literature demonstrating the efficacy of this technology in modifying the behavior of mentally retarded individuals. (p. 339)

Hundreds of similar studies have appeared since Scibak's chapter was written. We will consider two studies representative of this genre. One is a study by Azrin and Foxx (1971), who taught nine profoundly mentally retarded institutionalized adults (20 to 62 years of age) appropriate toileting skills. Before the treatment, all of them regularly urinated and/or defecated in their clothing. Within a few days of exposure to the treatment, incidents of incontinence had been reduced by about 90%, and by the end of the treatment, incontinence had been almost totally eliminated (Figure 11-2). Thus, the treatment obviously benefitted the residents, as well as the staff who cared for them.

The procedures used by Azrin and Foxx (1971) involved (1) increasing the frequency of urination (by having the residents drink water) to increase opportunities for learning; (2) positive reinforcement of correct toileting; (3) the use of an automatic apparatus to signal elimination; (4) shaping of independent toileting; and (5) cleanliness training. Steps were also taken to ensure the maintenance of appropriate toileting. Table 11-6 summarizes the procedure used by

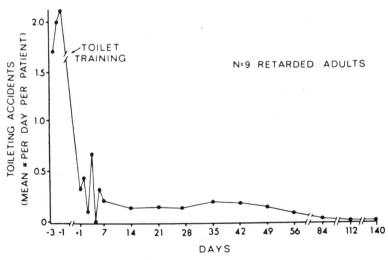

Figure 11-2. The effects of a toilet-training program on the mean frequency of accidents (urinating and defecating in clothing) in nine profoundly mentally retarded adults. (From "A Rapid Method of Toilet Training the Institutionalized Retarded" by N. H. Azrin & R. M. Foxx, 1971, *Journal of Applied Behavior Analysis, 4,* 96. Copyright 1971 by the Society for the Experimental Analysis of Behavior. Reproduced by permission.)

Table 11-6

Summary of Procedures Used by Azrin and Foxx
to Toilet-Train Mentally Retarded Residents of an Institution[a]

Procedures Used in Training

I. When No Accidents Occur
  1. Resident seated in chair when not seated on toilet bowl
  2. Resident drinks fluids every half-hour
  3. Scheduled toileting of resident every half-hour
  4. Resident given edible and social reinforcer every 5 min while dry
  5. Resident given edible and social reinforcer following elimination in toilet bowl and returned to chair

II. When Accidents Occur
  1. Trainer disconnnects pants alarm
  2. Trainer obtains resident's attention
  3. Resident walks to laundry area to obtain fresh clothing
  4. Resident undresses himself
  5. Resident walks to nearby shower, receives shower, and dresses himself
  6. Resident obtains mop or cloth and cleans soiled area on chair or floor
  7. Resident handwashes soiled pants, wrings pants out, and hangs pants up to dry
  8. Trainer removes resident's chair from use
  9. 1-hour timeout procedures:
    a. no edibles or social reinforcers every 5 min
    b. no fluids every 30 min
    c. chair not available
    d. continue 30-min scheduled toilet periods

Post Training Ward Maintenance Procedure

I. General Procedure
  1. Advance assignment of one attendant for Toilet Responsibility each shift
  2. Snack period between breakfast and lunch and between lunch and dinner
  3. Resident's pants inspected at mealtime, snacktime and bedtime (6 times daily)
  4. Attendant initials record sheet when residents checked; record sheet sent directly to supervisor
  5. Discontinued use of both apparatuses for detecting eliminations

II. When Accidents Occur
  1. Cleanliness training whenever an accident is detected:
    a. Resident walks to laundry area to obtain fresh clothing
    b. Resident undresses himself
    c. Resident walks to nearby shower, receives shower, and dresses himself
    d. Resident obtains mop or cloth and cleans soiled area on chair or floor
    e. Resident handwashes soiled pants, wrings pants out, and hangs pants up to dry
  2. Delay of meal for 1 hour if accident prior to meal
  3. Omission of snacks if accident prior to snack
  4. Attendant initials and records each accident

Minimal Maintenance—Starts Eight Weeks After Training
  1. Inspections only at mealtime and bedtime
  2. Cleanliness training given for accidents

Termination of Maintenance Procedure—When resident is continent for at least one month
  1. No regular inspections for that patient
  2. Cleanliness training given for accident when detected

[a]From "A Rapid Method of Toilet Training the Institutionalized Retarded" by N. H. Azrin and R. M. Foxx (1971), *Journal of Applied Behavior Analysis, 4,* 91, 94, 116. Copyright 1971 by the Society for the Experimental Analysis of Behavior. Reproduced by permission.

Azrin and Foxx. These procedures, based entirely on principles of operant conditioning, are noteworthy for their completeness and efficacy.

A study by Dorsey, Iwata, Ong, and McSween (1980) provides another good example of the use of operant procedures to treat behavior problems in mentally retarded people. These authors treated self-injurious behavior (e.g., hand biting, head banging, and skin tearing) in seven profoundly mentally retarded residents (5 to 37 years of age) of a private nursing facility. Self-injury is surprisingly common among mentally retarded people; one survey indicated, for example, that approximately 14% of all residents of state schools for the mentally retarded in Texas (about 10,000 people) engaged in some form of self-injurious behavior (Griffin, Williams, Stark, Altmeyer, & Mason, 1984)—and it obviously constitutes a problem. Dorsey *et al.* substantially reduced self-injurious behavior (Figure 11-3) through the use of a simple punishment procedure in which a fine mist of water at room temperature was sprayed in the resident's face each time the self-injurious behavior occurred. In the second phase of the study, the water mist was paired with the word *no*. As a result of this pairing, self-injurious behavior could be suppressed by saying, "No" when the response occurred, even in a situation where the water mist had never been applied.

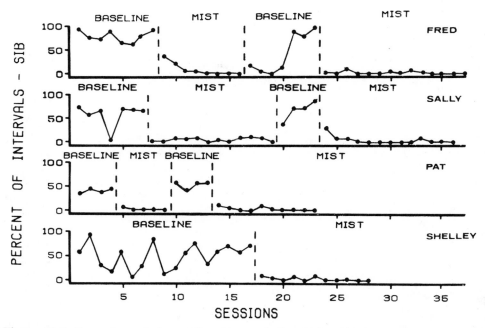

Figure 11-3. Percentage of observational intervals in which self-injurious behavior (SIB) was observed in each of four mentally retarded people across experimental conditions. (From "Treatment of Self-Injurious Behavior Using a Water Mist: Initial Response Suppression and Generalization" by M. F. Dorsey, B. A. Iwata, P. Ong, & T. E. McSween, 1980, *Journal of Applied Behavior Analysis, 13,* 348. Copyright 1980 by the Society for the Experimental Analysis of Behavior. Reproduced by permission.)

Much of the applied research conducted by behaviorists has involved mentally retarded participants, and as the foregoing examples illustrate, efforts with this population have yielded noteworthy successes. That this is so should not be interpreted to mean that procedures based on operant conditioning are intrinsically more effective with mentally retarded people than with other individuals. That is untrue. If it is possible to use operant conditioning procedures systematically, it is possible to change a wide range of behaviors in any human. These procedures have been widely used with mentally retarded people for two reasons: (1) some mentally retarded people exhibit problem behaviors that are resistant to other treatments, and (2) the residential, educational, and vocational placements of some mentally retarded people are structured so that it is possible to use behavioral procedures systematically.

Drug Abuse[1]

Drug abuse is any pattern of drug self-administration that produces harmful behavioral or physiological effects without producing compensatory medical benefit. It is an ancient problem, as indicated by the presence of many biblical cautions against excessive alcohol use. Among them:

> Wine is a mocker, strong drink a brawler; and whoever is led astray by it is not wise. (Proverbs 21:1)

> Happy are you, O land, when your king is the son of free men, and your princes feast at the proper time, for strength and not for drunkedness. (Ecclesiastes 10:17)

> . . . let us conduct ourselves becomingly as in the day, not in reveling and drunkenness. (Romans 13:13)

> Woe to those who rise early in the morning, that they may run after strong drink, who tarry late into the evening till wine influences them! (Isaiah 3:11)

Wise council notwithstanding, the production and abuse of alcohol began in the United States well before the Union was formed. The use and abuse of opiates (opium, morphine, heroin, and other drugs derived from opium) gained popularity some time later, after the Civil War, and was by 1880 widely recognized as rampant. Three factors appear to have contributed to the increased use of opiates in this country (Ray & Ksir, 1987). The first was the development of the hypodermic syringe in 1856. The hypodermic syringe allowed Civil War soldiers to inject morphine with ease, and they frequently did so to allay the pain, dysentery, and other miseries of war. As a consequence, many soldiers returned home physically dependent on, and highly inclined to use, morphine.

A second factor that contributed to the use of opiates was the importation of Chinese laborers, many of whom smoked opium, as they had in their homeland. The wide distribution of patent medicines—potions with such enticing labels as "Swain's Panacea" and "Dr. A. L. Taylor's Oil of Life"—was the third factor that increased the use and abuse of narcotics (and other drugs) in the United States, for many of them contained opium or another narcotic in addition to alcohol

---

[1]A significant portion of the material in this section is adapted from *A Primer of Human Behavioral Pharmacology* (Poling, 1986).

and, in some cases, cocaine. The techniques used to market these concoctions were so effective that may upstanding citizens who would never knowingly take "drugs" used them regularly.

In part because of the problems associated with patent medicines, Congress passed in 1906 the Pure Food and Drug Act, which required that drugs be pure and accurately labeled. This act did not, however, limit the import of opium or other drugs. The Opium Exclusion Act of 1909 rendered illegal the importation and manufacture of opium or its derivatives for nonmedical purposes. The Harrison Act of 1914 affirmed the principles set forth in the acts of 1906 and 1909 and further specified that dispensers of narcotics must register with the Bureau of Internal Revenue. At the time this act was passed, 1 American in 400 was addicted to opium or its derivatives (Ray & Ksir, 1987).

U.S. Supreme Court decisions in 1919 and 1922 established that physicians could not prescribe opiates to addicts even in the context of treatment. This precedent, along with the stipulations of the Opium Exclusion Act, ensured that there would be no way for an addict to obtain a narcotic legally. One result was the establishment of an illegal and profitable drug market. A second result was to make criminals of a sizable number of otherwise law-abiding citizens: one third of all individuals imprisoned in 1928 were guilty of breaking drug-control laws (Ray & Ksir, 1987).

Recognition of the problems created by imprisoning drug abusers without treatment goaded Congress into establishing, in 1929, two centers for the treatment of persons who had broken a federal law and who were also addicted to

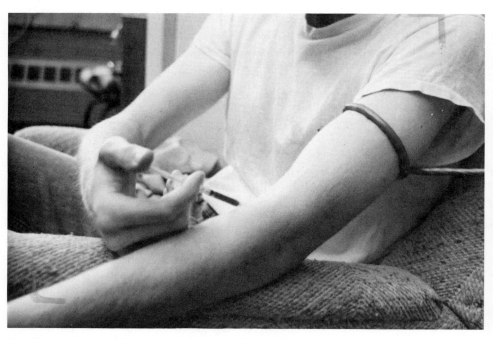

Despite the risks to the user, intravenous drug administration is popular in some social groups. (Photo courtesy of Sue Keller.)

habit-forming drugs, which were defined as including opium and its derivatives, as well as marijuana and peyote.

In 1919, 10 years before the establishment of these treatment centers, Congress had attempted to deal with abuse of another kind of drug, ethanol (beverage alcohol), by passing the Eighteenth Amendment to the Constitution (also known as the Volstead Act). This amendment made it illegal within the United States to manufacture, sell, transport, or import intoxicating liquors. Although the Eighteenth Amendment reduced per capita ethanol consumption immediately following its passage, by 1930 intake had returned to pre-Volstead levels. In addition, enforcement of the amendment was costly and difficult, and the ready market for illegal booze that the amendment had created had filled the coffers of organized criminals, who were delighted to supply it. After a brief and tumultuous life, the Eighteenth Amendment was repealed by the Twenty-First Amendment to the Constitution. Prohibition, in effect from 1920 to 1933, had failed to control alcohol abuse.

Legislation designed to control the abuse of other substances, including the acts described above, also failed to prevent significant trafficking in opiates, cocaine, and marijuana, and the federal treatment centers faired little better in habilitating drug abusers. In fact, from 1900 to 1960, a number of new drugs came to be popular on the street, bringing with them significant abuse problems. Amphetamines, for example, were first used in the 1930s; 20 years later, they were recognized as having considerable abuse potential. Barbiturates and anxiolytics, too, came to the public's attention as drugs capable of harming the incautious user and society at large, as did LSD, phencyclidine (PCP, or angel dust), and cocaine.

As indicated in Table 11-7, which presents data for reported drug use by high school seniors in the class of 1983, many people use drugs for nonmedical purposes. Some of them develop drug-related problems—enough, in fact, to make drug abuse[2] one of the world's great problems. Consider the following statistics:

1. Alcohol abuse costs the nation about $50 billion each year in lost employment and productivity, health care, property loss, and crime (Cruze, Harwood, Kristiansen, Collins, & Jones, 1981). Approximately 10 million adults and 3 million adolescents in the United States experience problems related to their alcohol use (Kinney & Leaton, 1983).

2. Cigarette smoking is associated with almost all deaths due to lung cancer, 30% of deaths due to all types of cancer, 30% of deaths due to coronary heart disease, and 80%–90% of deaths from chronic obstructive lung disease. Overall, cigarette smoking in the United States is associated with about 360,000 premature deaths per year, and it is the number-one avoidable cause of death. Nonetheless, 3 of 10 Americans smoke (Ray & Ksir, 1987; Witters & Venturelli, 1988).

3. The illegal drug industry in the United States is estimated to have yearly sales of $70–$90 billion (L.A.W. Publications, 1985). Each year, about $50 billion is also spent on alcohol and $20 billion on tobacco (Witters & Venturelli, 1988).

[2]Drug abuse includes the abuse of alcohol, which is obviously a drug. Phrases like "alcohol and drug abuse" are nonsensical, but they do indicate the special status that our society gives to alcohol.

Table 11-7
Reported Drug Use by High School Seniors in the Class of 1983[a]

Drug	Percentage who had ever used[b]	Percentage who had used in the past month[c]
Marijuana/hashish	57.0	27.0
Hallucinogens	14.7	2.8
LSD	8.9	1.9
PCP	5.6	1.3
Cocaine	16.2	4.9
Other stimulants	26.9	7.9
Heroin	1.2	0.2
Other opiates	9.4	1.8
Alcohol	92.6	69.4
Other sedatives	14.4	3.0
Barbiturates	9.9	2.1
Methaqualone	13.3	2.5
Inhalants	18.8	2.7
Amyl and butyl nitrates	8.4	1.4

[a]From *Highlights from Drugs and American High School Students 1975–1983* by L. D. Johnston, P. M. O'Malley, and J. G. Bachman. Washington, DC: U.S. Government Printing Office, 1984, p. 19.

[b]All data are based on responses to a questionnaire by a sample of approximately 16,300 students selected to provide an accurate cross-section of high school seniors throughout the United States.

[c]Data in this column refer to drug use in the month immediately before questionnaire administration.

A wide range of substances create problems of some who use them and, in that sense, have abuse potential. For many abused drugs that are illegal, Table 11-8 provides information concerning (1) medical uses; (2) physical dependence; (3) psychological dependence; (4) tolerance; (5) duration of action; (6) usual methods of administration; (7) possible effects; (8) overdose effects; and (9) withdrawal symptoms. Each of the drugs listed is classified as a controlled substance under the Comprehensive Drug Abuse Prevention and Control Act of 1970, which regulates drugs with recognized abuse potential. This act assigns drugs to one of five schedules (classes) according to their potential for abuse and whether or not they have medical uses. Penalties for unlawful possession and possession with intent to distribute are determined by the schedule to which a drug is assigned. Cocaine, for example, is a Schedule II drug; it has high abuse potential but recognized medical uses. First-offense unlawful possession of cocaine can result in up to 1 year of imprisonment and/or fines up to $5,000; penalties increase to a maximum of 15 years' imprisonment and/or fines to $25,000 plus 3 years' mandatory parole for possession with intent to distribute. Penalties double for second offenses, or when the unlawful distribution is by a person over 18 years old to someone under 21 years old.

A number of terms must be understood if Table 11-8 is to be meaningful. **Physical dependence** describes the state of an organism in which an abrupt termination of chronic (repeated) drug administration is followed by a withdrawal syndrome. The **withdrawal syndrome** is a confluence of signs (observable changes) and symptoms (changes reported by the individual) that emerge following the abrupt termination of drug administration. An implication of the term **physical dependence** is that the chronic presence of the drug has altered the individual in such a way that normal functioning requires the continued presence of the drug. The measurable disruption of normal activity induced by drug withdrawal includes physiological responses (e.g., diarrhea and vomiting when heroin administration is discontinued), overt behavioral responses (e.g., drug-seeking behavior), and subjective responses (e.g., self-reported craving for the drug).

Physical dependence is usually accompanied by **tolerance,** which occurs when chronic exposure to a drug reduces sensitivity to its effects. Tolerance is evident when either (1) the repeated administration of a given dose produces a progressively smaller effect or (2) a response of the magnitude initially produced by a given dose is produced only by the administration of a higher dose. For instance, an individual who is tolerant to heroin must administer more of it to produce euphoria than a person who is not tolerant.

Psychological dependence is a term that is ill-defined. It generally refers to a strong tendency to repeat the use of a drug (Ray & Ksir, 1987). In other words, **psychological dependence** occurs when a substance serves as a powerful positive reinforcer for an individual. Psychological dependence in this sense is not necessarily harmful; a person can, in some cases, regularly self-administer a substance without harming anyone. For example, many people ingest caffeine in coffee, tea, or cola on a daily basis, but they are not usually considered drug abusers.

A final term that is often encountered in the context of drug abuse is *addiction.* Over time, the term has been used in so many ways as to have become essentially meaningless. As noted by Nelson, Pearson, Sayers, and Glynn (1982), **addiction** is

> generally used in the drug field to refer to chronic, compulsive, or uncontrollable drug use, to the extent that a person (referred to as an "addict") cannot or will not stop the use of some drug. Beyond this, the term is ambiguously used with a wide variety of often arbitrary meanings and connotations. (p. 5)

The arbitrary connotations are often mentalistic and focus attention away from the empirical causes of drug-related problems.

It is important to recognize that these problems take many forms. A college freshman busted twice for driving under the influence of alcohol has a drug-related problem, but it differs from that of a prostitute physically dependent on heroin, or of an executive whose excessive cocaine use has led to financial ruin. There is, however, one element common in these and all other examples of drug abuse: Inappropriate drug-seeking and drug-taking behaviors harm someone, and the harm can be lessened only if these behaviors are changed.

Causes of Drug Abuse

Drug abuse encompasses an immense and heterogeneous set of problems with no single cause. In times past, drug abuse was commonly considered an ethical weakness or a sin. This attitude allowed others to blame those with drug-

Table 11-8
Characteristics of Abused Drugs[a]

	Drugs	Trade or other names	Medical uses	Physical dependence	Psychological dependence
Narcotics	Opium	Dover's Powder, Paregoric, Parepectolin	Analgesic, anti-diarrheal	High	High
	Morphine	Morphine, Pectoral Syrup	Analgesic, anti-tussive		
	Codeine	Tylenol with Codeine, Empirin Compound with Codeine, Robitussin A–C	Analgesic, anti-tussive	Moderate	Moderate
	Heroin	Diacetylmorphine, horse, smack	Under investigation	High	High
	Hydromorphone	Dilaudid	Analgesic		
	Meperidine (pethidine)	Demerol, Mepergan	Analgesic		
	Methadone	Dolophine, Methadone, Methadose	Analgesic		High–low
	Other narcotics	LAAM, Leritine, Numorphan, Percodan, Tussionex, Fentanyl, Darvon, Talwin,[†] Lomotil	Analgesic, anti-diarrheal, anti-tussive	High–low	
Depressants	Chloral hydrate	Noctec, Somnos	Hypnotic	Moderate	Moderate
	Barbiturates	Phenobarbital, Tuinal, Amytal, Nembutal, Seconal, Lotusate	Anesthetic, anti-convulsant, sedative, hypnotic	High–moderate	High–moderate
	Benzodiazepines	Ativan, Azene, Clonopin, Dalmane, diazepam, Librium, Xanax, Serax, Tranxene, Valium, Verstran, Halcion, Paxipam, Restoril	Antianxiety, anti-convulsant, sedative, hypnotic	Low	Moderate / High
	Methaqualone	Quaalude	Sedative, hypnotic	High	Low
	Glutethimide	Doriden	Sedative, hypnotic	High	
	Other depressants	Equanil, Miltown, Noludar Placidyl, Valmid	Antianxiety, sedative, hypnotic	Moderate	Moderate
Stimulants	Cocaine	Coke, flake, snow, crack	Local anesthetic	Possible	High

Table 11-8
(*Continued*)

Tolerance	Duration (in hours)	Methods of usual administration	Possible effects	Effects of overdose	Withdrawal syndrome
Yes	3–6	Oral, smoked	Euphoria, drowsiness, respiratory depression, constricted pupils, nausea	Slow and shallow breathing, clammy skin, convulsions, coma, possible death	Watery eyes, runny nose, yawning, loss of appetite, irritability, tremors, panic, chills and sweating, cramps, nausea
		Oral, injected, smoked			
		Oral, injected			
		Injected, sniffed, smoked			
		Oral, injected			
	12–24				
	Variable				
Yes	5–8	Oral	Slurred speech, disorientation, drunken behavior without odor of alcohol	Shallow respiration, clammy skin, dilated pupils, weak and rapid pulse, coma, possible death	Anxiety, insomnia, tremors, delirium, convulsions, possible death
	1–16				
	4–8				
Yes	4–8				
Yes	4–8				
Yes	4–8				
	1–2	Sniffed, smoked, injected	Increased alertness, excitation, euphoria,	Agitation, increase in body temperature,	Apathy, long periods of sleep, irritability,

(*continued*)

Table 11-8
(Continued)

	Drugs	Trade or other names	Medical uses	Physical dependence	Psychological dependence
	Amphetamines	Biphetamine, Delcobese, Desoxyn, Dexedrine, Mediatric, ice	Hyperkinesis, narcolepsy, weight control		
	Phenmetrazine	Preludin			
	Methylphenidate	Ritalin			Moderate
	Other Stimulants	Adipex, Bacarate, Cylert, Didrex, Ionamin, Plegine, Pre-Sate, Sanorex, Tenuate, Tepanil, Volanil			High
Hallucinogens	LSD	Acid, microdot	None	None	Degree unknown
	Mescaline and peyote	Mesc, buttons, cactus			
	Amphetamine variants	2,5-DMA, PMA, STP, MDA, MDMA, TMA, DOM, DOB		Unknown	
	Phencyclidine	PCP, angel dust, hog	Veterinary anesthetic	Degree unknown	High
	Phencyclidine analogues	PCE, PCPy, TCP	None		
	Other hallucinogens	Bufotenine, Ibogaine, DMT, DET, psilocybin, psilocyn		None	Degree unknown
Cannabis	Marijuana	Pot, Acapulco gold, grass, reefer, sinsemilla, Thai sticks	Under investigation	Degree unknown	Moderate
	Tetrahydrocannabinol	THC			
	Hashish	Hash	None		
	Hashish oil	Hash oil			

related problems and to feel superior to them, but it did not offer a rational explanation of the problems or a basis for their treatment. Much the same can be said of mentalistic theories of drug abuse. The framers of these theories construe inappropriate drug-taking as a reflection of aberrant psychodynamic function, or of a personality disorder (e.g., Chein, Gerard, Lee, & Rosenfeld, 1964; Hill, Haertzen, & Glazer, 1960). A major weakness of such conceptions is a lack of agreement on what kinds of personality traits, or intrapsychic maladies, cause drug abuse. For example, Jaffee (1985) noted:

Table 11-8
(*Continued*)

Tolerance	Duration (in hours)	Methods of usual administration	Possible effects	Effects of overdose	Withdrawal syndrome
Yes	2–4	Oral, injected	increased pulse rate and blood pressure, insomnia, loss of appetite	hallucinations, convulsions, possible death	depression, disorientation
Yes	8–12	Oral	Illusions and hallucinations, poor perception of time and distance	Longer, more intense "trip" episodes, psychosis, possible death	Withdrawal syndrome not reported
	Variable	Oral, injected			
	Up to days	Smoked, oral, injected			
	Variable	Oral, injected, smoked, sniffed			
Yes	2–4	Smoked, oral	Euphoria, relaxed inhibitions, increased appetite, disoriented behavior	Fatigue, paranoia, possible psychosis	Insomnia, hyperactivity, and decreased appetite occasionally reported

aThe primary source of this information is *Drugs of Abuse*, published by the Drug Enforcement Administration, 1985.

Certain psychiatric diagnostic categories are regularly overrepresented among those who seek treatment for alcoholism and drug dependency. These include depressive disorders, anxiety disorders, and antisocial personality. . . . Despite these findings, no single recognized addictive personality or constellation of traits has been identified that is equally applicable to all varieties of compulsive drug users. Indeed, given the different pharmacological effects of various drugs, it would be surprising if all compulsive drug users were similar. (p. 540)

Even when a single drug is considered, abusers are relatively heterogeneous. For instance, a notion currently popular is that the character disorder termed *antisocial personality* (previously known as *sociopathy*) leads to alcoholism. But the majority of alcohol abusers do not meet the diagnostic criteria for antisocial personality. Moreover, it is not clear what causes the disorder, or how it could produce alcoholism.

Personality-based models of drug abuse lead attention away from the inappropriate drug-taking and drug-seeking behaviors that are the crux of all drug abuse, and they ignore the physical events that cause these behaviors to occur. An alternate model, that favored by behaviorists, posits that drug self-administration is an operant response, hence learned, and that it can be studied and explained in the same manner as other learned responses. At the heart of this position is the fact that self-administered drugs can function as positive reinforcers; they strengthen responses that lead to their delivery. That many abused drugs serve as powerful positive reinforcers has been demonstrated in laboratory studies with nonhuman subjects. In these studies, conditions are arranged so that a rat or monkey can self-administer the drug of interest when it emits an operant response such as a lever press. Over 100 compounds have been tested for whether they serve as positive reinforcers for nonhumans (Griffiths, Bigelow, & Henningfield, 1980). In general, there is good correspondence between those drugs that serve as positive reinforcers in nonhumans and those that are self-administered, and abused, by humans. Hallucinogenic compounds such as LSD, mescaline, and psilocybin are exceptions to this pattern. No data indicate that nonhumans will behave in ways leading to the delivery of these drugs; instead, behavior that prevents their delivery is strengthened. Of course, these relations may not obtain in all circumstances: LSD might well serve as a positive reinforcer for nonhumans given special, and as yet unspecifiable, training. It has been suggested that social variables, primarily the way in which a group reacts to drug taking by its members, are uniquely important in controlling humans' intake of hallucinogens. Such social variables are not manipulated in nonhuman studies.

Nonetheless, a variety of opiates, CNS depressants, stimulants, and other drugs maintain the drug taking of nonhumans in environments devoid of obvious predisposing factors. That is, rats and monkeys will take certain drugs without being stressed, food-deprived, provided with nondrug reinforcement, or treated in any unusual manner to learn drug self-administration. All that is needed is exposure to a situation in which a response leads to drug delivery. Given this exposure, the behavior leading to drug delivery occurs often, and high levels of intake result. For example, monkeys allowed to press a bar producing intravenous injections of morphine self-administer enough of the drug to produce physical dependence (Thompson & Schuster, 1964). Moreover, unless protective contingencies that limit drug intake are arranged, monkeys, under some conditions, self-administer enough morphine or *d*-amphetamine to kill themselves (Johanson, Balster, & Bonese, 1976).

Studies of drug self-administration by nonhumans are important for two reasons. First, by extrapolation, they provide information about the variables that control human drug use and abuse. Second, they indicate that many drugs can exercise powerful control over behavior in the absence of any obvious psychopathology. It does not appear reasonable to assume that the average rat or monkey is mentally ill or aberrant in personality, but they will nonetheless self-administer many drugs at high and harmful levels. All that is required is exposure to the drug under certain conditions.

As a rule, in humans and nonhumans alike, the same classes of variables that affect operant responses maintained by other reinforcers control drug-maintained behavior. These variables sometimes act to produce a pattern of self-administration that, in one way or another, constitutes a drug abuse problem.

Obviously, no one abuses a drug without having been exposed to it. If a drug is available, the initial decision to self-administer it and the early pattern of use depends on at least three factors: (1) the kind of rules concerning appropriate drug intake and expected drug effects given to or generated by the person; (2) the extent to which historical events favor following these rules; and (3) the degree to which current circumstances (i.e., contingencies of reinforcement and punishment) support or weaken drug taking. When first presented with the option of trying a drug, every person will have been given, or will have self-generated, rules concerning its proper use and likely effects. Consider a college sophomore to whom a date offers cocaine at a party, saying, "It's great stuff; no hangover. Try it." This isn't quite like Mom and Dad's rule: "Cocaine use is bad—it's an expensive road to ruin. Just say no." Which rule is followed—that is, whether or not cocaine is self-administered—depends on the sophomore's experience with respect to drugs and parents' versus dates' pronouncements, as well as the circumstances in which the drug is offered. If all the party goers are snorting cocaine and encouraging the novice to do so, the likelihood that the response will occur is increased.

The variables that are responsible for the maintenance of drug abuse often differ from those responsible for initial use. Many drugs that are not positively reinforcing on early exposure come to be so if self-administration continues. Cigarette smoking is a case in point. Early exposures to cigarettes are not in themselves positively reinforcing, but they may be repeated because of nonpharmacological reinforcers (e.g., peer approval) associated with the experience. With continued exposure, tolerance develops to certain unpleasant effects of smoking (e.g., nausea), and cigarette use may become positively reinforcing, largely because of the nicotine administered. Self-talk may also play a role in early drug administration, as when a young person positively evaluates his or her own smoking, perhaps saying, "Cigarette smoking is great; it makes me look cool and grown-up." Note that there is nothing capricious in how someone responds when first offered a drug; this behavior is a function of historical and concurrent variables that, although complex, act in lawful fashion.

Variables with orderly actions continue to control drug self-administration once a compound is serving as a positive reinforcer in and of itself. As operant behavior, drug seeking and drug taking come under the control of discriminative stimuli and establishing operations. Discriminative stimuli, which nearly always include individuals who have provided the drug in the past, are historically correlated with successful drug seeking, and their presence increases the likelihood that such behavior will occur given the momentary effectiveness of the drug as a reinforcer. One potent determinant of the reinforcing effectiveness of a given drug is the degree of drug deprivation, an establishing operation. The effects of deprivation are most apparent in physically dependent users. For them, drug blood levels fall as time passes without exposure to the drug, withdrawal symptoms ensue, and the value of the drug as a positive reinforcer grows. Changes in the level of the drug in the blood (i.e., relative deprivation) can also influence patterns of self-administration in the absence of physical dependence. Studies with rats and humans given limited access to cocaine show, for example, that typical subjects rapidly self-administer enough drug to reach a moderately high level of the drug in the blood, then space administrations so that this level is maintained. When constantly available, cocaine and similar stimulants are usually self-administered in a cyclic pattern in which periods of high drug intake alternate with periods of low intake, during which much time is spent eating and sleeping (Griffiths *et al.*, 1980). Other drugs are associated with different characteristic patterns of self-administration. Opioids, for example, when constantly available, are typically administered in increasing

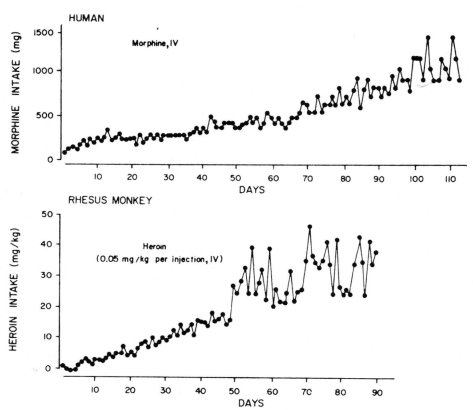

Figure 11-4. Similar patterns of opioid intake in a human and a rhesus monkey under conditions of continuous drug availability. Each graph shows the amount of drug taken over successive days. The human data are replotted from an experiment in which a volunteer with a history of drug abuse was permitted to self-regulate his intraveneous (IV) morphine intake (Wikler, 1952). The monkey data are from an unpublished study in which lever-press responses produced intraveneous injections of heroin. (From "Similarities in Animal and Human Drug-Taking Behavior" by R. R. Griffiths, G. E. Bigelow, & J. E. Henningfield, 1980, p. 17. Copyright 1980 by JAI Press. Reproduced by permission.)

quantities over a period of several weeks, after which a fairly stable level of intake is maintained. This pattern is evident in Figure 11-4, which shows morphine intake by a human and heroin intake by a rhesus monkey as a function of days of exposure.

Like other operant responses, drug-seeking and drug-taking behavior is controlled in part by the schedule of delivery. When the drug is scarce or expensive, much drug-seeking behavior may be required before drug delivery. For example, an average heroin user can easily self-administer $100 or $200 worth of the drug each day. Much of such a person's time is necessarily devoted to a long chain of drug-seeking behavior. For instance, theft, fencing stolen items, contacting a dealer, and preparing a fix may all precede drug injection. Although the effects of actual heroin use, including the possibility of accidental death by overdose, are troublesome, a significant part of the general heroin-abuse problem reflects the fact that the behavior required to obtain the drug cause trouble for society and the user.

As noted earlier, the nonpharmacological consequences of drug seeking and drug taking strongly affect these behaviors. In some instances, drug use provides access to valued objects or activities that would not otherwise be available. The seducer's maxim, "Flowers are good, but liquor is quicker," emphasizes that, in certain circles, drug (alcohol) use is associated with the increased likelihood of a particular kind of nonpharmacological reinforcer: sexual activity. Although this need not be the case, it sometimes is. Moreover, the *rule*, "alcohol + potential partner = sex," can foster drinking in a person for whom sexual activity is a potent reinforcer, even if the rule is untrue.

The pharmacological consequences of drug self-administration surely play a major role in the development and maintenance of abusive drug use. Remember that studies with nonhumans show beyond a reasonable doubt that many drugs are very potent reinforcers. Why, then, are such drugs not abused by all humans who come into contact with them? The general answer is straightforward: Environmental contingencies foster responsible use by many people. These contingencies, which are arranged by society at large, as well as by intimates of the drug user, involve short-term consequences of drug-seeking and drug-taking behaviors: nonabusive self-administration (or abstinence) is reinforced, and abusive self-administration is punished. In addition, rules describing appropriate drug use are provided, and voicing and following these rules are rewarded. Finally, concurrent behaviors incompatible with drug abuse are encouraged and reinforced. The contingencies that a group arranges to prevent abusive drug intake by its members are effective only to the extent that they involve consequences more powerful than those working to produce abusive self-administration.

Unfortunately, the reinforcing properties of a drug, coupled with a lack of contingencies sufficiently powerful to reduce drug use, sometimes lead to an abusive pattern of intake. As drug self-administration increases and progresses toward abuse, drug-related behaviors can weaken the contingencies that would otherwise discourage abusive intake. Envision a newly married coupled, one of them recently employed as a construction laborer. Neither has a drug abuse problem, but the newly hired spouse begins to stop regularly after work to have a few beers with fellow workers. At first, the stops use up little time or alcohol, for the reinforcers associated with home and spouse are preferred to those associated with bar and friends. As the days pass, however, the homebound mate wearies of waiting and begins to behave differently when the companion returns from work. No longer is dinner cooked nor are romantic evenings planned. Arguments, beginning with "Where the hell have you been?" become commonplace as the evening hour grows less pleasant for both partners. As the home environment becomes less rewarding, the bar grows relatively more so. Hence, more time is spent at the bar and more beer is drunk. This activity, in turn, further increases marital discord in a downward spiral that may well end in a drug abuse problem.

The scenario just described is oversimplified, but it does emphasize an important point: Drug-related behaviors may reduce an individual's access to other reinforcers and thereby increase the relative time and effort spent in drug seeking and drug taking. Moreover, at least some people who experience drug-related problems have never acquired a behavioral repertoire adequate for attaining any of a range of significant positive reinforcers, including those associated with a good job, a comfortable home, close friends, and satisfying lovers. In the absence of strong competing reinforcers, the relative power of drugs to control behavior is magnified immensely.

The foregoing discussion has emphasized that environmental variables play a major role in drug abuse. This should not be taken to mean that everyone is equally sensitive to these variables or is equally likely to develop drug-related problems. A substantial body of information suggests that genetic variables play a role in determining the risk that a person will develop drug-related problems, at least with respect to alcohol. Among the data suggesting such a relation are those from Danish and Swedish studies of adopted children of alcoholics (e.g., Bohman, 1978; Goodwin, Schulsinger, Mopller, Hermansen, Winokur, & Guze, 1973). These studies found that (1) adopted sons of alcoholics were significantly more likely than control subjects to develop drinking problems, but (2) sons of nonalcoholic biological parents raised by alcohol-abusing foster parents did not show elevated rates of alcohol abuse. Other correlational data further support the notion of a heritable predisposition to ethanol abuse. The mechanism of this predisposition is unclear. As Petrakis (1985) indicated in a review of the role of genetics in alcoholism:

> The studies described in preceding sections observed only a behavioral phenomenon—alcoholism—and provided strong evidence that it can have a genetic basis. But strictly speaking, behavior, as such, cannot be inherited. Only genes can, and the immediate products of genes are proteins. Behavioral characteristics arise from the genes and their products, but remotely, and furthermore they are strongly influenced by environment.
>
> It is therefore insufficient merely to say that the risk of the behavior pattern, alcoholism, is inherited and let it go at that. We need to know what *physical* characteristics people inherit that make them vulnerable to develop the alcoholic behavior pattern. Specifically, how do their anatomical, physiological, and biochemical systems differ from those of people who are not susceptible? And by what mechanisms do these differences become expressed as alcoholism? Such questions have more than theoretical importance; they can lead to discoveries that help us understand how alcoholism develops and devise better ways to treat and prevent it. Merely proving that alcoholism can have a genetic basis, and asking no further questions, gets us nowhere. (p. 18)

Further questions are being asked, and we may someday understand fully the biochemical and genetic basis of alcoholism and other forms of drug abuse, and we may then develop treatments that work at these levels. At the present time, however, there are no genetic treatments and few biochemical ones, but there are a multitude of interventions that involve some kind of manipulation of the client's environment.

Treating Drug Abuse

There are many approaches to the treatment of drug abuse. It is beyond our purpose to detail specific drug-abuse treatment-programs, or to consider their efficacy. Those programs that are consistent with the behavioral orientation are based on the assumption that drug abuse results in large part from exposure to a particular kind of environment, one in which contingencies support a troublesome pattern of drug self-administration. Altering these contingencies must therefore be a part of treatment.

Treatment characteristically begins with detoxification. **Detoxification** involves safely weaning a physically dependent person from a drug and can be accomplished easily with current technology (Jaffee, 1985). After an individual is detoxified, dramatic steps must be taken to alter the consequences of drug taking, so that abusive patterns of intake are not supported. How consequences should be changed to deal with a drug abuse problem depends on the kind of drug involved, the nature of the abuse problem, the circumstances of the abuser's life and the kind of contingency management they allow, and the person's overall behavioral repertoire. Abusive patterns of intake typically harm the user, but the harm is often much delayed beyond the time of drug intake. In contrast, the positively reinforcing effects of drug administration occur with little delay. Because delayed consequences have little direct effect on behavior, most behavioral approaches to the treatment of drug abuse attempt, in part, to arrange short-term consequences that weaken inappropriate drug use and that strengthen appropriate drug-related behavior. Effective treatment programs are also likely to teach appropriate rule-governed behavior concerning drugs. Moreover, training new responses appropriate to gaining nonpharmacological reinforcers may be necessary. Finally, conditioning factors in the client's daily environment that foster inappropriate drug use will probably have to be altered. These include aspects of the environment that increase drug taking by acting as discriminative stimuli and establishing operations, as well as nonpharmacological reinforcers associated with drug self-administration.

It is easy to eliminate inappropriate drug use in inpatient settings (Griffiths *et al.*, 1980). Like other operant behavior, drug self-administration is sensitive to punishment. For example, delivering shock or imposing a time-out dependent on drinking suppresses ethanol intake in a ward setting. Extinction, which can involve pharmacological blockade of a drug's effects or simple failure to deliver the drug, also reduces drug self-administration. Pairing the taste of a drug with nausea and vomiting in a conditioned taste-aversion procedure is also effective in reducing drug intake, and this procedure is sometimes used to treat cigarette smoking and ethanol abuse.

Although punishment, extinction, and taste-aversion conditioning are effective in reducing drug intake, the clinical utility of these procedures outside controlled settings is limited. None of these procedures produce permanent effects unless they are kept in effect; like all contingency management procedures, they affect behavior when they are operative and for a limited time thereafter. Once punishment or extinction ends, or the pairing of drug and nausea ceases, the behavior typically returns to pretreatment levels. Moreover, humans can discriminate conditions correlated with particular contingencies and behave accordingly. For instance, an alcohol abuser who is taking disulfiram (Antiabuse) as part of a treatment program may learn that drinking alcohol leads to sickness in the presence of disulfiram, but not in its absence. Sickness can be avoided by not drinking after taking disulfiram, or by not taking disulfiram before drinking. In the latter case, the client circumvents the intended treatment. Clients' avoiding therapeutic contingencies is a major problem in the outpatient treatment of drug abuse.

One tack that can be taken to increase the likelihood that clients will be exposed to therapeutic contingencies is to make these contingencies positively reinforcing. A study by McCaul, Stitzer, Bigelow, and Liebson (1984) provides a good example of the use of positive reinforcement in treating drug abuse. This investigation involved 20 male opiate abusers who were enrolled in an outpatient detoxification program in which methadone doses were gradually decreased over time. The contingency management treatment, which was arranged for 10 men (the experimental group), involved giving a patient $10 and a take-home methadone dose each time he produced an opiate-free urine specimen, as well as requiring him to participate in an intensive clinical procedure when an opiate was present in urine.

As shown in Figure 11-5, this treatment slowed the relapse to illicit opiate use relative to control subjects, who were paid for providing a urine sample regardless of its drug content. It should be noted that methadone was used in the McCaul *et al.* (1984) study to suppress withdrawal symptoms following the termination of illicit opiate use. This procedure should not be confused with chronic methadone-maintenance programs. By making an alternative opiate available dependent on appropriate behavior (e.g., appearing at the clinic on time), chronic methadone-maintenance programs are intended to reduce problems associated with procuring and administering heroin and similar opiates, which are both expensive and dangerous. As Jaffee (1985) indicated, "This treatment explicitly emphasizes law-abiding and productive behavior rather than abstinence per se, and its relative efficacy in reaching its goals is well documented" (p. 573). Although methadone maintenance programs are of recognized value, they do require chronic exposure to an opiate, a circumstance that is considered by many to be less than ideal.

Several other researchers have shown that contingency management procedures similar to those used by McCaul *et al.* (1984) are effective in reducing abusive drug intake. **Contingency contracting,** in which a therapist and a client formally agree that specified patterns of drug-related behavior (e.g., abstinence for a one-week period) will lead to particular consequences, has, for example, been demonstrated to be effective in reducing cigarette smoking, excessive caf-

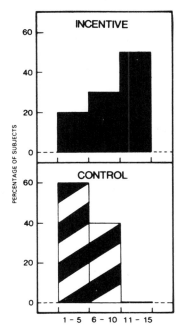

Figure 11-5. The longest opiate-free period achieved by patients in experimental and control groups, expressed as the number of consecutive opiate-free urine specimens. Patients provided two specimens per week during the 10-week intervention period; thus, they could achieve a maximum of 20 consecutive opiate-free specimens. Patients in the experimental group received money and methadone contingent on producing an opiate-free specimen; control patients did not. (From "Contingency Management Interventions: Effects on Treatment Outcome during Methadone Detoxification" by M. E. McCaul, M. E. Stitzer, G. E. Bigelow, & I. A. Liebson, 1984, *Journal of Applied Behavior Analysis, 17,* 40. Copyright 1984 by the Society for the Experimental Analysis of Behavior. Reproduced by permission.)

feine intake, cocaine intake, alcohol consumption, and, as shown in Figure 11-6, barbiturate use by inpatient sedative abusers.

Numerous other examples of the use of behavioral procedures to treat abusive drug intake are available (e.g., Harris, 1981). On balance, it is clear that altering the consequences of drug-related behaviors is an effective method for treating drug abuse in a variety of situations. The primary shortcoming of such procedures is that it is often difficult to arrange the environment so that appropriate consequences will occur. Although this can be done within a treatment facility, the client's return to his or her normal environment too often results in exposure to the same contingencies that originally produced the drug abuse, which reappears as a result of their actions.

A compelling example of the importance of the posttreatment environment in the reinstatement of drug abuse involves American military personnel who returned from Vietnam with a heroin abuse problem. After treatment and return

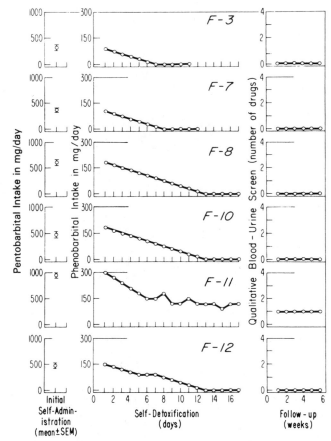

Figure 11-6. The effects of contingency contracting on the drug intake of six subjects with confirmed histories of sedative abuse. Graphs along the left side indicate levels of pentobarbital intake per day before treatment. At the start of detoxification, phenobarbital was substituted for pentobarbital (15 mg phenobarbital for 50 mg pentobarbital) for 3 days of self-administration. Subjects were then given points (exchangeable for a variety of reinforcers) for successfully reducing drug intake and lost points for failing to do so. Five of the six subjects met the requirements of the contract and became drug-free. Follow-up data (right panels) indicate that these patients had not returned to drug use 2 months after detoxification. (From "A Behavioral Program for Treatment of Drug Dependence" by R. Pickens, 1979, p. 50. Reproduced by permission.)

to their home country, the vast majority did not return to heroin abuse (Robins, 1974). The reason was that the environmental variables that had fostered abuse in Vietnam were not present in the posttreatment situation.

Study Questions

1. Name and give an example of each general category of troublesome behavior.

2. Causes of human behavior can be considered at three levels. What are the levels?

3. Distinguish between psychoses and neuroses.

4. Read the description of the John Hinckley case. What is the point regarding the differences in testimony of the defense and prosecution psychiatrists?

5. In what sense is psychiatric diagnosis a descriptive, not a prescriptive, process?

6. Name and describe three kinds of schizophrenia. Describe the explanatory model based on dopamine.

7. Is schizophrenia heritable? What is the evidence supporting your answer?

8. Briefly trace the history of the treatment of mental disorders. Include the following time frames: pre-Christianity, Christianity, the early 20th century, and the 1950s, when drug therapies were introduced.

9. Name four variables that influence the selection of an intervention.

10. What are the three elements that must be considered in the design of a token economy?

11. Name two treatment strategies that have reduced undesirable behavior exhibited by schizophrenics.

12. Many theories have been proposed to explain depression. Explain the four that are discussed (one is based on the lack of action of particular neurons, the second was suggested by behaviorists, the third is associated with learned-helplessness experiments, and the last is characterized by distorted covert verbal behavior).

13. What are the two primary treatments for managing depression?

14. What are the three behavioral components of anxiety? Is anxiety a thing? If not, what is it?

15. Explain how a phobia might arise through the process of respondent conditioning. How might a phobia persist over years?

16. Explain the three elements of systematic desensitization.

17. Read carefully the definition of mental retardation. Briefly explain each characteristic, including how it is assessed.

18. Name four causes of mental retardation. Is there an identifiable cause for the majority of cases?

19. Procedures derived from behavior analysis have been successfully used to treat inappropriate behavior exhibited by mentally retarded persons. Two applications of such procedures are presented. Describe one of them.

20. What three factors contributed to the increase in the use of opiates in the 1880s?

21. Many laws have been passed in an effort to limit the abuse of a variety of drugs. One such law was the Volstead Act. Explain the act and how it came to be repealed.

22. Cite some statistics that indicate that drug use is a problem.

23. What is the Comprehensive Drug Use Prevention and Control Act of 1970?

24. Personality-based models are sometimes used to explain drug abuse. Give an example. What are the weaknesses of such a model? What is the model most favored by behaviorists?

25. Why are studies of self-administration in nonhumans important?

26. What three factors can affect the initial decision to self-administer drugs? What variables can maintain drug use?

27. Self-administration of drugs can provide a variety of reinforcers. Why is it, then, that drugs are not abused by all humans who contact them?

28. Drug use can restrict the availability of a range of reinforcers, a process that, in turn, encourages more and more drug use. Give an example of this process.

29. Is alcoholism heritable? What is the evidence?

30. Discuss some elements involved in a behavioral treatment of drug abuse.

Recommended Readings

American Psychiatric Association. (1987). *Diagnostic and Statistical Manual of Mental Disorders* (3rd ed., rev.). Washington, DC: Author.

This standard reference book describes the nosological system currently used by many psychiatrists and clinical psychologists. Many people are interested in how people assigned a particular diagnostic label generally behave, and this information is available in the DSM-III-R.

Doleys, D. M., Meredith, R. L., & Ciminero, A. R. (1982). *Behavioral medicine: Assessment and Treatment Strategies.* New York: Plenum Press.

It is beyond debate that behavior plays a major role in the prevention and management of a variety of health problems, including drug abuse, sexual disorders, hypertensions, and eating disorders. This book provides expert coverage of many of the procedures commonly used to assess and treat patients with a wide range of health-related behavior problems.

Turner, S. M., Calhoun, K. S., & Adams, H. E. (1981). *Handbook of Clinical Behavior Therapy.* New York: Wiley.

This volume provides a good overview of the use of behavioral procedures to assess and treat a wide range of clinical conditions in adults and children. Many of the chapters provide reviews of research published in *Behaviour Research and Therapy, Behavior Therapy, Journal of Behavior Therapy and Experimental Psychiatry, Journal of Applied Behavior Analysis,* and *Behavior Modification.* These journals themselves are excellent sources of current information concerning clinical interventions.

CHAPTER 12

Applications of Behavioral Psychology

The field of psychology comprises many approaches to studying and explaining behavior, each with its own merits and shortcomings. One important characteristic of each approach is its usefulness in dealing with problems. Providing useful strategies for solving problems is one of the major strengths of behavioral psychology. The purpose of the present chapter is to give an overview of the practical applications of behavioral psychology. Several different applications are considered, but no attempt is made to review all of the research in a given area, or to consider the complex issues necessarily raised when psychologists attempt to solve behavioral problems.

Regardless of the problem at hand, applications of behavioral psychology are characterized by three features. First, actual behaviors that have some social significance, such as littering, electricity use, or worker productivity, are the focus of change. Moreover, some quantifiable feature of behavior is examined, such as gallons of gasoline consumed, minutes spent studying, or number of self-deprecating statements uttered. Second, events with real physical status, including both antecedent stimuli and consequences of behavior, are manipulated to change behavior. And third, researchers usually (but not always) arrange conditions so that changes in behavior can be attributed with confidence to the variable manipulated in a study. These characteristics appear to be largely responsible for the success of behavioral interventions.

Community and Environmental Problems

Human communities face many problems, some of which bear on their very survival. As this is written, the United States is struggling with the effects of severe drought. In the early 1970s, many Western nations were confronted with severe energy shortages as a result of the Arab oil embargo. Overuses of water and oil are among the problems studied by behavioral psychologists. Others that are considered here are littering, failure to use seat belts, failure to remove safety hazards from the home, and criminal activity.

Reducing Energy Use

That our energy sources are not limitless is now widely accepted. This fact has become part of the national scene as a result of shortages of resources such as gasoline and oil. One solution is to increase production; another is to encourage **conservation,** which is the approach taken by many researchers. For example, Foxx and Schaeffer (1981) attempted to decrease **gasoline consumption.** In a baseline condition,[1] the number of miles driven each day by two groups of employees was recorded. One group was then exposed to a lottery system. In the lottery, employees who reduced the number of miles they drove in a given week received lottery tickets; more tickets were given for larger reductions in the number of miles driven. A winning ticket was drawn each week, and the winner received up to $12. Employees who reduced the number of miles they drove in four consecutive weeks were eligible for a grand lottery, the winner of which earned $41. This condition was followed by another baseline period in which the lottery was discontinued. The number of miles driven and number of gallons of gasoline used were lower when the lottery was in effect than during the baseline conditions.

Many studies have investigated ways to reduce **electricity consumption.** For example, Hayes and Cone (1981) gave consumers information each month that specified whether they had consumed more or less electricity than the previous month and the amount of money lost or saved. The monthly "feedback" reduced electricity use by 4.7% at a savings of approximately $4 per month for each subject.

Other researchers have investigated **peaking,** which is high electricity use during particular times of the day (e.g., 7 to 9 A.M. and 4 to 7 P.M.). Peaking is a problem because auxiliary power generators must be activated during peak times; the use of the extra generators increases costs and stresses the production system. In an attempt to reduce peaking, Kohlenberg, Phillips, and Proctor (1976) installed in several houses a feedback light that was illuminated when electricity use in a 12-minute period exceeded a particular peak level. As depicted in Figure 12-1, this feedback procedure produced small reductions in peaking, which was defined as energy consumption above the peak level. The authors then combined the feedback with an incentive plan in which subjects could earn money for reducing peaking, and this combination reduced peaking more than feedback alone.

Littering

Littering is unsightly and is expensive to control. Recognizing this, Kohlenberg and Phillips (1973) developed a way to encourage people to deposit their litter. In this study, subjects who deposited litter in a trash receptacle received,

---

[1]Baseline is a condition in which the independent variable of interest is not present. Behavior during baseline is compared with that during the treatment condition (i.e., the condition in which the independent variable is present). One may make useful comparisons between the two conditions by ordering them in one of many experimental designs.

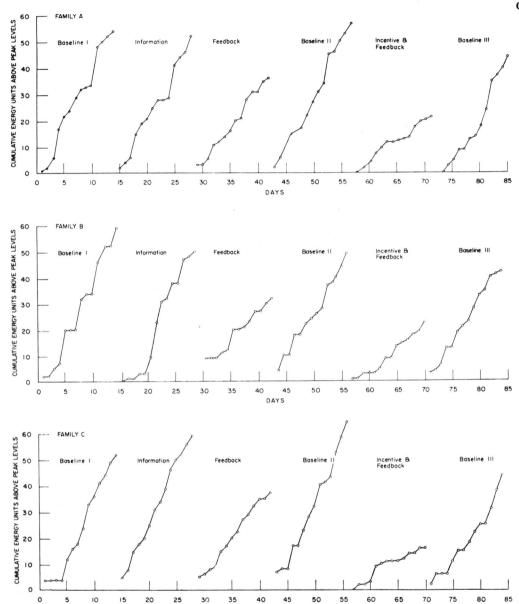

Figure 12-1. The cumulative number of energy units above peak levels in each experimental condition. (From "A Behavioral Analysis of Peaking in Residential Electrical-Energy Consumers" by R. Kohlenberg, T. Phillips, & W. Proctor, *Journal of Applied Behavior Analysis*, 1976, *9*, 17. Copyright 1976 by the Society for the Experimental Analysis of Behavior, Inc. Reproduced by permission.)

occasionally, a ticket exchangeable for a soft drink. This procedure substantially increased litter deposits compared to conditions in which the tickets were not given.

Other researchers have studied ways to encourage litter removal. For example, Powers, Osborne, and Anderson (1973) provided plastic garbage bags to park visitors, and visitors who filled the bag chose either a $0.25 reward or a chance to win a $20 lottery. This procedure increased the number of litter bags deposited and decreased litter on the park grounds compared to when the reward and lottery system were not in effect. Taken together, the above studies show that people can be induced with incentives to deposit their own litter and pick up that of others.

Safety Hazards in the Home

Safety is an important consideration for all communities. Accidental injury is costly in terms of dollars and the time of health care providers, as well as lost

Littering is a behavioral problem. Can we teach people to properly dispose of their trash?

productivity and wages. Safety hazards in the home were investigated in one study (Tertinger, Greene, & Lutzker, 1984). The presence in each home of many hazards, such as firearms, poisons, and accessible electrical outlets, was recorded. Parents were given information about how to eliminate hazards, feedback on the particular hazards in their own homes, and suggestions for improvements. After receiving the information and the feedback, all parents reduced the hazards in their home, some by more than 50%.

Safety in the Dental Office

Greene and Neistat (1983) studied ways to increase the use of lead shields (aprons) during X-ray examinations in dentists' offices (unshielded exposure to X rays may increase the risk of cancer). First, the authors instituted a baseline condition in which the percentage of patients provided with lead aprons during X-ray exams was tallied for each of eight dental offices. Then, offices that provided aprons less than 75% of the time received information concerning the effects of low-level radiation, a request to use lead aprons, stickers to remind office personnel to use aprons, and feedback that informed the office of how often lead aprons had been used in baseline. The information and feedback increased apron use to almost 100%, which, for most offices, was maintained nine months later.

Crime

Crime reduction was studied by Schnelle, Kirchner, Maerae, McNees, Eck, Snodgrass, Casey, and Uselton (1978). The number of burglary reports was recorded in a section of a major U.S. city. In one condition, police cars were used

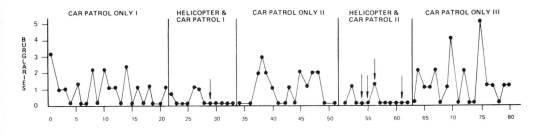

DAYS

Figure 12-2. The daily number of home burglaries in each experimental condition. Arrows indicate the days on which the helicopter did not fly. (From "Police Evaluation Research: An Experimental and Cost-Benefit Analysis of a Helicopter Patrol in a High Crime Area" by J. F. Schnelle, R. E. Kirchner, J. W. Macrae, M. P. McNees, R. H. Eck, S. Snodgrass, J. D. Casey, & P. H. Uselton, *Journal of Applied Behavior Analysis*, 1978, *11*, 15. Copyright 1978 by the Society for the Experimental Analysis of Behavior. Reproduced by permission.)

in normal patrols. In another condition, a helicopter also patrolled the area between the hours of 9 A.M. and 5 P.M.; the number of burglaries reported decreased from approximately 1 per day to 0.33 per day (see Figure 12-2). The authors noted that burglary rates in other sections of the city did not increase, a finding suggesting that the burglars did not merely shift the focus of their activity. Moreover, the benefits of the helicopter patrols (e.g., fewer burglaries and a reduction in property loss) outweighed the costs of the patrols (e.g., motor overhauls and helicopter fuel and oil). Thus, the patrols not only decreased crime but also saved money.

Unemployment

Unemployment is a problem that affects both workers and their family. Azrin, Flores, and Kaplan (1975) designed a program to teach out-of-work persons how to obtain a job. In this program, the subjects learned skills such as dressing, grooming, filling out applications and résumés, obtaining job leads, and appropriate behavior in a job interview. Some skills were rehearsed in role-playing exercises. There was a significant increase in the percentage of clients who obtained jobs over the percentage of jobs obtained by a control group who did not participate in the program.

The foregoing discussion of community applications is by no means exhaustive. There have been many other applications to problems such as lawn trampling, seat belt use, and the use of public transportation. But one thing is clear: The procedures described here, such as incentives and feedback, can improve community life in many ways.

Business and Industry

Although many Americans take great pride in our capacity to produce and distribute goods, our skills in this area have recently been questioned: Many businesses have moved overseas in search of cheaper labor, the quality of American goods has become suspect, and even the productivity of the vaunted American worker has been doubted. These developments, as well as competitive pressures at home and abroad, require that workers be as productive and efficient as possible. Thus, a worthwhile goal is to minimize tardiness, absenteeism, and accidents, while maximizing productivity and efficiency.

Worker Tardiness and Absenteeism

Hermann, deMontes, Dominguez, Montes, and Hopkins (1973) attempted to decrease worker **tardiness** in a manufacturing plant. Six employees each received a slip of paper when they arrived at work on time. Each slip could be cashed in for 16 cents at the end of the week. These "bonus" payments decreased tardiness from about 15% to 2%–3%. A group of employees who were not exposed to the bonus plan did not show reductions in tardiness. The authors suggested that the procedure was effective because it provided a more immediate consequence for punctuality than the system previously used at the plant. Under that system, the bonus for arriving on time was not delivered until the end of each year. Tardiness has also been decreased by self-monitoring, in which a worker is required to record the time of her or his arrival at and departure from work (Lamal & Benfield, 1978). The results were that the average arrival time changed from 10:45 A.M. during baseline to 8:15 A.M. during the self-monitoring condition.

Other researchers have attempted to decrease **absenteeism.** For example, Orpen (1976) worked with a group of employees at a fabric and garment factory. Baseline recording showed that the employees were absent 3.94% of the time. During the intervention, when an employee attended work he or she received a slip of paper. Each worker who attended work all five days of the week could then cash in the slips for a 50-cent bonus at the end of the week. The procedure was discontinued and then reintroduced at a later time. When the bonus system was in effect, absenteeism was significantly reduced, in some conditions by almost 50%. A control group that did not receive bonuses showed no such improvement. The authors noted that the success of the bonus plan may have resulted because the bonuses were given weekly; the plan that had been used previously, which was ineffective, gave bonuses only at the of the year.

Nonmonetary interventions for decreasing absenteeism were investigated by Kempen and Hall (1977) at two Western Electric plants. The authors implemented an attendance management system (AMS), which included a sequence of disciplinary procedures and incentives such as time off and not having to punch the time clock. The AMS procedure reduced absenteeism from 6.2% to under 3.4% in one plant, and from 7.8% to 6.7% in the other. Other plants, without the AMS, showed no comparable decrease in absenteeism.

Worker Productivity

Assuming that workers consistently arrive at work and do so on time, does this mean that they will be productive? No; we have all observed uninterested, unproductive, and malcontent employees. Fortunately, there are ways to increase **productivity.** For example, Anderson, Crowell, Sucec, Gilligan, and Wikoff (1982) attempted to increase the number of clients contacted by real-estate agents. The agents recorded and posted their client contacts, among other information, during an initial baseline period. A token system was then added. In this procedure, agents received tokens, or credits, for a particular number of client contacts. Credits could be exchanged for any of 60 items (e.g., gasoline or a pool table). The program was then withdrawn and was later reinstated. The number of client contacts, as well as the volume of sales, increased dramatically during the credit system.

The study just discussed showed that work output can be increased by behavioral procedures. It is possible, though, for workers to increase their output and still be inefficient. Thus, a worthy goal may be to increase **efficiency,** or the output per unit of time. Wikoff, Anderson, and Crowell (1982) studied efficiency in seven departments of a furniture manufacturing plant. Work efficiency (i.e., obtained output as a percentage of a standard) was measured in a baseline period. The workers in each department then received daily efficiency scores, which were also posted on a bulletin board. The efficiency scores increased in six of the seven departments during the feedback condition. In fact, the scores in some departments approached 100%. After the feedback condition, four departments were exposed to another procedure, in which the workers received, in addition to feedback, praise for improving their efficiency scores or for reaching or exceeding 100% efficiency. Of the four departments, two showed large increases in efficiency during the feedback condition; the other two showed somewhat smaller increases. At the conclusion of the study, the average plant efficiency was 92%, compared to 85% during baseline. Moreover, in the feedback-plus-praise condition, the company obtained an additional 800 hours per week of work without increased costs.

Worker Safety

Another important issue for business is safety. Although most businesses try to increase productivity and efficiency, few will accept safety hazards as a "cost of doing business." Sulzer-Azaroff and Santamaria (1980) investigated a method for decreasing industrial hazards (e.g., hazardous materials and the inappropriate storage of such materials). Workers were exposed to a procedure, implemented semiweekly, that included providing information concerning the number of hazards and their location, suggestions for improvement, and praise for reducing the hazards. This procedure substantially decreased the number of hazards.

Phone Use

Lest the reader assume that behavioral procedures are effective only on a small scale involving small amounts of money, communitywide studies have also been implemented. McSweeny (1978) reported the effects of charges for local directory-assistance calls imposed by Cincinnati Bell Telephone. When the charges were implemented, the calls decreased from 80,000 per day to 20,000 per day, and the number of long-distance directory-assistance calls, which were not subject to changes, remained unchanged (see Figure 12-3). Each consumer saved from $0.65 to $1.25 per month, which, because over 1 million consumers live in Cincinnati, involved significant amounts of money. In another study, Emory Air Freight implemented a feedback and reward system to increase the efficient use of freight containers (At Emory Freight, 1973). The system saved the company about $500,000 in the first year and $2 million over a three-year period.

Clinical Applications

For decades, psychologists have searched for ways to treat problems such as depression, anxiety, sexual dysfunction, and obsessions. Many of these prob-

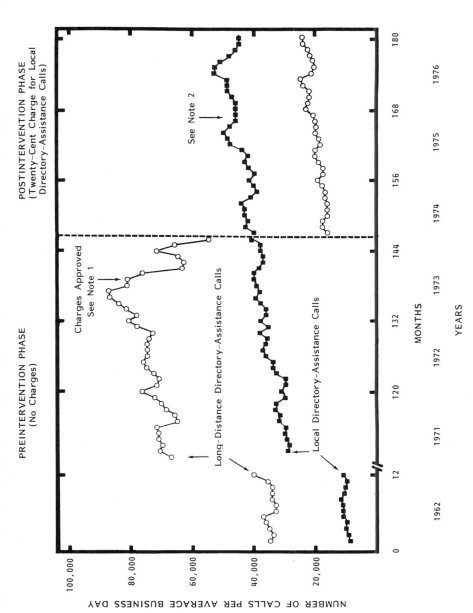

Figure 12-3. The average number of directory-assistance calls per day in the preintervention phase, when no charges were imposed, and in the postintervention phase, when a 20-cent charge was imposed for each local directory-assistance call. Note 1: Charges for local directory-assistance charges were approved by the Ohio Utilities Commission on August 19, 1973. Note 2: Long-distance directory-assistance calls from another city were added to Cincinnati Bell's area; this city averaged 3,000 calls per day. (From "Effects of Response Cost on the Behavior of a Million Persons" by A. J. McSweeney, *Journal of Applied Behavior Analysis*, 1978, *11*, 49. Copyright 1978 by the Society for the Experimental Analysis of Behavior. Reproduced by permission.)

lems are disabling: consider a phobic who is unable to leave his or her own home
or a depressed person who cannot hold a job or maintain friendships. Fortunately, there are effective treatments for many of these problems.

Anxiety Disorders and Phobias

Anxiety disorders, which are characterized by restlessness, muscle tension,
shortness of breath, dizziness, and, frequently, impairment of social and occupational functioning, were introduced in Chapter 11. There are many treatments
for anxiety that are based on behavioral principles. One such treatment is relaxation, in which the person learns to relax when she or he becomes anxious or is in
situations that often evoke anxiety. Rimm and Masters (1979) suggested that
"The most basic premise is that muscle tension is in some way related to anxiety,
and that an individual will experience a very marked and comforting reduction
in felt anxiety if tense muscles can be made loose and flaccid" (p. 35). With the
help of a therapist, clients typically learn to relax various body parts (e.g.,
hands, biceps, shoulders, forehead, thighs, calves, and feet), after which the
client may learn to relax on his or her own.

Relaxation is also often involved in the treatment of **phobias** (see Chapter
11), which involve anxiety, fear, and avoidance reactions to a particular object or
situation. In one form of treatment, called *desensitization,* the client learns to relax
while imagining the feared object or situation, or while actually being exposed
to it (see Chapter 11 for details).

Depression

Effective behaviorally based treatments of depression have been reported.
An important component of many behavioral approaches is the contention that
depression results from a sudden and dramatic decrease in positive reinforcement (Lewinsohn, 1975), perhaps because of the loss of a loved one, a job, or a
home. As a result, the person is sad, pessimistic, and generally inactive. Hersen,
Eisler, Alford, and Agras (1973) studied ways to increase activity level, in the
hope that, by virtue of increased activity, the depressed person would obtain
much-needed reinforcement. The depressive behavior of three clients was first
assessed in a baseline condition. In this condition, the clients received blue index
cards for completing tasks (e.g., work and personal hygiene), and reward activities were delivered independent of their performance. In the treatment condition, the rewards were dependent on the number of cards the clients earned.
When the reward activities depended on performance, there was an increase in
the number of tasks completed and a corresponding decrease in depressive
behaviors. The authors suggested that the card system increased opportunities
for the reinforcement of social (i.e., "nondepressive") behavior.

Other researchers who assume that depressed people experience a lack of
reinforcement have taken a different tack by teaching depressed clients how to
obtain social reinforcers. For instance, Hersen, Bellack, and Himmelhoch (1980)
identified clients' deficits in interactions with family and friends, with strangers,

and at work. Particular situations were then identified that caused trouble for each client. Through instructions, role-playing, feedback, and reinforcement from the therapist, the clients learned to obtain social reinforcement in these situations. The results showed decreases in depression, as measured by both rating scales and self-report inventories.

Hysteria

Hysteria, a loss or alteration of physical functioning without an organic cause, was made famous by Freud's pioneering work. The condition has not gone unnoticed by behaviorists. Hersen, Gullick, Matherne, and Harbert (1972) treated a man who, after a minor fall, was unable to walk, sit, or stand, and who complained of pain in his lower back and limbs. After ruling out physical damage, the authors instituted a reinforcement system in which walking was prompted and praised by a therapist. There was a rapid and large increase in the number of steps the client took per day, as well as a corresponding decrease in the number of requests for assistance. By the end of the study, the man was walking normally. Related behavioral interventions have been used to treat similar disorders, such as hysterical blindness (Parry-Jones, Sauter-Westrate, & Crawley, 1970) and vomiting (Alford, Blanchard, & Buckley, 1972).

Posttraumatic Stress Disorder

Victims or observers of a violent act, such as war veterans or rape victims, sometimes manifest a posttraumatic stress disorder (PTSD). The sufferers experience dreams, flashbacks, or other intrusive recollections that are related to the event; they also avoid stimuli associated with the event and exhibit other distressful behaviors such as insomnia, hypervigilance, outbursts of anger, and anxiety reactions to stimuli associated with the event (APA, 1987). According to many therapists, PTSD results from a respondent conditioning process in which trauma is paired with other stimuli. Keane, Zimmering, and Caddell (1985) suggested that

> humans exposed to a life threatening experience can become conditioned to a wide assortment of stimuli present during the trauma. For example, sounds, smells, terrain, time of day, the people present, and even cognitions can become conditioned to the traumatic event. Thus, each stimulus can evoke anxiety responses similar to those experienced during the event. (p. 10)

A treatment for this syndrome, which gained notoriety by publicity associated with the Vietnam war, was reported by Fairbank and Keane (1982). They treated a Vietnam veteran who reported anxiety and depression as a result of recurring nightmares about and flashbacks to combat experiences. The treatment was an **imaginal flooding** procedure in which the man repeatedly imagined the combat scenes and then imagined a positive, relaxing scene. When a particular scene was involved in treatment, there was a decrease in self-reported anxiety when he imagined that combat scene (see Figure 12-4), and there was a corresponding decrease in nightmares and flashbacks. Fairbank and Brown

(1987) suggested that such treatment procedures involve respondent extinction (see Chapter 6), in which the troublesome stimuli (CSs) are presented without the traumatic events (USs) until they no longer evoke distress and anxiety. Moreover, repeated presentation of the CSs also decreases their aversiveness and thereby decreases behavior that avoids these stimuli.

Obsessive-Compulsive Disorders

A form of flooding has also been used to treat obsessive-compulsive disorders, which involve repetitive thoughts and ritualized behavior to the extent that social and occupational functioning is impaired. The behavior is thought by some to allow the sufferer to avoid high-anxiety stimuli, such as contact with an object that the patient believes to be "contaminated." In treatment, the patient actually contacts the stimuli or perhaps only imagines them; such exposure to

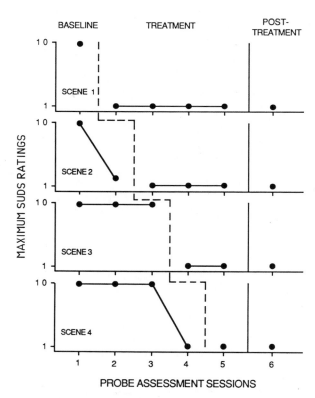

Figure 12-4. The maximum SUDS ratings in probe sessions during baseline, treatment, and posttreatment conditions. SUDS are subjective units of distress reported by the subject. (From "Flooding for Combat-Related Stress Disorders: Assessment of Anxiety Reduction across Traumatic Memories" by J. A. Fairbank & T. M. Keane, *Behavior Therapy*, 1982, *13*, 503. Copyright 1982 by Association for Advancement of Behavior Therapy. Reprinted by permission of the publisher and the authors.)

the stimuli continues until there is a "reported dimunition of anxiety to a relatively comfortable level" (Meredith & Milby, 1980, p. 45). Again, exposure to the stimuli decreases their aversiveness, and the excessive avoidance behavior decreases.

Another technique for decreasing obsessive-compulsive behavior is **contingency contracting,** used by Stern and Marks (1975) to treat a woman who incessantly checked and rechecked switches and gas taps in the house. The woman and her husband first identified behavioral goals for each other; for example, one goal for the woman was to complete more housework. When the goals were met, the partner provided particular rewards. The result was that, according to the husband's assessment, the housework was completed more often and the repetitive behavior decreased.

Marital Discord

Although not characterized by any particular bizarre behavior, marital discord is troublesome for many couples and families. Jacobsen and Margolin (1979) suggested that discord is largely a function of the low frequency of reinforcement delivered by each partner, which can arise from deficits in a wide range of skills. As a solution, many clients learn communication skills such as empathy and listening skills, assertiveness, and the expression of displeasure with the partner. To teach these skills, the therapist gives feedback concerning the couple's behavior, models or coaches more appropriate behavior, and sets up behavioral rehearsal sessions in which the couple practice the new skills.

Another important element in marital therapy is problem-solving training, in which clients learn to state problems, identify a solution, and implement the solution. A contingency contract is often the vehicle. A sample contract, from Jacobson and Margolin (1979), is shown below.

CONTRACT A
Wife agrees to stay home on as many nights as possible.
Reward: Husband will wash dishes and give baths to the children on all nights when wife is home.

CONTRACT B
Husband agrees to go out with wife on at least two week nights, although he can choose which nights.
Reward: Sex games of his choice, one for each week night he accompanies her. (p. 274)

The reader should recognize that the contract has the hallmarks of the behavioral approach, that is, a focus on specific behaviors and a manipulation of environmental variables.

Multiple Personalities

Kohlenberg (1973) studied an institutionalized patient who was thought to have multiple personalities. He characterized the personalities as "high" (e.g., rapid speech and movements, antisocial behavior, and "speaking" to deceased relatives), "middle," (e.g., socially appropriate behavior), and "low" (e.g., low-pitched voice, speaking of world destruction, and depression). During baseline, the patient was daily asked a series of questions, such as "How old are you?" "What is the date today?" and "Why are you in the hospital?" The answers were scored as being consistent with one of the three personalities. During a treatment phase, answers consistent with the "middle" personality were followed by tokens exchangeable for various activities. The token system increased the answers indicative of the "middle" personality and decreased those indicative of the other two personalities. A treatment program was then designed in which other behaviors indicative of the "middle" personality were reinforced. All other behaviors were ignored. This program was successful, and the patient was eventually discharged. These results suggest that the consequences of bizarre behavior and those of appropriate behavior may determine which pattern will occur. As Kohlenberg (1973) noted:

> The data clearly indicate that the relative frequency of occurrence of each type of repertoire is a function of the consequence attached to personality types. Thus it would appear to be more useful to consider multiple personality as a function of the consequence of multiple personality type behavior. (p. 139)

Behavioral Medicine

With the increasing concern about health and fitness, psychologists have become interested in problems such as eating disorders, chronic pain, hypertension, and smoking. Many such problems are life-threatening; consider the teenage girl with anorexia nervosa who is literally starving herself to death, or the smoker who is unable to stop smoking even while developing symptoms of emphysema. The focus on treating disease and disease-related behaviors through applications of behavioral principles defines the field of behavioral medicine (Doleys, Meredith, & Ciminero, 1982).

Obesity

Therapists often use behavioral procedures to treat **eating disorders,** including obesity. Stunkard (1979) described a weight-loss program that was developed at the University of Pennsylvania. To provide a complete description of the target behaviors, the clients record all eating behaviors and the time and place that they occur. Because eating occurs in many situations, the clients are asked to narrow the range of situations by eating in only one location and with one table setting. They also learn to limit the high-calorie food kept in the house, to eat slower, and to enjoy more fully the food that they do consume. A system of rewards is arranged in an effort to engender long-lasting changes in eating. Clients receive points for both particular behaviors (e.g., record keeping) and weight loss, and then they exchange the points for other rewards, such as preferred activities. Other weight-loss programs have added other elements, such as exercise and nutrition programs (Agras, 1987). In general, behavioral programs have produced substantial weight loss in many studies (e.g., Wollersheim, 1970).

Many behaviors have potentially adverse health-related consequences. Playing pool does not, but much that commonly goes on in a bar, including smoking and drinking, may. (Photo courtesy of Sue Keller.)

One problem in many weight-loss programs is that the clients sometimes drop out of the program. Contingency contracts, in which clients turn over to the therapist money or valuables that are then earned back, may be helpful in keeping clients from dropping out. The use of such contracts appears to contribute to the relatively low dropout rate characteristic of behavioral weight-loss programs (Stunkard, 1979).

Anorexia Nervosa

A second eating disorder, anorexia nervosa, is characterized by a reduction in food intake resulting in at least a 15% weight loss, fear of gaining weight, and disruption of the menstrual cycle in women. Sufferers usually report that they "feel fat," even though their weight loss is substantial; moreover, other symptoms appear, such as bradychardia (slowing of the heartbeat), hypotension, and vomiting (often self-induced). The disorder results in death in 5%–10% of all cases (APA, 1987).

Pentschuk, Edwards, and Pomerleau (1978) treated anorectic patients by means of a behavioral contract. In the contract, the patients were given access to ward privileges contingent on a weight gain of 0.5 pounds for a given day. The result was a median weight gain of 0.71 lb per day over a 13-day period. The subjects were then discharged, and follow-up contacts showed that most of them maintained or even continued to gain weight under a follow-up condition that included a family-enforced behavioral contract.

Bulimia Nervosa

Bulimia nervosa is a condition related to anorexia nervosa. Bulimia is characterized by frequent episodes of binge eating followed by "purging," such as self-induced vomiting or the use of laxatives or diuretics. Agras (1987) wrote, "It is widely agreed that dieting leads to a tendency to binge on sweet foods, and that in turn, binge eating leads to weight gain and hence purging in an attempt to reinstate control over weight and body shape" (p. 61). Thus, the disorder is characterized by repeated binge–purge cycles. The bulimic patient, although not suffering from extreme weight loss, is nonetheless at risk of other complications, such as heart arrythmias, damage to the teeth, electrolyte imbalance, and dehydration. One study of college-aged people reported that 4.5% of women and 0.4% of the men admitted to episodes of bulimia (Pyle, Mitchell, Eckert, Halvorson, Neuman, & Goff (1983).

Rosen and Leitenberg (1982) suggested that, because of the abnormal fear of weight gain, eating increases anxiety and vomiting decreases it. Using a procedure called **exposure and response prevention,** these authors attempted to decrease the anxiety evoked by eating and thereby to break the binge–purge cycle. Their patient consumed large quantities of food but was not permitted to vomit. After each meal, she was prompted to focus on the uncomfortable effects of the binge (e.g., bloated feelings and fear of gaining weight) until the urge to vomit passed. The amount of food she ate without vomiting increased dramatically, and the discomfort that she reported decreased. The patient was then given a schedule for decreasing vomiting at home, and within a year, her vomiting and binging both decreased to near-zero levels.

Hypertension

Treating high blood pressure, or hypertension, has become a focus in decreasing the incidence of cardiovascular disease, the most frequent cause of death in this country. Although the most common treatment is drug therapy, behavioral procedures are also used. Some patients learn relaxation techniques, such as those previously described. The assumption here is that environmental stress increases arousal and blood pressure; the learned relaxation responses are incompatible with these reactions. Some therapists use **biofeedback,** in which a device provides feedback to the patient concerning his or her blood pressure (in general, biofeedback involves giving the patient information about a bodily function such as blood pressure, heart rate, or temperature). For example, some devices provide visual displays of blood pressure, and the patient is instructed to lower the readings by whatever means possible (e.g., by relaxing). It is hoped that the patient will use this new skill outside therapy. Unfortunately, this is often not the case (Orton, Beiman, & Ciminero, 1982), perhaps because using the device is inconvenient in many situations. For this reason, biofeedback is often used as an adjunct to other forms of therapy, such as relaxation training.

Behavioral procedures have also been used to treat **Type A behavior,** which is characterized by time urgency, competitiveness, unwillingness to relax, and rushing pell-mell from task to task, and which is associated with an increased incidence of cardiovascular disease (Friedman & Rosenman, 1974). Suinn (1977) developed a cardiac-stress-management program to treat Type A behavior in the hope that the incidence of heart disease might be lowered. One component of the program involves **stress management,** in which the patient learns to avoid or limit exposure to stressful situations or to relax in those situations; this type of training often involves imagining the stressful situation and the more adaptive response. Participation in activities such as yoga, meditation, or exercise is commonly encouraged. Patients may also find other ways to change their Type A behavior, such as learning to speak and walk slower. Interestingly, Suinn reported that his patients experienced significant reductions in cholesterol and triglyceride levels after completing the program.

Chronic Pain

Chronic pain (e.g., lower back pain), an unpleasant and often unrelenting affliction that may dominate the sufferer's life, affects millions of people. Fordyce and Steger (1979) wrote that

> the pain experience persists and may eventually evolve into a feeling of helplessness and despair as the pain persists in spite of the health system's attempts to alleviate it. Without relief, the patient suffering from chronic pain begins to feel fatigued by constant pain and the relatively small amount of sleep which results [*sic*]. In addition, he or she feels hopeless and frustrated, and cannot see an end to the suffering. With continuation of this scenario, the patient becomes increasingly frustrated and angry at the health care system or his or her immediate family. (p. 130)

In the treatment of chronic pain, obvious physiological causes must be ruled out. When they are, one strategy is to teach the patient to cope with the pain. Some studies suggest that relaxation increases pain tolerance (Bobey & Davidson, 1970); thus, a patient might learn relaxation techniques to be used on the onset of pain.

Another strategy assumes that pain behavior (e.g., reports of pain and requests for medication) is maintained by consequences, such as attention from others, ingestion of medication, and escape from unpleasant tasks. Well behavior (e.g., physical activity and self-report of no pain), in contrast, produces no reinforcing consequences. If this is true, then a program should attempt to weaken pain behavior and to strengthen well behavior by changing the consequences of each behavior. Fordyce and Steger (1979) reported a treatment plan in which hospital staff deliver social reinforcers contingent on well behavior. Included in this plan is a contingency management procedure designed to increase exercise and activities (e.g., walking, climbing stairs, and cooking). Pain behavior, although not ignored, receives only minimal attention. For those addicted to pain medication, drugs are delivered in a single "pain cocktail," which is an oral form of all currently used medicines (the color and taste of the medicines are masked by dissolving the drugs in a substance such as cherry syrup). Pain cocktails are given at specific times during the day, not on request of the patient. Patients are weaned from the drugs by a slow decrease over many weeks in the drug dosage in the cocktail. This program appears to be very useful in managing chronic pain.

Headache

A particular kind of pain, **headache,** is experienced by all of us to varying degrees. For most of us, an occasional aspirin is all that is needed to control the pain. But this is not always the case. For example, **tension headaches,** which are associated with a chronic contraction of the muscles in the forehead, scalp, and neck (Stoyva, 1979), are often treated with the relaxation techniques previously described. Therapists also use frontal EMG (electromyogram) biofeedback, in which a device provides feedback to the patient concerning tension in the forehead muscles. Blanchard and Andrasik (1985) reported a typical procedure: Electrodes connected to the feedback apparatus are placed on the patient's forehead. The therapist instructs the patient to relax and "let your forehead become more relaxed." When the forehead muscles are tense, there is a particular kind of feedback, such as a clicking sound that occurs at a high rate. As the muscle tension decreases, the clicks occur at a lower and lower rate. During this time, the patient is reminded that, "as you relax, the clicks will occur slower and slower." At the end of the session, the feedback is turned off, and the patient attempts to relax without it. To encourage relaxation outside therapy sessions, Blanchard and Andrasik recommended that biofeedback training be used in conjunction with home relaxation exercises. These authors also recommended biofeedback and relaxation training for **migraine headaches,** which result from constriction followed by dilation of the cranial arteries and are accompanied by loss of appetite, nausea, sensory disturbances, and motor disturbances.

Asthma

Asthma, characterized by a temporary narrowing of the airways in the lungs and by shortness of breath, limits the activity of many sufferers. Although the disorder results from organic variables (Rainwater & Alexander, 1982), behavioral procedures have been used as a component in overall treatment. At the onset of an asthma attack, some patients become extremely anxious and frightened, thus exacerbating or prolonging the attack (Alexander, 1977). In such cases, the therapist teaches the patient to relax when the first symptoms arise. Neisworth and Moore (1972) showed that asthmatic symptoms may be decreased by a manipulation of their consequences. Their patient evidenced frequent wheezing and coughing episodes at bedtime, which were followed by heavy doses of parental attention. To reduce these episodes, a procedure was implemented in which (1) all asthmatic symptoms at bedtime were ignored, and (2) the child was given money to buy his lunch (instead of taking it from home) the next day if he coughed less often than during the previous night. As shown in Figure 12-5, the duration of the episodes was much longer during baseline (and reversal, which is a return to baseline) than during the treatment condition. The authors noted that:

This study . . . does not purport to obviate "organic" factors in the etiology or maintenance of asthmatic responses. Rather, it pinpoints the dramatic role that environmental
contingencies may have in the amplification and attenuation of the problem. (p. 98)

Sexual Dysfunction

Therapists have applied behavioral principles to treat various forms of sexual dysfunction. Many sexual problems are thought to result from excessive anxiety, and desensitization is therefore recommended. For example, Auerbach and
Kilman (1977) treated **erectile dysfunction,** or impotence, by teaching patients to
relax while imagining sexual situations that evoke anxiety. After many sessions,
the subjects reported little or no anxiety while imagining the scenes, as well as
improved sexual functioning at home. In another variation of the procedure, the
clients learn to relax while actually engaging in sexual activity (Walker, 1982).
Other dysfunctions are related to skill deficits. In these cases, clients learn behaviors such as stimulating their partner or themselves, controlling premature
ejaculation, and communicating sexual preferences.

Patient Compliance

In many medical treatments, patients must perform tasks such as taking
oral medications at a particular time, taking urine samples, or self-administering
shots. **Compliance with medical regimens** is often critical and has been investigated in many studies. For example, to achieve maximum recovery, burn victims
must consume nutritious foods, particularly foods high in calories and protein.

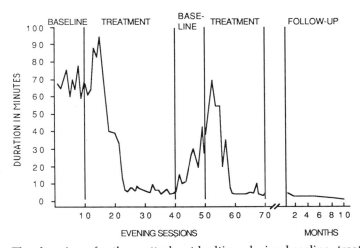

Figure 12-5. The duration of asthma attacks at bedtime during baseline, treatment, and
follow-up. (From "Operant Treatment of Asthmatic Responding with the Parent as Therapist" by J. T. Neisworth & F. Moore, *Behavior Therapy,* 1972, 3, 97. Copyright 1972 by
Academic Press. Reproduced by permission.)

To improve eating patterns in burn patients, Mahon, Neufeld, Mani, and Christophersen (1984) gave them information about the appropriate levels of protein and kilocalories, the protein and kilocalorie content of various foods, and the patients' actual intake of protein and kilocalories. Prescribed and actual intake were depicted on a graph adjacent to each patient's bed. This simple procedure increased protein and kilocalorie consumption.

The foregoing describes many ways of treating health-related behaviors by changing the environment. Interestingly, there is evidence that the environment may be involved in the *development* of diseases. For example, susceptibility to many diseases (e.g., cancer and viral infections) in nonhumans can be increased by individual housing, exposure to a flashing light, and exposure to "stressful" conditions (Riley, 1981). Moreover, it is thought that respondent conditioning may be involved in the suppression of the immune system, a phenomenon that is implicated in the development of many cancers (Ader, 1981). For example, Ader and Cohen (1975) showed that the ingestion of saccharine could, after a single pairing with a known immunosuppressant, also suppress the immune system in rats. The extent to which conditioned immunosuppression is a factor in human diseases is unknown. Nonetheless, it appears likely that learning mechanisms may be a fundamental element in the development of disease, as well as in treatment.

General Education

Behavioral applications have long been used in education. Techniques for improving learning have been studied in settings ranging from colleges to classrooms for developmentally disabled students. Some of the techniques used with intellectually normal students are discussed here, and then those used with developmentally disabled persons are presented.

Studying

Every student knows that good grades depend on studying. But how can students be encouraged to study amid the distractions of student life? Hall, Lund, and Jackson (1968) investigated a collection of classrooms and found that many grade-school teachers attended to students when they were not studying. In part because of this attention, studying occurred relatively infrequently, as depicted in the baseline condition in Figure 12-6. As a solution, the authors prompted the teachers to ignore nonstudy behavior and to attend instead to studying. As a result, the percentage of time engaged in studying increased from 30%–40% to well over 80%. Figure 12-6 shows the percentage of time that one student engaged in studying when the teacher attended to studying (i.e., the reinforcement condition) and when the teacher attended to nonstudy behavior (i.e., the reversal condition).

In a related study, Broden, Hall, and Mitts (1971) investigated the effects on study behavior of **self-monitoring,** or observing and recording one's own behavior. A student was asked to record a plus on a slip of paper when she was studying and a minus when she was not studying. The recording was to occur whenever the student remembered to mark the slip of paper during a 40-minute history period. This self-monitoring increased the percentage of time she spent studying from about 30% to over 75%.

Disruptive Behavior

Learning may be inhibited by disruptive behavior, both by the learner and by others. In an effort to manage the disruptive behavior of an entire class, Barrish, Saunders, and Wolf (1969) designed the "good behavior game." A class was divided into two teams. When a member of either team exhibited a disruptive behavior, that team received a mark on the chalkboard. The team with fewer marks received access to various privileges, unless both received fewer than five marks on a given day. In that case, both teams earned the privileges. The game reduced the percentage of time spent engaging in disruptive behavior from approximately 90% to about 15%.

Many studies have shown that disruptive behavior, like studying, may be influenced by teacher attention. Thomas, Becker, and Armstrong (1968) recorded disruptive behaviors in a class of 28 "well-behaved" children. When the

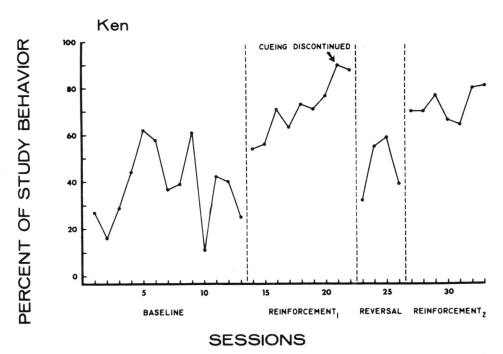

Figure 12-6. The percentage of time spent studying in baseline and reinforcement conditions. (From "Effects of Teacher Attention on Study Behavior" by R. Hall, D. Lund, & D. Jackson, *Journal of Applied Behavior Analysis*, 1968, *1*, 6. Copyright 1968 by the Society for the Experimental Analysis of Behavior. Reproduced by permission.)

teacher was asked to stop praising the children for appropriate behavior, the disruptive behavior increased. Moreover, when the teacher was asked to give more frequent disapproval for inappropriate behavior, some disruptive behavior increased further. The results of this and other studies show that teacher attention is a powerful reinforcer and must therefore be used with care.

Some schools have a high incidence of student violence, a problem investigated by Murphy, Hutchinson, and Bailey (1983). These authors first recorded the number of aggressive incidents over a 12-day baseline period. Following baseline, they tested an intervention in which the children participated in organized games. Frequent praise for appropriate behavior was delivered, and the children were required to sit quietly for two minutes for particularly unruly behavior. There was a fairly large reduction in aggressive acts during the intervention. The authors noted that the use of organized games seemed to be an important element in the intervention; one is reminded, perhaps, of the old adage "Idle hands are the devil's workshop."

Specific Skills

Even the most industrious student does not always produce high-quality work. Research has shown that the quality of academic output can usually be improved by contingency management systems. Rapport and Bostow (1976) defined performance requirements each day in four task categories. Students who correctly completed at least 80% of the requirements in each category were permitted to engage in that day's recreational activities. This arrangement produced significant increases in the performance of all subjects in the study.

Other studies have investigated methods of improving specific skills. For example, Foxx and Jones (1978) reported that spelling was improved by a procedure in which correct spelling was followed by social approval, prizes, and the posting of papers with high marks, and in which incorrect spelling resulted in a collection of spelling tasks involving the misspelled word. Many other skills, such as the correct use of prepositions, sharing, healthy snacking, reading, and mathematics have been taught by procedures based on behavioral principles.

Broad-Spectrum Applications

The aforementioned studies involved applications of behavioral principles to rather narrow problems. There are, however, larger scale applications. For example, **direct instruction** has behavioral principles as its foundation. In this approach, teachers teach a variety of skills by using carefully planned scripts that have been tested and found effective. The presentations are fast-paced and afford many opportunities for students to respond, providing ample opportunities for immediate corrective feedback and praise. Students initially work in small groups and later participate in larger groups or in individual sessions. This method has proved very successful when compared with a host of other approaches to education in the primary grades (Carnine, 1988).

Behavioral principles have also found their way into college education. Keller (1966) described a method, now called the **personalized system of instruction** (PSI), in which instruction and progress through the course are individualized. The course is divided into small units, each with specific learning objectives. Each student reads the material, learns the objectives for a particular unit, and then is tested on that material. The tests are scored immediately by a proctor, who also provides feedback concerning test answers. Students who do not master the material in a unit have additional opportunities to study the material and to retake the test. Only when a unit is mastered can the student progress to the next unit. Grades are assigned not by the comparison of a student's performance to that of others, but on the basis of the number of units mastered. Lectures and demonstrations are used infrequently and only as "inspiration" for students who have mastered enough material to guarantee their interest. A key element of PSI is the self-pacing feature: students decide when they will study and take the test for each unit. Although formal PSI is not used in most college courses, many instructors make use of some of its elements (e.g., learning objectives and small instructional units).

Educating Developmentally Disabled People

Although behavioral principles have been used successfully in many areas of education, in no area have they been more successful than in educating developmentally disabled students. As for any other student, a good educational plan for a developmentally disabled student involves training in many specific skills. For example, many students must learn self-care (e.g., dressing and showering), which is often taught by a procedure called **chaining** (see Chapter 6 and Figure 12-7). In chaining, the student first learns one small skill (e.g., tying a shoe), which is then "chained" to another skill (e.g., putting on a shoe), so that both are performed in the proper sequence. The two skills are then chained to a third and then to a fourth, and so on, until the entire sequence of skills can be executed. Along the way, the student receives guidance when necessary and rewards for correct performance. As discussed in Sidebar 12-1, long and elaborate sequences of behavior can be developed through chaining.

Communication Skills

To participate fully in life activities, developmentally disabled persons must learn some type of communication. Lutzker and Sherman (1974) taught three mentally retarded students to correctly describe various pictures when they were given tokens for correct responses; after incorrect responses, the teacher stopped the session for five seconds and then modeled the correct response. When speech training is not feasible, sign language is often taught. Faw, Reid, Schepis, Fitzgerald, and Welty (1981) instituted a program in which mentally retarded persons learned manual signs for a variety of objects in their environment through a combination of modeling, reinforcement, physical guidance, and corrective feedback. This procedure was effective in teaching the participants to use signs in individual sessions and in their natural environment.

Many developmentally disabled individuals can enjoy productive careers, so that training in vocational skills is important. Schepis, Reid, and Fitzgerald (1987) investigated a procedure designed to teach a vocational skill to a group of

---

Sidebar 12-1

Developing Complex Repertoires through Chaining: A Rat Example

Chaining is a procedure developed in the laboratory that has been adapted to applied settings. An impressive laboratory demonstration of chaining was reported by Pierrel and Sherman (1963), who taught a rat, named Barnabus, to perform a long complex series of behaviors (see Figure 12-7). The rat's task was to climb a staircase to a platform, cross a drawbridge, climb a ladder, retrieve a car by pulling a chain, pedal a car through a tunnel, climb another flight of stairs, run through a tube, enter an elevator, raise a Columbia University flag that caused the elevator to de-

scend to a lever, and, finally, press the lever, which resulted in the delivery of a pellet of food. The authors used backward chaining, in which the last behavior (pressing the bar) was taught first. Then the last two behaviors (operating the elevator and pressing the bar) were trained, followed by the last three, four, and so on, until all elements of the chain had been mastered. Chaining can be used effectively with both developmentally disabled and normal students (see Sulzer-Azaroff & Mayer, 1977).

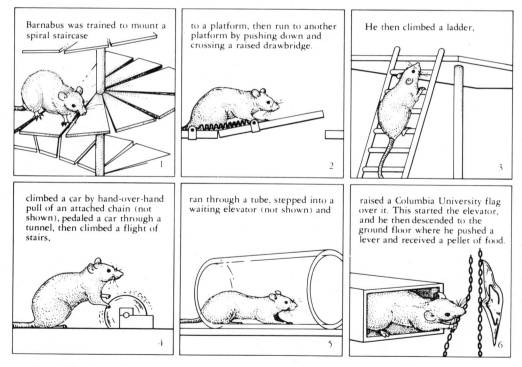

Figure 12-7. The behaviors taught to Barnabus the rat by means of a backward chaining procedure. (From *Psychology: The Science of Behavior* by N. R. Carlson, 1984, p. 138. Copyright 1984 by Allyn & Bacon. Reproduced by permission.)

profoundly mentally retarded students. The students, who learned to stamp envelopes with a return address, received task-related instructions as a group. Praise and physical guidance were presented to each student depending on performance, and the steps of the task were chained together as described previously. As seen in Figure 12-8, the students learned each of the three compo-

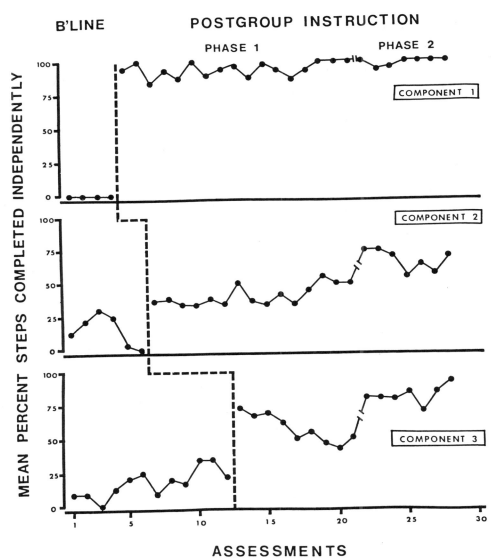

Figure 12-8. Mean percentage of steps of the address-stamping task completed for each component during baseline and instruction conditions. Data are presented for the entire group. (From "Group Instruction with Profoundly Retarded Persons: Acquisition, Generalization, and Maintenance of a Remunerative Work Skill" by M. M. Schepis, D. H. Reid, & J. R. Fitzgerald, *Journal of Applied Behavior Analysis*, 1987, 20, 101. Copyright 1987 by the Society for the Experimental Analysis of Behavior, Inc. Reproduced by permission.)

nents of the task. Moreover, their performance was good enough to permit them to earn money for the work. This study underscores an important point: When developmentally disabled persons learn marketable skills, they accrue many benefits, as does the community at large.

Community-Living Skills

Although developmentally disabled people may be encouraged to participate fully in community activities, they are often woefully unprepared to do so. Recognizing this, researchers have attempted to teach community-living skills. For example, Neef, Iwata, and Page (1978) used simulations with instructional slides, role playing, and the manipulation of small dolls to teach mentally retarded subjects bus-riding skills. For example, to teach the approach to a bus stop, a small doll and a miniature-sized bus route were used. Similarly, boarding skills were taught with a mock "bus" set up in the classroom. As a result of the training, the subjects learned the skills in the classroom and were then able to exhibit these skills by riding actual buses. The authors noted that the training was just as effective, and less time-consuming, than more traditional instruction that was delivered to subjects riding on actual buses. Many other community skills, including telephone dialing, the appropriate use of leisure time, and housekeeping, have been taught by means of behavioral procedures.

Disruptive Behavior and Self-Injury

Disruptive behavior, such as aggression, is often a problem, particularly in institutions where large numbers of people live with little to occupy their time. In many cases, **overcorrection** has proved effective in reducing aggressive responding. According to the general rationale of overcorrection (Foxx & Azrin, 1973), the aggressor should correct the environmental consequences of his or her actions (called **restitutional overcorrection**) and repeatedly practice appropriate behavior (called **positive-practice overcorrection**). For example, a physically assaultive client might be required to apologize profusely to the victim and to others who witnessed the attack, thereby mending hurt feelings. He or she might also be required to repeatedly practice correct forms of behavior, such as engaging in positive, friendly interactions with other people. Researchers have reported that overcorrection can decrease aggression, as well as many other disruptive behaviors such as stealing, public disrobing, and property destruction (Miltenberger & Fuqua, 1985).

As noted in Chapter 11, many developmentally disabled individuals engage in self-injury; in some cases, the behavior is particularly vigorous. For example, those afflicted with **Lesch-Nyhan syndrome,** which is associated with a metabolic deficiency, engage in biting and other forms of self-injury. The biting is so severe—tissue from the lips and the fingers may be torn off—that the person is restrained and, in some cases, the teeth are pulled. Many researchers have found that manipulating therapist attention influences self-injury. For example, Anderson, Dancis, and Alpert (1978) reported that, when a therapist provided attention after every bite attempt, the attempts increased dramatically. When attention was withdrawn after bite attempts, the biting decreased. Withdrawal of attention after biting was so effective that the subjects were restrained for only short periods of time, and their access to many activities was thus greatly increased.

Conclusions

Many of the principles of behavior accepted by psychologists were discovered, or at least refined, in laboratory investigations. It is common practice to extend terms and principles from the laboratory to applied situations. This practice is generally fruitful, but it is important to recognize that the extension is sometimes strained, even to the point of being metaphorical. For instance, it is tempting to call a weekly bonus that increases productivity a "reinforcer." Although the bonus resembles a "reinforcer" in laboratory research (e.g., food that follows a rat's lever press) in that both increase the rate of responding, the former probably depends on some uniquely human characteristics, such as the ability to make and be affected by statements like "You can earn extra money for working efficiently." This is not to say that fundamentally different behavioral processes control behavior in laboratory and applied settings, but only to point out that the procedures used in applied settings sometimes affect behavior through processes too complex to be described accurately by a single term.

In some cases, the procedures used to deal with applied problems may be difficult to describe in terms of precise behavioral principles. For example, "feedback" is often used to change behavior, but how it does so is rarely evident. *Feedback* is not a technical term in behavior analysis, and the information described as feedback may conceivably alter behavior by acting as a positive reinforcer, a negative reinforcer, a punishing stimulus, a discriminative stimulus, or an establishing operation. These different actions might, in principle be singled out by experimentation, but in practice such experiments are seldom attempted.

Although there is some terminological imprecision in applied behavior analysis, and although the relation of applied procedures to established behavioral principles may be hard to discern, it is clear that interventions developed by behaviorally oriented psychologists have proved effective in a wide range of areas. Why is this so? The answer appears to reflect the three elements of the behavioral approach mentioned at the beginning of this chapter.

First, the behavioral approach, as implied by its name, emphasizes *behavior*, and behavior is an essential factor in many problems such as crime, the dwindling supply of natural resources, and deficient worker productivity. An approach that emphasizes behavior, and not the activity of some hypothetical entity, is well suited to solving such problems.

Second, the behavioral approach emphasizes the manipulation of real objects and events in the environment. Interventions based on the manipulation of environmental events are apt to be straightforward and nonmystical; thus, their use is not restricted to a few experts. More important, much behavior is controlled by antecedent and postcedent stimuli and may be altered by a manipulation of these stimuli.

Third, the behavioral approach emphasizes that the efficacy of interventions should be documented through the use of appropriate experimental procedures. Although often expensive in terms of time and resources, adequate documentation of the effects of an intervention is necessary to satisfy **accountability** requirements, which hold that, when money is to be paid for a psychologist's services, evidence of patient improvement must be provided. What better way to demonstrate improvement than by pointing to verifiable changes in observable behavior? As Lutzker and Martin (1981) suggested, the behavioral approach "generates data that enable anyone to judge the success or failure of a behavior change intervention" (p. 12). For those who pay for psychological services, or who are in the position of choosing a strategy to deal with a current problem, such data are invaluable.

Although they are widely applicable, interventions based on behavioral principles are surely not the only ones effective in applied settings. There are many ways to deal with the problems that beset humanity, and it is naive to believe that any one approach will be consistently superior. It is equally naive to assume that interventions based on behavioral principles are applicable in all situations. In some cases, as when obvious physiological abnormalities lead to behavioral problems, they are ineffective. In others, they cannot be implemented. Treatments characteristic of applied behavior analysis rest on the assumption that the best way to change behavior is to change the environment in which it occurs. Practical and ethical restrictions sometimes make such changes difficult or impossible. Nonetheless, there are many settings in which the environment can be altered systematically to bring about desired changes in what people do. And as Skinner (1978) observed:

> By turning . . . to the external conditions of which man's behavior is a function, it has been possible to design better practices in the care of psychotics and retardates, in child care, in education (in both contingency management in the classroom and the design of instructional material), in incentive systems in industry, and in penal institutions. In these and many other areas we can now more effectively work for the good of the individual, for the greatest good of the greatest number, and for the good of the culture of mankind as a whole. (p. 55)

In the pursuit of these goals lies the future of behavior analysis, and of humanity.

Study Questions

1. Be able to describe the three features that characterize the applications of behavioral psychology.

2. Be able to give examples of behavioral applications with (a) community and environmental problems, (b) business and industry, (c) clinical applications, (d) behavioral medicine, (e) general education, and (f) educating developmentally disabled people. When possible, include the three features mentioned in Objective #1 (above).

3. It might be tempting to classify a weekly bonus that strengthens behavior a "reinforcer." What is the difference between this kind of process and the kind associated with a reinforcer in laboratory research (i.e., What human characteristic is necessary for weekly bonuses to affect behavior?)?

4. Give the three reasons why behaviorally-oriented procedures have proven effective in many areas.

Recommended Readings

Goldstein, A. P., & Krasner, L. (1987). *Modern Applied Psychology.* New York: Pergamon Press.

Goldstein and Krasner are renowned for their work in applied psychology. Community, clinical, educational, health, legal, industrial, and sports applications are discussed, and fictional and case studies illustrate important points. An interesting summary of the history of applied psychology is also provided.

Journal of Applied Behavior Analysis (1968–present).

The journal reports applications of behavioral principles in a host of areas. The articles are typically reports of research activities that meet minimum standards of internal validity, reliability, and relevance.

Lutzker, J. R., & Martin, J. A. (1982). *Behavior Change.* Monterey, CA: Brooks/Cole.

The authors present an excellent overview of applications of behavioral principles. They discuss representative studies in a wide range of areas, including education, business, clinical interventions, and health care. This text is just right for the beginning student, as an introduction to behavioral principles is also provided.

References

Abramson, L. Y., Seligman, M. E. P., & Teasdale, J. D. (1978). Learned helplessness in humans: Critique and reformulation. *Journal of Abnormal Psychology, 87*, 49–74.

Ader, R. (1981). Behavioral influences on immune responses. In S. M. Weiss, J. A. Herd, & B. H. Fox (Eds.), *Perspectives on behavioral medicine* (pp. 163–182). New York: Academic Press.

Ader, R., & Cohen, N. (1975). Behaviorally conditioned immunosuppression. *Psychomatic Medicine, 37*, 333–340.

Agras, W. S. (1987). *Eating disorders: Management of obesity, bulimia, and anorexia nervosa.* New York: Pergamon Press.

Alcock, J. (1984). *Animal behavior: An evolutionary approach.* Sunderland, MA: Sinauer Associates.

Alexander, A. B. (1977). Chronic asthma. In R. B. Williams, Jr., & W. D. Gentry (Eds.), *Behavioral approaches to medical treatment* (pp. 7–23). Cambridge, MA: Ballinger.

Alford, G. S., Blanchard, E. B., & Buckley, T. M. (1972). Treatment of hysterical vomiting by modification of social contingencies: A case study. *Journal of Behavior Therapy and Experimental Psychiatry, 3*, 209–212.

Allen, M. G. (1976). Twin studies of affective illness. *Archives of General Psychiatry, 33*, 1476–1478.

Allport, G. (1937). *Personality: A psychological interpretation.* New York: Holt, Rinehart, & Winston.

Allport, G. (1961). *Pattern and growth in personality.* New York: Holt, Rinehart, & Winston.

American Heritage Dictionary of the English Language. (1984). New York: Houghton Mifflin.

American Psychiatric Association. (1987). *Diagnostic and statistical manual of mental disorders* (3rd ed., rev.). Washington, DC: Author.

American Psychological Association. (1981). Ethical principles of psychologists. *American Psychologist, 36*, 633–638.

Anastasi, A. (1976). *Psychological testing.* New York: Macmillan.

Anderson, D. C., Crowell, C. R., Sucec, J., Gilligan, K. D., & Wikoff, M. (1982). Behavior management of client contacts in a real estate brokerage: Getting agents to sell more. *Journal of Organizational Behavior Management, 4*, 67–96.

Anderson, L. T., Dancis, J., & Alpert, M. (1978). Behavioral contingencies and self mutiliation in Lesch-Nyhan disease. *Journal of Consulting and Clinical Psychology, 46*, 529–536.

Asch, S. E. (1956). Studies of independence and conformity: A minority of one against a unanimous majority. *Psychological Monographs, 70* (Whole No. 546).

At Emory Air Freight: Positive reinforcement boosts performance. (1973). *Organizational Dynamics, 1*, 41–50.

Atkinson, R. C., & Shiffrin, R. M. (1968). Human memory: A proposed system and its control processes. *The Psychology of Learning and Motivation, 2*, 89–195.

Atkinson, R. L., Atkinson, R. C., Smith, E. E., & Hilgard, E. R. (1987). *Introduction to psychology.* San Diego: harcourt Brace Jovanovich.

Atthowe, J. M., & Krasner, L. A. (1968). A preliminary report on the application of contingent reinforcement procedures (token economy) on a chronic psychiatric ward. *Journal of Abnormal Psychology, 73*, 37–43.

Auerbach, R., & Kilman, P. R. (1977). The effects of group systematic desensitization on secondary erectile failure. *Behavior Therapy, 8*, 330–339.

Ayala, F. J. (1978). The mechanisms of evolution. *Scientific American, 239,* 56–69.

Ayllon, T., & Azrin, N. H. (1968). *The token economy: A motivational system for therapy and rehabilitation.* New York: Appleton-Century-Crofts.

Azrin, N. H., & Foxx, R. M. (1971). A rapid method of toilet training the institutionalized retarded. *Journal of Applied Behavior Analysis, 4,* 89–99.

Azrin, N. H., & Holz, W. C. (1966). Punishment. In W. K. Honig (Ed.), *Operant behavior: Areas of research and application* (pp. 380–447). New York: Appleton-Century-Crofts.

Azrin, N. H., & Lindsley, O. R. (1956). The reinforcement of cooperation between children. *Journal of Abnormal Social Psychology, 52,* 100–102.

Azrin, N. H., Hutchinson, R. R., & Hake, D. F. (1966). Extinction-induced aggression. *Journal of the Experimental Analysis of Behavior, 9,* 191–204.

Azrin, N., Flores, T., & Kaplan, S. J. (1975). Job-finding club: A group-assisted program for obtaining employment. *Behavior Research and Therapy, 13,* 17–26.

Bachrach, A. J. (1972). *Psychological research: An introduction.* New York: Random House.

Baldessarini, R. J. (1985). Drugs and the treatment of psychiatric disorders. In A. G. Gilman, L. S. Goodman, T. W. Rall & F. Murad (Eds.), *The pharmacological basis of therapeutics* (pp. 387–445). New York: Macmillan.

Bandura, A. (1969). *Principles of behavior modification.* New York: Holt, Rinehart & Winston.

Bandura, A. (1977). *Social learning theory.* New York: Prentice-Hall.

Barash, D. P. (1977). *Sociobiology and behavior.* New York: Elsevier.

Barber, T. X. (1976). *Pitfalls in human research.* New York: Pergamon Press.

Barnard, C. J. (1983). *Animal behavior: Ecology and evolution.* New York: Wiley.

Barrish, H. H., Saunders, M., & Wolf, M. M. (1969). Good behavior game: Effects of individual contingencies for group consequences on disruptive behavior in a classroom. *Journal of Applied Behavior Analysis, 2,* 119–124.

Beaumont, J. G. (1983). *Introduction to neuropsychology.* New York: Guilford Press.

Beck, A. T. (1976). *Cognitive therapy and the emotional disorders.* New York: International Universities Press.

Beck, K. H. (1979). The effects of positive and negative arousal upon attitudes, belief acceptance, behavioral intention, and behavior. *Journal of Social Psychology, 107,* 239–251.

Bekhterev, V. M. (1907). *Objective psychology.* Leipzig: B. G. Teubner.

Bem, D. (1967). Self-perception: An alternative interpretation of cognitive dissonance phenomena. *Psychological Review, 74,* 183–200.

Berger, P. A. (1978). Medical treatment of mental illness. *Science, 200,* 974–981.

Berkowitz, L., & Frodi, A. (1977). Stimulus characteristics that can enhance or decrease aggression. *Aggressive Behavior, 3,* 1–5.

Berscheid, E., & Walster, E. (1978). *Interpersonal attraction.* Reading, MA: Addison-Wesley.

Biachine, J. R. (1985). Drugs for Parkinson's disease, spasticity, and acute muscle spasms. In A. G. Gilman, L. S. Goodman, T. W. Rall, & F. Murad (Eds.), *The pharmacological basis of therapeutics* (pp. 473–490). New York: Macmillan.

Bijou, S. W. (1979). *Behavior analysis of the infantile stage of development.* Unpublished manuscript.

Bijou, S. W., & Baer, D. M. (1961). *Child development. Vol. 1: A systematic and empirical theory.* New York: Appleton-Century-Crofts.

Blanchard, E. B., & Andrasik, F. (1985). *Management of chronic headaches: A psychological approach.* New York: Pergamon Press.

Block, J. J. (1976). Issues, problems and pitfalls in assessing sex differences: A critical review of "The psychology of sex differences." *Merrill-Palmer Quarterly, 22,* 283–308.

Bloomfield, L. (1933). *Language.* New York: Henry Holt.

Bobey, J. J., & Davidson, P. O. (1970). Psychological factors affecting pain tolerance. *Psychomatic Research, 14,* 371–376.

Bochner, S., & Insko, C. A. (1966). Communicator discrepancy, source credibility, and opinion change. *Journal of Personality and Social Psychology, 4,* 614–621.

Bohman, M. (1978). Some genetic aspects of alcoholism and criminality: A population of adoptees. *Archives of General Psychiatry, 35,* 269–276.

Boring, E. G. (1942). *Sensation and perception in the history of experimental psychology.* New York: Appleton-Century.

Bowlby, J. (1973). *Separation and loss.* New York: Basic Books.

Brazelton, T. B. (1982). Behavioral competence in the newborn infant. In J. K. Gardner (Ed.), *Readings in developmental psychology* (pp. 79–90). Boston: Little, Brown.

Brewer, W. F. (1974). There is no convincing evidence for operant or classical conditioning in adult humans. In W. B. Wimer & D. S. Palermo (Eds.), *Cognition and the symbolic processes* (pp. 1–42). Hillsdale, NJ: Erlbaum.

Bridgeman, B. (1988). *The biology of behavior*. New York: Wiley.

Brill, A. A. (1909). Selected papers on hysteria and other psychoneuroses: Sigmund Freud. *Nervous and Mental Disease Monograph Series* (No. 4).

Broad, W. J., & Wade, N. (1982). *Betrayers of the truth*. New York: Simon & Schuster.

Brock, T. C. (1965). Communicator-recipient similarity and decision change. *Journal of Personality and Social Psychology, 1,* 650–654.

Broden, M., Hall, R. V., & Mitts, B. (1971). The effect of self-recording on the classroom behavior of two eighth grade students. *Journal of Applied Behavior Analysis, 4,* 191–199.

Brower, L. P., & Brower, J. V. (1964). Birds, butterflies, and plant poisons: A study in ecological chemistry. *Zoologica, 49,* 137–159.

Brown, J. L. (1975). *The evolution of behavior*. New York: Norton.

Brown, R. (1973). *A first language: The early stages*. Cambridge: Harvard University Press.

Brown, R., & Bellugi, U. (1964). Three processes in the child's acquisition of syntax. *Harvard Educational Review, 34,* 133–151.

Bryan, J. H., & Test, M. A. (1967). Models and helping: Naturalistic studies in aiding behavior. *Journal of Personality and Social Psychology, 6,* 400–407.

Butterfield, E. C., & Siperstein, G. N. (1974). Influence of contingent auditory stimulation upon non-nutritional suckle. In *Proceedings of third symposium on oral sensation and perception: The mouth of the infant*. Springfield, IL.: Charles C Thomas.

Byrne, D. (1971). *The attraction paradigm*. New York: Academic Press.

Campbell, B. G. (1985). *Humankind emerging*. Glenview, IL: Scott, Foresman.

Campbell, D. T., & Stanley, J. C. (1966). *Experimental and quasi-experimental designs for research*. Chicago: Rand McNally.

Campos, J. J., Langer, A., & Krowitz, A. (1970). Cardiac responses on the visual cliff in prelocomotor human infants. *Science, 170,* 196–197.

Campos, J. J., Svejda, M., Bertenthal, B., Benson, N., & Schmid, D. (1981, April). *Self-produced locomotion and wariness of heights: New evidence from training studies*. Paper presented at the meeting of the Society for Research in Child Development, Boston.

Carducci, B. J., Cosby, P. C., & Ward, C. D. (1978). Sexual arousal and interpersonal evaluations. *Journal of Experimental Social Psychology, 14,* 449–457.

Carlson, N. R. (1981). *Physiology of behavior*. Boston: Allyn & Bacon.

Carlson, N. R. (1986). *Physiology of behavior*. Boston: Allyn & Bacon.

Carlson, N. R. (1987). *Psychology: The science of behavior* (2nd ed.). Boston: Allyn & Bacon. First edition 1984.

Carlson, N. R. (1988). *Discovering psychology*. Boston: Allyn & Bacon.

Carnine, D. (1988, July). Breaking the failure cycle in the elementary school. *Youth Policy, 10,* 22–25.

Carr, H. (1925). *Psychology*. New York: Longmans, Green.

Carter, E. N. (1973). *The stimulus control of a response system in the absence of awareness*. Unpublished doctoral dissertation, University of Massachusetts.

Cash, T. F., Begley, P. J., McGown, D. A., & Weise, B. C. (1975). When counselors are heard but not seen: Initial impact of physical attractiveness. *Journal of Counseling Psychology, 22,* 273–279.

Cattell, R. B. (1946). *Description and measurement of personality*. New York: World Book.

Cattell, R. B. (1950). *Personality: A systematic, theoretical, and factual study*. New York: McGraw-Hill.

Cattell, R. B. (1957). *Personality and motivation structure and measurement*. New York: Harcourt Brace Jovanovich.

Cattell, R. B. (1965). *The scientific analysis of personality*. Harmondsworth, England: Penguin.

Cattell, R. B. (1979). *Personality and learning theory*. New York: Springer.

Cattell, R. B., & Kline, P. (1977). *The scientific analysis of personality and motivation*. New York: Academic Press.

Chein, I., Gerard, D. D., Lee, R. S., & Rosenfeld, E. (1964). *The road to H*. New York: Basic Books.

Chomsky, N. (1957). *Syntactic structures*. London: Mouton.

Chomsky,, N. (1965). *Aspects of the theory of syntax*. Cambridge, MA: MIT Press.

Chugani, H. T., & Phelps, M. E. (1986). Maturational changes in cerebral function in infants determined by 18FDG positron emission tomography. *Science, 231*, 840–843.

Cialdini, R. B., Vincent, J. E., Lewis, S. K., Catalan, J., Wheeler, D., & Darby, B. L. (1975). Reciprocal concessions procedure for inducing compliance: The door-in-the-face technique. *Journal of Personality and Social Psychology, 31*, 206–215.

Ciminero, A. R., Calhoun, K. S., & Adams, H. E. (1977). *Handbook of behavioral assessment.* New York: Wiley.

Conners, C. K. (1973). Rating scales for use in drug studies with children. *Psychopharmacology Bulletin (Special issue, Pharmacotherapy of children)*, 24–84.

Costello, C. G. (1972). Depression: Loss of reinforcers or loss of reinforcer effectiveness? *Behavior Therapy, 3*, 240–247.

Council Report. (1983). *Fifth special report on alcohol and health.* Washington, DC: U.S. Government Printing Office.

Craighead, W. E., Kazdin, A. E., & Mahoney, M. J. (1981). *Behavior modification: Principles, issues, and applications.* Boston: Houghton Mifflin.

Croyle, R. T., & Cooper, J. (1983). Dissonance arousal: Physiological evidence. *Journal of Personality and Social Psychology, 45*, 782–791.

Cruze, A. M., Harwood, H. J., Kristiansen, P. L., Collins, J. J., & Jones, D. D. (1981). *Economic costs to society of alcohol and drug abuse and mental illness—1977.* Rockville, MD: Alcohol, Drug Abuse, & Mental Health Administration.

Cuny, H. (1965). *Ivan Pavlov: The man and his theories.* New York: Paul S. Eriksson.

Darley, J. M., & Batson, C. D. (1973). From Jerusalem to Jerico: A study of situational and dispositional variables in helping behavior. *Journal of Personality and Social Psychology, 27*, 100–108.

Darley, J. M., & Latane, B. (1968, May). When will people help in a crisis? *Psychology Today,* pp. 54–57.

Darley, J. M., Glucksberg, S., Kamin, L. J., & Kinchla, R. A. (1981). *Psychology.* Englewood Cliffs, NJ: Prentice-Hall.

Darwin, C. (1859). *On the origin of species by means of natural selection.* London: Murray.

Darwin, C. (1872). *The expression of the emotions in man and animals.* London: John Murray.

Dawkins, R. (1986). *The blind watchmaker.* New York: Norton.

Dawkins, R. (1976). *The selfish gene.* New York: Oxford University Press.

Dayton, G. O., Jones, M. H., Aiu, P., Rawson, R. H., Steele, B., & Rose, M. (1964). Developmental study of coordinated eye movements in the human infant. *Archives of Opthamology, 71*, 865–870.

Deaux, K. (1976). *The behavior of men and women.* Monterey, CA: Brooks/ Cole.

Deaux, K., & Wrightsman, L. S. (1984). *Social psychology in the 80s* (4th ed.). Monterey, CA: Brooks/Cole.

Deguchi, H. (1984). Observational learning from a radical-behavioristic viewpoint. *The Behavior Analyst, 7*, 83–96.

Delgado, J. M. R. (1969). *Physical control of the mind.* New York: Harper & Row.

Dermer, M., & Pyszczynski, T. A. (1978). Effects of erotica upon men's loving and liking responses for women they love. *Journal of Personality and Social Psychology, 36*, 1302–1309.

de Solla Price, J. (1961). *Science since Babylon.* New Haven, CT: York University Press.

deVilliers, J. G., & deVilliers, P. A. (1978). *Language acquisition.* Cambridge, MA.: Marvard University Press.

Dickerson, R. E. (1978). Chemical evolution and the origin of life. *Scientific American, 239*, 1–9.

Dion, K. K., & Stein, S. (1978). Physical attractiveness and interpersonal influence. *Journal of Experimental Social Psychology, 17*, 97–108.

Dion, K. K., Berscheid, E., & Walster, E. (1972). What is beautiful is good. *Journal of Personality and Social Psychology, 24*, 285–290.

Dobzhansky, T. (1964). *Heredity and the nature of man.* New York: Harcourt, Brace & World.

Doleys, D. M., Meredith, R. L., & Ciminero, A. R. (1982). *Behavioral medicine: Assessment and treatment strategies.* New York: Plenum Press.

Dollard, J., Dobb, L., Miller, N., Mowrer, O., & Sears, R. (1939). *Frustration and aggression.* New Haven, CT: Yale University Press.

Dorsey, M. F., Iwata, B. A., Ong, P., & McSween, T. E. (1980). Treatment of self-injurious behavior using a water mist: Initial response suppression and generalization. *Journal of Applied Behavior Analysis, 13*, 343–353.

Dowling, H. F. (1977). *Fighting infection.* Cambridge: Harvard University Press.

Dutton, D. G., & Aron, A. P. (1974). Some evidence for heightened sexual attraction under conditions of high anxiety. *Journal of Personality and Social Psychology, 30,* 94–100.

Dworetzky, J. P. (1987). *Introduction to child development.* St. Paul: West.

Eacker, J. N. (1972). On some elementary physiological problems of psychology. *American Psychologist, 27,* 553–565.

Eisenson, J., Auer, J. J., & Irwin, J. V. (1963). *The psychology of communication.* New York: Appleton-Century-Crofts.

Ekman, P., & Oster, H. (1979). Facial expressions of emotion. *Annual Review of Psychology, 30,* 527–554.

Eldredge, N., & Gould, S. J. (1972). Punctuated equilibria: An alternative to phyletic gradualism. In T. J. M. Schopf (Ed.), *Models in paleobiology* (pp. 82–115). San Francisco: Freeman, Cooper.

Emswiller, T., Deaux, K., & Willits, J. E. (1971). Similarity, sex, and requests for small favors. *Journal of Applied Social Psychology, 8,* 72–83.

Esquirol, J. E. D. (1845). *Mental maladies* (E. K. Hunt, trans.). Philadelphia: Lea & Blanchard. (Original work published 1838.)

Evans, R. I. (1968). *B. F. Skinner: The man and his ideas.* New York: Dutton.

Fairbank, J. A., & Brown, T. A. (1987). Current behavioral approaches to the treatment of post-traumatic stress disorder. *The Behavior Therapist, 3,* 57–64.

Fairbank, J. A., & Keane, T. M. (1982). Flooding for combat-related stress disorders: Assessment of anxiety reduction across traumatic memories. *Behavior Therapy, 13,* 499–510.

Fantino, E., & Logan, C. A. (1979). *The experimental analysis of behavior: A biological perspective.* San Francisco: Freeman.

Fantz, R. L. (1961). The origin of form perception. *Scientific American, 204,* 66–72.

Farris, H. E. (1967). Classical conditioning of courting behavior in the Japanese quail, *Coturnix coturnix japonica. Journal of the Experimental Analysis of Behavior, 10,* 213–217.

Faw, G. D., Reid, D. H., Schepis, M. M., Fitzgerald, J. R., & Welty, P. A. (1981). Involving institutional staff in the development and maintenance of sign language skills with profoundly retarded persons. *Journal of Applied Behavior Analysis, 14,* 411–423.

Ferster, C. B. (1965). Classification of behavior pathology. In L. K. Krasner & L. P. Ullman (Eds.), *Research in behavior modification* (pp. 87–109). New York: Holt, Rinehart, & Winston.

Festinger, L. (1957). *A theory of cognitive dissonance.* Stanford, CA: Stanford University Press.

Festinger, L., & Carlsmith, J. M. (1959). Cognitive consequences of forced compliance. *Journal of Abnormal and Social Psychology, 58,* 203–210.

Finlay, D., & Ivinkis, A. (1984). Cardiac and visual responses to moving stimuli presented either successively or simultaneously to the central and peripheral visual fields in 4-month-olds. *Developmental Psychology, 20,* 29–36.

Ford, D. H., & Urban, H. B. (1963). *Systems of psychotherapy: A comparative study.* New York: Wiley.

Fordyce, W. E., & Steger, J. C. (1979). Chronic pain. In O. F. Pomerleau & J. P. Brady (Eds.), *Behavioral medicine: Theory and practice* (pp. 125–153). Baltimore: Williams & Wilkins.

Foxx, R. M., & Azrin, N. H. (1973). The elimination of autistic self-stimulatory behavior by overcorrection. *Journal of Applied Behavior Analysis, 6,* 1–14.

Foxx, R. M., & Jones, J. R. (1978). A remediation program for increasing the spelling achievement of elementary and junior high school students. *Behavior Modification, 2,* 211–230.

Foxx, R. M., & Schaeffer, M. H. (1981). A company-based lottery to reduce the personal driving of employees. *Journal of Applied Behavior Analysis, 14,* 273–285.

Frazier, K. (1984–1985). Gallup youth poll finds high belief in ESP, astrology. *The Skeptical Inquirer, 9,* 113–114.

Freedman, J. L., & Fraser, S. C. (1966). Compliance without pressure: The foot-in-the-door technique. *Journal of Personality and Social Psychology, 4,* 195–202.

Freud, S. (1933). *New introductory lectures on psychoanalysis.* New York: Norton.

Freud, S. (1963). *Introductory lectures on psycho-analysis.* In Standard Edition (Vols. 15, 16). London: Hogarth Press. (First German editions, 1916, 1917.)

Friedman, M., & Rosenman, R. (1974). *Type A behavior and your heart.* New York: Knopf.

Futuyma, D. J. (1979). *Evolutionary biology.* Sunderland, MA: Sinauer.

Futuyma, D. J. (1986). *Evolutionary biology* (2nd ed.). Sunderland, MA: Sinauer.

Gadow, K. D., & Poling, A. (1988). *Pharmacotherapy and mental retardation.* San Diego: College-Hill.

Garcia, J., Kimeldorf, D. J., & Koelling, R. A. (1955). Conditioned aversion to saccharin resulting from exposure to gamma radiation. *Science, 122,* 157–158.

Gardner, R. A., & Gardner, B. T. (1978). Comparative psychology and language acquisition. *Annals of the New York Academy of Sciences, 309*, 37–76.

Geen, R. G. (1980). The effects of being observed on performance. In P. B. Paulus (Ed.), *Psychology of group influence*. Hillsdale, NJ: Erlbaum.

Geldard, F. A. (1972). *The human senses* (2nd ed.). New York: Wiley.

Gelman, R. (1969). Conservation acquisition: A problem of learning to attend to relevant attributes. *Journal of Experimental Child Psychology, 7*, 167–187.

Gericke, O. L. (1965). Practical use of operant procedures in a mental hospital. *Psychiatric Studies and Projects, 3*, 2–10.

Geschwind, N. (1979). Specializations of the human brain. *Scientific American, 241*, 180–199.

Gibson, E. J., & Walk, R. D. (1960). The "visual cliff." *Scientific American, 202*, 64–71.

Glanzer, M., & Cunitz, A. R. (1966). Two storage mechanisms in free recall. *Journal of Verbal Learning and Verbal Behavior, 5*, 351–360.

Gleitman, H. (1988). *Psychology.* New York: Norton.

Glenn, S. S. (1986). Metacontingencies in Walden Two. *Behavior Analysis and Social Action, 5*, 2–8.

Goddard, H. H. (1928). Feeblemindedness: A question of definition. *Journal of Psycho-Asthenics, 33*, 219–227.

Goldberg, M. E., & Gorn, G. J. (1979). Television's impact on preferences for non-white playmates: Canadian Sesame Street inserts. *Journal of Broadcasting, 23*, 27–32.

Goodwin, D. W. (1983). *Phobias: The facts.* London: Oxford.

Goddard, H. H. (1920). *Human efficiency and levels of intelligence.* Princeton, NJ: Princeton University Press.

Goldhaber, D. (1986). *Lifespan human development.* New York: Harcourt Brace Jovanovich.

Goodwin, D. W., Schulsinger, F., Mopller, P., Hermansen, L., Winokur, G., & Guze, S. B. (1973). Alcohol problems in adoptees raised apart from alcoholic biological parents. *Archives of General Psychiatry, 28*, 238–243

Goodwin, F. K., Wirz-Justice, A., & Wehr, T. A. (1982). Evidence that the pathophysiology of depression and the mechanisms of action of antidepressant drugs both involve alterations in circadian rhythms. In E. Costa & G. Racagni (Eds.), *Typical and atypical antidepressants: Clinical practice* (pp. 136–179). New York: Raven.

Gordon, H. (1987). *Extrasensory deception.* Buffalo, NY: Prometheus.

Gould, J. L. (1982). *Ethology: The mechanisms and evolution of behavior.* New York: Norton.

Gould, S. J. (1977). *Ever since Darwin: Reflections in natural history.* New York: Norton.

Gould, S. J. (1981). *The mismeasure of man.* New York: Norton.

Gould, S. J. (1987–1988). The verdict on creationism. *The Skeptical Inquirer, 12*, 184–187.

Greene, B. F., & Neistat, M. D. (1983). Behavior analysis in consumer affairs: Encouraging dental professionals to provide consumers with shielding from unnecessary X-ray exposure. *Journal of Applied Behavior Analysis, 16*, 13–27.

Greenough, W. T., & Green, E. J. (1981). Experience and the aging brain. In J. L. McGaugh, J. G. March, & S. B. Kiesler (Eds.), *Aging: Biology and behavior.* New York: Academic Press.

Griffin, D. R. (1981). *The question of animal awareness.* Los Altos, CA: William Kaufman.

Griffin, J. C., Williams, D. E., Stark, M. T., Altmeyer, B. K., & Mason, M. (1984). Self-injurious behavior: A state-wide prevalence survey, assessment of severe cases, and follow-up of aversive programs. In J. C. Griffin, M. T. Stark, D. E. Williams, B. K. Altmeyer & H. K. Griffin (Eds.), *Advances in the treatment of self-injurious behavior* (pp. 1–26). Richmond: Texas Developmental Disabilities Program.

Griffiths, R. R., Bigelow, G. E., & Henningfield, J. E. (1980). Similarities in animal and human drug-taking behavior. In N. Mello (Ed.), *Advances in substance abuse* (pp. 1–90). Greenwich, CT: JAI.

Grossman, H. J. (1983). *Classification in mental retardation.* Washington, DC: American Association on Mental Deficiency.

Gustafson, G. E. (1984). Effects of the ability to locomote on infants' social and exploratory behaviors: An experimental study. *Developmental Psychology, 20*, 397–405.

Guze, S. B., & Robins, E. (1970). Suicide and primary affective disorders. *British Journal of Psychiatry, 117*, 437–438.

Haith, M. M. (1966). The response of the human newborn to visual movement. *Journal of Experimental Child Psychology, 3*, 235–243.

Haith, M. M. (1969). Infrared television recording and measurement of ocular behavior in the human infant. *American Psychologist, 24*, 279–283.

Haith, M. M. (1976). Visual competence in early infancy. In R. Held, H. Leibowitz, & H. L. Teuber (Eds.), *Handbook of sensory physiology* (Vol. 8). New York: Springer-Verlag.

Hake, D. F., Olvera, D., & Bell, J. C. (1975). Switching from competition to sharing or cooperation at large response requirements: Competition requires more responding. *Journal of the Experimental Analysis of Behavior, 24,* 343–354.

Hall, C. S., & Lindzey, G. (1985). *Introduction to theories of personality.* New York: Wiley.

Hall, R. V., Lund, D., & Jackson, D. (1968). Effects of teacher attention on study behavior. *Journal of Applied Behavior Analysis, 1,* 1–12.

Hansel, C. E. M. (1980). *ESP and parapsychology: A critical re-evaluation.* Buffalo, NY: Prometheus.

Harkins, S. G., & Petty, R. E. (1982). Effects of task difficulty and task uniqueness on social loafing. *Journal of Personality and Social Psychology, 43,* 1214–1229.

Harlow, H. F. (1958). The nature of love. *American Psychologist, 13,* 673–685.

Harlow, H. F., & Suomi, S. J. (1970). The nature of love—Simplified. *American Psychologist, 25,* 161–168.

Harris, E. L., Noyes, R., Crowe, R. R., & Chaundry, D. R. (1983). A family study of agoraphobia: Report of a pilot study. *Archives of General Psychiatry, 40,* 1065–1070.

Harris, L. S. (1981). *Problems of drug dependence, 1981.* Washington, DC: U.S. Government Printing Office.

Hartl, E. M., Monnelly, E. P., & Elderkin, E. S. (1982). *Physique and delinquent behavior.* New York: Academic Press.

Hathaway, S. R., & McKinley, J. C. (1951). *Manual for the Minnesota Multiphasic Personality Inventory.* New York: Psychological Corp.

Hayes, C. (1952). *The ape in our house.* London: Gollancz.

Hayes, S. C., & Cone, J. D. (1981). Reduction of residential consumption of electricity through simple monthly feedback. *Journal of Applied Behavior Analysis, 14,* 81–88.

Heider, F. (1958). *The psychology of interpersonal relations.* New York: Wiley.

Hermann, J. A., de Montes, A. I., Dominguez, B., Montes, F., & Hopkins, B. L. (1973). Effects of bonuses for punctuality on the tardiness of industrial workers. *Journal of Applied Behavior Analysis, 6,* 563–570.

Hersen, M., & Barlow, D. H. (1976). *Single case experimental designs.* New York: Pergamon Press.

Hersen, M., & Bellack, A. S. (1976). *Behavioral assessment: A practical handbook.* New York: Pergamon Press.

Hersen, M., & Bellack, A. S. (1982). Perspectives in the behavioral treatment of depression. *Behavior Modification, 6,* 95–106.

Hersen, M., Gullick, E. L., Matherne, P. M., & Harbert, T. L. (1972). Instructions and reinforcement in the modification of a conversion reaction. *Psychological Reports, 31,* 719–722.

Hersen, M., Eisler, R. M., Alford, G. S., & Agras, W. S. (1973). Effects of token economy on neurotic depression: An experimental analysis. *Behavior Therapy, 4,* 392–397.

Hersen, M., Turner, S. M., Edelstein, B. A., & Pinkston, S. G. (1975). Effects of phenothiazines and social skills training in a withdrawn schizophrenic. *Journal of Clinical Psychology, 31,* 588–594.

Hersen, M., Bellack, A. S., & Himmelhoch, J. M. (1980). Treatment of unipolar depression with social skills training. *Behavior Modification, 4,* 547–555.

Hess, E. H. (1958). Imprinting in animals. *Scientific American, 198,* 81–89.

Hester, P., & Hendrickson, J. (1977). Training functional expressive language: The acquisition and generalization of five-element syntactical responses. *Journal of Applied Behavior Analysis, 10,* 316.

Hetherington, E. M., & Parke, R. D. (1986). *Child psychology: A contemporary viewpoint.* New York: McGraw-Hill.

Hill, H. E., Haertzen, C. A., & Glazer, R. (1960). Personality characteristics of narcotic addicts as indicated by the MMPI. *Journal of General Psychology, 62,* 127–139.

Hinde, R. A., & Stevenson-Hinde, J. (1973). *Constraints on learning: Limitations and predispositions.* London: Academic Press.

Hines, T. (1988). *Pseudoscience and the paranormal.* Buffalo, NY: Prometheus.

Hoff-Ginsburg, E., & Shatz, M. (1982). Linguistic input and the child's acquisition of language. *Psychological Bulletin, 92,* 3–26.

Holland, J. G., & Skinner, B. F. (1961). *The analysis of behavior.* New York: McGraw-Hill.

Hollon, S. D., Spoden, F., Chastek, J. (1986). Unipolar depression. In M. Hersen (Ed.), *Pharmacological and behavioral treatment: An integrative approach* (pp. 199–239). New York: Wiley.

Honig, W. K. (1966). *Handbook of operant behavior.* New York: Appleton-Century-Crofts.

Houston, J. P., Bee, H., Hatfield, E., & Rimm, D. C. (1979). *Invitation to psychology.* New York: Academic Press.

Hoveland, C. I., Lumsdaine, A. A., & Sheffield, F. D. (1949). *Experiments on mass communication: Studies in social psychology in World War II* (Vol. 3). Princeton, NJ: Princeton University Press.

Hubel, D. H. (1979). The brain. *Scientific American, 241,* 45–53.

Huitema, B. E. (1986). Statistical analysis and single-subject designs: Some misunderstandings. In A. Poling & R. W. Fuqua (Eds.), *Research methods in applied behavior analysis: Issues and advances* (pp. 209–232). New York: Plenum Press.

Hull, C. L. (1952). *A behavior system.* New Haven, CT: Yale University Press.

Hutchinson, R. R. (1977). By-products of aversive control. In W. K. Honig & J. E. R. Staddon (Eds.), *Handbook of operant behavior.* Englewood Cliffs, NJ: Prentice-Hall.

Insko, C. A., & Wilson, M. (1977). Interpersonal attraction as a function of social interaction. *Journal of Personality and Social Psychology, 15,* 294–301.

Israel, A. C., & Brown, M. S. (1977). Correspondence training, prior verbal training, and control of nonverbal behavior via control of verbal behavior. *Journal of Applied Behavior Analysis, 10,* 333–338.

Isaacson, R. L., Douglas, R. J., Lubar, I. F., & Schmaltz, L. W. (1971). *A primer of physiological psychology.* New York: Harper & Row.

Jacobson, N. S., & Margolin, G. (1979). *Marital therapy: Strategies based on social learning and behavior exchange principles.* New York: Brunner/Mazel.

Jaffee, J. H. (1985). Drug addiction and drug abuse. In A. G. Gilman, L. S. Goodman, T. W. Rall, & F. Murad (Eds.), *The pharmacological basis of therapeutics* (pp. 532–571). New York: Macmillan.

Jensen, A. R. (1969). How much can we boost IQ and scholastic achievement? *Harvard Educational Review, 33,* 1–123.

Johanson, C. E., Balster, R., & Bonese, S. (1976). Self-administration of psychomotor stimulant drugs: The effects of unlimited access. *Pharmacology Biochemistry and Behavior, 4,* 45–51.

Johnston, J. M., & Pennypacker, H. S. (1980). *Strategies and tactics of human behavioral research.* Hillsdale, NJ: Erlbaum.

Johnston, J. M., & Pennypacker, H. S. (1986). The nature and functions of experimental questions. In A. Poling & R. W. Fuqua (Eds.), *Research methods in applied behavior analysis: Issues and advances* (pp. 55–84). New York: Plenum Press.

Johnston, L. D., O'Malley, P. M., & Bachman, J. G. (1984). *Highlights from drugs and American high school students.* Washington, DC: U.S. Government Printing Office.

Jones, E. E., & Harris, V. A. (1967). The attribution of attitudes. *Journal of Experimental Social Psychology, 3,* 2–24.

Kagan, J. (1970). The distribution of attention in infancy. In D. H. Hamburg (Ed.), *Perception and its disorders.* Baltimore: Williams & Wilkins.

Kalnins, I. V., & Bruner, J. S. (1973). The coordination of visual observation and instrumental behavior in early infancy. *Perception, 2,* 307–314.

Kamin, L. J. (1974). *The science and politics of IQ.* Potomac, MD: Erlbaum.

Kanfer, F. H., & Saslow, G. (1969). Behavioral diagnosis. In C. M. Franks (Ed.), *Behavior therapy: Appraisal and status* (pp. 417–444). New York: McGraw-Hill.

Kanner, L. (1964). *A history of the care and study of the mentally retarded.* Springfield, IL: Charles C. Thomas.

Karabenick, S. A., Lerner, R. M., & Beecher, M. D. (1973). Relation of political affiliation to helping behavior on election day, November 7, 1972. *Journal of Social Psychology, 91,* 223–227.

Karen, R. L. (1974). *An introduction to behavior theory and its applications.* New York: Harper & Row.

Kazdin, A. (1981). The token economy. In G. Davey (Ed.), *Applications of conditioning theory.* London: Methuen.

Kazdin, A. E. (1982). *Single-case research designs.* New York: Oxford University Press.

Keane, T. M., Zimmering, R. T., & Caddell, J. M. (1985). A behavioral formulation of posttraumatic stress disorder. *The Behavior Therapist, 8,* 9–12.

Keller, F. S. (1966). A personal course in psychology. In R. Ulrich, T. Stachnik, & J. Mabry (Eds.), *The control of behavior* (pp. 91–93). Glenview, IL: Scott, Foresman.

Keller, F. S., & Schoenfeld, W. N. (1950). *Principles of psychology.* New York: Appleton-Century-Crofts.

Kelly, H. H. (1967). Attribution theory in social psychology. In D. Levine (Ed.), *Nebraska Symposium on Motivation.* Lincoln: University of Nebraska Press.

Kempen, R. W., & Hall, R. V. (1977). Reduction of industrial absenteeism: Results of a behavioral approach. *Journal of Organizational Behavior Management, 1*, 1–21.

Kempthorne, O. (1978). Logical, epistemological and statistical aspects of nature-nuture data interpretation. *Biometrics, 34*, 1–23.

Kenny, D. A., & Nasby, W. (1980). Splitting the reciprocity correlation. *Journal of Personality and Social Psychology, 38*, 249–256.

Kenrick, D. T., & Cialdini, R. B. (1977). Romantic attraction: Misattribution versus reinforcement explanations. *Journal of Personality and Social Psychology, 35*, 381–391.

Kettlewell, H. B. D. (1973). *The evolution of melanism.* Oxford: Clarendon.

Kety, S. S., Rosenthal, D., Wender, Ph. H., Schulsinger, F. (1968). The types and prevalence of mental illness in the biological and adoptive families of adopted schizophrenics. In D. Rosenthal & S. S. Kety (Eds.), *The transmission of schizophrenia* (pp. 1–88). Elmsford, NY: Pergamon Press.

Kinney, J., & Leaton, G. (1983). *Loosening the grip: A handbook of alcohol information.* St. Louis: Mosby.

Kohlenberg, R., & Phillips, T. (1973). Reinforcement and rate of litter depositing. *Journal of Applied Behavior Analysis, 6*, 391–396.

Kohlenberg, R., Phillips, T., & Proctor, W. (1976). A behavioral analysis of peaking in residential electrical-energy consumers. *Journal of Applied Behavior Analysis, 9*, 13–18.

Kohlenberg, R. J. (1973). Behavioristic approach to multiple personality: A case study. *Behavior Therapy, 4*, 137–140.

Kolb, B., & Whishaw, I. Q. (1985). *Fundamentals of human neuropsychology* (2nd ed.). San Francisco: Freeman.

Krasner, L., & Ullmann, L. P. (1973). *Behavior influence and personality: The social matrix of human action.* New York: Holt, Rinehart & Winston.

Krebs, B., & Blackman, R. (1988). *Psychology: A first encounter.* San Diego: Harcourt Brace Jovanovich.

Kroll, N. E. A., Parks, T., Parkinson, S. R., Bieber, S. L., & Johnson, A. L. (1970). Short-term memory while shadowing: recall of visually and of aurally presented letters. *Journal of Experimental Psychology, 85*, 220–224.

Kuhn, T. (1970). *The structure of scientific revolutions.* Chicago: University of Chicago Press.

Kurtz, P. (1985a). Introduction: More than a century of psychical research. In P. Kurtz (Ed.), *A skeptic's handbook of parapsychology* (pp. xi–xxiv). Buffalo, NY: Prometheus.

Kurtz, P. (1985b). Is parapsychology a science? In P. Kurtz (Ed.), *A skeptic's handbook of parapsychology* (pp. 503–518). Buffalo, NY: Prometheus.

Kurtz, P. (1985c). *A skeptic's handbook of parapsychology.* Buffalo, NY: Prometheus.

Kurtz, P. (1987). Is there intelligent life on earth? *The Skeptical Inquirer, 12*, 2–5.

Lagerspetz, K. (1964). Studies on the aggressive behaviour of mice. *Suomalainen Tudeakatemia* (Helsinki), *131*, 1–131.

Lamal, P. A., & Benfield, A. (1978). The effect of self-monitoring on job tardiness and percentage of time spent working. *Journal of Organizational Behavior Management, 1*, 142–149.

Landy, D., & Sigall, H. (1974). Beauty is talent: Task evaluation as a function of the performer's physical attractiveness. *Journal of Personality and Social Psychology, 36*, 886–893.

LaPiere, R. T. (1934). Attitudes and actions. *Social Forces, 13*, 230–237.

Leahey, T. H. (1987). *A history of psychology: Main currents in psychological thought* (2nd ed.). Englewood Cliffs, NJ: Prentice-Hall.

Lefton, L. (1979). *Psychology.* Boston: Allyn & Bacon.

Leitenberg, H. (1976). Behavioral approaches to treatment of neuroses. In H. Leitenberg (Ed.), *Handbook of behavior modification and behavior therapy* (pp. 124–167). New York: Appleton-Century-Crofts.

Lenneberg, E. H., Rebelsky, F. G., & Nichols, I. A. (1965). The vocalizations of infants born to deaf and hearing parents. *Human Development, 8*, 23–37.

Lerner, R. M. (1984). *On the nature of human plasticity.* New York: Cambridge University Press.

Lewinsohn, P. M. (1975). The behavioral study and treatment of depression. In M. Hersen, R. M. Eisler, & P. M. Miller (Eds.), *Progress in behavior modification* (pp. 335–374). New York: Academic Press.

Lewontin, R. C., Rose, S., & Kamin, L. J. (1984). *Not in our genes.* New York: Pantheon.

Liberman, R. P., King, L. W., & DeRisi, W. J. (1976). Behavior analysis and therapy in community mental health. In H. Leitenberg (Ed.), *Handbook of behavior modification and behavior therapy* (pp. 566–603). Englewood Cliffs, NJ: Prentice-Hall.

Lickey, M. E., & Gordon, B. (1983). *Drugs for mental illness.* New York: W. H. Freeman.

Lieberman, S. (1956). The effects of changes in roles on the attitudes of role occupants. *Human Relations, 9,* 385–402.

Lindsly, D. F., & Holmes, J. E. (1984). *Basic human neurophysiology.* New York: Elsevier.

Lord, C. (1975). *Is talking to baby more than baby talk? A longitudinal study of the role of linguistic input to young children.* Unpublished paper presented at the Biennial Conference of the Society for Research in Child Development, Denver.

Lutzker, J. R., & Martin, J. A. (1981). *Behavior change.* Monterey, CA: Brooks/Cole.

Lutzker, J. R., & Sherman, J. A. (1974). Producing generative sentence usage by imitation and reinforcement procedures. *Journal of Applied Behavior Analysis, 7,* 447–460.

Maccoby, E. E., & Alexander, J. (1980). Use of media in lifestyle programs. In P. O. Davidson & S. M. Davidson (Eds.), *Behavioral medicine: Changing health lifestyles.* New York: Brunner/Mazel.

Mackintosh, N. (1974). *The psychology of animal learning.* New York: Academic Press.

MacMillan, D. L. (1982). *Mental retardation in school and society.* Boston: Little, Brown.

Mahon, L. M., Neufeld, N., Mani, M. M., & Christophersen, E. R. (1984). The effect of informational feedback on food intake of adult burn patients. *Journal of Applied Behavior Analysis, 17,* 391–396.

Martens, R. (1969). Palmar sweating and the presence of an audience. *Journal of Experimental Social Psychology, 5,* 371–374.

Maruyama, G., & Miller, N. (1980). Physical attractiveness, race, and essay evaluation. *Personality and Social Psychology Bulletin, 40,* 962–975.

Maslow, A. H. (1970). *Motivation and personality* (2nd ed.). New York: Harper & Row.

Matson, J. L., & Mulick, J. A. (1983). *Handbook of mental retardation.* New York: Pergamon Press.

Mayr, E. (1974). Behavior programs and evolutionary strategies. *American Scientist, 62,* 650–659.

Mayr, E. (1978). Evolution. *Scientific American, 239,* 46–55.

McCain, G., & Segal, E. M. (1988). *The game of science.* Pacific Grove, CA: Brooks/Cole.

McCaul, M. E., Stitzer, M. L., Bigelow, G. W., & Liebson, I. A. (1984). Contingency management interventions: Effects on treatment outcome during methadone detoxification. *Journal of Applied Behavior Analysis, 17,* 35–43.

McSweeney, A. J. (1978). Effects of response cost on the behavior of a million persons. *Journal of Applied Behavior Analysis, 11,* 47–51.

Mead, M. (1928). *Coming of age in Samoa.* Chicago: University of Chicago Press.

Medawar, P. B. (1984). *The limits of science.* New York: Harper & Row.

Meredith, R. L., & Milby, J. B. (1980). Obsessive-compulsive disorders. In R. J. Daitzman (Ed.), *Clinical behavior therapy and behavior modification* (Vol. 1, pp. 21–80). New York: Garland STPM.

Meyers, D. G. (1983). *Social psychology.* New York: McGraw-Hill.

Michael, J. L. (1975). Positive and negative reinforcement, a distinction that is no longer necessary; or a better way to talk about bad things. *Behaviorism, 3,* 33–44.

Michael, J. L. (1980). Flight from behavior analysis. *The Behavior Analyst, 3,* 1–24.

Michael, J. L. (1982). Distinguishing between discriminative and motivational functions of stimuli. *Journal of the Experimental Analysis of Behavior, 37,* 149–155.

Michael, J. L. (1984). Behavior analysis: A radical perspective. In B. L. Hammonds, & C. J. Scheirer (Eds.), *Master lecture series, Vol. 4: Psychology of learning.* Washington, DC: American Psychological Association.

Milgram, S. (1963). Behavioral study of obedience. *Journal of Abnormal and Social Psychology, 67,* 371–378.

Miller, G. A. (1956). The magical number seven, plus or minus two: Some limits on our capacity for processing information. *Psychological Review, 63,* 81–97.

Miltenberger, R. G., & Fuqua, R. W. (1985). Overcorrection: A review and critical analysis. *The Behavior Analyst, 4,* 123–141.

Mims, P. R., Hartnett, J. M., & Nay, W. R. (1975). Interpersonal attraction and help volunteering as a function of physical attractiveness. *Journal of Psychology, 89,* 125–131.

Moore, D. L., & Baron, R. S. (1983). Social facilitation: A physiological analysis. In J. T. Cacioppo & R. Petty (Eds.), *Social psychophysiology.* New York: Guilford Press.

Moore, J. (1987). The roots of the family tree: A review of four books on the history and nature of behaviorism. *The Psychological Record, 37,* 449–470.

Moore, K. L. (1989). *Before we are born.* Philadelphia: W. B. Saunders.

Moss, G. R., & Boren, J. J. (1972). Depression as a model for behavioral analysis. *Comprehensive Psychiatry, 13,* 581–590.

Murphy, H. A., Hutchinson, J. M., & Bailey, J. S. (1983). Behavioral school psychology goes outdoors: The effect of organized games on playground aggression. *Journal of Applied Behavior Analysis, 16*, 29–35.

Neef, N. A., Iwata, B. A., & Page, T. J. (1978). Public transportation training: In vivo versus classroom instruction. *Journal of Applied Behavior Analysis, 11*, 331–344.

Neisworth, J. T., & Moore, F. (1972). Operant treatment of asthmatic responding with the parent as therapist. *Behavior Therapy, 3*, 95–99.

Nelson, G. L., & Cone, J. E. (1979). Multiple-baseline analysis of a token economy for psychiatric inpatients. *Journal of Applied Behavior Analysis, 12*, 255–272.

Nelson, J. E., Pearson, H. W., Sayers, M., & Glynn, T. J. (1982). *Guide to drug abuse research terminology*. Washington, DC: U.S. Government Printing Office.

Nietzel, M. T., & Bernstein, D. A. (1981). Assessment of anxiety and fear. In M. Hersen & A. S. Bellack (Eds.), *Behavioral assessment* (pp. 215–245). New York: Pergamon Press.

Nisbett, R. E., Caputo, G. C., Legant, P., & Mareck, J. (1973). Behavior as seen by the actor and the observer. *Journal of Personality and Social Psychology, 35*, 250–256.

Nowrey, J. E. (1945). A brief synopsis of mental deficiency. *American Journal of Mental Deficiency, 49*, 319–357.

Nye, M. J. (1980). N-rays: An episode in the history and psychology of science. *Historical Studies in the Physical Sciences, 11*, 125–156.

Olds, J., & Milner, P. (1954). Positive reinforcement produced by electrical stimulation of septal areas and other regions of rat brains. *Journal of Comparative and Physiological Psychology, 41*, 419–427.

Opitz, J. M., & Sutherland, G. R. (1984). Conference Report: International workshop on the fragile X and X-linked mental retardation. *American Journal of Medical Genetics, 17*, 5–94.

Orpen, C. (1978). Effects of bonuses for attendance on the absenteeism of industrial workers. *Journal of Organizational Behavior Management, 1*, 118–124.

Orton, I. K., Beiman, I., & Ciminero, A. R. (1982). The behavioral assessment and treatment of essential hypertension. In D. M. Doleys, R. L. Meredith, & A. R. Ciminero (Eds.), *Behavioral medicine: Assessment and treatment strategies* (pp. 175–198). New York: Plenum Press.

Overmeier, J. B., & Seligman, M. E. P. (1967). Effects of inescapable shock upon subsequent escape and avoidance learning. *Journal of Comparative and Physiological Psychology, 63*, 23–33.

Owens, R. E. (1984). *Language development: An introduction*. Columbus, OH: Charles E. Merrill.

Parry-Jones, W. L., Sauter-Westrate, H. C., & Crawley, R. C. (1970). Behavior therapy in a case of hysterical blindness. *Behavior Research and Therapy, 8*, 79–85.

Parsonson, B. S., & Baer, D. M. (1986). The graphic analysis of data. In A. Poling & R. W. Fuqua (Eds.), *Research methods in applied behavior analysis: Issues and advances* (pp. 157–186). New York: Plenum Press.

Parton, D. A., & DeNike, L. D. (1966). Performance hypotheses of children and response to social reinforcement. *Journal of Personality and Social Psychology, 4*, 444–447.

Patterson, C. (1978). *Evolution*. Ithaca, NY: Cornell University Press.

Pavlov, I. P. (1927). *Conditioned reflexes* (G. V. Anrep, trans.). Oxford, England: Clarendon.

Pertschuk, M. J., Edwards, N., & Pomerleau, O. F. (1978). A multiple-baseline approach to behavioral intervention in anorexia nervosa. *Behavior Therapy, 9*, 368–376.

Pervin, L. A. (1984). *Personality*. New York: Wiley.

Peterson, N. (1960). Control of behavior by presentation of an imprinted stimulus. *Science, 132*, 1395–1396.

Petrakis, P. L. (1985). *Alcoholism: An inherited disease*. Washington, DC: U.S. Government Printing Office.

Pettijohn, T. E. (1989). *Psychology: A concise introduction*. Guilford, CT: Dushkin Publishing Group.

Phillips, J. R. (1973). Syntax and vocabulary of mother's speech to young children: Age and sex comparisons. *Child Development, 44*, 182–185.

Piaget, J. (1952). *The origins of intelligence in children*. New York: International Universities Press.

Piaget, J., & Inhelder, B. (1969). *The psychology of the child*. New York: Basic Books.

Pickens, R. (1979). A behavioral program for treatment of drug dependence. In N. A. Krasnegor (Ed.), *Behavioral analysis and treatment of substance abuse* (pp. 44–54). Washington, DC: U.S. Government Printing Office.

Pierrel, R., & Sherman, J. G. (1963, February). J. G. Barnabus, the rat with college training. *Brown Alumni Monthly*, 8–14.

Plomin, R., Defries, J. C., & McClearn, G. E. (1980). *Behavioral genetics: A primer.* San Francisco: W. H. Freeman.

Poling, A. (1986). *A primer of human behavioral pharmacology.* New York: Plenum Press.

Popper, K. (1978). Natural selection and the emergence of the mind. *Dialectica, 32,* 339–355.

Powers, R. B., Osborne, J. G., & Anderson, E. G. (1973). Positive reinforcement of litter removal in the natural environment. *Journal of Applied Behavior Analysis, 6,* 579–586.

Premack, D. (1959). Toward empirical laws. Part 1: Positive reinforcement. *Psychological Review, 66,* 219–233.

Pyle, R. L., Mitchell, J. E., Eckert, E. E., Halvorson, P. A., Neuman, P. A., & Goff, G. M. (1983). The incidence of bulimia in freshman college students. *The International Journal of Eating Disorders, 2,* 75–85.

Rachman, S., & Hodgson, R. J. (1968). Experimentally-induced sexual fetishism: Replication and development. *Psychological Record, 18,* 25–27.

Rainwater, N., & Alexander, A. B. (1982). Respiratory disorders: Asthma. In D. M. Doleys, R. L. Meredith, & A. R. Ciminero (Eds.), *Behavioral medicine: Assessment and treatment strategies* (pp. 435–446). New York: Plenum Press.

Randi, J. (1982). *The truth about Uri Geller.* Buffalo, NY: Prometheus.

Rapport, M. D., & Bostow, D. E. (1976). The effects of access to special activities on the performance in four categories of academic tasks with third-grade students. *Journal of Applied Behavior Analysis, 9,* 372.

Ray, O. (1983). *Drugs, society, and human behavior.* St. Louis: Mosby.

Ray, O., & Ksir, C. (1987). *Drugs, society, and human behavior.* St. Louis: Times Mirror/Mosby.

Report to the National Advisory Child Health and Human Development Council. (1981, May). Washington, DC: Program of Mental Retardation and Developmental Disabilities Branch.

Reschly, D. J. (1979). Nonbiased assessment. In G. D. Phye & D. J. Reschly (Eds.), *School psychology: Perspectives and issues* (pp. 201–259). New York: Academic Press.

Reschly, D. J. (1981). Psychological testing on educational classification and placement. *American Psychologist, 36,* 1094–1102.

Rheingold, H. L., & Eckerman, C. O. (1973). The fear of strangers hypothesis: A critical review. In H. Reese (Ed.), *Advances in child development and behavior* (Vol. 8, pp. 185–222). New York: Academic Press.

Rheingold, H. L., Gewirtz, J. L., & Ross, H. W. (1959). Social conditioning of vocalizations in the infant. *Journal of Consulting and Clinical Psychology, 52,* 67–73.

Riley, V. (1981). Biobehavioral factors in animal work on tumorigenesis. In S. M. Weiss, J. A. Herd, & B. H. Fox (Eds.), *Perspectives on behavioral medicine* (pp. 183–206). New York: Academic Press.

Rilling, M., & Caplan, H. (1973). Extinction-induced aggression during errorless discrimination learning. *Journal of the Experimental Analysis of Behavior, 20,* 85–91.

Rimm, D. C., & Masters, J. C. (1979). *Behavior therapy: Techniques and empirical findings.* New York: Academic Press.

Robbins, L. N., Helzer, J. E., Weissman, M. M., Orvaschel, H., Gruenberg, E., Burke, J. D., & Regier, D. A. (1984). Lifetime prevalence of specific psychiatric disorders in three sites. *Archives of General Psychiatry, 41,* 949–958.

Robins, L. N. (1974). *The Vietnam drug user returns.* Washington, DC: U.S. Government Printing Office.

Robinson, N. M., & Robinson, H. B. (1976). *The mentally retarded child: A psychological approach.* New York: McGraw-Hill.

Roediger, H. L., III, Rushton, J. P., Capaldi, E. D., & Paris, S. G. (1984). *Psychology.* Boston: Little, Brown & Co.

Rogers, C. R. (1951). *Client-centered therapy: Its current practice, implications, and theory.* Boston: Houghton Mifflin.

Rogers, C. R. (1959). A theory of therapy, personality, and interpersonal relationships as developed in the client-centered framework. In S. Koch (Ed.), *Psychology: A study of a science* (Vol. 3). New York: McGraw-Hill.

Rogo, D. S. (1985). J. B. Rhine and the Levy scandal. In P. Kurtz (Ed.), *A skeptic's handbook of parapsychology* (pp. 313–326). Buffalo, NY: Prometheus.

Rollin, B. E. (1986). Animal consciousness and scientific change. *New Ideas in Psychology, 4,* 141–152.

Roosens, E. (1979). *Mental patients in town life.* Beverly Hills, CA: Sage.

Rosen, J. C., & Leitenberg, H. (1982). Bulimia nervosa: Treatment with exposure and response-prevention. *Behavior Therapy, 13,* 117–124.

Rosenhan, D. L. (1973). On being sane in insane places. *Science, 179,* 250–258.

Rosenzweig, M. R. (1966). Environmental complexity, cerebral change, and behavior. *American Psychologist, 21,* 321–332.

Rosenzweig, M. R., & Bennet, E. L. (1970). Effects of differential environments on brain weights and enzyme activities in gerbils, rats, and mice. *Developmental Psychobiology, 2,* 87–95.

Rosenzweig, M. R., & Leiman, A. L. (1982). *Physiological psychology.* New York: Norton.

Ross, L. (1977). The intuitive psychologist and his shortcomings. In L. Berkowitz (Ed.), *Cognitive theories in social psychology.* New York: Academic Press.

Rothenbuhler, W. C. (1964). Behavior genetics of nest cleaning in honeybees. Part 4: Responses of F1 and backcross generations to disease-killed brood. *American Zoologist, 4,* 111–123.

Rubin, Z. (1970). Measurement of romantic love. *Journal of Personality and Social Psychology, 16,* 265–273.

Rubin, Z. (1973). *Liking and loving: An invitation to social psychology.* New York: Holt, Rinehart & Winston.

Rychlak, J. F. (1981). *Personality and psychotherapy: A theory-construction approach.* Boston: Houghton Mifflin.

Saegert, S., Swap, W., & Zajonc, R. B. (1973). Exposure, context, and interpersonal attraction. *Journal of Personality and Social Psychology, 25,* 234–242.

Sagan, C. (1987). The burden of skepticism. *The Skeptical Inquirer, 12,* 38–46.

Salapatek, P. (1975). Pattern perception in early infancy. In L. B. Cohen & P. Salapatek (Eds.), *Infant perception: From sensation to cognition* (Vol. 1). New York: Academic Press.

Salvia, J., & Ysseldyke, F. E. (1981). *Assessment in special and remedial education.* Boston: Houghton Mifflin.

Salzinger, K. (1978). Language behavior. In A. C. Catania & T. A. Brigham (Eds.), *Handbook of applied behavior analysis: Instructional processes.* New York: Irvington.

Schachter, S., & Singer, J. E. (1962). Cognitive, social and physiological determinants of emotional state. *Psychological Review, 69,* 379–399.

Schepis, M. M., Reid, D. H., & Fitzgerald, J. R. (1987). Group instruction with profoundly retarded persons: Acquisition, generalization, and maintenance of a remunerative work skill. *Journal of Applied Behavior Analysis, 20,* 97–105.

Schlinger, H., & Blakely, E. (1987). Function-altering effects of contingency-specifying stimuli. *The Behavior Analyst, 10,* 41–45.

Schneider, A. M., & Tarshis, B. (1975). *An introduction to physiological psychology.* New York: Random House.

Schnelle, J. F., Kirchner, R. E., Macrae, J. W., McNees, M. P., Eck, R. H., Snodgrass, S., Casey, J. D., & Uselton, P. H. (1978). Police evaluation research: An experimental and cost-benefit analysis of a helicopter patrol in a high crime area. *Journal of Applied Behavior Analysis, 11,* 11–21.

Schultz, D. P. (1975). *A history of modern psychology.* New York: Academic Press.

Schultz, F. (1971). Pragung des sexual Verhaltens von Enten und Gansen durch Sozialeindrucke wahrend der Jugendphase. *Journal of Neurovisceral Relations, Supplementum, 10,* 357–399.

Scibak, J. W. (1983). Behavioral treatment. In J. L. Matson & J. A. Mulick (Eds.), *Handbook of mental retardation* (pp. 339–350). New York: Pergamon Press.

Searle, L. V. (1949). The organization of hereditary maze-brightness and maze-dullness. *Genetic Psychology Monographs, 39,* 279–335.

Sears, R. R., Maccoby, E. E., & Levin, H. (1957). *Patterns of childrearing.* Evanston, IL: Row, Peterson.

Sebeok, T., & Umiker-Sebeok, J. (1979, November). Performing animals: Secrets of the trade. *Psychology Today,* pp. 77–91.

Seligman, M. E. P., Klein, D. C., & Miller, W. R. (1976). Depression. In H. Leitenberg (Ed.), *Handbook of behavior modification and behavior therapy* (pp. 168–210). New York: Appleton-Century-Crofts.

Shatz, M., & Gelman, R. (1973). The development of communication skills: Modifications in the speech of young children as a function of the listener. *Monographs of Social Research in Child Development, 38* (152), 157.

Sheldon, W. H. (with collaboration of S. S. Stevens). (1942). *The varieties of temperament: A psychology of constitutional differences.* New York: Harper & Row.

Sheldon, W. H. (with the collaboration of C. W. Dupertuis & E. McDermott). (1954). *Atlas of men: A guide for somatotyping the adult male at all ages.* New York: Harper & Row.

Shirley, M. M. (1933). *The first two years.* Minneapolis: University of Minnesota Press.

Sidman, M. (1960). *Tactics of scientific research.* New York: Basic Books.

Sigel, I. F., Roeper, A., & Hooper, F. H. (1966). A training procedure for acquisition of Piaget's conservation of quantity: A pilot study and its replication. *British Journal of Educational Psychology, 36,* 301–311.

Skinner, B. F. (1938). *The behavior of organisms.* New York: Appleton-Century-Crofts.

Skinner, B. F. (1945). The operational analysis of psychological terms. *Psychological Review, 52,* 270–277.

Skinner, B. F. (1948). *Walden two.* New York: Macmillan.

Skinner, B. F. (1953). *Science and human behavior.* New York: Macmillan.

Skinner, B. F. (1957). *Verbal behavior.* Englewood Cliffs, NJ: Prentice-Hall.

Skinner, B. F. (1969). *Contingencies of reinforcement.* New York: Meredith.

Skinner, B. F. (1974). *About behaviorism.* New York: Random House.

Skinner, B. F. (1978). *Reflections on behaviorism and society.* Englewood Cliffs, NJ: Prentice-Hall.

Skinner, B. F. (1987). *Upon further reflection.* Englewood Cliffs, NJ: Prentice-Hall.

Spitzer, R. L. (1975). On pseudoscience in science, logic in remission, and psychiatric diagnosis: A critique of Rosenhan's "On being sane in insane places." *Journal of Abnormal Psychology, 84,* 442–452.

Springer, S. P., & Deutsch, G. (1984). *Left brain, right brain.* San Francisco: Freeman.

Sroufe, L. A., & Cooper, R. G. (1988). *Child development: Its nature and course.* New York: Knopf.

Stapp, J., Tucker, A. M., & VandenBos, G. R. (1985). Census of psychological personnel: 1983. *American Psychologist, 40,* 1317–1351.

Stern, R. S., & Marks, I. M. (1975). Contract therapy in obsessive-compulsive neurosis with marital discord. In C. M. Franks & G. T. Wilson (Eds.), *Annual Review of Behavior Therapy: Theory and Practice* (pp. 733–740). New York: Brunner/Mazel.

St. John, J. A. (1905). *The philosophical works of John Locke.* London: G. Bell.

Stokes, D. M. (1985). Parapsychology and its critics. In P. Kurtz (Ed.), *A skeptic's handbook of parapsychology* (pp. 379–424). Buffalo, NY: Prometheus.

Stoyva, J. M. (1979). Musculoskeletal and stress-related disorders. In O. F. Pomerleau & J. P. Brady (Eds.), *Behavioral medicine: Theory and practice* (pp. 279–298). Baltimore: Williams & Wilkins.

Stunkard, A. J. (1979). Behavioral medicine and beyond: The example of obesity. In O. F. Pomerleau & J. P. Brady (Eds.), *Behavioral medicine: Theory and practice* (pp. 279–298). Baltimore: Williams & Wilkins.

Suinn, R. M. (1977). Type A behavior pattern. In R. B. Williams, Jr., & W. D. Doyle (Eds.), *Behavioral approaches to medical treatment* (pp. 55–65). Cambridge, MA: Ballinger.

Sulzer-Azaroff, B., & Mayer, G. R. (1977). *Applying behavior-analysis procedures with children and youth.* New York: Holt, Rinehart, & Winston.

Sulzer-Azaroff, B., & Santamaria, M. (1980). Industrial safety hazard reduction through performance feedback. *Journal of Applied Behavior Analysis, 13,* 287–295.

Swap, W. C. (1977). Interpersonal attraction and repeated exposure to rewarders and punishers. *Personality and Social Psychology Bulletin, 3,* 248–251.

Taylor, S. E., & Fiske, S. T. (1978). Salience, attention, and attribution: Top of the head phenomena. In L. Berkowitz (Ed.), *Advances in experimental social psychology* (Vol. 11). New York: Academic Press.

Tertinger, D. A., Greene, B. F., & Lutzker, J. R. (1984). Home safety: Development and validation of one component of an ecobehavioral treatment program for abused and neglected children. *Journal of Applied Behavior Analysis, 17,* 159–174.

Thomas, C. L. (1981). *Taber's cyclopedic medical dictionary.* Philadelphia: F. A. Davis.

Thomas, D. R., Becker, W. C., & Armstrong, M. (1968). Production and elimination of disruptive classroom behavior by systematically varying teacher's behavior. *Journal of Applied Behavior Analysis, 1,* 35–45.

Thompson, T. (1963). Visual reinforcement in Siamese fighting fish. *Science, 141,* 55–57.

Thompson, T. (1964). Visual reinforcement in fighting cocks. *Journal of the Experimental Analysis of Behavior, 7,* 45–49.

Thompson, T., & Schuster, C. E. (1964). Morphine self-administration, food-reinforced, and avoidance behaviors in rhesus monkeys. *Psychopharmacologia, 5,* 87–94.

Thorndike, E. L. (1905). *The elements of psychology.* New York: Seiler.

Todd, G. A., & Palmer, B. (1968). Social reinforcement of infant babbling. *Child Development, 39,* 591–596.

Triplett, N. (1897). The dynamogenic factors in peacemaking and competition. *American Journal of Psychology, 9,* 507–533.

Trivers, R. (1985). *Social evolution.* Menlo Park, CA: Benjamin/Cummings.

Tryon, R. C. (1940). Genetic differences in maze-learning in rats. *Yearbook of the National Society for the Study of Education, 39,* 111–119.

Ullmann, L. P., & Krasner, L. (1965). *Case studies in behavior modification.* New York: Holt, Rinehart, & Winston.

Ulrich, R., Stachnik, T., & Mabry, J. (1966). *Control of human behavior* (Vol. 1). Glenwood, IL: Scott, Foresman.

van Lawick-Goodall, J. (1971). *In the shadow of man.* New York: Dell.

Walker, C. E. (1982). Sexual disorders. In D. M. Doleys, R. L. Meredith, & A. R. Ciminero (Eds.), *Behavioral medicine: Assessment and treatment strategies* (pp. 371–406). New York: Plenum Press.

Wardhaugh, R. (1977). *Introduction to linguistics.* New York: McGraw-Hill.

Washburn, S. L. (1960). *Tools and human evolution.* New York: Scientific American.

Watson, J. B. (1929). Behaviorism. *Encyclopedia Britannica, 3,* 327–329.

Watson, J. B. (1930). *Behaviorism.* New York: Norton.

Watson, J. B., & Rayner, R. (1920). Conditioned emotional reactions. *Journal of Experimental Psychology, 3,* 1–14.

Watson, J. D., & Crick, F. H. C. (1953). Molecular structure of nucleic acid: A structure for deoxyribose necleic acid. *Nature, 171,* 737–738.

Watson, J. S. (1973). Smiling, cooing and the "game." *Merrill-Palmer Quarterly, 18,* 323–339.

Watson, J. S., & Ramey, C. T. (1972). Reactions to responsive contingent stimulation in early infancy. *Merrill-Palmer Quarterly, 18,* 219–227.

Weinmann, G. (1982). Dealing with bureaucracy: The effectiveness of different persuasive appeals. *Social Psychology Quarterly, 45,* 136–144.

Weiten, W. (1989). *Psychology: Themes and variations.* New York: Brooks/Cole.

West, S. G., & Brown, T. J. (1975). Physical attractiveness, the severity of the emergency and helping: A field experiment and interpersonal simulation. *Journal of Experimental Social Psychology, 11,* 531–538.

White, B. L. (1967). An experimental approach to the effects of environment on early human behavior. In J. P. Hill (Ed.), *Minnesota symposium on child psychology* (Vol. 1). Minneapolis: University of Minnesota Press.

White, B. L., & Held, R. M. (1966). Plasticity of sensorimotor development in the human infant. In J. Rosenblith & W. Allinsmith (Eds.), *The causes of behavior: Readings in child development and educational psychology* (pp. 60–70). Boston: Allyn & Bacon.

White, B. L., Castle, P., & Held, R. M. (1964). Observations on the development of visually directed teaching. *Child Development, 35,* 349–364.

White, G. L., Fishbein, S., & Rutsein, J. (1981). Passionate love and the misattribution of arousal. *Journal of Personality and Social Psychology, 41,* 56–62.

Whitehurst, G. J. (1972). Production of novel and grammatical utterances by young children. *Journal of Experimental Child Psychology, 13,* 502–515.

Wikler, A. (1952). A psychodynamic study of a patient during experimental self-regulated re-addiction to morphine. *Psychiatry Quarterly, 26,* 270–293.

Wikoff, M., Anderson, D. C., & Crowell, C. R. (1982). Behavior management in a factory setting: Increasing work efficiency. *Journal of Organizational Behavior Management, 4,* 97–127.

Wilford, J. N. (1985). *The riddle of the dinosaur.* Knopf: New York.

Wilson, E. O. (1975). *Sociobiology: The new synthesis.* Cambridge: Harvard University Press.

Wilson, E. O. (1978). *On human nature.* Cambridge: Harvard University Press.

Winograd, T. (1975). Frame representations and the declarative-procedural controversy. In D. Bobrow & A. Collins (Eds.), *Representation and understanding: Studies in cognitive science.* New York: Academic Press.

Witters, W., & Venturelli, P. (1988). *Drugs and society.* Boston: Jones & Bartlett.

Wollersheim, J. P. (1970). Effectiveness of group therapy based upon learning principles in the treatment of overweight women. *Journal of Abnormal Psychology, 76,* 562–574.

Wolpe, J. (1958). *Psychotherapy by reciprocal inhibition.* Stanford, CA: Stanford University Press.

Woodruff, M. L. (1984). Operant conditioning and behavioral neuroscience. In A. C. Catania & L. Harnard (Eds.), *The behavioral and brain sciences* (Vol. 7, pp. 652–653). New York: Cambridge University Press.

Worell, J., & Nelson, C. M. (1974). *Managing instructional problems: A case study workbook.* New York: McGraw-Hill.

Zajonc, R. B. (1965). Social facilitation. *Science, 149,* 269–274.

Zeiler, M. (1977). *Schedules of reinforcement.* In W. K. Honig & J. E. R. Staddon (Eds.), *Handbook of operant behavior* (pp. 201–232). Englewood Cliffs, NJ: Prentice-Hall.

Zelazo, P. R., Zelazo, N. A., & Kolb, S. (1972). "Walking" in the newborn. *Science, 176,* 314–315.

Zimbardo, P. G. (1988). *Psychology and life.* Glenview, IL: Scott, Foresman.

Index